African Studies

Psychology of Emotions, Motivations and Actions

nova science publishers

www.novapublishers.com

African Studies

Child Mortality in Eritrea: An Overview of History and Progress
Fikresus Amahazion, PhD (Editor)
2022. ISBN: 979-8-88697-041-8 (Softcover)
2022. ISBN: 979-8-88697-095-1 (eBook)

African History: One of the Original Seven Liberal Arts
William S. Cook (Editor)
2022. ISBN: 978-1-68507-962-8 (Hardcover)
2022. ISBN: 979-8-88697-065-4 (eBook)

More information about this series can be found at
https://novapublishers.com/product-category/series/african-studies/

Psychology of Emotions, Motivations and Actions

A Guide to Clinical Psychology: Psychopathology
Suprakash Chaudhury, PhD (Editor)
2023. ISBN: 979-8-88697-932-9 (Hardcover)
2023. ISBN: 979-8-88697-951-0 (eBook)

Mindfulness: An Alternative Perspective for the Management of Anxiety Symptoms
Fleura Shkëmbi, PhD (Editor)
2023. ISBN: 979-8-88697-738-7 (Softcover)
2023. ISBN: 979-8-88697-797-4 (eBook)

More information about this series can be found at
https://novapublishers.com/product-category/series/psychology-of-emotions-motivations-and-actions/

Tina Marie Glover
Editor

How Did We Survive?

African-American Women and the Trauma Within

nova
science publishers

www.novapublishers.com

Library of Congress Cataloging-in-Publication Data

ISBN: 979-8-88697-918-3

Published by Nova Science Publishers, Inc. † New York

Contents

Preface

The preface of this book articulately encapsulates the profound mission and purpose it embodies - the culmination of the endeavors of numerous Black/African American therapists and scholars. Each contributor brings their unique perspective and dedication to addressing trauma in Black/African American women. My own passion for this subject arises from a profound awareness of the stark reality of trauma, including generational trauma, which is an intrinsic part of the lives of Black women. In clinical terms, it might be labeled as posttraumatic stress disorder (PTSD) or transgenerational trauma, but for the women we serve, it is an enduring facet of their existence. They grapple with the burden of oppression and microaggressions daily.

The core vision of this book is to shine a spotlight on the enduring legacy of trauma that Black/African American women bear and perpetuate through generations. It is essential to recognize that, for many, this trauma is a distant echo from its origins, yet it remains palpable and demands attention. African American women have weathered exposure to trauma, from the shackles of slavery to the contemporary microaggressions and oppression they confront.

This book takes a comprehensive view of various aspects of this trauma. It delves into the historical and cultural contexts, exploring the origins of trauma in African-American women and the social and cultural factors that sustain it. As readers progress through its pages, they will encounter the notion of contrary trauma and its conceptualization, diagnosis, and treatment. Some authors will advocate for considering specific factors when assessing and treating posttraumatic stress disorder (PTSD), while others may refer to it as race-based trauma. Irrespective of terminology, the overarching objective remains constant: to enhance the competence of mental health professionals in diagnosing and treating trauma, PTSD, and generational trauma in Black/African American women.

The book's structure is thoughtfully organized into four parts. Part one offers an examination of historical trauma, exploring the etiology of trauma in African-American women and the historical and social underpinnings of this phenomenon. Part two shifts the focus to contemporary trauma, dissecting the role of African-American women in today's society and the dynamics of the change process. Part three delves into the intricacies of diagnosing and treating trauma, encompassing the challenges of underdiagnosis, misdiagnosis, and the dissemination of best practices when working with African-American women. Finally, part four delves into the healing process of trauma, scrutinizing systemic issues and the racially sensitive approaches that women must navigate.

In essence, this book emerges as a vital contribution to the mental health field, shedding light on the often-overlooked experiences of Black/African American women and their resilience in the face of enduring trauma. It is a clarion call for mental health professionals to be attuned to the unique needs of this demographic and to cultivate a deeper understanding of their lived experiences to provide effective care and support.

Part 1. Historical Trauma

Chapter 1

The Etiology of Trauma in African-American Women

Tiffany Brannon*, PhD
University of the Cumberlands, Williamsburg, Kentucky, USA

Abstract

In pursuit of a more comprehensive interpretation of Trauma, theories of etiology have emerged from essentially every theoretical influence. Many provide a framework helpful in understanding facets of the disorder. However, based on current knowledge, a model must be comprehensive enough to include the collection of symptoms that contain the disorder, the differential severity of symptoms, the presence of Trauma in African American women but not others facing similar trauma, and recent empirical research relevant to these factors. This chapter reviews the etiology of Trauma among African American women. This review includes a reflection on the role of biological and psychological susceptibilities, adverse life events, alarms (fear reactions), perceptions of control, social support, and coping tactics. Empirical research advocating the inclusion of these components is presented. Finally, etiological and phenomenological similarities between anxiety disorders and Trauma are discussed.

Keywords: African American women, black women, trauma, etiology of trauma

---

* Corresponding Author's E-mail: Tiffany.Brannon@lindsey.edu.

In: How Did We Survive?
Editor: Tina Marie Glover
ISBN: 979-8-88697-918-3

Historical Background

Slavery

The slave experience for women was different from men. During this time, African Americans lacked rights under U.S. law; therefore, enslaved women could not control their bodies. Slaveholders were invested in reproducing African American women decades before the Civil War. African American enslaved women were pertinent in the plantation south regarding their ability to bear children. All the while, they were expected to complete their daily workloads often while conducting significant physical labor, whether pregnant or not. Whites dominating African American women's wombs to maintain a system of slavery supplied an early model for reproductive control.

A law was developed in 1662, making enslaved women's children the enslaver's property. This meant that plantation owners could increase their wealth by controlling their slaves' ability to reproduce. Plantation owners wanted to enhance their profits by breeding and increasing the fertility of enslaved women. In 1808 importing enslaved people were banned, making the reproduction of enslaved people more profitable. Thomas Jefferson expressed the significance of childbearing enslaved women in his book, *Thomas Jefferson's Farm Book,* where he stated that a woman who brings a child every two years is more worthy than the best man on the farm. The reproduction of enslaved people contributed to the increase of the slave population to 1.75 million by 1825.

Techniques were used to enhance fertility, including rewarding pregnancy with relief from fieldwork and improving food and clothing (Taylor, 2020). Women who did not have children were often punished by being forced to get pregnant or through manipulated marital practices. Other enslaved people were threatened to be sold off to other plantations, which meant removal from family and friends. Women who were considered damaged goods were physically abused and tormented by their owners. Enslavers believed the failure to bear children was a profit loss. Some enslaved women who did deliver many children in short timeframes were rewarded with freedom.

Forced mating and reproductive control became significant (Taylor, 2020). This was popular among enslavers, so enslaved people were perceived as prime stock and were coerced to produce children for purchase in the labor market. These enforced breeding practices included interfering with the sexual activity of enslaved people to ensure that women's fertility increased.

Unfortunately, offspring were raised solely to sell for profit, and enslaved women were expected to be pregnant every eighteen months to two years. The infant mortality rate among enslaved people in 1850 was twice that of whites, and less than two out of three African American children lived to see the age of ten.

Plantation owners became familiar with new training practices and medical doctors' sophisticated surgical procedures to reproductive organs by the mid-nineteenth century (Taylor, 2020). The new surgical procedures in women's health enhanced plantation productivity as the United States ceased importing enslaved people in 1808. Using a scientific approach to plantation management transitioned into a new era of slave breeding, coercion, medical experimentation, and the neglect of reproductive freedom.

In the 1800s, infertility treatment of enslaved African American women was often experimental, injurious, and painful. At the time, physicians depended a great deal on experience and observation for studying gynecology; however, the support of the scientific method was made impossible. As a result, African American enslaved women experimented with different surgical instruments, not using anesthesia in most cases. Morphine was abused in the way it was administered to drug African American enslaved women to decrease significant pain and related screams resulting from extreme vaginal surgeries. Despite adverse outcomes, physicians were ordered to make sure that these mothers could reproduce and that they experienced no negative impacts on their ability to have children on the plantation.

The African American enslaved woman was controlled by physicians, experiencing excruciating pain as their genitals were sutured without anesthesia. At times, other enslaved people were ordered to help restrain the women undergoing surgical procedures. As a result, enslaved women became addicted to morphine from their experimental surgeries. These examples contribute to the decades-long history of mistreatment, experimentation, and exploitation of African American women (Taylor, 2020). These practices have led to inferior treatment practices and poor medical care, even in maternal health today, which will be articulated later in this chapter. As the nineteenth century came, the reproductive injustice of African American women transformed into something institutionalized through sterilization and eugenic control.

The South became the first region to perform forced sterilizations, although sterilization abuse occurred in other regions. In 1972, the *Boston Globe* reported that Boston City Hospital performed hysterectomies on African American mothers at increased rates. Other incidents were reported at

New York municipal hospital where low-income African American, Puerto Rican, and Native American women were targeted and given unauthorized hysterectomies. Unfortunately, hospitals lacked policies addressing informed consent. Physicians, social workers, and members of state eugenics boards worked together to sterilize low-income African American women to reduce the number of African American women eligible for public aid (Taylor, 2020).

Post-Traumatic Slave Syndrome

The etiology of many adaptive survival practices in African American communities across the United States and the Diaspora is explained by Post Traumatic Slave Syndrome (PTSS). PTSS is a phrase established by globally known researcher Joy DeGruy, Ph.D., to characterize the multigenerational trauma and injustices faced by African Americans from the beginning of slavery to recent police killings of Black civilians. It is a situation that has arisen because of decades of chattel slavery, which has resulted in the oppression of Africans and their descendants over generations. This is a form of slavery based on the assumption that African Americans were genetically and fundamentally inferior to whites. Institutionalized racism has continued to cause harm, thus resulting in the development of M.A.P, which is (M)multigenerational trauma together with continued oppression; (A)absence of opportunity to heal or access the benefits available in the society, leading to (P)Post Traumatic Slave Syndrome.

Under such circumstances, predictable behavior patterns tend to occur, including vacant esteem, a marked propensity for rage and violence, and racist socialization. Vacant Esteem is characterized by a lack of growth of primary esteem, as well as sentiments of pessimism, melancholy, and a self-destructive outlook, according to Dr. DeGruy. A marked propensity for rage and violence can be explained as suspicion of others and negative motivations of others. Additionally, self-harm, property destruction, and violence towards others, including members of one's group, i.e., friends. *Racist Socialization and (internalized racism) are learned helplessness, literacy deprivation, and distorted self-concept. It is also antipathy or aversion for the following: the members of one's own identified cultural/ethnic group, the morals and customs associated with one's own identified cultural/ethnic heritage, and the physical characteristics of one's own identified cultural/ethnic group.*

Hypervigilance and arousal are signs of PTSS, which occur when a trauma survivor is repeatedly exposed to the stimulus or originator of the traumatic experience. The trauma recovery process is divided into stages, requiring the victim of trauma to flee a dangerous situation and seek refuge in a safe environment to minimize trauma responses (Herman, 2015). Due to the victims' continued exposure to the dangerous environment of chattel slavery, they experienced retraumatization for many years, even though they were still in the same area and were subjected to the perpetrator's continued violence. The epigenetics research confirmed the physiological evidence of PTSS as intergenerational trauma across generations. Epigenetics studies heritable gene expression changes that do not need changes to the genome's DNA sequence. Exposure to trauma by environmental stressors such as rape, torture, murder, and other forms of violence resulted in a change in the genetic makeup of trauma victims. These transmuted traits are then passed down to the children of the trauma victims. Thus, the trauma of chattel slavery has been continually transmitted throughout multiple generations (DeGruy, 2005). Additionally, intergenerational trauma research includes biological theories that explain the predispositions of the offspring of traumatized parents based on symptomatic patterns from one generation to the next. (Bowers &Yehuda, 2016). Children of parents who have been diagnosed with a trauma-based disorder have a greater likelihood of developing a similar trauma history, regardless of whether they have experienced trauma themselves or not, according to research.

African American Childhood

The history of racial discrimination in the United States has included an increasingly severe response to the behavior of African American children (Epstein et al., 2017). Beginning with slavery, African American children were treated as property and forced to work as early as two or three years old (Dumas & Nelson, 2016). Children face the same dehumanization that African American adults do; as a result, African American children are rarely considered deserving of playtime and are sometimes abused for acting like children. Adultification is a type of age compression in which young African American girls' mannerisms are assigned to more mature characteristics; this has been a problem for African American girls. As a result, presently, African American girls are compared to adults rather than children. They are considered to be intentionally engaging in behaviors often associated with African American women (Morris, 2016). This compression has stripped African American girls of their childhood privileges, making African

American girlhood and African American womanhood interchangeable. Loosen (2015) lays out the following points: Three main paradigms of African-American femininity that emerged in the South during slavery have made their way into modern culture, where African-American women are viewed by society as hypersexual, noisy, aggressive, and unscrupulous: Jezebel (e.g., emasculating, loud, aggressive, angry, stubborn, and unfeminine); Sapphire (e.g., hypersexualized, seductive, and exploiter of men's weasels); Mammy (e.g., self-sacrificing, nurturing, loving, asexual). These beliefs and historical prejudices of African American women have real-world ramifications for African American girls today. These prejudices are at the root of many adults' unconscious biases about African American women as sexually promiscuous, hedonistic, and needing socialization (Losen, 2015).

The sexualization of African American girls is a culturally ingrained feature of adultification (Morris, 2007). Stereotypes portray African American women as hypersexualized, and society interprets this as an acceptance of sex as a natural role for African American women and girls. As African American young ladies are often misperceived as older than their chronological age, adultification is direct and views African American girls as adults. According to researchers, the adultification of African American girls may contribute to more unequal levels of school punishment. Schools serve as settings for the formation of race, class, and gender identities and the perpetuation of standing inequities in their communities. The disproportionate treatment of African American girls in the juvenile justice system is an example of how schools enhance and amplify the inequities that children bring to school (Morris, 2007). Gender and race discrimination legacies have been encrusted upon African American women to add to elevated rates of criminality by greater society (Ocen et al.,2015). The historical relevance of racial and gender subjugation, including slavery and Jim Crow, has been combined with childhood classification to create a threshold category that leaves African American women vulnerable to criminalization.

According to research, African American women are viewed by society as more mature than their white counterparts at practically all stages of life, beginning at the age of five, peaking between the ages of ten and fourteen, and continuing through their teenage years (Epstein et al., 2017). The significance of this finding lies in the potential that adultification is to blame for the more complex treatment of African American women compared to their white counterparts. Adultification contributes to inequity in school punishment outcomes, more brutal law enforcement treatment, and the distinctive practice of judgment by officials across the continuum of the juvenile justice system for African American girls.

Adverse Childhood Experiences

According to Felitti et al., 1998 African American individuals have experienced more childhood adversity than Latinos and European Americans. While the Adverse Childhood Experience (ACE) study expanded the investigation of interpersonal events, it excluded the prevalence, nature, and consequences of childhood adversity in single African American mothers. Developing preventive interventions and policies that potentially alter the landscape is also essential, as African American individuals are more vulnerable to early adversity due to environmental factors. Researchers recently discovered a relationship between ACEs and community-based experiences, not only those that are personal or familial. Poverty, neighborhood violence, and racism may contribute to a person's likelihood of developing similar health problems (Sobol, 2019). Multiple childhood adverse experiences are more common among African American children than among their European American peers. Except for drug use or parents' mental illness, this paradigm applies to all adverse childhood experiences (Maguire-Jack et al., 2020). Nonetheless, race/ethnicity and income are intertwined to where racial/ethnic disparities in childhood adversity are most significant in the highest-income group.

Trauma Disparities in African American Women

Prevalence

Women are twice as likely as men to have had lifetime trauma and three times as likely to have experienced exposure to gender-based violence (Silove et al., 2017). Women are twice as likely as men to choose a network trauma as the index trauma, resulting in full PTSD symptoms. African American women are more likely than other racial/ethnic groups to be sexually assaulted and have a high lifetime prevalence of sexual assault (Ullman et al., 2020). The lifetime prevalence of PTSD is around 10–12% in women and 5–6% in men (Olff, 2017). Men and women are exposed to distinct traumas, with women experiencing more high-impact trauma (e.g., sexual trauma) at a younger age than men. Trauma experienced early in life has a more significant impact, particularly when type II trauma interferes with neurobiological development and personality.

According to the 2010-2012 National Intimate Partner and Sexual Violence Survey, 45% of African American women experienced contact sexual violence, physical violence, or stalking by an intimate partner in their lifetime. The same survey found that 40% of African American men experienced contact with sexual violence, physical violence, or stalking by an intimate partner in their lifetime. Almost one in every five African American women is stalked at some point in their lives. According to the survey, roughly 45% of African American women experience stalking by an intimate partner at some point in their lives.

In the United States, roughly 9% of African American women have been raped by an intimate partner over their lifetime (Breiding, 2014). In the United States, around 17% of African American women have suffered sexual violence other than rape by an intimate partner in their lifetime. According to the National Coalition Against Domestic Violence, African American men and women have more reported incidences of intimate partner violence because of systemic racism, racist legislation, and racist cultural structures. Intimate partner physical violence, intimate partner sexual violence, or intimate partner stalking have all been reported by 45.1% of African American women in their lifetime. Fear, safety concern, PTSD symptoms, injury, need for medical care, housing services, victim advocate services, or legal services, missing at least one day of work or school, and calling a crisis hotline are all experiences that 31.8% of African American women have had because of intimate partner violence. Intimate partner physical abuse affects 41.2% of African American women at some point in their lives. 53.8% of African American women experienced psychological aggression from an intimate partner in their lifetimes. Intimate relationship rape has happened to 8.8% of African American women at some point in their lives. Intimate partner sexual violence (other than rape) has been experienced by 17.4% of African American women throughout their lifetimes. Intimate partner stalking affects 9.5% of African American women at some point in their lives. Intimate partner violence is associated with 51.3% of African American adult women homicides (National Coalition Against Domestic Violence, 2020).

The Ujima National Center on Violence Against Women (2018) supplied the following statistics, for every African American woman who reports a rape, there are at least 15 women who stay silent. Before the age of 18, one out of every four African American women will be a victim of a sexual assault. One in five African American women has been raped. 35% of African American women have been subjected to some contact with sexual violence. By the age of 18, 40% to 60% of African American women report being subjected to forceful sexual contact. Other than rape by an intimate partner, 17% of African American women have experienced sexual violence in their lifetime by a stranger (Ujima: The National Center on Violence Against Women in the African American Community, 2018).

According to the Institute for Women's Policy Research (2017), more than 20% of African American women are raped at some point in their lives, a more significant percentage than for all women. African American women were two and a half times more likely than white women to be murdered by men. Furthermore, more than 9 out of 10 African American women victims knew their assailants. African American women also face much greater rates of psychological abuse than women in general, including humiliation, taunts, name-calling, and coercive control.

The Harvard & Brown Anxiety Research Projet suggested that increased trauma exposure toward African American individuals, compared to White adults, shows that therapeutic interventions for PTSD in this minority group are lacking. As a result of this study, sociocultural and racial stressors promote a higher prevalence and worse outcomes in this population, including experiences with prejudice. However, there has been little research examining the link between discrimination and the risk of PTSD and much less research on the pattern of PTSD among African American individuals (Sibrava et al., 2019).

Chronicity

Chronic trauma occurs after a series of occurrences, including suffering protracted child abuse, extended exposure to war and warfare, continual sexual assault, direct experience of or exposure to ongoing domestic violence, and experiencing many natural disasters. Mental health and socioeconomic status explain childhood trauma's association with chronic disease in adulthood, with mental health showing a more substantial effect (Mock & Arai, 2011). Additionally, cumulative disadvantage following trauma may lead to chronic illness. This may guide the need for public health expenditures on resources such as counseling, and income supports to prevent or reduce psychological harm and chronic disease resulting from traumatic events.

In contrast to acute trauma, where symptoms appear in weeks, PTSD symptoms can sometimes take years to manifest. People who have experienced chronic trauma are more prone to engage in maladaptive coping techniques, prompting them to feel obligated to respond to their chronic trauma, according to the National Health Service in 2018. Chronic trauma symptoms are severe, interfering with regular everyday functions and resulting in deviant behaviors. Anxiety, melancholy, sadness, confusion, wrath, rage, violent outbursts, overreactions to routine occurrences, damaged or distorted memories, low self-worth, weariness, sleep problems, a skewed viewpoint of one's environment, nightmares, and flashbacks are all common symptoms among survivors.

Childhood trauma is a substantial predictor of depression in adulthood (Herts et al., 2021). A history of emotional abuse and neglect, and physical abuse in childhood were significant predictors of persistent depression in adults (Negele et al., 2015). Compared to other traumatic events (e.g., sexual abuse), studies analyzing childhood trauma as a predictor of subsequent depression showed that experiencing emotional abuse or neglect as a child increases the likelihood of depression (Springer et al., 2003). Survivors with chronic trauma are more likely to engage in destructive and damaging behaviors, such as high-risk conduct, sexual avoidance, violence, dysfunctional relationships, and substance misuse, to manage and reestablish normalcy without professional therapy.

Comorbidity

Reliving the experience through flashbacks, recollections, thoughts, and dreams are common trauma symptoms. These symptoms are often connected with hyperarousal pupil dilation, muscular tremors, and perspiration. Triggers produce a significant stress response, and sensory signals often lead a trauma patient to believe the experience is repeating itself (Substance Abuse and Mental Health Services Administration, 2014). Hypervigilance is a behavioral habit that can be regulated by avoiding triggers. Up to 80% of PTSD patients have a comorbid disorder, with depression, anxiety, alcoholism, and substance misuse as the most prevalent comorbidities (Gradus et al., 2015). Trauma-related comorbidity may result in a diminished health-related value of life.

An Example of Prevalence & Chronicity

Personal Narrative : Anonymous

My childhood trauma included molestation by my father, brother, two male cousins, and others. I remember being molested by the neighbor's son after my mom left my dad in another country. We lived with her sister in California and her three daughters when I was four. I then had an encounter with my elementary school classmate involving her being aggressive with me and wanting to role-play sexually. This involved scenarios where she was the victim of an aggressor or in a home invasion involving rape. My brother only did what he saw or started because our middle sister molested him. My father was previously married, so my five brothers and three sisters were in and out over the years.

When my father molested me, my mother told a friend when I told her what he did to me. The friend removed all the children from home, and we stayed a few days with my aunt. My father was in the military at the time, so she went to the military base and sought discipline for him. He was sent to the quarters for single military personnel barracks, and he was eventually court marshaled, and we returned to the family home. Once it was time for trial, my mother lied on the witness stand. A person came to our house with anatomically correct dolls, and I had to simulate what he had done to me and make a statement, but that did not matter. He was allowed to return home on his promise to my mother that he would never do it again, but he did. At the trial, I remember my brother screaming through the window that he hated me because of the entire ordeal. My brother was in and out of prison most of his life. It was not until he was out of prison, right before he died, he apologized to me.

I have tried to tell other family members about the things happening to me at different times. One year, I told my favorite male cousin about what another cousin had been doing to me, and he encouraged me to tell my mother. I told her, and she became agitated with me while I was telling her what had happened, and she told my dad. The next time all of us were together again, Thanksgiving. I had imagined in my head all day into the night that they would do something to my cousin about what he did to me. However, everyone gathered their coats and said goodbye. I knew then that nothing had been done or would be. At this point, I felt no point in talking about the other cousin or my brother.

I am unsure how everything that has happened has impacted others in my family. The only people who have expressed disappointment or anger at our father are my oldest brother and my middle sister. However, they only seem to do that when drunk or high.

As a result, I had no self-esteem, and sports were my only outlet. My mother has always been obsessed with how everything looks, which is very important in the military and the church, especially since my father was a pastor. I found out later that my father also molested my two female cousins.

I was alone and always felt like I could not be myself. I know my sexual abuse history at such a young age has impacted my sex life as an adult drastically. As a result, I was always attention-seeking when I was younger and started smoking weed. I was always heavily under my parent's influence and watch. I lived with them until my mid-twenties, and at that time, I met my ex-husband, and we married. I was finally able to leave that dreadful house! Looking back, I believe I was subconsciously seeking familiarity. I had three children with my ex-husband, and he controlled everything I did throughout our marriage. He abused me emotionally and physically over the years significantly. I finally found the courage to leave him and divorce him. I struggle with going to therapy and hope I find the courage to go one day.

Transgenerational Trauma

Trauma that is passed down through generations is referred to as transgenerational trauma. Not only can someone be traumatized, but they can also carry the signs and behaviors of trauma survival to their children, who can then pass them down the family line. Intergenerational trauma is another term for transgenerational trauma. Childhood abuse is a classic example of transgenerational trauma, perpetuating a cycle of abuse and anxiety across generations. Extreme poverty, a sudden or violent loss of a family member, a parent who fought in a war, and the torture of a family member are all examples of trauma that can produce intergenerational trauma.

Transgenerational trauma is a type of historical trauma. Historical trauma, unlike transgenerational trauma, affects many people or perhaps an entire generation and is sometimes referred to as "collective trauma." Slavery, the Holocaust, and the displacement of Native American children in the United States are all examples of historical trauma. Other kinds of trauma that cause historical trauma could include famine, natural disaster, war, terrorism, and displacement.

The trauma cannot be passed on; no one else can truly experience what another has gone through. However, they pass on trauma symptoms, such as post-traumatic stress disorder (PTSD), anxiety, and anxiety disorders. Learned behavior is usually how these symptoms are handed down to the following generation. *Trauma affects how someone's parents and parenting affect how a child thinks and behaves into adulthood (barring intervention). Trauma has an impact on how someone's parents and parenting has an impact on how a child thinks and behaves as an adult. Trauma impacts a parent's capacity to provide adequate attachment to their child, the activities a parent chooses to do or not do with their child, the stories a parent tells their child, and the perspective, personal values, and fundamental beliefs a parent teaches their child. According to research, even if a child of someone with post-traumatic stress disorder grows up to be psychologically well, they are more likely to develop PTSD if they are exposed to or witness anything upsetting.*

An Example of Transgenerational Trauma

Personal Narrative: Anonymous

At the age of 20, my grandmother Lily fell in love with a married man and conceived my mother. Lily was heartbroken and in love, but he returned to his wife. Lily then married a military man she did not love so my mother could have a father. At 21, she gave birth to her son, who was quickly adopted. She then left my mother with my cousin for months because she was not emotionally ready to be a mother. My mother ended up being raised by my great-grandmother Ruth.

My mother, Cheryl, yearned for affection and love from my great-grandparents. They took care of her but did not give her much attention. At age 6-7, my mother told our family that an unidentified family member sexually abused her. As a result, she was told to keep it a secret by my family. My mother then met a man, so she started using birth control. My grandmother told her she could not have sex until marriage and that she could not use birth control. Physical threats and slaps to the face were discipline used to stop her from using birth control. My mother obliged but became pregnant with my brother Steve; his paternity was unknown. My mother then met my father at her job when my brother Steve was a baby. They quickly became a couple, and I was born shortly after, followed by my sister. My mother had three children before she turned 21.

My father often cheated on my mother, and my brother began to have behavioral issues. My grandmother Lily took my brother in. During this time, I discovered my mother smokes marijuana. Everyone kept telling me I looked like my father, which drove my mother crazy. I was often the target of her anger. I was spanked daily for minor incidents, such as improper cleaning up. My mother noticed I had a stronger bond with my father, which infuriated her.

During this time, my mother left me alone often so she could go out. The police came to our house, and due to accusations of physical abuse that left detectable signs of bruises, I had repeated social work visits at my school, but nothing was ever done. As time went on, we moved about to different areas and schools. My mother's anger became more extreme. She met a guy who eventually moved in with us. He was very controlling. They fought every night, resulting in multiple black eyes and concussions.

My mother began using crack cocaine and stealing from department stores soon after. My mother would take my sister and me to the mall and have us try on things while she loaded her jeans with goods. She was arrested, and we had to stay with my father. My mother became involved with a married white man. He gave narcotics to my mother to sell in our neighborhood. She gave him all her money and made a small profit. We were evicted because she became addicted to drugs and could not pay her bills. He returned to his wife, my mother moved to another county with my sister, and I moved in with my father. My grades deteriorated at this point because I was exhausted. I neglected my skills as a star athlete because I was angry and tired. I then met a boy who was the first to show interest in me, and I focused all my time on him.

He was sweet and affectionate initially, which was new to me. He became increasingly toxic as our relationship evolved. He was obnoxious, arrogant, insulting, and disrespectful. I put up with him cheating, lying, choking me, embarrassing me, and taking me for granted from age 16 to 21. I stayed because, despite the abuse, he told me he loved me and always showered me with presents after he abused me. Emotionally I suppressed my emotions because I was told crying is weak. I grew into a deep depression, and my father told me to get over it. At this time, my mother was at the deep end of her addiction, and my 16-year-old sister worked in high school to pay the bills while having no electricity or running water.

Anger, aggression, and resentment soon fueled my sadness and exhaustion. I trusted no one because I felt no one cared about me and my life experiences. At 19, I got a retail job, which saved me because I learned how to care for myself. I was taught my value and worth and soon began to make friends. I was determined not to make the same choices as my grandmother and mother did by getting pregnant, unmarried, and young.

Epigenetics

Epigenetics can cause a pregnant mother's trauma to alter her baby's stress hormone levels at the genetic level (Williams, 2014). The fetus' ground zero stress levels are permanently changed by a surge in cortisol levels from the mother, making it hyperresponsive to stimuli once it is born. The pressures a pregnant woman faces and the pre-existing pressure her body is under cause epigenetic markers on the fetus' DNA to alter (Sullivan, 2013). As seen by a change in cortisol levels, the repercussions of white racism in America are passed down through the generations. This phenomenon explains why a pregnant enslaved woman's pain can still be felt by her descendants hundreds of years later and why the reaction to race-related stress is like that of PTSD.

The term epigenetics refers to a series of potentially heritable changes in the genome triggered by environmental factors (Yehuda et al., 2018). These changes affect the function of genomic DNA, histone proteins, and noncoding RNAs, collectively known as chromatin, without requiring a change in DNA sequence. Epigenetics is the science of gene expression and cannot be written in pencil since DNA cannot be changed or removed. Gene expression is edited, which means it can vary throughout time. Nature-inherited genes from parents, nurture, and life experiences form the basis of epigenetics. The type of genes passed down from parents, developmental stage, and overall environment influence how genes are expressed. During menopause or pregnancy, the body changes, and genes are influenced by inherited biological variables and the environment. The inherited genetic code, life events, and environment can all influence gene expression. Epigenetic modifications caused by toxins exemplify how the environment influences gene expression. According to research, epigenetic changes linked to toxins are passed on from mother to child (McIntosh, 2019).

Epidemiology of Trauma in the African American Community

According to epidemiological surveys, exposure to childhood adversity is a severe public health problem; about two-thirds of adults report having had at least one adverse childhood event or three or more adverse childhood experiences (Merrick et al., 2018). Hardship in childhood varies by race, although most studies show that African American individuals are more likely than European Americans to report childhood adversity (Slopen et al., 2016). Adults who identify as African American, Latinx, or mixed race experience higher rates of childhood adversity than adults who identify as other racial/ethnic groups (Merrick et al., 2018). Multiple childhood adverse experiences are more common among African American and Latinx children than among their European American peers (Slopen et al., 2016). When analyzed, African American children experience adverse childhood experiences compared to European American or Latinx children. When analyzing rates of childhood adversity across racial and ethnic groups, other social identities, such as socioeconomic status (SES), require consideration. Children from low-SES backgrounds report more childhood adversity than children from higher-SES homes across all racial/ethnic groups (Slopen et al., 2016).

Biological Correlates of Trauma

A sizeable body of data shows that childhood adversity has enduring effects on one's neurological, endocrine, immune, and metabolic functions (Danese & Lewis, 2017). Likely because of the interaction of childhood adversity with genes via sequence variation and epigenetic effects (Jiang et al., 2019). The ACE study presented the first evidence of a graded association between cumulative exposure to childhood adversity and a broad range of adult physical health outcomes (e.g., ischemic heart disease, cancer, chronic lung disease, skeletal fractures, or liver disease autoimmune disorders.

Numerous studies with low-income African American families living in urban environments have discovered that fear physiology, autonomic function, and elevated inflammation are correlated with trauma exposure and childhood adversity (Michopoulos et al., 2015). Together, these data emphasize the heterogeneity of changes in secondary stress physiology in trauma-exposed African American individuals. These changes may, exclusively or in combination, increase the allostatic load and the combined risk of creating stress-related physical and psychological disorders.

Cognitive Affective Deficits Related to Trauma

Researchers associate childhood adversity with unfavorable cognitive outcomes that affect more advanced cognitive abilities linked to continuous working memory, inhibitory control, and cognitive flexibility (Guinosso et al., 2016). These influences continue into adulthood for African American individuals and European Americans. Even after accounting for demographics, general intellectual performance, psychopathology, and alcohol use, researchers believe that childhood neglect predicted executive functioning insufficiencies in adulthood in a large, mixed-race population (Nikulina & Widom, 2013).

The timing of childhood adversity exposure plays a role in creating cognitive-affective deficits. During sensitive times in brain development, including pre-and peri-pubertal periods, childhood adversity alters regions experiencing the highest rise in development (e.g., amygdala, hippocampus, or prefrontal cortex). These regions, which are accountable for more advanced cognition and emotion regulation, are vulnerable to the effects of stress. Childhood adversity negatively affects basic emotion processing, which can cause biases in attention and the precise identification of emotions in adulthood (Young & Widom, 2014). In African American families, researchers link childhood maltreatment to biases in attention to emotional cues such as threat-related facial expressions (Lakshman et al., 2020).

Social Correlates of Trauma

In low-income African American children, those subjected to childhood abuse have more challenges with social functioning compared to those who did not experience abuse (Lamis et al., 2014); therefore. Notably, these relational difficulties make it challenging to find and sustain social support over time (Segrin et al., 2016). A history of childhood abuse is linked to lower levels of social support among low-income African American women. Childhood maltreatment is related to more challenges with emotion regulation, weaker social support, and more adult interpersonal violence; therefore, social aid helps women connect the dots between childhood trauma and adult PTSD symptoms. This lack of social support in the context of childhood adversity is alarming; social support is an important protective factor against the development of biopsychosocial disorders in African American people.

Cultural Process that Impact Trauma

As a result of childhood trauma, cultural elements may affect biological, psychological, and/or social functioning (Hampton-Anderson et al., 2021). African American cultural strategies include a focus on socioeconomic position and culture-specific coping. This is problematic because it may impact persons who have endured childhood adversity's ability to function. African American women who experienced sexual abuse as children employ spirituality, community support, activism, and racial reframing/racial attribution, among other culturally relevant coping techniques. Furthermore, when embracing spirituality as a coping method, African American women with a history of childhood maltreatment are less likely to develop PTSD (Zhang et al., 2015). Spiritual coping is a subset of Africultural coping that includes culture-specific coping methods used in stressful situations, all of which are founded on an African-centered conceptual framework. The theories of ritual-centered coping, collective coping, and cognitive/emotional debriefing are also relevant to childhood adversity in Agricultural coping. Community support and hobbies are examples of culture-specific coping.

The strong African American woman/superwoman paradigm is another helpful approach to culture-specific coping (Donovan & West, 2015). This paradigm connects one's tendency to cope with stress by presenting it as powerful, self-sacrificing, and dispassionate. Researchers found a correlation between a history of childhood adversity (such as abuse) and a propensity to adopt the superwoman role, which leads to a reduced willingness to express feelings or seek help. Implementing the solid African American woman notion is one way to draw the link between trauma exposure and early struggle (Harrington et al., 2010). Furthermore, the role of superwomen entwines itself with racial prejudice and exposes African American women to physical health issues such as binge eating.

It is important to remember that the role of biological and psychological susceptibilities, childhood adversity, cultural effects, social support, and more are discussed in this chapter. There is a link between transgenerational trauma and the prevalence and chronicity of trauma in African American women. Through anonymous personal narratives that highlight African American women's unique experiences of trauma and their adventures navigating trauma throughout their lives. Counseling and associated professions need to know more about the etiology of trauma in African American women. Examining the historical consequences of trauma in this community is essential to provide culturally appropriate counseling techniques. Looking at the historical effects of trauma in this population is necessary to offer counselors culturally relevant approaches that can help advance counseling as a diverse and equitable profession.

References

Bowers, M., Yehuda, R. Intergenerational Transmission of Stress in Humans. *Neuropsychopharmacol* 41, 232–244 (2016). https://doi.org/10.1038/npp.2015.247

Breiding, M. J. (2014). *Prevalence and characteristics of sexual violence, stalking, and intimate partner violence victimization—National Intimate Partner and Sexual Violence Survey,* United States, 2011.

Danese, A., & Lewis, S. J. (2017). Psychoneuroimmunology of early-life stress: The hidden wounds of childhood trauma? *Neuropsychopharmacology*, *42*(1), 99–114. https://doi.org/10.1038/npp.2016.198

Donovan, R. A., & West, L. M. (2015). Stress and mental health: Moderating role of the strong black woman stereotype. *Journal of Black Psychology*, *41*(4), 384–396. https://doi.org/10.1177/0095798414543014

Dumas, M. J., & Nelson, J. D. (2016). (Re)Imagining Black boyhood: Toward a critical framework for educational research. *Harvard Educational Review*, *86*(1), 27–47. https://doi.org/10.17763/0017-8055.86.1.27

Epstein, R., Blake, J., González, T. (2017). Girlhood interrupted: The erasure of Black girls' childhood. Center on Poverty and Inequality.

Gradus, J. L., Antonsen, S., Svensson, E., Lash, T. L., Resick, P. A., & Hansen, J. G. (2015). Trauma, comorbidity, and mortality following diagnoses of severe stress and adjustment disorders: a nationwide cohort study. *American journal of epidemiology*, *182*(5), 451–458. https://doi.org/10.1093/aje/kwv066

Guinosso, S. A., Johnson, S. B., & Riley, A. W. (2016). Multiple adverse experiences and child cognitive development. *Pediatric Research*, *79*(1), 220–226. https://doi.org/10.1038/pr.2015.195Herts, K. L., & Evans, S. (2021). Schema Therapy for Chronic Depression Associated with Childhood Trauma: A Case Study. *Clinical Case Studies*, *20*(1), 22–38. https://doi.org/10.1177/1534650120954275

Hampton-Anderson, J. N., Carter, S., Fani, N., Gillespie, C. F., Henry, T.L., Holmes, E., Lamis, D. A., LoParo, D., Maples-Keller, J. L., Powers, A., Sonu, S., & Kaslow, N. J. (2021). Adverse childhood experiences in African Americans: Framework, practice, and policy *American Psychologist*, *76*(2), 314–325. https://doi.org/10.1037/amp0000767

Hill, S. A. (2006). Marriage among African American Women: A Gender Perspective. *Journal of Comparative Family Studies*, *37*(3), 421-440. https://doi.org/10.3138/jcfs.37.3.421

Jiang, S., Postovit, L., Cattaneo, A., Binder, E. B., & Aitchison, K. J. (2019). Epigenetic modifications in stress response genes associated with childhood trauma. *Frontiers in Psychiatry*, *10*, 808. https://doi.org/10.3389/fpsyt.2019.00808

Lakshman, M., Murphy, L., Mekawi, Y., Carter, S., Briscione, M., Bradley, B., Tone, E. B., Norrholm, S. D., Jovanovic, T., & Powers, A. (2020). Attention bias toward threat in African American children exposed to early life trauma. *Behavioural Brain Research, 383*. https://doi.org/10.1016/j.bbr.2020.11251

Lamis, D. A., Wilson, C. K., Shahane, A. A., & Kaslow, N. J. (2014). Mediators of the childhood emotional abuse–hopelessness association in African American women. *Child Abuse & Neglect, 38*(8), 1341–1350. https://doi.org/10.1016/j.chiabu.2013.11.006

Leary, Joy DeGruy. (2005). Post traumatic slave syndrome : America's legacy of enduring injury and healing. Milwaukie, Oregon :Uptone Press,

Losen, D. J. (2015). *Closing the School Discipline Gap: Equitable Remedies for Excessive Exclusion*. Teachers College Press.

Maguire-Jack, K., Lanier, P., & Lombardi, B. (2020). Investigating racial differences in clusters of adverse childhood experiences. *American Journal of Orthopsychiatry, 90*(1), 106–114. https://doi.org/10.1037/ort0000405

Merrick, M. T., Ford, D. C., Ports, K. A., & Guinn, A. S. (2018). Prevalence of adverse childhood experiences from the 2011–2014 Behavioral Risk Factor Surveillance System in 23 states. *Journal of the American Medical Association Pediatrics, 172*(11), 1038–1044. https://doi.org/10.1001/jamapediatrics.2018.2537

Michopoulos, V., Rothbaum, A. O., Jovanovic, T., Almli, L. M., Bradley, B., Rothbaum, B. O., Gillespie, C. F., & Ressler, K. J. (2015). Association of CRP genetic variation and CRP level with elevated PTSD symptoms and physiological responses in a civilian population with high levels of trauma. *The American Journal of Psychiatry, 172*(4), 353–362. https://doi.org/10.1176/appi.ajp.2014.14020263

Mock, S. E., & Arai, S. M. (2011). Childhood trauma and chronic illness in adulthood: mental health and socioeconomic status as explanatory factors and buffers. *Frontiers in psychology, 1*, 246. https://doi.org/10.3389/fpsyg.2010.00246

Morris, M. W. (2016). *Pushout: The Criminalization of black girls in Schools*. New York: The New Press.

Negele, A., Kaufhold, J., Kallenbach, L., & Leuzinger-Bohleber, M. (2015). Childhood Trauma and Its Relation to Chronic Depression in Adulthood. *Depression research and treatment, 2015*, 650804. https://doi.org/10.1155/2015/650804

Nikulina, V., & Widom, C. S. (2013). Child maltreatment and executive functioning in middle adulthood: A prospective examination. *Neuropsychology, 27*(4), 417-427. https://doi.org/10.1037/a0032811

Olff, M. (2017). Sex and gender differences in post-traumatic stress disorder: an update. *European Journal of Psychotraumatology, 8*(4). https://doi.org/10.1080/20008198.2017.1351204

Segrin, C., McNelis, M., & Swiatkowski, P. (2016). Social skills, social support, and psychological distress: A test of the social skills deficit vulnerability model. *Human Communication Research, 42*(1), 122–137. https://doi.org/10.1111/hcre.12070

Silove, D., Baker, J. R., Mohsin, M., Teesson, M., Creamer, M., O'Donnell, M., Forbes, D., Carragher, N., Slade, T., Mills, K., Bryant, R., McFarlane, A., Steel, Z., Felmingham, K., & Rees, S. (2017). The contribution of gender-based violence and network trauma to gender differences in Post-Traumatic Stress Disorder. *PLoS ONE, 12*(2). https://doi.org/10.1371/journal.pone.0171879

Slopen, N., Shonkoff, J. P., Albert, M. A., Yoshikawa, H., Jacobs, A., Stoltz, R., & Williams, D. R. (2016). Racial disparities in child adversity in the U.S.: Interactions with family immigration history and income. *American Journal of Preventive Medicine, 50*(1), 47–56. https://doi.org/10.1016/j.amepre.2015.06.013

Sobol, M. (2019, August 20). How Adverse Childhood Experiences Shape Your Life Today. *Well Clinic*.

Springer, K. W., Sheridan, J., Kuo, D., & Carnes, M. (2003). The long-term health outcomes of childhood abuse. An overview and a call to action. *Journal of general internal medicine, 18*(10), 864–870. https://doi.org/10.1046/j.1525-1497.2003.20918.x

Su, W. M., & Stone, L. (2020). Adult survivors of childhood trauma: Complex trauma, complex needs. *Australian Journal of General Practice, 49*(7), 423–430. https://doi.org/10.31128/AJGP-08-19-5039

Sullivan, S. (2013). Inheriting Racist Disparities in Health: Epigenetics and the Transgenerational Effects of White Racism. Critical Philosophy of Race, 1(2), 190–218.

Taylor, J. K. (2020). Structural Racism and Maternal Health Among Black Women. *Journal of Law, Medicine & Ethics, 48*(3), 506–517. https://doi.org/10.1177/1073110520958875

Ullman, S. E., & Lorenz, K. (2020). Correlates of African American sexual assault survivors' medical care seeking. *Women & Health, 60*(5), 502–516. https://doi.org/10.1080/03630242.2019.1671947

Williams, M. T., Malcoun, E., Sawyer, B. A., Davis, D. M., Nouri, L. B., & Bruce, S. L. (2014). Cultural Adaptations of Prolonged Exposure Therapy for Treatment and Prevention of Posttraumatic Stress Disorder in African Americans. *Behavioral Sciences,* 4(2), 105–106. https://doi.org/10.3390/bs4020102

Yehuda, R., & Lehrner, A. (2018). Intergenerational transmission of trauma effects: Putative role of epigenetic mechanisms. *World Psychiatry*, 17(3), 243–257. https://doi.org/10.1002/wps.20568

Young, J. C., & Widom, C. S. (2014). Long-term effects of child abuse and neglect on emotion processing in adulthood. *Child Abuse & Neglect, 38*(8), 1369–1381. https://doi.org/10.1016/j.chiabu.2014.03.008

Chapter 2

The Trauma of Colorism across a Lifespan

Kerri McCullough[*]
University of Southern California, Los Angeles, California, USA

Abstract

This chapter will focus on the role of colorism in the socialization of African American women across decades and its impact on their role in the community. Colorism is a symptom of internalized racism in the African American community for both men and women. This chapter will examine literature and provide insight into how the concept of colorism affects one's self-esteem and the way one interacts with others within and outside of their ethnc group.

Keywords: African American women, black women, trauma, colorism

"If you are light, you are all right; If you are brown, stick around; If you are black, get back."

Introduction

Colorism is a symptom of internalized racism in the African American community, affecting both men and women. Numerous studies have been conducted to examine the effects of colorism on both light and dark-skinned women (Elmore 2009; Fegley, Spence, Goss, Harpalani, & Charles 2008).

[*] Corresponding Author's Email: kclegette@gmail.com.

In: How Did We Survive?
Editor: Tina Marie Glover
ISBN: 979-8-88697-918-3

However, research indicates that colorism affects men and women differently. Research suggested that colorism affects African American females' self-concept and self-esteem different than any other racial group. The darker the skin color the more significant adverse self-esteem effects (Thompson & Keith, 2001).

In 1983, Alice Walker invented colorism to refer to the prejudice and preference for African Americans with more European characteristics. Colorism has infiltrated everyday terms and actions used by Family, friends, and social contexts, perpetuating, and reinforcing the discrimination associated with skin tone. Numerous skin terms, ranging from "bright yellow" to "blue-black," are used to characterize the tones found in the African American community. In the African American community, lighter skin has traditionally been associated with increased opportunity, access to resources, and general privilege as a black person in society today (Thompson & Keith, 2001).

This has been noted most prominently in regions with a disproportionate impact on women. These aspects included penalties in criminal justice, job selection, perceived beauty, and opportunities for mate selection (Thompson & Keith, 2001). According to some studies, these interracial attitudes foster a competitive dynamic. This competition's growth has resulted in hostility amongst skin color groups. A darker complexion is associated with negative color symbolism because of a post-colonial American civilization. Additionally, the notion of attractiveness as a source of capital for women is inextricably linked to the historical devaluation of women's strength and potential (Thompson & Keith, 2001).

Colorism has a long history in the African Diaspora (Africa, the Caribbean, Central, and South America) and the United States (Russell, Wilson, and Hall, 1992). The history of skin color discrimination against African Americans dates back to their colonization and enslavement. Additionally, it is sustained by community members' internalization of these experiences (Russell, Wilson, and Hall, 1992). As a result, the most critical section of the literature review is an examination of the color complex's historical context and development. Numerous studies have examined the influence of colorism on African Americans' functioning and self-esteem; however, this study presents findings from a deficit perspective (Parrish, 1944; Russell, Wilson, and L Hall, 1992;).

The history of colorism among African Americans demonstrates that, like racism, colorism was evident and overt in the lives of black Americans before the civil rights movement. Having a lighter skin tone explains why, according to Wade (1996), "skin color became a criterion for achieving prestige in the African-American community" at this time (p. 359). Skin tone and socioeconomic class became focal points for black social scientists studying various facets of black life. Gunnar Myrdal's study on the nature of class and skin tone among African Americans was reported in An American Dilemma. St. Clair Drake and Horace Cayton (1945) demonstrate that racial differences in employment, occupation, and mate selection translate into differences in employment, occupation, and mate selection. Additionally, the authors provide candid criticism on prevailing attitudes around skin tone and how they affect Black women.

Racism and Colorism Relationship

Since the founding of the United States, race has been at the core of power and privilege discourse. While institutional racism persists, the discussion is more significant than the Black-White dichotomy. The evidence of racism's detrimental effects on the African American population is rising. The effort to enhance Black Americans' quality of life is a continuing tale with no conclusion. Much of Black America's struggle for racial equality is directed against mainstream White America's bigotry. Research reveals that beliefs about race and identity are embedded relationships that begin in childhood, starting with Kenneth and Mamie Clark's (1947) doll study, which was significant in the Brown v. Board Supreme Court decision.

For more than a century, professionals, researchers, and everyday black people have been seized by colorism. In the mid-1800s, the first scholarly study about colorism was published. In his 1853 masterpiece Clotel, author William Wells Brown was the first to chronicle the complexity of skin tone (Kerr, 2006). Since then, color consciousness has been discussed in the following works: The Blacker the Berry (1929), The Bluest Eye (1970), The Color Purple (1983), The Color Complex (1992), and Do Not Play in the Sun (2004); Black Bourgeoisie and Black Metropolis; and films such as Spike Lee's School Daze (1988), Oprah Winfrey's The Wedding (1998), and CC Stinson's Light, Bright, Damn Near White (2004). (2007). This extensive corpus of literature demonstrates the persistence of skin tone prejudice and discrimination in black American society over time.

Colorism in America is a historical issue that dates to enslavement. It manifests in societal structures and impacts how African Americans feel and develop their identities. Color bias also influences how many African

Americans interact with other group members. Colorism is perpetuated because of internalized racism and the influence of the majority culture on African Americans' self-perceptions. Russell, Wilson, and Hall (1992) believe that the black community suffers from a color disparity in privilege, which dates to the mixed-race sexual relationships between slaves and their masters. These unions exacerbated color disparities and distanced lighter and darker-skinned Africans in America regarding status. This social divide was exacerbated by the white supremacist ideology imported by European colonists, which associated Blackness with primitivism, lack of civilization, unrestricted sexuality, pollution, and dirt. (Glenn, 2008, p. 284) Thus, colorism is an important phenomenon worth studying and analyzing since it has influenced the internalization of century-old racist practices.

Skin tone and socioeconomic class became focal points for black social scientists studying various facets of black life. Gunnar Myrdal's study on the nature of class and skin tone among African Americans was reported in An American Dilemma. St. Clair Drake and Horace Cayton (1945) demonstrate that racial differences in employment, occupation, and mate selection translate into differences in employment, occupation, and mate selection. Additionally, the authors provide candid criticism on prevailing attitudes around skin tone and how they affect Black women.

Fears (1998) defined colorism as a pattern of interaction in which lighter-skinned African Americans reject darker Blacks and then blame their lighter-skinned colleagues for not being "black enough." She touched on the attitudes and beliefs linked with lighter skin, such as the impression of lighter-skinned Blacks as more intelligent and attractive due to their skin tone and hair texture being like Whites. Banks and Grambs (1972) emphasize the detrimental effect of intergroup racism on African Americans' self-concept. They believe that racial prejudice has historically and continues to impact Black people's self-concept profoundly. Additionally, the authors believe that racial socialization begins in childhood and influences black children's future development. If intergroup racism has this effect, it is reasonable to assume that intragroup racism has a comparable impact on racial identity and self-concept.

This issue continues to be explored because many researchers are interested in learning about and comprehending the subject's significance. Additionally, they wish to determine whether colorism has the same influence today as it did in the past. This, suggested in the literature, is why colorism continues to be explored. Throughout this era, slogans such as "Black is Beautiful" and "I am Black and proud" fostered an acceptance of darker skin tones and natural hair (Brown, 2000; Hall, 1998, 2005; Hughes & Hertel,

1990; Hunter, 1998, 2002, 2005; Jones, 2000; Keith & Herring, 1991, 2004; Kerr, 2006; Patton, 2006; Seltzer & Smith, 1991; Wade, 1996; Zook, 1990). These movements were significant because they rejected the concept that everything light or remotely European was superior.

Colorism Pre-Civil Rights

"Following the Civil War, light-skinned African Americans sought to isolate themselves from their darker-skinned brothers and sisters by establishing exclusive civic and cultural groups, fraternities, sororities, schools, and institutions (Russell, Wilson, and Hall 1992, 24-40)." (Glenn, 2008, p. 287). Lake (2003) provides an overview of America's history of colorism, beginning with its origins in slavery. As many other authors have done, she locates the origins of color consciousness in masters' inter-racial sexual practices with their slaves. She cites maternity issues, family structures, and community divide because of the birth of "mulattoes" in America.

Colorism was as overt and pervasive as racism during the Jim Crow era. As a result, African Americans with more European characteristics enjoyed a greater degree of opportunities. Wade (1996) says that during the Jim Crow era, "skin color became a criterion for African American communal prestige" (p. 359). As a result of this sociological element, scholars such as Anna Julia Cooper (1892) and W.E.B DuBois (1903) began to investigate the reality of colorism. Drake & Cayton (1945), E. Franklin Frazier (1957), Gunnar Myrdal (1944), and Charles Parrish (1944) all followed suit in this work (1946). Drake and Cayton also investigated the effect of black women's skin tone. Herring (2002) asserts that these early studies and observations were critical in understanding how colorism affects social outcomes such as employment, occupation, and partner selection.

Charles Parrish (1946) researched the terms and labels used by African Americans to refer to various skin tones and the associated stereotypes. His investigation discovered that African Americans who are extremely light or extremely dark did not obtain pleasant names or stereotypes. Interestingly, African Americans with a medium complexion were given good names and preconceptions. E. Franklin Frazier (1957) explored the views and values of middle-class African Americans in The Black Bourgeoisie. Frazier (1957) writes on page 23 that people of the African American community with lighter skin are more than likely members of the African American middle class. Frazier's central claim was that these middle-class African Americans enjoy a false sense of security because of their access to mainstream white society. It should be mentioned that several works were produced during this era; nevertheless, the results discussed here address the psychological and sociological roots and consequences of colorism.

Colorism during Civil Rights and Post-Civil Rights

Numerous movements were formed throughout the civil rights struggle to elevate and alter African Americans' perceptions of themselves. The challenges of self-perception transformation and persistence were crucial for the "Black is Beautiful" and "Black Power" movements to emerge. These movements rose to prominence in the 1960s and promoted black pride. These movements were critical because they reflected a fundamental shift in how African Americans allowed themselves to be perceived by themselves and others. As a result, this worldview accepted darker complexion and natural hair to the point that skin tone bias was diminishing (Wilder, 2010). As a result, colorism research undertaken during and after the civil rights struggle was conducted to determine whether there has been a substantial shift in how Blacks regard themselves and whether there have been noticeable gains in other life outcomes.

Goering performed a 1972 survey with 200 African American males to ascertain their attitudes toward the significance of skin color. Goering discovered that the "Black is Beautiful" concept resulted in a shift toward skin tone. Additionally, this study revealed that participants desired to wear their hair naturally and were open to marrying women of darker color. Additional researchers discovered similar results in 1970 and 1973. As previously stated, these findings gave the researcher hope that colorism would be eradicated. However, contemporary studies reveal that colorism continues to influence African Americans' life outcomes.

The post-civil rights era was characterized by covert systematic segregation and limited access to large-scale economic and educational possibilities. However, throughout this historical period, the opportunities available to African Americans were reserved for the Black Elite. This meant that the study of colorism would center on skin tone and the Black community's class differences. While some believe that colorism has little effect on African Americans' life results, recent research indicates that the experience of colorism influences self-esteem and life outcomes. Hughes & Hertel (1990) conducted a study in which they discovered that blacks with lighter skin have "greater educational achievement, occupational prestige, personal income, and family income than blacks with darker skin" (p. 1109). Similarly, Keith & Herring (1991) and Seltzer & Smith (1991) investigations resulted in Hughes & Hertel's conclusions (1990).

While these 1990s findings corroborate previous research, some researchers contend that light skin has reduced. Gullickson is one scholar who makes this argument, stating in 2005 that there had been a drop in light skin advantage associated with education and occupation. Gullickson (2005) noted that skin tone is not a significant determinant for African Americans born after 1963. Additionally, he emphasized that one factor that has remained constant is the importance of perceived attractiveness in mate selection. According to Thompson and Keith (2001) and Hill (2002), gender is a factor in physical beauty, self-esteem, and self-efficacy.

According to Hill (2000), the importance of gender and colorism resulted in the coining of a new term, "gendered colorism." Hill (2000) defines gendered colorism as "the belief that skin color has a greater impact on African American women's lives than it does on African American men's lives" (p. 5). Gendered colorism research demonstrates that dark African American women have disadvantages in appearance, mate selection, and self-esteem. Additionally, because of the created phrase gendered colorism, black feminism and black feminist philosophy have developed. Black feminism emerged in the 1980s, and the consciousness gained from this movement emphasizes the experiences shaping African American women's lives. Bell Hooks (1981;1989), Audre Lorde (1984), Patricia Hill Collins (1986;1990; 2000), and Deborah K. King are just a few examples of black feminist authors (1988). This explains why many contemporary works on colorism are produced by African American women who employ Black feminist theory as their primary theoretical and conceptual framework. Additionally, much colorism research has been conducted across multiple academic areas (Pearson-Trammell, 2014).

While most colorism research focuses on gender, other scientists focus on age and others on geography. Goering (1972), Holtzman (1973), and Jones (1973) argue that as racism evolves, younger African Americans' opinions of colorism will change and be changed. The findings of these numerous investigations result in a plethora of conclusions. Bond and Cash (1992) discovered that many African American women were content with their skin color.

Hall (1998) also found that African American college students identify beauty with skin tone through an analysis of skin color bias. According to Hall

(1998), This finding demonstrates that the 1960 movements and ideology had little lasting impact. Coard, Breland, and Raskin recognized that something was amiss in their 2001 research on college students. African Americans, it was believed, favored medium complexion tones, and had no preference for light skin tones. These new findings demonstrate that opinions about the effects of colorism on the African American community remain divided. Additional studies should be conducted to examine generational disparities in the experience of colorism and the impact of resiliency following colorism exposure.

Colorism: Current Research (2013–present)

Wilder (2015) discovered that nine color terms for light, medium, and dark brown skin tones remained in common usage between the two studies, including "high yellow," "bright," "light," and "yellow." Thus, while the term "colorism" has not been fully integrated into everyday Black American language and culture, the color names and concepts that have persisted since slavery constitute a commonsense knowledge of color that perpetuates a divisive and psychologically damaging intercommunal regime of color hierarchy (Wilder 2015, pp. 6-7, 69)- 70). Wilder's research delves deeper into the subject, revealing how gendered colorism exerts an especially pernicious strain on the lives of Black women, who are mercilessly classified into hierarchies of beauty and Blackness that attempt to destroy their self-esteem and feeling of value.

Wilder surveyed Black women about their associations with various skin tone terms and discovered that "blue-black," "purple," "burnt," and other terms associated with darker skin tones were primarily associated with negative connotations such as "suspicious," "loud," "ghetto," "less intelligent," and "unattractive" (p. 75). In comparison, phrases such as "redbone" and "high yellow" associated with lighter skin tones connoted attractiveness, amiability, and trustworthiness (p. 70). Nonetheless, Wilder's talks indicated that darker skin tones were positively associated with African ancestry and a post-Black Power sense of Black pride, in addition to demonstrating the continuity of positive and negative traits associated with lightness and darkness. In comparison, lighter-skinned women in the conversations stressed the importance of overcompensating to explain their Blackness (pp. 73, 75). Despite these advantages, lighter-skinned participants expressed emotions of limitation, exposure to stereotyping, self-doubt, and a belief that they had never encountered racial discrimination (Ibid., p. 73).

Steele (2016) examines the influence of children's media on self-esteem and identity concepts. In her study, she asserts that children's cartoons (media) influence children's opinions on attractiveness, skin tone, and racial identity from an early age. In her analysis, Steele (2016) claims that "The Proud Family is a children's show that honors African American families and presents varied perspectives on the Black community." However, it continues to rely significantly on colorist conceptions of beauty and social position. The Proud Family's female characters' beauty is inextricably linked to their conformity to Eurocentric standards. Proud Family's portrayals of feminine attractiveness are eerily like colorist ideals of beauty. This essay, written and developed by an African American man, contributes to the media's sexist portrayals of Black women (p. 63)."

Hall, in her 2017 article on "gendered colorism." Hunter (2007) invented this term to describe colorism's profound effect on women. Hall (2017) claims that various research studies have consistently found that colorism has a more significant impact on African American women's lives than on African American men. Keith et al. (2010) addresses this concept in detail, arguing that "questions of racial identity, skin color, and attractiveness are fundamental considerations for women" (p. 54). Hall (2017) explores and concludes that gendered colorism experiences had a detrimental influence on the psychosocial outcomes of her study's participants. She promotes the idea that future scholars need to recognize and accept the unique problems associated with being black, female, and dark-skinned in a society that does not value these features (p. 77)."

Because skin tone is integral to an African American woman's self-image and attractiveness, it is critical to view oneself positively. Gender-based colorism can be detrimental to darker-skinned women, as society rewards those who appear more Eurocentric. As a result, Keith et al. (2010) state that "a dark-skinned Black woman who is self-conscious about her appearance may believe she has nothing to contribute to society" (p. 48). According to Maxwell (2013), the appearance of one's skin can be more critical to one's self-esteem than one's accomplishment. According to Mathews (2013), people of color face both primary and secondary marginalization. Personal interactions with discriminatory treatment also play a significant role in the lives of African American women (Wilder & Cain, 2011).

Being a lady from an ethnic minority group is a complicated experience. According to historical and contemporary research on colorism, one binding effect of the experience is self-esteem. According to Keith et al. (2010)'s study, 82% of African American women had experienced at least one episode of everyday prejudice in their lifetime, such as being treated rudely or being called insulting names. In their research, Wilder and Cain (2011) state that women are disproportionately harmed since attractiveness is associated with pale skin and is more significant for women in our society.

McCullough (2018) studied the experience of colorism among African American women across three generations. The authors posit that the experience of colorism for African American women, no matter the generation is traumatic and can have a lasting psychological impact.

Respondents expressed that the experience of colorism could happen every day but mostly during their younger years (McCullough, 2018). This study also illuminated contemporary, distinctive features of colorism. First, it is essential to underscore that colorism is a byproduct of racism. Second, it is imperative to note that although colorism is a derivative of racism, colorism exists as its structure operates at the individual, interactional, and institutional levels. The women in this study discussed the distinct experiences of colorism and racism. Nevertheless, colorism functions as a structure that interacts and co-exists with the larger structures of race, gender, and class (McCullough, 2018).

The recurring point was that while many participants have learned to challenge colorism, they still find themselves in positions of prejudice and discrimination. McCullough (2018) asserts that colorism operates as a three-tiered structure rather than a binary one. Most scholarly research (past and present) has situated colorism within an opposing, twofold hierarchy: light and dark skin. As a result, colorism should be understood within the context of these other societal structures.

The next feature of colorism concerns the classification of the structure as a one-dimensional hierarchy. This framing of colorism assumes that the interactions and experiences are one-directional. Dark-skinned women are always noted as the victims, partly because of their lower place in the color hierarchy. However, the literature on colorism suggests that while light-skinned women occupy the highest rung of the color ladder, they are also victimized for their position (McCullough, 2018). The results of this research point to a different pattern of colorism where victimization occurs at all levels.

Ultimately light and dark-skinned women find themselves in the position of proving, disproving, legitimizing, and delegitimizing the socially constructed perceptions of who and what they should (or should not) be because of their skin tone. However, research illustrates that women have dual roles as victims and victimizers (McCullough, 2018). This points to variable relations of control within the system of colorism. As Bell Hooks (1989) points out, "women can and do participate in politics of domination, as perpetrators as well as victims—that we dominate, that we are dominated" (p. 20). To that end, colorism is a multi-directional (and perhaps, multi-positional) hierarchy that exhibits unsteady relations of domination (McCullough, 2018).

Self-Esteem

Lake (2003) provides an overview of America's history of colorism, beginning with its origins in slavery. As many other authors have done, she locates the origins of color consciousness in masters' inter-racial sexual practices with their slaves. She cites maternity issues, family structures, and community divide because of the birth of "mulattoes" in America.

Lake uses this backdrop to elucidate the Black community's attitude on good and terrible hair. She refers to hair as a manifestation of America's color consciousness. She also discusses women's strategies for overcoming "kinky" hair, ranging from Madame C.J. Walker's straightening treatments to contemporary tactics for adding extensions.

The author describes the underlying topic as the Black community's conviction that whiteness is the ideal of beauty; hence, lighter complexion and longer, silkier hair were preferred, even among siblings. Additionally, the author explains how internalized racism has created a negative association between African American women and traditional African characteristics. Further, the author discusses the lengths to which Black women strive to eliminate characteristics that have earned them stigma in American society, particularly within the Black community.

While many dark-skinned African Americans view their skin tone positively and with pride, Coard et al. (2001) imply that others are ambivalent and may regard their Blackness as a "mark of oppression." On the other hand, many light-complexed African Americans, considered more attractive, have been marginalized because they do not appear or act "black enough." According to Thompson and Keith (2001), 24 skin color and physical beauty are inextricably related. Because women are held to a higher standard of physical appeal across all cultures, preconceptions of attractiveness and color preference are especially pervasive among Black women.

These prejudices influence African American women's general self-esteem based on their impressions of others' opinions. Thompson and Keith analyze the effect of limited possibilities on both dark-skinned African American males' and women's self-efficacy. The scientists discovered that skin tone was a more accurate predictor of men's perceived self-efficacy than women's self-esteem. The findings indicated that clinical populations of dark-skinned African American women frequently struggle with self-esteem and confidence issues. Additionally, the study discovered that Black women expect to be judged based on their skin tone, while women who identify as dark-skinned had more negative expectations about their perceived worth. Another way that regular color discrimination might affect one's self-esteem is through its long-term effect.

Falconer and Neville (2000) examined the total body satisfaction of African American female college students. They discovered a link between skin tone and body pleasure. Unhappiness with one's color, regardless of other traits, results in dissatisfaction with one's appearance (i.e., weight or ethnic identification). According to the author, increased internalization of external beauty standards causes women to be more critical of their bodies (i.e., hips, lips, and thighs).

On average, the sample's composition judged themselves to be fair skinned. The findings indicate that light-skinned African American women may experience decreased self-esteem because of self-comparison with the other 25 light-skinned African American women (in-group) or Caucasian women (out-group). The effect on African American women is a topic that may be discussed during treatment. Parker (2008) argues that because colorism severely affects black women, it should be given special consideration in therapeutic interventions. The author proposes that colorism be considered to improve cultural competence and intervene successfully with this community. Recent research, such as Pearson-Trammell (2014) and others, has begun to examine protective variables such as resilience and their significance in the phenomenon of colorism.

Resilience

Werner (2005) employs Suniya Luthar's (2003) definition of resilience, which is "a dynamic process that results in positive adaptation, even in the face of adversity" (Luthar, 2003). Resilience possesses three characteristics from this perspective: adaptive resilience, intrinsic resilience, and learned resilience. These three categories of resilience are critical for comprehending how resilience is internalized. Adaptive resilience can be defined as the capacity to adapt to any environmental condition. According to Southwick and colleagues (2014), "when you consider young children, for example, they are evolutionary products who are extremely adaptable" (Southwick, Bonanno, Masten, Panter-Brick, Yehuda, 2014, p. 5).

The two types of resilience, inherent and adaptive, are inextricably linked. Inherent resilience can work effectively in non-crisis situations (Tierney, Bruneau 2007, p. 14). Inherent resilience might be considered a static or snapshot phenomenon (Kais & Islam, 2016, p. 4).

The snapshot/static state captures an individual's current stressed state. This concept of resilience helps us make sense of current adversity and its relationship to resilience. Learned resilience occurs in the context of the Family, school, or community. Internalize the concept of conquering hardship. Resilience can be acquired through a traumatic experience (Southwick et al., 2014, p. 11). Observing family members adapt to a difficult situation can be an example of learned resilience in this area. Adversity can teach resilience by observing, living, and experiencing it. Although there is no uniform definition of resilience, these definitions may appear disparate, and numerous parallels exist among the qualities believed to define resilience. There are three types of support systems: (1) psychological and dispositional characteristics, (2) family support and cohesion, and (3) external support systems (Campbell-Sills et al., 2006; Connor and Davidson, 2003; Friborg et al., 2003; Masten, 2001.) Personal competency, social competence, and personal structure are all psychological and dispositional characteristics. Personal competencies can be characterized as an individual's confidence in their abilities, accomplishments, determination, and realistic viewpoint (White, Driver, and Warren, 2008).

Social competence refers to an individual's belief in their capacity to function in social contexts and comprises social communication skills and adaptation in social situations (White Driver & Warren, 2008). Personal structure is a term that relates to an individual's capacity for planning and organizing their everyday activities (White, Driver, and Warren, 2008). Family support and cohesion concern how families resolve conflict, collaborate to accomplish goals, and sustain stability. External support systems briefly described above refer to an individual's capacity to provide and receive support from Family and friends and cultivate intimacy with individuals in their immediate circle. Additionally, spirituality is viewed as a critical source of external support for someone who has conquered adversity (Connor & Davidson, 2003; Hodge, 2003).

Variation in resilience is a necessary component of the resilience notion. Resilience will manifest differently for individuals exposed to various sorts of hardship. Additionally, it is critical not to disregard systemic concerns such as racism, socioeconomic inequality, and racial discrimination, contributing to resilience variations. These adversities can influence development. Resilience can shape an individual's identity, and lacking resilience contributes to inadequate identity development. Werner's (2005) notion of identification exaggerates the reality of African Americans. According to Werner (2005), "resilient males tended to come from households with structure and regulations, where a man served as a model of identification, and where emotional expressiveness was encouraged" (Werner, 2005, p. 12). African Americans' emotional and psychological toll in their search for identity must be addressed.

The Intersection of Resilience, Racism, and Colorism

Romero, Edwards, Fryberg, and Orduna (2014) propose that minorities will be resilient to discriminating stress based on their racial/ethnic identity formation stage. African Americans must acquire resiliency. Their development of self-worth and self-image is greatly influenced by family, community, society, and educational influences. Possessing resilience enables you to overcome adversity (Zolkoski, Bullock, 2012, p. 2295). Familiarizing oneself with African Americans and developing an awareness of their colorism experiences is critical for identifying areas of weakness in one's resistance. According to the resiliency literature, resilience education starts during childhood years. This is not to say that adults cannot build resilience; teaching children allows for developing the skill over time. Hopefully, by the time children reach adulthood, teaching them how to be resilient will become second nature.

Colorism's Traumatic and Psychological Effects

According to Akbar (1984), color consciousness is a psychological repercussion of American slavery. He describes color consciousness as "the erroneous assignment of mental or moral characteristics based on one's physical skin color" (p. 35). He portrays colorism in this essay as a "ghost" of slavery that haunts the African American community, arguing that this profoundly rooted concept survives in society. He explains an "abnormal correlation" between typically Caucasian traits and intelligence, beauty, and authority and contends that this idea is still valid today. Additionally, he observes that a disproportionate number of professional, educated, and "so-called 'beautiful'" African Americans exhibit prominent Caucasian traits. Throughout his examination of the impact of slavery on African Americans' beliefs, Akbar tries to dispel the popular notion of inferiority due to darker skin. However, this disparaging and extremely biased attitude toward darker skin tones and features continues to influence the Black community and displays itself in various ways.

There is a dearth of studies on African Americans' well-being following their experiences with colorism in the rising collection of research on colorism. On the other hand, considerable research has been conducted on the impact of prejudice based on race on African Americans. Pinkston (2015) stated that the psychological effects experienced by African Americans because of racial discrimination would be identical if they encountered colorism. On the other hand, perceived colorism can profoundly negatively influence a Black person's mental health and well-being. These events can contribute to developing mental illnesses such as depression and anxiety (Dawson-Andoh, & BeLue, 2011). Additionally, persistent exposure to this discrimination has a detrimental effect on one's physical health and coping abilities (Borrell et al., 2006).

If colorism is perpetuated (by Family, media, and society), it may influence how African Americans conceive their worth (Conrad et al., 2009; Mathews, 2013). Biases against specific skin tones may affect a person's self-concept (Stephens & Fews, 2007a), resulting in lower levels of self-efficacy (Thompson & Keith, 2001). Thornton and Moore (1993) discovered that when people are shown photographs deemed appealing compared to themselves, they rank themselves lower. Hill conducted a similar study with African Americans in 2002 and discovered that skin tone influenced what is considered attractive.

When all the studies are reviewed, it appears that Blacks who face discrimination due to colorism are at risk of experiencing poor self-esteem, which is associated with various adverse life outcomes. These life outcomes include but are not limited to personal relationships, career achievement, criminal justice system treatment, and perceived physical beauty. Wilder (2010) discovered that African Americans had a negative attitude toward one another depending on their skin tone. African Americans with dark skin frequently face the most disparaging labels. While labels for light-skinned African Americans are pejorative, such as light, bright, redbone, and red syndrome, most names are more pleasant. Midnight, darkness, charcoal, tar baby, and jigaboo are just a few of these names. According to the literature, this study hypothesizes that the perspectives of distinct generations will differ. African American women with dark skin may have a less favorable impression than light-skinned African American women. Additionally, as African American women build resilience, they create a stronger and more favorable opinion.

Clinical Implications

This section is likely the most pertinent, as it presents novel strategies for applying fundamental research and theory discoveries in clinical practice. First, suggestions are made regarding recognizing colorism in patients and the specific concerns to keep in mind. Clinicians working with African American women who struggle with poor self-esteem would be wise to educate themselves on colorism and be willing to discuss it (McCullough, 2018). As a result of this information, the therapist may speak intelligently about issues of colorism and the far-reaching influence it can have on the self-esteem of African American women. The outcomes of this study show that colorism has a detrimental and, in some cases, traumatic effect on the self-esteem of African American women.

Clinicians must consider the impacts of colorism when diagnosing and treating patients. A therapist could utilize this knowledge to ascertain the patient's self-esteem development and resilience stage and the severity of colorism's influence and protective variables. For instance, a patient who continues to struggle with a negative self-image and is placed in an unsupportive setting may benefit from resources that educate her about colorism and provide a platform for her to begin her path toward self-awareness. The therapist must remember that colorism is prevalent, and the therapeutic goal is to assist the patient in developing their inherent resilience (McCullough, 2018).

Clinicians who work with African American women may find the findings in this study beneficial in creating more robust and healthy self-esteem. Addressing the emotional impact of colorism on the self-esteem of African American women may need a combination of measures.

Cognitive Behavioral Therapy (CBT) is one type of therapy that may be beneficial in resolving this type of internalized oppression. Beck (1967) proposed a cognitive triad consisting of a negative view of self—in which the self is viewed as defective or insufficient—a negative view of the world—in which events are interpreted negatively, and there is an expectation of failure and punishment—and a negative view of the future—in which there is an expectation of continued negative appraisal of the future. CBT would provide a logical framework for resolving these internalized negative thinking habits.

Colorism is a loaded subject that is so ingrained in the lives of African Americans that they may be unaware of the phenomenon or its significant impact on their self-esteem growth. The culturally sensitive therapist faces difficulty validating a patient's real-world experience of colorism while confronting and challenging negative thought patterns. While negative thinking patterns may have developed in response to real-world experiences of colorism, it is apparent that negative thinking and internalization of those experiences are detrimental to the patient, suffocating their ability to grow and prosper in several ways (McCullough, 2018). Allowing patients to delve deeply into their negative cognitions by discovering habitual and maladaptive thought patterns while simultaneously producing alternate and more self-affirming statements may be an effective strategy to activate their resilience and healing.

Conclusion

Colorism is a sort of internalized oppression in which one's skin tone is used to determine stereotypes, privilege, and discrimination. Colorism can arise interracially when individuals of one racial group create distinctions between members of another racial group based on their skin color (Herring, 2004). Colorism is likely to affect most ethnic groups influenced by colonization and European beauty standards (Herring, 2004). However, because colorism is rarely discussed intra-racially, it remains taboo. In the case of persons of African heritage, this phenomenon contains ancestral experiences and racist elements that have been internalized and sustained by community members (Russell, Wilson, and Hall, 1992).

Colorism is a phenomenon that is largely neglected in culture, particularly in treatment. This is partly due to a need for more awareness and research on the subject. The influence of colorism on the self-esteem of African American women has a significant impact, and the development of resilience has positive effects. While the past study has examined the effects of colorism on African Americans and their self-esteem, this prior research has primarily taken a deficit viewpoint, offering no therapeutic strategies for assisting African

Americans in recovering (Alford, 1997; hooks, 2003; Neal & Wilson, 1989; Parrish, 1944; Russell, Wilson, and L Hall, 1992; Thompson & Keith, 1992).

This paper seeks to make helping professionals aware of the phenomenon of colorism and provide suggestions on how to work with clients who have had the experience of colorism. The research has demonstrated that colorism has a detrimental effect on the self-esteem of African American women, particularly throughout adolescence. This occurs because of the pervasiveness of colorism and the inevitable negative messages (McCullough, 2018). The rejection by the dominant society and the African American community and the numerous forms and venues through which women encountered colorism can leave women desiring to avoid the culture of the people who caused that experience. Spirituality, faith, and actively fighting colorism's influence through education about the African American ethnicity contributed to resilience. The development of resilience can work to protect African American women and girls that have experienced colorism.

References

Anderson, C., and Cromwell, R. (1977). "Black is Beautiful" and the Color Preferences of Afro-American Youth. *Journal of Negro Education,* 46, 76–88.

Brown, D. L. (2008). African American resiliency: Examining racial socialization and social support as protective factors. *Journal of Black Psychology*, 34(1), 32–48. doi:10.1177/0095798407310538.

Burton, L. M., Bonilla-Silva, E., Ray, V., Buckelew, R., and Freeman, E. H. (2010). Critical race theories, Colorism, and the decade's research on families of color. *Journal of Marriage and Family*, 72(3), 440–459. doi:10.1111/j.1741-3737.2010.00712.x.

Bachrach, D. (Producer), and Burnett, C. (1998). *The Wedding*. [Motion Picture]. United States: Harpo Productions.

Bailey, B. (2001). Dominican-American Ethnic/Racial Identities and United States Social Categories *International Migration Review*, (35) 3, 677–708.

Bates, K. G. (1994). The Color Thing: Why, in the Midst of Our Afrocentric Renaissance, Should There Still Be a Better Shade of Black? *Essence*, 25, 79-80+

Bond, S., and Cash, T. F. (1992). Black Beauty: Skin Color and Body Images among African American College Women. *Journal of Applied Social Psychology*, 22, 874–888.

Boyd-Franklin, N. (2003). *Black Families in Therapy: Understanding the African American Experience*. New York: Guilford Press.

Bowman, P., Muhammad, R., and Ifatunji, M. (2004). Skin Tone, Class, and Racial Attitudes Among African Americans. In Herring, C., Keith, V.M. & Horton, H.D. (Eds.) *Skin Deep: How Race and Complexion Matter in the "Color-Blind" Era*. Chicago: University of Illinois Press.

Charles, C. D. (2003). Skin Bleaching, Self-Hate, and Black Identity in Jamaica. *Journal of Black Studies*, 33, 6, 711-728.

Charmaz, K. (2006). *Constructing Grounded Theory: A Practical Guide Through Qualitative Analysis*. London: Sage Publications.

Coard, S. I., Breland, A. M., and Raskin, P. (2001). Perceptions of and Preferences for Skin Color, Black Racial Identity, and Self-Esteem among African Americans. *Journal of Applied Social Psychology*, 31, 2256–2274.

Cooper, A. J. (1892). A Voice from the South: By a Black Woman of the South. Xenia: Aldine.

Cox, O. C. (1948). *Caste, Class, and Race: A Study in Racial Dynamics*. New York: Monthly Review Press.

Cross, W. E., Jr., and Vandiver, B. J. (2001). Nigrescence theory and measurement: Introducing the Cross Racial Identity Scale (CRIS). In J. G. Ponterotto, J. M. Casas, L. A. Suzuki, C. M. Alexander (Eds.), *Handbook of multicultural counseling* (pp. 371-393). Thousand Oaks, CA, US: Sage Publications, Inc.

Daniel, G. (2002). *More than Black? Multiracial Identity and the New Racial Order*. Temple University Press: Philadelphia.

Drake, S., and Cayton, H. (1945). *Black Metropolis*. New York: Harcourt Brace. DuBois, W.E.B. (1903). *The Souls of Black Folk*. New York: Vintage Books. Emerson, R.A. (n.d.). African-American Teenage Girls and the Construction of Black Womanhood in Mass Media and Popular Culture. *Perspectives*, 85-102.

Elmore, T. G. (2009). Colorism in the classroom: An exploration of adolescents' skin tone, skin tone preferences, perceptions of skin tone stigma and identity.

Fegley, S. G., Spence, M. B., Goss, T. N., Harpalani, V., and Charles, N. (2008). Colorism embodied: Skin tone and psychological well-being in adolescence. In W. Overton & U. Muller (Eds), *Body in mind, mind in body: Developmental perspectives on embodiment and consciousness* (pp. 281–312). Mahwah, NJ: Erlbaum.

Freeman, H., Armor, D. J., Ross, M., and Pettigrew, T. F. (1966). Color Gradation and Attitudes Among Middle Income Negroes. *American Sociological Review*, 31, 365–74.

Gallagher, C. (2006). *Rethinking the Color Line: Readings in Race and Ethnicity*. Mountain View, CA: Mayfield.

Golden, M. (2004). *Do not play in the Sun: One Woman's Journey through the Color Complex*. New York: Doubleday.

Goering, J. M. (1972). Changing Perceptions and Evaluations of Physical Characteristics among Blacks: 1950-1970. *Phylon*, 33, 3, 231-241.

Gomez, C. (2000). The Continual Significance of Skin Color: An Exploratory Study of Latinos in the Northeast. *Hispanic Journal of Behavioral Sciences*, 22, 1, 94–103.

Fultz, L. A. (2016). *CORE scholar the Psycho-Social impact of Colorism among African American women: Crossing the divide*. Retrieved from http://corescholar.libraries.wright.edu/cgi/viewcontent.cgi?article=1909&context=etd_ all.

Hunter, M. (2007). The persistent problem of Colorism: Skin tone, status, and inequality. *Sociology Compass*, 1(1), 237–254. doi:10.1111/j.1751-9020.2007.00006.x.

Haizlip, S. T. (1994). *The Sweeter the Juice: A Family Memoir in Black and White*. New York: Simon and Schuster.

Hall, R. E. (1992). Bias Among African-Americans Regarding Skin Color: Implications for Social Work Practice. *Research on Social Work Practice*, 2, 479–486.

Harris, V. (1994). Prisoner of Color. In Adelman, A. & Enguidanos, G. *(Eds.). Racism in the Lives of Women: Testimony, Theory, and Guides to Antiracist Practice.* New York: The Haworth Press.

Harvey, A. (1995). The Issue of Skin Color in Psychotherapy with African Americans. Families in Society: *The Journal of Contemporary Human Services*, 76, 1, 3-15.

Hernandez, D., and Rehman, B. (Ed.) (2002). *Colonize This! Young Women of Color on Today's Feminism.* Emeryville: Seal Press.

Herring, C., Keith, V., and Horton, H. D. (Eds.). (2004). *Skin Deep: How Race and Complexion Matter in the "Color-Blind" Era.* Urbana and Chicago: University of Illinois Press.

Hesse-Biber, S. N., Howling, S. A., Leavy, P., and Lovejoy, M. (2004). Racial Identity and the Development of Body Image Issues among African American Adolescent Girls. *The Qualitative Report*, 9, 1, 49-79.

Hill, M. (2000). Color Differences in the Socioeconomic Status of African American Men: Results of a Longitudinal Study. *Social Forces*., 78, 4, 1437–1460.

Hill, M. (2002). Skin Color and the Perception of Attractiveness among African Americans: Does Gender Make a Difference? *Social Psychology Quarterly*, 65, 1, 77–91.

Hunter, M. (1998). Colorstruck: Skin Color Stratification in the Lives of African American Women. *Sociological Inquiry*, pp. 68, 4, 517–535.

Hunter, M. (2002). 'If You're Light, You're Alright': Light Skin Color as Social Capital for Women of Color. *Gender and Society*, 16, 2, pp. 175–193.

Hunter, M. (2004). Light Bright and Almost White: The Advantages and Disadvantages of Light Skin. In Herring, C., Keith, V.M., & Horton, H.D. *(Eds.) Skin Deep: How Race and Complexion Matter in the "Color-Blind" Era*. Chicago: University of Illinois Press.

Hunter, M. (2005). *Race, Gender, and the Politics of Skin Tone.* New York: Routledge.

Hunter, M. (2007). The Persistent Problem of Colorism: Skin Tone, Status, and Inequality. *Sociology Compass*, 1, 1, pp. 237–254. 200

Kelly, L., Burton, S., and Regan, L. (1994). Researching Women's Lives or Studying Oppression? Reflections on What Constitutes Feminist Research. In Maynard, M. & Purvis, J. (Eds.). *Researching Women's Lives from a Feminist Perspective.* London: Taylor & Francis. pp. 27–48.

Kerr, A. E. (2006). *The Paper Bag Principle: Class, Colorism, and Rumor in the Case of Black Washington*, D.C. Knoxville: University of Tennessee Press.

Lee, S. (Director & Producer). (1988). *School Daze*. [Motion Picture]. United States: Columbia Pictures.

Lynn, R. (2002a). Skin Color and Intelligence in African Americans. *Population and Environment*, 23, 365–75.

Mathews, T. J. (2013). *The relationship between skin complexion and social outcomes: How colorism affects the lives of African American women.* Retrieved from http://digitalcommons.auctr.edu/cgi/viewcontent.cgi?article=2286&context=dissertations.

Mathews, T., and Johnson, G. (2015). Skin Complexion in the 21st Century: Impact of Colorism on African American Women. *Race, Gender & Class*, 22(1/2), 248–274. Retrieved from http://search.proquest.com.libproxy.edmc.edu/central/docview/1757045044/fulltext/8. D4C75B40957405CPQ/2?accountid=34899.

Monk, E. P. (2014). Skin tone stratification among black Americans, 2001-2003. *Social Forces*, 92(4), 1313–1337. doi:10.1093/sf/sou007.

Myrdal, G. (1944). *An American dilemma: The Negro problem and modern democracy*. New York: Transaction Publishing.

Neal, A. M., and Wilson, M. L. (1989). The Role of Skin Color and Features in the Black Community: Implications for Black Women and Therapy. *Clinical Psychology Review*, 9, 323–333.

Nobles, M. (2002). Racial Categorization and Census. In Kertzer, D.I. & Arel, D. (Eds.). *Census and Identity: The Politics of Race, Ethnicity, and Language in National Censuses*. Cambridge: Cambridge University Press, p. 43-70.

Omi, M., and Winant, H. (1986*). Racial Formation in the United States: From the 1960s to the 1980s.* New York: Routledge.

Ozakawa-Rey, M., Robinson, T., and Ward, J. (1987). Black women and the politics of skin color and hair. *Women and Therapy*, 6, 89–102.

Pearson-Trammell, N. (2010). Colorism, self-esteem, and resiliency: A qualitative study of dark-skinned African American women. Retrieved November 24, 2016, from http://gradworks.umi.com/34/07/3407390.html.

Pinkston, T. M. (2015). "Cues of Colorism: The Psychological, Sociocultural, and Developmental Differences between Light-skinned and Dark-skinned African-Americans." *Electronic Theses & Dissertations*. http://digitalcommons.georgiasouthern.edu/etd/1300.

Parrish, C. H. (1946). Color Names and Color Notions. *The Journal of Negro Education*, 15, 1, 13–20.

Russell, K., Wilson, M., and Hall, R. (1993). *The Color Complex: The Politics of Skin Color Among African Americans*. New York: Anchor Books.

Stinson, C. C., and Velis, N. (Directors). (2007). *Light, Bright, Damn Near White* [Documentary]. United States: CC Squared Productions.

Tademy, L. (2001). *Cane River*. New York: Warner Books.

Tatum B. D. (1997). *Why Are All the Black Kids Sitting Together in the Cafeteria? And Other Conversations about Race*. New York: Basic Books.

Thompson, M. S., and Keith, V. M. (2001). The Blacker the Berry: Gender, Skin-Tone, self-esteem & Self-Efficacy. *Gender & Society*, 15, 336–357.

Viglione, J., Hannon, L., and DeFina, R. (2011). The impact of light skin on prison time for black female offenders. *The Social Science Journal*, 48(1), 250-258.

Wade, T. J. (1996). The Relationships between Skin Color and Self-Perceived Global, Physical, and Sexual Attractiveness, and Self-Esteem for African Americans. *Journal of Black Psychology*, 22, 3, 358–373.

Walker, A. (1983). *In Search of Our Mothers' Gardens*. San Diego: Harcourt Brace Jovanovich, Publishers.

Walker, A. (1983). *The Color Purple*. Women's Press Limited.

Ward, J. V., and Robinson, T. L. (1995). African American Adolescents and Skin Color. *Journal of Black Psychology*, 21, 256–274.

Wilder, J. (2008). Everyday Colorism in the lives of young black women: Revisiting the continuing significance of an old phenomenon in a new generation. Retrieved from http://etd.fcla.edu/UF/UFE0022480/wilder_j.pdf.

Wilder, J., and Cain, C. (2010). Teaching and learning color consciousness in black families: Exploring family processes and women's experiences with Colorism. *Journal of Family Issues*, 32(5), 577–604. doi:10.1177/0192513x10390858

Worrell, F. C. (2012). Chapter one forty years of Cross's Nigrescence Theory: From stages to profiles, from African Americans to all Americans. *African American identity: Racial and cultural dimensions of the Black experience*, 3-28.

Chapter 3

The African-American Woman's Historical Trauma: Our Inability to Heal

Nakpangi Thomas[1,*], PhD
and Tezonia Morgan[2,†], PhD
[1]Southern New Hampshire University, Manchester, New Hampshire, USA
[2]Wings of Virtue Counseling and Research Institute, Southfield, Michigan, USA

Abstract

The inequalities African_American women endure include disparities in housing, education, adequate salary, quality of life for self and family, and the institutional and systemic challenges they face daily, leading to higher stress and anxiety (Perry, Harry & Oser, 2013). There is a strong need to increase ethical sensitivity to racial and gender intolerance within the workplace and community. Research shows that African American women are more likely to be denied access to jobs and training and offered lower pay than their male counterparts. The deniability to be provided fair wages left African_American women vulnerable to abuses such as forced labor, loss of jobs, and left dealing with racial microaggression in the workplace. The African American woman's healing process is a never-ending journey due to constant trauma. Patel (2021) noted that the severe consequences of failing to address this consistent discrimination include the broken cycle and leaving African American women to protect themselves. Solutions include developing policies and programs for African-American women and allocating finances to assist African American women in education, housing, and employment (Patel, 2021). In addition to program development, there

* Corresponding Author's Email: nakpangi.thomas@gmail.com.
† Corresponding Author's Email: tezonia@wingsofvirtue.org.

In: How Did We Survive?
Editor: Tina Marie Glover
ISBN: 979-8-88697-918-3

needs to be a safe place for African American women to address their inequalities and discrimination without negative recourse (Thompson, 2016).

> For an orderly future, special and particular attention must be paid to the FEMALE and the YOUNGEST offspring…Both must be taught to respond to a peculiar new LANGUAGE. Psychological and physical instruction of CONTAINMENT must be created for both…YOU MUST KEEP YOUR EYE AND THOUGHTS ON THE FEMALE and the OFFSPRING of the horse and the nigger. A brief discourse on offspring development will shed light on the key to sound economic principles. Pay little attention to the generation of original breaking but CONCENTRATE ON FUTURE GENERATION. Therefore, if you break the FEMALE mother, she will BREAK the offspring in its early years of development; and when the offspring is old enough to work, she will deliver it up to you, for her normal female protective tendencies will have been lost in the original breaking process."
>
> ~ Lynch (1712).

Keywords: African American women, Black women, trauma, etiology of trauma

Introduction

Trauma within the African-American community has been an uphill battle for over 400 years. Historically, trauma for African-American people in the United States has its foundation in slavery. During slavery, there was a distinct motive to dismantle African-American families, starting with women (Morrow, 1991). It could be argued that this is still a silent motive today. During slavery, the women were forced to watch the men be beaten, sodomized, and sold. While at the same time, the women were raped, and their children were taken and sold. As a result, African-American women developed strength and endurance to insurmountable pain. The horrendous acts of slavery have kept the African-American community in a psychological hold that bleeds through the seams of their souls. Since slavery, the African-American home has never fully reestablished itself. The African_American community was never given the liberty to restore but was forced to move on. African-American women are not only the foundation of the African-American family but the glue that holds everyone together; however, the struggles to heal are never-ending. African-American women continue to rise to the occasion in higher education, entrepreneurship, and leadership; the journey to those positions has proven itself to be more strenuous and tedious than men and women of other cultures. The inequalities of African-American women spread in every area of life, including, but not limited to, housing, education, adequate salary, family life, and the institutional and systemic arena, which lead to higher stress and anxiety levels (Perry, Harry & Oser, 2013). There is a strong need to increase ethical sensitivity to racial and gender intolerance within the workplace and community. Research shows that African-American women are more likely to be denied access to jobs and training and offered lower pay than their male counterparts. The deniability of offering fair wages left African- American women vulnerable to abuses such as forced labor, loss of jobs, and dealing with racial microaggression. The African-American woman's healing process is a never-ending journey due to the constant trauma. For true healing, African-American women must feel safe in the workplace, community, and home.

Institutional and Systemic Inequalities

The United States has developed many institutions and systems that are supposed to promote the growth and security of all Americans. These systems continuously fail African-American women, whose voices continuously go unheard. According to Sociologists, there are five primary institutions of life: family, government, economy, education, and religion. Each primary institution can have secondary institutions. Although these primary institutions are the same for African-American women, the areas of success and achievement are entirely different. African-American women have suffered in all five areas but tend to keep their struggles within their community of friends. African-American women have become the head of the household, learned to live on welfare, struggled in economic growth, overcame educational disparities, and relied on religion to survive.

Family Life

Based on the U.S. classification, the family consists of one man, one woman, and their offspring (Capuzzi, Stauffer, & Eber-LaPierre, 2021). The unit is formed in a ceremony where vows are taken, and the couple becomes united before God and witnesses. According to Lewis (1989), the women's primary role is to be the caregiver and nurture their spouse, children, and aging family members. Unfortunately, this natural order has hindered African- American women. Common barriers facing African-American women can be traced back to 1619 when the first slave ship landed in Jamestown. Veering from this natural order has hindered African- American/Black women in the Kingdom of Ndongo (Leary-DeGruy, 2005). Arriving in bondage, those "20 and odd" bondage enslaved Africans brought valuable skills such as artisans, blacksmiths, herding, and farming that were necessary for the survival of the early English colony. Thus, marking the beginning of the slave trade in the North Americas.

As the slave trade increased, more African families were separated. The women were paired with a man for the sole purpose of bearing children, hence, increasing the revenue of the slave owner (Perry, Harry & Oser, 2013; Truth, 1997). If no children were produced within a year, the woman was sold, and the man was paired with another slave. Often, the slave children were sold to another slave owner. Annie L. Burton (2006), a formerly enslaved person, recalls her time as a child on the plantation:

> If a slave man and woman wished to marry, a party would be arranged some Saturday night among the slaves. The marriage ceremony consisted of the pair jumping over a stick. The wife was sold if no children were born within a year or so. At New Year's, if there was any debt or mortgage on the plantation, the extra slaves were taken…and sold at the courthouse. In this way, families were separated (p. 4).

In the *Women's Slave Narratives,* Mattie J. Jackson tells her childhood memory:

> Mr. Canory resided in St. Charles County for five years after he purchased my mother. During that time, my father and mother were in the same neighborhood but a short distance from each other…Her master moved twenty miles away…Two years after this separation, my father was sold and separated from us…He was not her's, for cruel hands had separated them. My mother was then left with two children (Burton, 2006, p. 48).

Testimonies from slaves bear witness to rape and ill-treatment of the African enslaved women. African women were even sent to nurse white children when their mothers could not (Leary-DeGruy, 2005; Truth, 1997). African mothers watched as their children suffered from a lack of care as they were forced to tend to the needs of their master first. On the auction block, slave children have torn away in tears from their mothers as they were sold and carted off to a new master. Watching one child to the next being sold off and the possibility of never seeing your child again had an emotional toll on African women (Perry, Harry & Oser, 2013).

Post Slavery Era

After emancipation, slaves had the option of staying on the plantation and working the land for pay or leaving and fending for themselves. Sometimes, being free meant being captured and illegally sold back into slavery. The war and lack of jobs forced African men to leave their families. Some men went North to source for work and then sent for their families. Others found work and started a new life. Thousands of African men fought and lost their lives during World War II. Marriage rates declined at the end of the 1800s and peaked in 1950 for African-American women. Ricketts (2007) argued that African-American women married at higher rates than white women until 1950 (Table 1). Furthermore, the rate of African-American female Heads of Household increased due to the African-American male mortality rate increased, not low marital rates.

Table 1. Rate of Marriage of Black and White Women

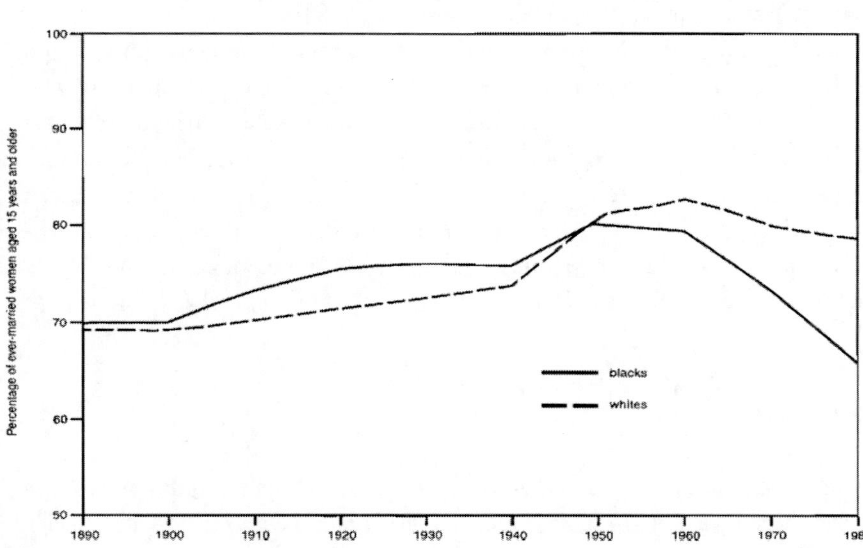

Housing

Slavery was a major contributor to the unstable African-American families because of the lack of legal marriage among slaves and the constant separation of families as males and older children were sold. Frazier argued that family instability among African-Americans resulted from the effects of slavery on African-American family life. According to Frazier, slavery destroyed all family bonds except those between mother and child, leading to a pattern of African-American families centered on the mother (Ricketts, 2007). As such, the percentage of African-American female Heads of Households increased. Between 1960 and 1985, African-American female-headed families grew from 20.6 to 43.7 percent in contrast to 8.4 to 12 percent for white female-headed families (Ross & Sawhill, 1975; Walker, 1988).

Available African-American female Heads of Households experience higher poverty rates than other women. According to the 2021 report from the U.S. Census Bureau, African-American women represent 22.3 percent of women in poverty but makeup only 12.8 percent of all women in the U.S. population. Currently, over half of the African-American families are headed by females, while females headed 22% in 1960 (Sudarkasa, 2007), mainly due to housing disparities and the lack of affordable housing. The Fair Housing Act was passed in April 1968 as Title VIII of the Civil Rights Act to eliminate overt discrimination and disparities in the housing market. However, these unlawful practices continue to persist (Julian, 2019).

Additionally, policies established by the federal government allowed legal forms of discrimination, and racially biased policies have played an essential role in the formation and endurance of segregated African-American neighborhoods, particularly households led by African-American females. African-Americans were excluded from homeownership as lenders targeted White borrowers. African-American single mothers were deemed at high-risk for home loans, thus, relegating them to low-income communities and subsidized housing (Julian, 2019).

Education

It was once said, "If you want to keep a Black person down, put the information in a book because they do not read" (Unknown Author). The desire for education for African-American women has been growing for several decades. Many women strive to obtain higher education to assist with catapulting their families out of poverty. African-American women tend to make life decisions for the betterment of their family; this is due to them more likely taking on the matriarchal role in the family unit. Although this is a financial decision, there is evidence that African-American women are less likely to be tenured in faculty positions and have lower wages than their white counterparts. The National Center for Educational Statistics (2018) noted an increase in African-American women obtaining terminal degrees in various fields of study. Although this is an increase, only 5% of people with terminal degrees are African-American women, which is a 1% increase since 2016. The challenges that African-American woman face to reach the goal of a terminal degree the hurdle starts before elementary school and often continues throughout their academic career. One of the most notable challenges is the hyper-segregation African-Americans face due to residing in ghettos. African-American women are more likely to come from a lower socioeconomic class, living in ghettos and receiving less than equal education to their counterparts. According to Putnam (2015)

> Poor kids, though no fault of their own, are less prepared by their families, schools, and communities to develop their God-given talents as fully as rich kids. For economic productivity and growth, our country needs as much talent as we can find, and we certainly can't afford to waste it. The opportunity gap imposes on all of us both real costs and what economists term "opportunity costs." (p. 230).

Due to the opportunity gap, higher education is more difficult for African-American women because the academic expectation within a program does not consider a privilege. Research shows that obtaining a degree will provide an opportunity for higher salaries (The Bureau of Labor Statistics, 2020). The Bureau of Labor Statistics (2020) noted that having a bachelor's degree will earn a person nearly $25,000 more than having a high school diploma. They also indicated that the average bachelor's degree earns almost $61,000. This is untrue for African-American women, who earn an average of $36,694 (The Journal of Blacks in Higher Education, 2021). Many disparities within the institution of education leave African-American women with the daunting task of survival of the fittest. This fight begins in elementary school.

According to Weir (2016), AfricanAmerican students are 54% less likely to be recognized and recommended for gifted education programs. On the other hand, African-American students are three times more likely to be recommended if their teacher is African-American. In addition, white teachers tend to have different expectations for their African-American students. Weir (2016) explained that white teachers were 12% less likely to predict if their students would graduate. Additionally, white teachers were likelier to give less critical feedback if an African-American student wrote a paper. This leaves the student without the same growth opportunities as their white peers. It also poses a problem when African-American women begin their higher education journeys. African-American students tend to have more brutal disciplinary action within the school system, including 3.8 times as likely to be suspended than other students. Students with higher success are less likely to finish school and go to college. The caveat to this research is that African-American males are more likely to get suspended, which leaves the burden of educational freedom on African-American women.

Labor Market

Duncan, Morris, and Rodrigues (2011) argued that the family structure and education level play an integral part in a family's earning potential. Furthermore, the family's economic standing affects access to immediate needs, services, resources, and asset building. Moreover, parental earnings predict where the family lives; time with family; the services and resources accessible such as schools, grocery stores, hospitals, and transportation; and learning outcomes for children. Research shows that African-Americans participate in the U.S. workforce at high rates, yet this does not translate to high-wage earnings, which can lead to higher stress levels (Mutari, Power & Figart, 2002; Williams & Rubin, 2003). African-Americans continue to face fewer job opportunities, higher unemployment rates, access to higher-paying jobs, lower wages, lower job stability, and poor benefits, which hinder economic prosperity (Duncan, Morris, and Rodrigues, 2011; Moras et al., 2018; Solomon, Maxwell, & Castro, 2019). Historically, the labor market has been worse for African-Americans. According to Solomon, Maxwell, and Castro (2019), factors that contributed to the dismantling of the African-American workforce include repeated violent oppression of African-Americans, such as the riots that destroyed Black business owners' wealth on the African-American Wall Street in Tulsa, Oklahoma in 1921, codified segregation, legal racial terrorism during the almost century-long period from Reconstruction to the civil rights era, systematic exclusions of African-Americans from better-paying jobs, and continued occupational segregation.

In addition to the "redevelopment" of Black communities such as Detroit's Black Bottom (Detroit Historic Society, 2021). Despite increased access to the labor market and higher education, African-American females remain the lowest earners.

Historically, African-American women have always been among the highest participants in the labor market (Goldin, 1977). Furthermore, in 1880, 35.4 percent of married black women and 73.3 percent of single black women were in the labor force, compared with only 7.3 percent of married white women and 23.8 percent of single white women. However, African-Americans face unique challenges in the workforce due to employment practices and government policies that hinder black women compared to white, Asian, and Latinx women and men (Moras et al., 2018). They are more likely to work (even while married) than other ethnic races, yet, have a more challenging time securing long-term employment. African-American working mothers make up one-third of the workforce, making them the primary economic provider. Despite the growing number of college-educated African-American females, economic well-being and security remain elusive. This disparity can be linked to the single-female Heads of Households and employment instability. African-American women are burdened with shouldering the financial responsibility of the household as more than 80 percent of African-American women are the family's breadwinners compared with 50 percent of white women. Between 2004 and 2014, the median annual earnings declined, resulting in higher unemployment rates among African-American women regardless of marital status and education level. (U.S. Bureau of Labor Statistics, 2015).

Many African-American are employed in low-earning jobs with few benefits such as adequate health care, childcare, and paid sick leave, with approximately 28 percent in the service sector (Moras et al., 2018; U.S. Bureau of Labor Statistics, 2015). Traditionally, African-American women's value in the labor market has been considered worthy. After emancipation, African-American women could only seek employment as a cook or in housekeeping (Burton et al., 2006; Diner, 1995; Moras et al., 2018). Ironically, white women devalue African-American women as mothers, yet African-American women have been charged with caring for white children since slavery. To the point of neglecting their children. Even as the 20th century ushered more African-Americans to the North, African-American women were only hired as domestic service workers. The 1950s and '60s saw more white females entering the labor market. While this provided more opportunities in the work sector for women, the acceptance of African-American women in this labor market was slow. In the 21st century, African-American women remain the largest group in the labor market-62.2 percent, higher than 57 percent of white women or 59 percent of Asian women who work. However, they continue to be the lowest earners in the labor market (U.S. Bureau of Labor Statistics, 2021). Additionally, African-American women are more likely to be fired or laid off and have the highest unemployment rate. As of May 2021, African-American females account for 8.2 percent of the unemployment rate in contrast to white women, who account for 5.8 percent.

Workplace

The work environment can be a pleasant place for many individuals. While for others, it is a place of war. African-American women must code-switch to make their peers feel comfortable. It is known that African-American people have been taught how to understand, interact, and adjust to the white race (Brown, 2018). Unfortunately, the same work environment obligation is not demanded of others. This means a daily struggle of hiding evidence of being an African-American woman in the workplace while making everyone else feel comfortable. African-American women endure higher racial microaggressions while at their jobs. Wing et al. (2007) define racial microaggressions as brief and commonplace daily verbal, behavioral, or environmental indignities, whether intentional or unintentional, that communicate hostile, derogatory, or harmful racial slights and insults toward people of color. Perpetrators of microaggressions are often unaware that they engage in such communications when interacting with racial/ethnic minorities. Microaggressions appear in three forms: micro assault, microinsult, and microinvalidation. Almost all interracial encounters are prone to microaggressions (Wing et al., 2007). Although subtle, racial microaggressions make it harder for African-American women to stay motivated. Racial microaggression against African-American women is prevalent in all work situations. In a study on African-American female faculty members, Pittman (2012) discovered that African-American female faculty members have experienced racial assaults (micro assaults), been insulted, or told they only have their position due to their race (microinsults), and have their experiences invalidated (microinvalidation). As a result of these racial attacks, many university institutions have difficulty recruiting and retaining African-American female faculty members. Even though African-American women are the victims of racial microaggressions, they must be "nice" or else they will be perceived as the "angry black woman." To sustain employment, African-American women stay silent and remain nice. Author Austin Channing Brown described the distortion of the be excellent concept in the following excerpt.

> When you believe that niceness disproves the presence of racism, it's easy to start believing bigotry is rare and that the label racist should be applied only to mean-spirited, intentional acts of discrimination. The problem with this framework – besides being a gross misunderstanding of how racism operates in systems and structures enabled by friendly people – is that it obligates me to be excellent in return rather than truthful. I am expected to come close to the racists. Be nicer to them. Coddle them. (p. 101)

This lets us *make everyone happy* game creates exhaustion, insecurity, and workplace burnout in African-American women. Pittman (2010) researched coping strategies for racial stressors within the workplace. The study revealed that the only coping strategy was to "play the game," meaning they changed parts of themselves to appease others (p.67). In addition, support was sought outside of the institutions from other people of color. African-American women are advised to use racial stressors as teachable moments; however, this modality puts the burden of education on the victim. This perpetuates the thought process that African-American women must hold all accountability in the workplace setting.

Implications

Post-Traumatic Slave Syndrome

Dr. Joy DeGruy (2005) findings from a twelve-year study implementing both quantitative and qualitative methods coined the term Post Traumatic Slave Syndrome (PTSS). DeGruy describes Post Traumatic Slave Syndrome or PTSS as the "multigeneration trauma resulting from centuries of slavery and continues to experience oppression and institutional racism today (p. 121). The real or imagined belief accompanied them that the benefits of their society are not obtainable to them. DeGruy postulated that the long-term effects of slavery have a multigenerational impact on the self-esteem, attitudes, and socialization that have crippled African-American women. During slavery, African-American women had to submit their bodies to the well of their masters. The worth of African-American women has been perceived as a low value among other ethnicities. Negative, degrading images of African-American women have been depicted in films, music, television, and social media. Even African-American men view African-American women as less valuable, unloving, less nurturing, and rigid (Lewis, 1989; Moras et al., 2018; Perry, Harp, Oser, 2013). However, African-American women are labeled as "strong" or less acceptable to pain or emotionless. As such, African-American women are forced to grin and bear the continued trauma stemming from slavery. When a mother raising children possesses little to no self-esteem or believes they have little to no value, that behavior is subconsciously instilled in the offspring(s). According to DeGruy, this learned behavior or conditioning "is transmitted from generation to generation through the family, community, and society" (p. 125).

African-American women have been labeled "The Angry Black Women." In part due to the boisterous methods of the African-American women to remain silent about the mistreatment of themselves, their families, and African-American people. The aftermath of slavery has resulted in negative economic, social, and political stereotypes of African-American women that endorse these women as aggressive, ill-tempered, illogical, overbearing, hostile, and ignorant without provocation (Ashley, 2014). Ashley agreed that many of these characteristics developed in response to historical factors and external stressors significantly affecting African-American women intra-psychically and interpersonally. On and Milan (2018) posited that African-American women place a high value on the attributes of the "Strong Black Women" while other races deem these attributes as assertive and external problems. Additionally, African-American women pass these attributes down to their daughters and reinforce the importance of self-reliance; further exacerbating the multigenerational effects of the "Angry Black Woman" syndrome.

Re-Traumatization

In the African-American community, there is a saying, "Strong Black Women" Syndrome. To be a "Strong Black Woman" means denying or avoiding your true feelings. Clinging to the phenomenon of a strong black woman may have caused more harm to African-American women and the black community. Women have learned that painful experiences are considered shameful or should have been kept secret. African-American women face more stress in the workplace, family responsibilities, finances, sexism and racism, and other trauma, increasing the potential for re-traumatization (Ashley, 2014; Duncan et al., 2011; Julian, 2019). No matter the obstacle; a sick child; a friend needing a ride, or a work project, African-American women lace up their boots and finish the job. Over time, if left unaddressed, the emotional toll causes physical and emotional distress and little time to meet one's own needs.

The invisible Superwoman cloak worn by African-American women contributes to the disadvantages faced by this population. For example, police tend to ignore reports of missing African-American women. The media paints these women as promiscuous or a plague on society. Alternatively, the media fails to report critical incidents in the news. One of the researchers recalled working with a family whose child had been missing for over a year. We had been working with local authorities in multiple counties and the FBI. We held a vigil supporting bringing the teen home, but the news falsely reported that she had been found. It took weeks to fix their mess, and the information never retracted the story of the girl being found. In the workplace, African-American experience higher rates of sexual harassment and microaggressions than their White counterparts (Knighton et al., 2020; Perry, Harp, Oser, 2013; Solomon et al., 2019).

Additionally, the entertainment industry's depiction of African-American women as prostitutes, promiscuous, angry, cold, and more aids in the re-traumatization. These images are dehumanizing, undermining, and dismissive and often unfairly describe African-American women as superhuman. Black women have struggled to be seen as humans who experience diverse emotions, feelings, challenges, highs, and lows.

Mental Distress

Research has provided empirical support for the notion that African-American women experience psychological distress due to family and social ills such as racism, sexism, and classism (Julian, 2019; Moras et al., 2018; Perry, Harry & Oser, 2013; Ward & Heidrich, 2009). Landrine, Klonoff, Alcaraz, Scott, and Wilkins (1995) argued that racism might intensify the impact of sexism, and sexism may intensify race. Greene (1994) suggested racist events may strain stress factors, leaving few resources for African-American women to cope with sexist events. Landrine, Klonoff, Gibbs, et al. (1995) used the Schedule of Sexist Events (SSE) (Klonoff & Landrine, 1995) to examine the link between self-reports of sexist events and psychological distress for 551 community women (approximately 183 women of color) the findings indicated that lifetime and recent sexist events were related to premenstrual symptoms, real psychological distress, obsessive-compulsivity, interpersonal sensitivity, and anxiety above and beyond daily hassles and other stressful life events. According to Knighton, Dogan, Hargons, and Stevens-Watkins (2020), an estimated 8 out of 10 African-American women have experienced at least one traumatic event in their lifetime. African-American women silently suffer from anxiety, loneliness, depression, unresolved childhood trauma, family drama, dissatisfaction with their relationships, poverty, microaggressions, racism and sexism at work, feeling not good enough, and more (Duncan et al., 2011; Julian, 2019; Knighton et al., 2020; Moras, A., Shehan, C., Berardo; 2018; Perry, Harry & Oser, 2013; Ward & Heidrich, 2009). Not acknowledging and addressing the historical trauma and stressors has caused physical and mental problems for African-American women. These traumas and mental distress are continually passed down from generation to generation with little access to support, including family and support networks.

The Healing Process

To begin the healing process of African-American women, we must first understand the method of breaking. William "Willie" Lynch (1712) outlined "Cardinal Principles" for the breaking process of the African Women that will be passed down for generations. In his speech given on the banks of the James River in Virginia, he exclaimed:

> Take the female and run a series of tests on her to see if she will submit to your desires willingly. Test her in every way because she is the most critical factor for good economics. If she shows any resistance in submitting completely to your will, do not hesitate to use the bullwhip on her to extract that last bit of [b----] out of her. Take care not to kill her, for in doing so; you spoil good economics. When in complete submission, she will train her offspring in the early years to submit to labor age. Understanding is the best thing. Therefore, we shall go deeper into this area of the subject matter concerning what we have produced here in this breaking process of the female nigger. We have reversed the relationship; in her natural uncivilized state, she would have a strong dependency on the rough nigger male, and she would have a limited protective tendency toward her independent male offspring and would raise male offspring to be dependent like her. Nature had provided for this type of balance. We reversed nature by burning and pulling a civilized nigger apart and bullwhipping the other to the point of death, all in her presence. By her being left alone, unprotected, with the

> *MALE IMAGE DESTROYED*, the ordeal caused her to move from her psychologically dependent state to a frozen, independent state. In this frozen, psychological state of independence, she will raise her *MALE* and female offspring in reversed roles. For *FEAR* of the young male's life, she will psychologically train him to be *MENTALLY WEAK* and *DEPENDENT*, but *PHYSICALLY STRONG*. Because she has become psychologically independent, she will train her *FEMALE* offspring to be psychologically independent. What have you got? You've got the nigger *WOMAN OUT FRONT AND THE* nigger *MAN BEHIND AND SCARED*. This is a perfect situation of sound sleep and economics. Before the breaking process, we had to be alertly on guard at all times. Now, we can sleep soundly, for out of frozen fear his woman stands guard for us. He cannot get past her early slave-molding process. He is a good tool, now ready to be tied to the horse at a tender age. By the time a nigger boy reaches the age of sixteen, he is soundly broken in and ready for a long life of sound and efficient work and the reproduction of a unit of good labor force. Continually through the breaking of uncivilized savage niggers, by throwing the nigger female savage into a frozen psychological state of independence, by killing the protective male image, and by creating a submissive dependent mind of the nigger male slave, we have created an orbiting cycle that turns on its axis forever, unless a phenomenon occurs and re-shifts the position of the male and female slaves…(p. 31-32).

The powerful effects of this letter still ring true in modern society. All must understand the psychological warfare that African-American women have endured for centuries. The steps toward healing are not just for African-American women to do but for all those who encounter these women. This community healing theme provides safety and understanding for African-American women to receive the much-needed break to heal truly.

Internal Healing

Trauma memories are encoded in the body and can manifest physically through selective memory, collective forgetting, and denying testimony that threatens its harmony (Mikkelsen, 2012). A growing number of studies support the ideology that the effects of trauma can be encoded and modify DNA in future generations through epigenetics. Epigenetic regulation occurs throughout the lifespan and can be induced by random changes or environmental factors. (Guerrero-Bosagna, Skinner; Massicotte, Whitelaw, Angers, 2011). Additionally, human epigenome changes correlate with adaptation and evolution processes. As such, African-American women must self-evaluate their value and worth to themselves and others (DeGruy, 2005). They develop a positive self-image, and self-love impacts how others treat them. Focusing on the positive aspects of life over the negative helps to ameliorate anxiety, depression, and other mental distress (Nichols, Gringle, & Pulliam, 2015). Engaging in healthy self-care and re-shaping past traumatic experiences, either experienced, witnessed, or vicariously, can foster the healing of African-American women and build their families and outlook on the future.

According to the researchers, the concept of self-care sometimes carries a different definition from person to person, but on a fundamental level, practicing self-care means taking care of yourself above others. To be able to care for others, you must first take care of yourself. Self-care is crucial for our physical, emotional, and mental well-being. While you are supporting and helping others as a "strong black woman," it is essential for you to also take care of yourself. It means that you are simply being mindful of your needs to support them better and meet their needs. Engaging in self-care helps you and others value your worth. It produces positive feelings and boosts your confidence and self-esteem. Also, self-care is necessary to remind yourself and others that you and your needs are essential too. The researchers posited that as working professionals, parents, students, and contributing members of your family and society, you must develop a self-care plan. With that said, think about developing a self-care plan. The researchers suggested that a self-care plan can help you enhance your mental health and well-being, manage stress, and maintain balance. Overworking and the accompanying stress and exhaustion can make you less productive, disorganized, and emotionally depleted. It can also lead to all sorts of health problems, from anxiety and depression to insomnia, heart diseases, and various medical and physical ailments. Positive self-care habits ensure that you stay sharp, motivated, and healthy.

Support

Most people will not understand the emotional toll African-American women experience with historical oppression, systemic racism, sexism, being over-sexualized, and being undervalued. For African-American women, the survivor of generations of oppression and discarded in society, sharing her/their experience helps to validate their experience. It helps to bring awareness and insight into abuse. She must tell her story in her own words; then be validated and affirmed (DeGruy, 2005). Developing healthy support systems creates a sense of belonging and deeper connections in relationships with family, friends, community, and society. The researchers suggest seeking support from a licensed, trained mental health provider aids in fostering awareness and cognitive restructuring to identify the issues; help to process thoughts, feelings, and emotions; develop new coping skills, and change negative mindsets. Multiple studies suggest the vital role of support systems in African-American women's life (Ashley, 2014; DeGruy, 2005; Porter & Dean, 2015; Ward, & Heidrich, 2009; Williams, 2008).

Legislative Engagement

The most impactful healing of African-American women can be implemented through legislative policies. Policy changes that would generally improve wages, health coverage, and paid leave could particularly help black women (Duncan et al., 2011; Julian, 2019; Moras et al., 2018; Solomon, Maxwell, & Castro, 2019). Another factor is increasing the representation of African-American women in politics, and policy could help create a political system that addresses the problems that black women face. Some African American community members feel monetary reparations will aid in building wealth and contribute to the building of generational wealth. It is unclear if monetary reparations will help make African American women whole; it is apparent that financial wealth leads to better physical and mental access as well as health (Duncan et al., 2011; Julian, 2019; Knighton et al., 2020; Moras et al., 2018; Perry, Harry & Oser, 2013; Ward & Heidrich, 2009). Legislatives have the power to pass slavery reparations bills. The U.S. Congress revisited this on April 14, 2021, first introduced by the last Honorable Congressional Representative John Conyers of Michigan's 13th District back in 1989 (Sotomayor, 2021). The 46th President, Joseph Biden, supported the idea of a committee to study reparations for Black Americans but has yet to officially sign a bill that would create a commission to investigate the idea of paying the descendants of enslaved citizens. It is noteworthy to highlight the language. President Biden supported the "idea" of a committee to study reparations but not to "endorse" reparations. The advancement of legislative policies could potentially dismantle how others negatively perceive African American women's value to their families and society. However, it appears that African-

American women have a long way to go before seeing any true legislative reform that benefits them.

Community Call to Action – Building a Safe Place

Imagine breaking a bone and going to the hospital. The physician will set the bone and place a cast to stop moving so the bone can heal properly. When someone has a cast on, everyone inside and outside of their circle begins to carry the burden of tasks that cannot be completed with the unspoken understanding that this person needs help. This same concept must be applied to the healing process of African-American women. The community must acknowledge that there are several broken bones, and the steps mentioned above are the areas where African-American women are cast. White people must use their privilege within the workplace to provide a voice for African-American women. All men must protect African-American women by ensuring they are safe within their communities. The housing systems must dismantle the redlining, so there is an equal opportunity for affordable housing. Institutions should take multicultural competence and diversity, as well as inclusion more seriously. Multicultural competence cannot be taught without white people feeling judged or defensive; thus, it mustbe experienced to fully understand the injustices of the Black community. Most of all, all people must be willing to listen to the experiences of African-American women with the intent to help. This individualized approach offers an opportunity for inclusion in all institutions.

Conclusion

African-American women are known as the heartbeat of their community. This magnificent group of women is the target of all forms of discrimination without any protection from the community. Patel (2021) noted that the severe consequences of failing to address this consistent discrimination include the broken cycle and leaving African- American women to protect themselves. Solutions include developing policies and programs for African-American women and allocating finances to assist African-American women in education, housing, and employment (Patel, 2021). In addition to program development, there needs to be a safe place for Black women to address their inequalities and discrimination without negative recourse (Thompson, 2016). Due to the soil of pain and anguish, all community members are responsible for supporting African- American women. Malcolm X stated, "*The most disrespected person in America is the black woman. The most unprotected person in America is the black woman. The most neglected person in America is the black woman.*" (X.M. & Haley, A, 1962). His words have been a statement of truth for 59 years, and there is a call to action for protection. Healing must be a community effort because the traumas were community-based. Healing allows African-American women a freedom that is deserved. The direct ramifications of African-American women healing are the ability to walk without shame, to be heard when speaking, and to be loved unconditionally. African-American women have been a part of monumental changes while carrying the load of pain; imagine what more they can do when they are trauma-free.

References

Ashley, W. (2014). The angry black woman: The impact of pejorative stereotypes on psychotherapy with black women. *Soc Work Public Health,* 29(1):27–34. Doi: 10.1080/19371918.2011.619449. PMID: 24188294.

Beal, F. M. (1970). Double jeopardy: To be Black and female. In T. Cade (Ed.), The *Black woman: An anthology* (pp. 90–100). New York: Signet.

Burton, A. L., Thompson, L. S., Delaney, L. A. & Drumgoold, K. (2006). *Women's slave narratives.* Dover Publishing Co., Mineola, N.Y. ISBN-10: 0486445550.

Bowman, B. T., Comer, J. P., & Johns, D. J. (2018). Addressing the African American Achievement Gap: Three Leading Educators Issue a Call to Action. *Young Children, 73*(2).

Capuzzi. D., Stauffer, M. D., Eber-Lapierre, N. (2021). Variations in family systems and family life cycles. In Capuzzi. D., Stauffer, M. D., (2 nd Ed). *Foundations of couples, marriage, and family counseling. John Wiley & Sons, Inc.* ISBN-10: 1119686083.

DeGruy, J. (2005). Post traumatic slave syndrome. *Uptone Press.* ISBN-13: 978-0-9852172-0-4.

Detroit Historic Society. (2021). *Black Bottom neighborhood.* Retrieved July 23, 2021, from https://detroithistorical.org/learn/encyclopedia-of-detroit/black-bottom-neighborhood.

Diner, H. (1985). Black women in families: From field to factory. *Reviews in American History, 13*(4), 551–556. doi:10.2307/2702587.

Duncan, G. J., Morris, P. A., & Rodrigues, C. (2011). Does money really matter? Estimating impacts of family income on young children's achievement with data from Random-assignment experiments. *Developmental psychology, 47*(5), 1263–1279. https://doi.org/10.1037/a0023875.

Feagin, J., & Bennefield, Z. (2014). Systemic racism and U.S. health care. *Social Science & Medicine*, *103*, 7–14. https://doi.org/10.1016/j.socscimed.2013.09.006.

Gilbert, O. (1997). *Narrative of Sojourner Truth*. Dover Publication, Inc., Mineola, N.Y. ISBN-10: 048629899X.

Goldin, C. (1977). Female labor force participation: The origin of black and white differences, 1870 and 1880. *Journal of Economic History,* 37(1): 87–108.

Greene, B. (1994). African American women. In L. Comas-Diaz & B. Greene (Eds.), *Women of color: Integrating ethnic and gender identities in psychotherapy* (pp. 10–29). New York: Guilford.

Guerrero-Bosagna, C. M., Skinner, M. K. (2014). Environmental epigenetics and phytoestrogen/phytochemical exposures. *J Steroid Biochem Mol Biol,* 139, 270–6. doi: 10.1016/j.jsbmb.2012.12.011.

Henry, W. J., & Glenn, N. M. (2009). Black Women Employed in the Ivory Tower: Connecting for Success. *Advancing Women in Leadership Journal*, *29*(2). https://doi.org/https://doi.org/10.18738/awl.v29i0.271.

Joint Economic Committee. (2019). *Full employment and stable prices: Pursuing the dual mandate in a changing economy*. Retrieved July 23, 2021, from https://www.jec.senate.gov/public/_cache/files/0fc5c5fd-8c02-4d26-a11a31c6d9d99353/full-employment-and-stable-prices-final-version1.pdf.

Julian, E. (2019). The fair housing act at fifty: Time for a change. *Cardozo Law Review,* 40 (3), 1133–1148.

Jones, C. (2006). Falling between the cracks: What diversity means for black women in higher education. *Policy Futures in Education*, *4*(2), 145–159. https://doi.org/10.2304/pfie.2006.4.2.145.

Pedro A. Noguera (Guest Editor) (2017) Introduction to "Racial Inequality and Education: Patterns and Prospects for the Future," *The Educational Forum*, 81:2, 129–135, doi: 10.1080/00131725.2017.1280753.

Knighton, J. S., Dogan, J., Hargons, C., Stevens-Watkins, D. (2020). Superwoman Schema: a context for understanding psychological distress among middle-class African American women who perceive racial microaggressions. *Ethn Health*, 15:1-17. doi: 10.1080/13557858.2020.1818695. Epub ahead of print. PMID: 32931323; PMCID: PMC7956919.

Landrine, H., & Klonoff, E. A. (1996). The Schedule of Racist Events: A measure of racial discrimination and a study of its negative physical and mental health consequences. *Journal of Black Psychology*, 22, 144-168.

Landrine, H., Klonoff, E. A., Alcaraz, R., Scott, J., & Wikins, P. (1995). Multiple variables in discrimination. In B. Lott & D. Maluso (Eds.), *The social psychology of interpersonal discrimination* (pp. 183-224). New York: Guilford.

Landrine, H., Klonoff, E. A., Gibbs, J., Manning, V., & Lund, M. (1995). Physical and psychiatric correlates of gender discrimination: An application of the Schedule of Sexist Events. *Psychology of Women Quarterly*, 19, 473–492.

Lewis, E. (1989). Role strain in African American women: The efficacy of support networks. *Journal of Black Studies, 20*(2), 155–169. Retrieved July 23, 2021, from http://www.jstor.org/stable/2784697.

Leibowitz-Nelson, S. B., Baker, S. B., & Nassar, S. C. (2020). Multicultural and social justice counseling competencies: Institutional interventions for professional school counselors. *Journal of Counselor Leadership and Advocacy*, *7*(1), 42–54.

Lynch, W. (2009). *The Willie Lynch letter and the making of A slave.* BN Publishing.

Marina, B. L. H. (2016). *Beyond retention: Cultivating spaces of equity, justice, and fairness for women of color in U.S. higher education*. Information Age Publishing.

Massicotte, R., Whitelaw, E., Angers, B. (2011). DNA methylation: a source of random variation in natural populations. *Epigenetics*, 6(4), 421–7. doi: 10.4161/epi.6.4.14532.

McDaniel, A., DiPrete, T. A., Buchmann, C., & Shwed, U. (2011). The black gender gap in educational attainment: Historical trends and racial comparisons. *Demography*, *48*(3), 889–914. https://doi.org/10.1007/s13524-011-0037-0.

Mikkelsen, N. (2010). [Review of the book Traumatic Possessions: The Body and Memory in African American Women's Writing and Performance]. *MELUS: Multi-Ethnic Literature of the U.S.* 35(4), 195-196. https://www.muse.jhu.edu/article/407345.

Moras, A., Shehan, C., Berardo, F. M. (2018). African American families: Historical and contemporary forces shaping family life and studies. In: Batur P., Feagin J. (eds) Handbook of the Sociology of Racial and Ethnic Relations. *Handbooks of Sociology and Social Research.* Springer, Cham. https://doi.org/10.1007/978-3-319-76757-4_6.

Morgan, T. & Twine, S. (May, 2021). *Social justice advocacy: Hearing the voices of female African American faculty* [Video webinar].

Mutari, E., Power, M. & Figart, M. D. (2002). Neither mothers nor breadwinners: African American women's exclusion from US minimum wage policies, 1912–1938. *Feminist. Economics* 8(2),37–61.

Nichols, T., Gringle, M., & Pulliam, R. (2015). You have to put your children's needs first or you're really not a good mother: Black motherhood and self-care practices. *Women, Gender, and Families of Color*, 3(2), 165–189. doi:10.5406/womgenfamcol.3.2.0165.

Oshin, L. A., Milan, S. (2019). My strong, Black daughter: Racial/ethnic differences in the attributes mothers value for their daughters. *Culture Divers Ethnic Minor Psychol.*, 25(2):179-187. doi: 10.1037/cdp0000206. Epub 2018 Dec 3. PMID: 30507209; PMCID: PMC6438745.

Perry, B. L., Harp, K. L., Oser, C. B. (2013). Racial and gender discrimination in the stress process: Implications for African American women's health and well-being. *Social Perspect.* Spring; *56*(1):25–48. PMID: 24077024; PMCID: PMC3783344.

Porter, C. J & Dean, L. A. (2015). Making meaning: Identity development of black undergraduate women, *NASPA Journal About Women in Higher Education*, 8(2), 125-139, doi: 10.1080/19407882.2015.1057164.

Ricketts, E. (2007). *The origin of black female-headed families.*

Ricks, S. A. (2014). Falling through the Cracks: Black Girls and Education. *Interdisciplinary Journal of Teaching and Learning*, *4*(1), 10–21.

Ross, H. L. & Sawhill, I. V. (1975). *Time of transition: The growth of families headed by women*. Washington, D. C.: Urban Institute Press.

Skubikowski, C., Wright, C., & Graf, R. (2009). *Inviting faculty to transform their institutions.* Stylus Publications.

Solomon, D., Maxwell, C. & Castro, A. (2019). *Systematic inequality and economic opportunity.* Washington: Center for American Progress. Retrieved from: https://www.americanprogress.org/issues/race/reports/2019/08/07/472910/systematic-inequality-economic-opportunity/. Lasted viewed: July 28, 2021.

Sotomayor, M. (April, 2021). House panel approves bill to create commission on slavery reparations. The Washington Post.

Sudarkasa, N. (2007). African American female-headed households: some neglected dimensions. In H. P. McAdoo (Ed.), *Black families* (pp. 172-183). SAGE Publications, Inc., https://www.doi.org/10.4135/9781452226026.n12.

Tabbye Chavous, & Courtney D. Cogburn. (2007). Super invisible Women: Black Girls and Women in Education. *Black Women, Gender Families, 1*(2), 24–51. Retrieved August 10, 2021, from https://www.jstor.org/stable/10.5406/blacwomegendfami.1.2.0024.

U.S. Bureau of Labor Statistics. (2015). Data Retrieval: Labor Force Statistics (CPS). Table 1. Union affiliation of employed wage and salary workers by selected characteristics. https://www.bls.gov/webapps/legacy/cpslutab1.htm; U.S. Bureau of Labor Statistics. (2019). TED: The Economics Daily. "*Union membership rate 10.5 percent in 2018, down from 20.1 percent in 1983.*" https://www.bls.gov/opub/ted/2019/union-membership-rate-10-point-5-percent-in-2018-downfrom-20-point-1-percent-in-1983.htm.

U.S. Census Bureau. (2021). *Poverty Thresholds.* 11111retrieceved from: https://www.census.gov/data/tables/time-series/demo/income-poverty/historical-poverty-threshlds.html (Last accessed July 2021).

Wade, J. M., Bean, A., Teixiera-Poit, S. (2019). Students, universities, and employers: Why we all win when we promote social justice through SoTL. *International Journal for the Scholarship of Teaching and Learning,* 13(3), 1-7.

Walker, H. A. (1988). *Black-White differences in marriage and family patterns.* in S. M. Dornbush and M. H. Strober, eds., Feminism, Children, and the New Families New York: Guilford Press.

Ward, E. C., & Heidrich, S. M. (2009). African American women's beliefs about mental illness, stigma, and preferred coping behaviors. *Research in nursing & health, 32*(5), 480–492. https://doi.org/10.1002/nur.20344.

Washington, H. A. (2006). Medical Apartheid: The Dark History of Medical Experimentation on Black Americans from Colonial Times to the Present. *Harlem Moon.* ISBN-10: 076791547X.

Weir, K. (2016, November). Inequality at school. *Monitor on Psychology, 47*(10). http://www.apa.org/monitor/2016/11/cover-inequality-school.

Williams, T. B. (2008). Pain: It Just Looks Like We're Not Hurting. *Scribner.* ISBN-10: 0743298837.

Williams-Reid, L. & Rubin, B. A. (2003). Integrating economic dualism and labor market segmentation: The effects of race, gender, and structural location on earnings, 1974–2000. *The Sociological Quarterly,* 44 (3), 405–432, doi: 10.1111/j.1533-8525.2003.tb00539.x.

Whitaker, I. P., Whitaker, M. M., & Jackson, K. A. (2014). Single parenting in the African American Community: Implications for public policy and practice. *Journal of Human Behavior in the Social Environment, 24*, 230 - 249.

X, M., & Haley, A. (1965). The autobiography of Malcolm X. New York: Grove Press.

Part 2. Contemporary Trauma

Chapter 4

Treatment Practices of Black/African-American Women Dealing with Race-Based Trauma

Tina Marie Glover*
Keiser University, Fort Lauderdale, Florida, USA

Abstract

The cultural demands of mental health counseling require considering all cultural factors when assessing and treating mental illness. Traditional assessment and counseling techniques do not serve Black/African Americans well (Dana, 2008). Sue, Arredondo, and McDavis (1992), Sue and Sue (2008), and Ridley (2005) indicate that clinicians without adequate cross-cultural skills may find it challenging to establish and maintain the necessary relationship with individuals from ethnocultural groups. Clinicians lacking these skills result in a lack of long-standing client engagement or decreased efficacy. Authors (Dana, 2008; DeGruy-Leary, 2005; Sue et al., 1992) describe how multicultural awareness, knowledge, and skills are essential to counseling and assessing culturally different clients, particularly Black/African Americans. Despite this knowledge, few professionals in the mental health field explore the assessment and treatment practices of culturally similar, culturally competent counselors who effectively engage with Black/African American clients. This manuscript included reports of a study of the assessment and treatment practices of a Black/African American clinician identified as successful in engaging and maintaining engagement with Black/African American clients.

* Corresponding Author's Email: tglover@keiseruniversity.edu.

In: How Did We Survive?
Editor: Tina Marie Glover
ISBN: 979-8-88697-918-3

Keywords: African American women, black women, trauma, etiology of trauma, mental health, counseling, multi culture, therapeutic alliance, generational trauma

The current trend in mental health practice demands considering culturally specific factors when assessing and treating mental illness (Sue, Arredondo, and McDavis, 1992). Much of the multicultural counseling literature suggests that traditional assessment and counseling techniques do not serve Black/African Americans well (Dana, 2008). Authors such as Sue and Sue (2004) and Ridley (1995) highlight how the necessary therapeutic alliance may be difficult to establish or maintain without culturally sensitive relationship building. Many authors describe how multicultural knowledge, awareness, and skills are essential to assessing and treating culturally different clients, particularly Black/African American women (Dana, 2008; DeGruy-Leary, 2005; Sue et al., 1992). Furthermore, the literature suggests that therapists with the same cultural background are more likely to assess and treat women of color effectively than non-Black/African Americans (Ford, Bullard, McKeever, Toler, Neighbors & Jackson, 2007; DeGruy-Leary, 2005). The overall goal is to continually explore the assessment and treatment practices of culturally similar, culturally competent counselors who effectively engage with Black/African American clients (Glover, 2012).

The reference to multicultural knowledge as specific knowledge about the historical background, sociopolitical influences, and cultural heritage of diverse cultural groups, Glover, (2012) Sodowsky (1996) and Sue et al., (1992). Multicultural knowledge is different for each client. What remains consistent is the cultivation of the relationship. In some cases, counseling may represent another form of cultural oppression for diverse clients, leaving them feeling unsafe engaging with helping professionals (Ridley, 1995).

Other factors that affect the mental health of Black/African American women include economic, social, and political status. U.S. Department of Health and Human Services (2001) noted that Black/African Americans are 50% more likely to drop out of counseling following the second session than 30% of White Americans (Sue, 1977). The underuse of mental health services is primarily associated with the fear and anxiety of self-exposure or possible re-traumatization (Lawson, 2003). This begs the question if clinicians' have a lack of awareness of cultural issues or bias, does this increase their inability to speak the clients' language and decrease the client's fears and mistrust of the therapy process (Carter, 2007; Glover, 2012; DeGruy-Leary, 2005).

Scholars such as Carter (2007), Comas- Diaz (2007), and DeGruy-Leary (2005) have proposed that historically oppressed people such as Black/African Americans may have trauma responses specific to their historical experience(s). Both Carter (2007) and Cross (1998) have indicated that Black/African Americans have unique stressors. Specifically, racially based may include racial violence, discrimination, and micro-aggressions (Kearney, Draper, & Baron, 2005). Along with more commonly known stressors, the literature suggests that generational trauma (e.g., that associated with survivors of African slavery or the Jewish Holocaust) should be included in the list of racially based stressors (Danieli, 1998; Rosenthal & Rosenthal, 1980; Rubenstein, et al., 1990).

Engagement in the therapeutic process of Black/African American women should address racially based trauma, racial violence, discrimination, social and economic barriers, and micro-aggressions. The overall goal is to assist clients in developing socio-culturally acceptable coping strategies (Glover, 2012). Previously learned techniques of coping can cause the individual to function in a way wherein they feel hopeless or powerless about their life or circumstances (Pinderhughes,1990). Understanding the worldviews of our clients is a priority; thus, professionals need to understand the Black/African American women's experience, also known as the "Black experience." These professionals must be willing to adjust their practice to include all the micro-aggressions and oppression the Black/African American women experiences daily. A large part of understanding the "black experience is continued education surrounding cultural competencies and standard methods of incorporating this knowledge in the assessment and treatment process, particularly for Black/African American women.

There is an increased need for clinician awareness of the social climate of Black/African Americans. With events such as the deaths of George Floyd, Brianna Taylor, and many more, the Black/African American community has shown that the trauma they endure is still accurate. The women that are heads of the Black household are traumatized almost daily. With this and other untold stories, the social context in which Black/African American women live and different life experiences should and could dictate variance in theoretical approaches to treatment (Cooke & Shear, 2001). How a therapist engages with Black/African American clients should include exploring one's individual, environmental, and generational influences (Glover, 2012; DeGruy-Leary, 2005; Sue et al., 1992). Although mental health professionals should be trained to be culturally skilled, there appears to be a disconnect between their skills and cultural sensitivity when working with racially or culturally different clients (Sue et al., 1992).

Cultural competence in counseling and assessment has been conceptualized as encompassing knowledge, awareness, and skills (Sue et al., 1992 & Glover, 2012). Knowledge and awareness should include sensitivity to generational and environmental trauma or life experiences. These practices should increase engagement and treatment success (Glover, 2012). Arredondo et al. (1996) highlighted areas important in working with culturally specific clients, including 1) beliefs, 2) knowledge, and 3) skills. Mental health professionals should be aware of one's cultural values and biases, the client's worldview, and culturally appropriate intervention strategies. The assertion is that these areas can assist professionals in identifying, assessing, and treating individual, familial, and environmental barriers that may be intergenerational with Black/African American women.

Best Practices in Counseling

Best practices hold clinicians of the American Counseling Association (ACA) and American Psychological Association (APA) accountable to a code of ethics, commanding practitioners to be qualified and competent when applying interventions (ACA, 2005; APA, 2002). In working with Black/African American clients, talented professionals should be aware of the need to incorporate skills and knowledge of varied cultures into the assessment and treatment process. However, combining multicultural skills and awareness of environmental, generational, or individual factors that affect Black/African Americans during the assessment process can routinely be omitted (Glover, 2012).

In prior research, I examined two interrelated areas of clinical practice. First, I explored the current assessment and treatment techniques of a Black/African American professional (a female therapist) identified by peers as culturally competent/proficient with Black/African American clients. Second, the research examined and defined the context of this practice. The research queries: "What are the assessment and treatment practices of a culturally proficient Black/African American therapist working with Black/African American clients?" and "What are the intrapersonal and interpersonal, experiential, educational, social, and institutional contexts surrounding these practices?" It is my belief that a practitioner's cultural proficiency in the assessment and treatment process when working with Black/African Americans equal a greater success in the treatment process..

In prior research looking at the treatment process of a culturally proficient professional, I used a single case study method with semi-structured interviews with a Black/African American clinician identified as successful in engaging Black/African American clients. My interview focus included assessment and treatment practices and considered the contextual development of these practices. I found this research to be helpful in answering the "how" and "why" questions related to the therapist's approach to engaging and treating clients. I augmented my findings by interviewing clinical supervisors, clients, and colleagues who were knowledgeable of the therapist's practices and ability to develop a therapeutic alliance and the therapist's multicultural competence to provide additional perspectives surrounding the clients' concerns and needs.

By exploring what works and what continues to be worked on in a successful engagement of Black/African American clients in therapy with a culturally similar clinician. The goal of the therapist is to be culturally competent. The goal for the client is to find a therapist who is recognized as a culturally competent mental health professional and can engage the client through all parts of the treatment process. This would include the initial contact and all ongoing assessment and treatment processes.

Clients seeking help need to feel that the therapist is culturally proficient. This would include the language they use to communicate with the client. Is the therapist using language that is familiar to the client rather than the language therapist and other professionals use in the field? By doing so, professionals can build rapport before the assessment begins; by doing so, therapists can develop a therapeutic alliance (Glover. 2012).

Therapeutic Alliance is developed by being present with the client and listing their concerns. If they are open and descriptive, incorporate language familiar to the individual rather than the field terminology. By including this, the professional equalizes the power differentials by putting self 'out there regarding culture and what the therapist has to offer the client. The therapist has to take a 'service-oriented' stance from the first interaction. Therapists must be aware of differences in culturally specific experiences between therapists and clients—the ability to understand the local environment and culture and how it might impact the client. Culturally-proficient clinicians explore past reasons for lack of engagement – with sensitivity to client culture (individual and familial experiences with psychological treatment). Culturally proficient clinicians identify issues in the client's social environment that may or may not be perceived as traumatic in mainstream culture. Culturally proficient clinicians continue these behaviors and attitudes through ongoing assessment and treatment. Culturally proficient clinicians explore new themes and emerging information throughout the evaluation and treatment, focusing on identifying individual coping skills that might be familial, generational, culturally specific, or related to racial stress.

Working Alliance is critical in developing the engagement of a strong working alliance with clients. Working on the client's goals is essential to create a strong working alliance with the client. Identified goals require tasks or steps to achieve the goals and bond. Bonding can be achieved through therapeutic alliance.

Cultural knowledge and awareness in counseling are a large part of the success of the treatment process. What enhances the treatment process is when there is a Black/African American mental health professional. Research has found that he has encouraged and maintained engagement while assessing and treating Black/African American clients (Glover, 2012). Clients are open to addressing the issue at hand and the ability to name and place identification with the culturally specific and proficient clinician. Culturally proficient clinicians can identify with the client and encourage connections based on real-world issues when working with Black/African American clients.

Culturally Proficient Therapist

Research shows that a culturally proficient counselor communicates a strong sense of cultural self. They are experienced in having a strong cultural understanding of clients. They are experienced in effectively engaging with clients throughout the counseling process. The culturally proficient counselor continuously gathers and makes sense of work and educational experiences to better work with clients. The relationship's success relates to how the therapist successfully engages the Black/African American client. Does the therapist have a strong sense of cultural self-knowledge and display pride in who they are? This cultural pride can be illustrated to the client by artwork displayed in the work environment. These can be less than apparent displays of cultural pride. The therapist dresses in clothing that indicates professionalism, cultural knowledge, and pride. Cultural pride can be as simple as incorporating jewelry, kente cloths/wraps, or other items of clothing made with traditional African print or inspiration. How one develops a line of communication, and a personal worldview includes a firm belief in the essential resilience of the

African American people. The deeper the therapist can connect with the client, the more they can understand and relate to current and historical oppression. The message to Black/African American women should be that they are survivors and have the potential to be prosperous and healthy against all odds (Glover, 2012).

Supervisors of trauma and other mental health want to feel that they can have a deeper connection with their therapist. The journey to a healthy, happy life is a gift they deserve, and the therapist can help clients obtain it. The shared world views can be of power and strength while looking through how to be successful in a time of oppression. The goal is to help the client see that oppression is not their identity but a set of circumstances they are experiencing.

Cultural Knowledge and Awareness

Research has shown that a culturally proficient counselor understands the clients' race, ethnicity, and culture. In this case, being a Black/African American counselor aids in successfully working with Black/African American clients. Professionals need to have the ability to understand and acknowledge the existence of oppression, racism, and microaggressions. The ability to know how this microaggression and oppression may play. A role in local and national events. How do these local and national events impact the client, their family, and the community in which they reside? They are intensely aware of the daily issues Black/African Americans face, including problems accessing services and how this may be a part of their experiences.

Understanding the cultural implications for the client's family dynamics and functioning is central, particularly to the client. The ability to know the client's choice of language and comfort with how the client may use and view language. The goal is to understand the cultural differences within the community and the broader concepts of oppression and racism through verbal and nonverbal language. As previously noted, to be culturally competent, you must understand the dynamics of racism in this county and have a strong foundation. Then you must understand the systematic approach to oppression in this country and how it is in the systems, not just racism alone but its multi-levels (Glover, 2012).

Engaging with Clients Throughout the Process

The engagement and the ability to maintain engagement with Black/African American clients are vital to the healing process. Research has shown that clients respond more4 to the initial meeting, are viewed as warm, and the therapist is perceived as trustworthy and representing the clients' own culture. The therapist should be considered an extension of an organization that prioritizes and promotes equity of services for clients of color. A therapist who is actively engaged with their clients assists and empowers clients by helping them better understand mental health systems, thereby reducing the shame and stigma associated with receiving services.

The culturally proficient counselor works with the client's needs within a cultural context. The therapist examines all aspects of the clients' lives (social, environmental, familial) that may have brought the client into services. During treatment, they are responsive to systemic oppression, regional and national racism, micro-aggressions, and internalized racism and how they may, directly and indirectly, affect the clients. The therapist utilizes techniques that engage clients and address cultural aspects of their issues.

Gaining Initial Trust Through Authenticity and Cultural Identification

A culturally proficient counselor can successfully engage Black/African American clients while working on client-identified issues. They can engage clients skeptical of mental health counseling while building a healthy therapeutic alliance. Engagement starts at the first contact, where they can gain initial trust with a skeptical client of mental health services. It is important that clients feel connected to authentic counselors and represent their culture to some extent. It is also fair to note that when the professional is also a member of another organization that prioritizes services to clients of color, which is meaningful to the clients.

It Is Reducing Skepticism and Stigma through Education

Upon initial contact, the therapist should begin to work with the client to reduce the stigma associated with mental health services and demystify mental health systems. This can be obtained by utilizing personal knowledge of Black/African American culture and educating clients on how mental health and human service systems work and how they can benefit the client. This can be achieved by educating the client about your professional history and years of experience working with African Americans, adolescents, adults, and families. It can also include educating the clients on the approach utilized when working with clients; for example, do you use a systems approach to work with clients, or is your theoretical approach from a multi-theoretical approach? Whatever the method, educate the client about your theoretical practice and assist the client in feeling as if they are part of the process. Use language that is accessible and inform clients about language that may be used in the field so that it is not a foreign language to the client. Providing examples that closely mirror their experiences reassures clients and reduces stigma.

They Are Empowering by Involving Clients in Treatment Planning

Client engagement by actively involving Black/African American clients in treatment planning is essential to the success of the treatment. A successful therapist needs to engage the client and empower the client to take an active role in the therapeutic process. It is believed that this is an extension of explaining the process of helping. It is a form of understanding and validating the client's understanding of their problems and the goals that they may bring with them. As the treatment process continues, the therapist should revisit the treatment plan to review and revise progresswith the client.

Research has shown that clients feel unheard of or devalued when they are not part of the process. Therefore, the ability to demonstrate the ability to use the treatment planning process to meet with a client, hear their story and assist clients in understanding the problems they face. It helps the client feel like they are in a nonjudgment place and that the therapist understands what is going on with the client.

They Are Working with the Cultural Context of the Client's Issues

As a culturally proficient therapist, you should be able to keep Black/African American clients engaged throughout the counseling process by understanding and working with the client's needs within a cultural context. In essence, knowledge of the client's race, ethnicity, and culture, as well as the many layers of a supersystem, is demonstrated in the actions she takes with clients throughout counseling. The ability to establish a proper understanding and not be reliant solely upon one's education, training, and experience, but the ability to use one's identification and pride as a person of color or acknowledge that they are working outside the context of their culture but have the willingness to learn is essential. This can be achieved by examining all aspects of the clients' lives (social, environmental, familial) that may have brought the client into services. This culturally proficient counselor often seeks collateral information to understand the dynamics that affect the client, past and present.

By seeking collateral information, the therapist can be responsive to systemic oppression, regional and national racism, micro-aggressions, and internalized racism and how all of these things may, directly and indirectly, affect the clients' needs. When a counselor has a strong awareness of client perceptions and relates to the dynamics of racism, oppression, or any form of discrimination or microaggressions clients may present with, they can normalize a situation. This can also be achieved through storytelling, building support systems, and addressing the issues. The goal is to work with clients to dismantle oppressive conditions and aid them in understanding systems, including the mental health system. In the case of micro-aggressions, help them interpret how the client sees the aggression and assists them in shifting their thinking. They can develop a plan of action to deal with current or past racial stress.

Gathering and Processing of Experiences and Education to Benefit Clients

The therapist should be purposeful in seeking continued education as a part of being a culturally proficient therapist. To gain competence, therapists should have experience working with Black/African American clients. Additionally, they should seek continued education through national conferences and training specific to the African American professional and client and more general training around diversity. A culturally proficient counselor is viewed as continuously gathering information about Black/African American culture beyond graduate-level studies to make sense of past and present issues within that culture. It is important to note that culturally proficient therapists do not just work with Black/African American clients but also with clients who identify as Caucasians, Asians, Latinos, and others. A culturally proficient therapist is willing to learn and discoverhow culture plays a role in any client issues.

Conclusion

Culturally proficient therapists can work with clients from assessment and throughout the treatment process by communicating a strong sense of cultural self, having a strong cultural understanding of clients, being experienced in effectively engaging with clients throughout the counseling process, and continuously gathering and making sense of work and educational experiences to better work with clients.

The literature suggests that descendants of Black/African Americans acculturate to the dominant culture; they tend to lose their cultural self (Comas-Diaz, 2007; Grier & Cobbs, 1968; DeGruy-Leary, 2007; Glover, 2012). Therefore, the ability to communicate a strong sense of cultural self. Communicating and supporting a strong understanding of one's cultural norms and worldview. It is believed that the ability to identify with Black/African Americans aids in the ability to make a client feel comfortable about opening up, thereby helping in the engagement process.

Cultural norms, also identified as standards, affect the coping strategies of Black/African Americans. How one displays anger rather than depression may be a more socio-culturally acceptable and preferred expression of feeling for some members of Black/African culture. Other external factors can often resemble the acculturation process, such as socially acceptable coping skills found within the dominant culture. These coping skills may subconsciously reflect the dominant culture's mores, values, myths, fantasies, and beliefs. This factor has much to do with acculturation and belief systems about coping with stress, trauma, or other present mental health symptoms. A culturally proficient clinician can identify the cultural norms that prompt these learned coping strategies and knows that patterns are often formed by familial behaviors and the variations of response to onset events (Danieli, 1998).

Clinicians achieving master's level education often learn how to be culturally competent. Cultural competence in assessment and treatment has been conceptualized as encompassing knowledge, awareness, and skills (Sue et al., 1992). Scholars such as Sue et al., (1992), Dana (2008), and DeGruy-Leary (2007) describe knowledge and awareness as specific historical background, sociopolitical influences, and cultural heritage of diverse cultural groups. Having a strong sense of cultural awareness enhances the understanding needed to address the issues facing Black/African Americans. Awareness goes above and beyond the level of competence. It is a strong cultural understanding of the issues that Black/African Americans face daily that cause a feeling of oppression, racism, and other microaggressions. Belief heightens knowledge and is essential in developing a culturally sensitive relationship between counselor and client. Furthermore, building a therapeutic alliance may be difficult (Ridley, 1995). With strong cultural awareness, the clinician can work with the client to develop a strong therapeutic alliance while creating a relationship to acknowledge cultural differences (Sodowsky, 1996; Sodowsky et al., 1998).

It is recommended that clinicians consider all factors (environmental, familial, and individual) when counseling clients of color (e.g., African Americans) (Carter, 2007; Sue et al., 2008). Considering these factors allows for the initial and sustained engagement of the client within the therapeutic alliance. Sue et al., (2008) shared that culturally different therapeutic relationships can be developed if clinicians know clients' cultural issues. Considering all factors, clients face an increased possibility that the client will answer questions related to their experience. A clinician's knowledge of historical events may predict the symptoms and also aids in engagement. Knowledge of specifics related to the culture and experiences of Black/African Americans and, in particular, assessment and treatment of Black/African Americans is essential to the engagement process.

Continuous gathering and making sense of work and educational experiences to work with clients of color effectively is critical. Understanding the historical context and the current issues facing Black/African Americans is a crucial component of being a culturally proficient clinician. Although much of the diagnostic process is based on measures such as demographics, biological information, and, often, self-reported events, those factors need to be captured in more assessment tools andprocesses (Brewin, 2005). This challenges current assessment tools that do not look at the differences *within* cultural groups, specifically Black/African Americans. Therefore, continued education and training enhance the probability of correct assessment and engagement in treatment. Cultural competency does not equate to being culturally proficient, nor does it imply the ability to successfully engage or maintain engagement with clients of color (e.g., Black/African Americans). However, the desire to work with communities of color and keep clients engaged from initial and ongoing assessment, engagement, and treatment practices of Black/African Americans and other communities of color require continued efforts on the therapist's belief.

Mental health professionals are encouraged to seek advanced training that addresses oppression, racism, and micro-aggression with more venues to solidly train in the knowledge of culture and the awareness of the various challenges individuals in communities of color (e.g., African Americans) face. Training in conjunction with culturally specific assessments to address the cultural constructs will aid in the initial and ongoing evaluation and enhance the probability of continued engagement/treatment of Black/African Americans.Culturally competent clinicians can gain cultural awareness and make themselves culturally proficient through continued education, training, and supervision, explicitly addressing the cultural experiences (challenges, needs, and issues) related to that racial/ethnic population (e.g., African Americans). With this advanced education, training, and supervision, there is a higher probability of properly inclusive assessment, engagement, and treatment of clients of color (e.g., African Americans). Finally, it is essential to be aware of personal limitations concerning the client's ethnic culture and worldview verse one's own ethnic culture and worldview. The ability to bring this knowledge and awareness of the challenges and limitations into the session can/will aid in building a healthy therapeutic alliance.

References

American Counseling Association. (2005). *Code of ethics and standards of practice.* Alexandria, VA: American Counseling Association.

American Psychiatric Association (2000). *Diagnostic and statistical manual of mental disorders* (4th ed., text rev.). Arlington, VA: American Psychiatric Publishing.

American Psychological Association. (2002). *Ethical principles of psychologists and code of conduct.* Washington, DC: American Psychiatric Publishing.

Anastasi, A., & Urbina, S. (1997). *Psychological testing (7th ed.).* Englewood Cliffs, NJ: Prentice-Hall.

Arredondo, P., Toporek, M. S., Brown, S., Jones, J., Locke, D. C., Sanchez, J. & Stadler, H. (1996). Operationalization of the multicultural counseling competencies. *AMCD*: Alexandria, VA: American Counseling Association.

Baxter, S. & Jack, S. (2008). Qualitative Case Study Methodology: Study Design and Implementation for Novice Researchers. The Qualitative Report, 13 (4), 544–559. Retrieved 01/10/11 from http://www.nova.edu/sss/QR/QR 13-4/baster.pdf.

Boyd-Franklin, N. (2003). *Black/African families in therapy: Understanding the African American experience* (2nd ed.). New York, NY: Guilford Press.

Brewin, C. R. (2005). A systematic review of screening instruments for adults at risk of PTSD. *Journal of Traumatic Stress, 18*(1), 53–62.

Carter, R. T. (2007). Racism and psychological and emotional injury: Recognizing and assessing race-based traumatic stress. *The Counseling Psychologist, 35,* 15–99. 287-318). New York: Guilford Press.

Comas-Diaz, L. (2007). An ethnopolitical approach to working with visible minorities. *American Psychological Association*, pp. 55, 1319-1325.

Cooke, A. L., & Shear, M. K. (2001). Treatment of a 50-year-old African American woman whose chronic post-traumatic stress disorder went undiagnosed for over 20 years. *American Journal of Psychiatry, 158*(6), 866–870.

Cross, W. E., Jr. (1998). Black/African psychological functioning and the legacy of slavery: Myths and realities. In Danieli, Y. (Ed.), *International Handbook of Multigenerational Legacies of Trauma* (pp. 387-400); New York, NY: Plenum Press.

Dana, R. H. (2008). Clinical diagnosis in multicultural populations. In L. A Suzuki & J. G. Ponterotto (Eds.), *Handbook of multicultural assessment: Clinical, psychological, and educational applications* (pp. 107–131), San Francisco, CA: Jossey-Bass.

Danieli, Y. (1998). *International handbook of multigenerational legacies of trauma*. New York, NY: Plenum Press.

Ford, B. C., Bullard, K., McKeever, T., Toler, A. K., Neighbors, H. W., & Jackson, J. S. (2007). Lifetime and 12-month prevalence of *Diagnostic and Statistical Manual of Mental Disorders, Fourth Edition* disorders among older African Americans: Findings from the National Survey of American life. *American Journal of Geriatric Psychiatry,* 15(8), 8.

Gall, J. P., Gall, M. D., & Borg, W. R. (2005). *Applying educational research: A practical guide* (5th ed.). New York: Longman.

Glover, T. M. (2012). Exploration of Culturally Proficient Mental Health Assessment and Treatment Practices of Black/African American Clients. ProQuest Dissertations, Oregon State University.

Grier, W. H., & Cobbs, P. M. (1968). *Black rage*. New York: Basics Books.

Horvath, A. O., & Greenberg, L. S. (1986). Development of the Working Alliance Inventory. In L. S. Greenberg & W. M. Pinsoff (Eds.), *The psychotherapeutic process: A research handbook* (pp. 529-556). New York: Guilford.

Horvath, A. O., & Greenberg, L. S. (1989). Development and validation of the Working Alliance Inventory. *Journal of Counseling Psychology*, *36*, 223–233.

Jennings, L., & Skovholt, T. M. (1999). The cognitive, emotional, and relational characteristics of master therapists. *Journal of Counseling Psychology, 46,* 3-11.

Kearney, L. K., Draper, M., & Baron, A., (2005). Counseling utilization by ethnic minority college students. *Cultural Diversity and Ethnic Minority Psychology, 11,* 272-285.

Lawson, W. B. (2003). Mental health issues in African Americans. In G. Bernal, J. E. Trimble, A. K. Burlew, & F. T. L. Leong (Eds.), *Handbook of Racial and Ethnic Minority Psychology* (pp. 561–569). Thousand Oaks, CA: Sage.

DeGruy-Leary, J. D. (2005). *Post-traumatic slave syndrome: America's legacy of enduring injury and healing*. Milwaukie, OR: Upton Press.

Loborsky, L., McLellan, T. A., Woody, G. E., O'Brien, C. P., & Auerbach, A. (1985). Therapist success and its determinants. *Archive of General Psychiatry, 42,* 602-611.

Pinderhughes, E. (1990). Legacy of slavery: The experience of Black/African families in America. In M. P. Mirkin (Ed.), *The social and political contexts of family therapy* (pp. 289–305). Needham Heights, MA: Allyn and Bacon.

Ponterotto, J. G., Gretchen, D., Utsey, S. O., Riger, B. P., & Austin, R. (2002). A revision of the multicultural counseling awareness scale. *Journal of Multicultural Counseling and Development, pp. 30,* 153–181.

Ridley, C. (1995). *Overcoming unintentional racism in counseling and therapy: A practitioner's guide to intentional interventions.* Thousand Oaks, CA: Sage.

Rosenthal, P., & Rosenthal, S. (1980). Holocaust effect in the third generation: Child of another time. *American Journal of Psychotherapy, 34*(4), 572-580.

Rubenstein, I., Cutter, R., & Templer, D. I. (1990). Multigenerational occurrence of survivor's syndrome symptoms in families of Holocaust survivors. *Omega Journal of Death and Dying, 20*(3), 239-244.

Sodowsky, G. R. (1996). The Multicultural Counseling Inventory: Validity and applications in multicultural training. In G. R. Sodowsky & J. C. Impara (Eds.), *Multicultural assessment in counseling and clinical psychology* (pp. 283-324). Lincoln: University of Nebraska-Lincoln, Buros Institute of Mental Measurements and Department of Education Psychology.

Sue, D. W., Arredondo, P., & McDavis, R. J. (1992). Multicultural counseling competencies and standard: A call to the profession. *Journal of Counseling & Development*, 70, 477-486.

Sue, D. W, Nadal, K. L, Capodilupo, C. M., Lin, A. I., Torino, G. C., & Rivera, D. P., (2008). Racial Microaggressions against Black/African Americans: Implications for counseling. *Journal for Counseling & Development, 86*, 330-338.

Sue, S (1977). Community mental health services to minority groups: Some optimism, some pessimism. *American Psychologist, 32,* 616–624.

Sue, D. W. & Sue, D. (2004). *Counseling the culturally diverse: Theory and practice*. (4th ed).

Tichenor, V., & Hill, C. E. (1989). A comparison of six measures of the working alliance. *Psychotherapy, 26*, 195-199.

Tracey, T. J., & Kokotovic, A. M. (1989). Factor structure of the Working Alliance Inventory. *Psychological Assessment, 1*, 207-210.

U.S. Department of Health and Human Services. (2001). *Mental health: Culture, race, And ethnicity: A supplement to mental health: A report of the Surgeon General.* Washington, DC: Author.

Yin, R. K. (2003). *Case study research: Design and methods* (3rd ed.). Thousand Oaks: Sage.

Yin, R. K. (2009). *Case study research: Design and methods* (4th ed.). Los Angeles: Sage.

Chapter 5

Deconstructing Negative Stereotypes About Black Women: Implications for Clinical Treatment

Portia X. Allie-Turco*, **PhD, LMHC, NCC**
University of New York Plattsburgh, Plattsburgh, New York, USA

Abstract

As a result of the enduring legacies of generational slavery and the associated socio-political traumatization of people of African descent, Black women have become the victims of destructive stereotyping in mainstream American culture. Five psychologically harmful and pervasive stereotypes abound: the Mammy, the Strong Black Woman, the Welfare Queen, the Jezebel, and the Sapphire, or Angry Black Woman, characterize Black women as aggressive, overbearing, emasculating, or sexually depraved. These stereotypes significantly affect how Black women are understood, engaged, and treated in a therapeutic context. Furthermore, this prevailing anti-Black woman misogynoir contributes to intersectional discrimination and is associated with maladaptive coping strategies. This chapter will explore the implications of these enduring stereotypes about Black womanhood and the interpersonal, health, and professional consequences. Successful mental health intervention requires cultural competence and trauma-informed skills to directly address the complexities of providing therapy to Black women subjected to these tropes.

* Corresponding Author's Email: turc9866@plattsburgh.edu.

In: How Did We Survive?
Editor: Tina Marie Glover
ISBN: 979-8-88697-918-3

Keywords: African American women, Angry Black Woman, Black women, Jezebel, Mammy, trauma, generational slavery, Sapphire, stereotypes, Strong Black Woman, tropes, Welfare Queen

Introduction

What image comes to mind immediately when people think of a Black woman? Is it a finger-wagging, yelling, in-your-face personality or a scantily clad, sashaying temptress? Perhaps the image is of a tireless, sexless nurturer or a lazy gold-digger. Quite often, the image relates to one of five pervasive stereotypes of Black women that are ubiquitous in American culture: the Mammy, the Strong Black Woman, the Welfare Queen, the Jezebel, and the Sapphire or Angry Black Woman, all of which characterize Black women in harmful ways. Increasingly, evidence points to the role of discrimination and stereotypes as significant contributors to adverse health outcomes of Black women (Geronimus et al., 2010; Duvall et al., 2013; Rosenthal & Lobel, 2011; Rosenthal & Overstreet, 2016). Allostatic load from various causes damages the body's physiological systems, especially in vulnerable populations, and has been linked to heart disease, aggressive breast cancer, Post-traumatic Stress Disorder (PTSD), and other severe conditions (Guidi et al., 2020). Racial discrimination is a social stressor linked to detrimental long-term effects of increasing the allostatic load and is associated with the stress response leading to a shortened life span for Black women (Allen et al., 2019; Duru et al., 2012; Seeman et al., 2010; Peek et al., 2010). Chronic exposure to racism and discrimination overwhelms the body's coping regulatory systems and increases the chances of using coping strategies such as emotional eating and substance use (Major et al., 2013). As a result, Black women in the United States face greater physical and emotional health disparities than white women (Chinn & Redmond, 2021). They are more likely to suffer from higher rates of preventable illnesses and to suffer complications leading to death from treatable conditions such as diabetes, hypertension, and obesity (Mcsweeney et al., 2010; DeVon et al., 2014; Obeng-Gyasi et al., 2021; Siegel et al., 2021; Xing et al., 2020). Black women also report elevated mental health disorders such as anxiety, depression, and PTSD (Hicken et al., 2013). Simultaneously, racism and discrimination have been associated with restricted access to health care and poorer quality of care for Black women (Williams & Mohammed, 2013; Williams et al., 2019), making the situation even more dire. To respond to these challenges and treat Black women effectively in therapy, clinicians must understand and then help to deconstruct the negative stereotypes that drive the debilitating racial and gender-based stress Black women experience.

The Role of Racism and Stereotypes on Black Women's Wellbeing

That racism is ingrained into the fabric of American culture and rooted in the history of slavery in this country is axiomatic. Race is a social construct where the white race is elevated arbitrarily, and the Black race is juxtaposed as inferior and deviant because societal standards presume whiteness as the ideal. Racial discrimination is associated with internalized beliefs or stereotypes towards Black culture, manifesting as differential treatment at individual and systemic levels (Bonilla-Silva, 2015). As people who have been devalued for their race, Black Americans have faced oppression in myriad ways that are now so routine and banal that discrimination is an ordinary part of daily life.

Furthermore, the overlay of patriarchy onto existing racism results in additional discrimination against Black women. While all women suffer under a patriarchal system, Women of Color sustain even more injury because the inherent racism subjugates them doubly. Scholars such as Kimberlé Crenshaw (1990) discuss that Black women experience unique marginalization due to the intersection of gender and race.

This intersectional oppression is reflected in what scholars, such as Patricia Hill Collins (Hill-Collins, 1990; 1991; 2004) conceptualize as controlling images. These are oppressive stereotypes created during slavery that function to ensure Black women's subordination and continue to shape the experiences of subjugation in Black women's lives (Harris-Perry, 2011; Jerald et al., 2017). Stereotypes are beliefs about the innate characteristics, attributes, or behaviors associated with members of groups (Kite et al., 2022). Stereotypes often reflect inaccurate or harmful overgeneralizations about members of a specific group and fail to account for individual differences, leading to adverse consequences (Kite et al., 2022; Rosenthal & Overstreet, 2016; Rosenthal & Lobel, 2016). The literature describes five particularly damaging controlling images or archetypes about Black women: the Mammy, the emotionally challenging Strong Black Woman, the morally deficient Welfare Queen, the hypersexual Jezebel, and the verbally aggressive and domineering Sapphire/Angry Black Woman (Collins, 1991).

The Mammy

The Mammy is a stereotype traced back to slavery in the Antebellum South and is reinforced in media images and films (Collins, 2005). The Mammy character depicts an obese, sexually unattractive, dark-skinned Black female loyal servant in a white household. She is portrayed as a motherly, self-sacrificing, and asexual housekeeper who eagerly and lovingly takes care of her white family. The Mammy is understood as a mother whose children are on the periphery. This portrayal of willing servitude and devotion was created to minimize Black women's enslavement by promoting the idea of happy and contented subservience. (Collins, 2005). Although the Mammy is characterized as devoted, it is implied that service to the white family takes precedence over her own family. Therefore, she will relegate her own Black family to save her energy for the well-being of the white children (Collins, 2005). The Mammy is a chronic and uncomplaining caregiver who demonstrates effortless and endless patience, wisdom, and understanding.

The Mammy and Black Women's Body Image and Weight

The image of white femininity as the idealized standard of beauty intersects with the Mammy stereotype to influence two significant areas for Black women: skin color and body size (Collins, 2005). Black women in the United States are disproportionately affected by obesity, with almost two-thirds considered obese based on body mass index. Obesity has been directly linked to cardiovascular morbidity and mortality in Black women. Earlier studies concluded that obesity in Black women was related to the social buffer against the desire for thinness (Awad & Cokley, 2010; Cash et al., 2004). Black women report less negative body evaluation, experiencing body satisfaction at larger weights than white women; even at larger sizes, they perceive their body size to be smaller. Research demonstrates that Black women are less likely to diet, less motivated to exercise to reduce weight, and have fewer concerns about gaining weight or experiencing weight fluctuations (Cash et al., 2004; Flowers et al., 2012; Gordon et al., 2010; Lowy et al., 2021; Rucker & Cash, 1992;). Other scholars highlight concerns with studies that explore Black women's desire for thinness (Awad et al., 2015; Johnson et al., 2017). They posit that body image assessment geared towards measuring ideals of thinness fails to account for the beauty standards Black women internalize.

Historically, Black women have been permitted to be larger, curvier, or "thick-bodied" (Dunn et al., 2019) due to the demands of manual work and childbearing during slavery. Foundationally, women of African descent live into ancient cultural preferences for curvier, larger bodies that represent beauty, prosperity, and well-being.

Colorism and Skin Tone Preference

Slavery and colonialism were founded on the idea of white supremacy, which normalized the idea that individuals who are lighter in skin tone are superior. White supremacy was evident in "the one drop rule," which mandated that even one drop of African blood was enough to define a person as Black and, therefore lesser. Enslaved people who had proximity to whiteness or who could pass as white, gained more access to privilege (Jordan, 2014). Black people with a lighter skin tone and Eurocentric features were closer to the white cultural assumption of civility and advancement and therefore were assigned a higher social standing (Hill-Collins, 1991). Colorism, as Alice Walker (1983) named this phenomenon, is infused in the American culture generally, but has also developed as an aspect of racial trauma response manifested as intra-race discrimination (Russell et al., 2013). This is an oppressive intragroup classification system that is reflected in the internalized racism of oppressed racial groups when they privilege individuals of the same race based on their skin tone (Matthews & Johnson, 2015).

Proximity to whiteness continues to have social and economic implications for Black women due to the dominant cultural preference for fair skin tone, blond hair, and blue eyes (Cain, 2008). Skin complexion affects the perception of Black women's physical attractiveness and social status. A lighter skin complexion is associated with attractiveness and desirability in Black women and often translates to success (Monk, 2021; Reece, 2021). The lightness of a Black woman's skin has been linked to higher self-esteem compared to women of darker complexion (Hall, 2017). Research on skin tone stratification reveals that for Black women, a light skin tone impacts access to higher education (Saperstein & Penner, 2012), income (Hannon & DeFina, 2014), relationships (Landor & Halpern, 2016), pregnancy (Slaughter-Acey, 2019), and mental health (McCleary-Gaddy & James (2020).

The problem of colorism has been so internalized that the Black family of origin often provides a critical model for how women view their skin complexion and influences the transmission of colorism (Landor et al., 2013; Wilder & Cain, 2011). For example, family members may comment negatively about darker skin tones girls, such as "You are so pretty for a dark girl," and even use disparaging characterizations and name-calling. Within Black families, colorism is linked to a higher quality of parenting for light-skinned females (Landor et al., 2013), and lighter skin and Eurocentric features are often fetishized. In contrast, darker-skinned girls experience less preferential treatment and are often more subject to ridicule based on their skin complexion (Landor et al., 2013).

Black Women and Hair

Like skin color, Black women's relationship with their hair has been equally impacted by systemic oppression. It is related to a failure to live up to the dominant white narrative of beauty. Black hair is contentious as a political symbol and a representation of selfhood. Black women's relationship with their hair and skin tone was cultivated under colonialism and racism, and Black hair was deemed sub-standard compared to white hair (Randle, 2015). Hair texture is associated with significant historical and cultural trauma for Black women stemming from the internalization of white supremacy and the racial stratification of slavery. Black women's hair is judged against the impossible-to-attain standards of long straight white hair. Internalized racism within the Black community associated with the distinction between "good" and "bad" hair (Byrd & Tharps, 2014) has perpetuated the disdain for textured hair. It influences women's view of themselves as unattractive, impacts self-esteem related to hair texture and length, and damages the idea of self as beautiful (Robinson, 2011).

The Black Power movement of the 1960s was the first national attempt to reclaim pride in Blackness (Bellinger, 2007). Malcolm X led the fight for the redefinition of the selfhood of Black bodies and reconnected Black women to their natural beauty. In contemporary society, many Black women continue advocating in private and public spaces for the acceptance of natural hair (Randle, 2015). However, this movement has been met with obstacles, both from the Black culture and the wider society. Black women who choose to wear their hair in its natural texture as a form of self-acceptance (Jeffries & Jeffries, 2014; Johnson & Bankhead, 2014) are often faced with backlash and sanctions dictating how they should wear their hair, particularly in professional spaces (Thompson, 2009).

Demonstrating Strength Against All Odds: The Strong Black Woman

In response to limiting portrayals, Black women sought to rewrite the damaging stereotypes of Black womanhood (Harris-Perry, 2011; Beauboeuf-Lafontant, 2007; Collins, 1990, 2000) by showcasing strength in the face of adversity. Demonstrating strength is a particularly redeeming coping skill that protects the Black woman's esteem and highlights her ability to persevere through adversity (Collins, 2000; 2005). Prominent historical figures such as Harriet Tubman represent strong Black women figures (Collins, 2000; 2005) and are celebrated symbols of prevailing against all odds in adversity (Beauboeuf-Lafontant, 2007). It is crucial to highlight that Black women's masking of their emotions and demonstrating strength was necessary for survival and protection against the trauma of slavery, Jim Crow laws, and systemic racism to sustain their communities (Collins, 2000, 2005). The Strong Black Woman also discredits the derogatory association of Black womanhood with sexual promiscuity and rage and endorses respectable, self-contained, and self-reliant femininity associated with both positive and detrimental qualities (Beauboeuf-Lafontant, 2005; Collins, 2000; Harris-Perry, 2011).

Although the Strong Black Woman image was created to reclaim the positive aspects of Black womanhood, the internalization of this image has been linked to damaging self-neglect (Watson & Hunter, 2015) and detrimental negative consequences, including emotional dysregulation, stress, sleep disturbance; smoking (Beauboeuf-Lafontant, 2003; Woods-Giscombé, 2010); depression (Donovan & West, 2015), anxiety (Watson & Hunter, 2015b) and binge eating (Beauboeuf-Lafontant, 2016; Harrington et al., 2010).

Stigmatization of Black Motherhood: The Welfare Queen

The Welfare Queen is another controlling stereotype of Black women that further alienates them from the broader society. Black motherhood represents the intersection of class, race, and gender discrimination and dates back to the early stereotypes of Black women as 'breeders' during slavery (Collins, 2009). American Black women's bodies have always lacked protection; Black women were routinely subjected to medical experimentation without consent. For example, J. Marion Sims, a plantation doctor in South Carolina, who is considered the "father of modern gynecology," developed the modern vaginal speculum by performing dozens of surgeries on enslaved women without consent or anesthesia (Cronin, 2020).

Black single motherhood also has deep roots in slavery because enslaved Black people were often forbidden to marry, and mothers and fathers were routinely separated. Black women have had to work despite their status as mothers to service the institution of slavery long before white women's entrance into the workforce (Glenn, 1992; Jones, 2010). Black women's status as head of the household has been subject to vilification in mainstream society (Collins, 2009; Hancock, 2004), as exemplified by Senator Patrick Moynihan's announcement that Black women's role as matriarchs was emasculating men and was the reason for the current state of Black families (U.S. Department of Labor, Office of Policy Planning and Research 1965).

Former Republican President Ronald Reagan intensified the sentiment against Black motherhood and cemented negative views of Black single mothers, notably when he coined the term 'Welfare Queen' to gain support during his 1976 Republican presidential campaign (Hancock, 2004). In his campaign speech, he described an unwed and promiscuous Black woman from the South Side of Chicago who cunningly manipulated the system claiming benefits for her multiple illegitimate children to support an extravagant and materialistic life (Hancock, 2004). This speech exaggerated Black women's use of government welfare by providing a single example of a woman of undetermined ancestry, Linda Taylor (Hancock, 2004), rumored to use several aliases and racial identities to collect government benefits. Taylor (Hancock, 2004) was eventually sentenced and convicted of welfare fraud; unfortunately, her story confirmed the controlling image of Black motherhood as immoral, greedy, promiscuous, and lazy (Blake, 2012; Kohler-Hausmann, 2015; Stein, 2013). Rosenthal and Lobel (2016) confirm that the Welfare Queen stereotype affects individual perceptions and negative judgments about Black pregnant women, leading to the assumption that pregnant Black women are single, promiscuous, poor, and on welfare.

Today, the implications of the Welfare Queen breeder stereotype persist with the belief that a Black single mother only has children to scam the welfare system. This trope undermines Black women's attachment to their children, their caretaking and responsiveness as mothers, devalues the lives of Black children and has devastating implications for perinatal and maternal care. As a result of racism, Black neighborhoods have lacked adequate health services, which limits access to timely quality care. At the same time, even when services are available, studies indicate that racial mistreatment is responsible for Black women having disproportionately grave health outcomes, especially in childbirth. Data from the Center for Disease Control shows, for example, that Black women are three to four times more likely than white women to experience life-threatening complications in childbirth and to suffer medical neglect and abuse, regardless of social class. (Markin & Coleman, 2023). High death rates for Black women have made the United States one of the worst among developed nations in maternal mortality (Tikkanen et al., 2020; MacDorman et al., 2016). The Kaiser Foundation similarly emphasizes racial disparities in maternal and infant health (Hill et al., 2022).

The Jezebel

Out of slavery and the commercialization of Black women's bodies grew the stereotype of Jezebel (Collins, 1991). Jezebel is a female biblical figure (Windsor et al., 2011), representing a fallen woman who seduces men to their sexual demise and falls from the grace of God (Windsor et al., 2011). During slavery, it was beneficial for enslavers to depict Black women as sexually insatiable seductresses who lured 'good men'; this nullified the white men's dissonance in committing sexual assault. The Jezebel stereotype was used to justify legalized rape against Black women as a form of sexual gratification and for building wealth. In many states, laws regarding rape protected only white women, even though this crime more often victimized Black women. The earliest account of the court siding with the perpetrator is reflected in the story of Celia (Griffin, 2018; McLaurin, 1991; Whites, 1993), a 19-year-old Missouri enslaved woman who was bought at the age of 14 and then routinely sexually violated until she killed her owner and was later charged and hanged for manslaughter.

Because race-based sexual violence and legalized sexual and reproductive exploitation were the norm during enslavement (1619–1865), Black women had no reproductive or sexual rights and could not choose their sexual relationships. Childbearing during slavery was associated with economic profit for white enslavers who would forcibly "breed Black women for offspring" (Sublette & Sublette, 2015). This abuse of Black women's bodies, contrasted with the protection of white women's femininity, justified and reinforced the view of Black women as uncivilized, immodest, and sexually deviant (Harris-Perry, 2011). The pervasive Jezebel stereotype that Black women are naturally sexually promiscuous developed during colonialism and was reinforced by several aspects of chattel slavery (Harris-Perry, 2011). Again, contrasting cultural experiences of white and Black women help explain this view. During the 18th and 19th centuries, white women were expected to be fully clothed as a sign of civility, purity, and modesty (Harris-Perry, 2011). The expectations that women are sexually chaste and protected contrasted starkly with the condition of enslaved Black women, who were often subjected to forceful removal of their clothing and physical inspection in public spaces.

The tragedy of Sarah Baartman (Neeto, 2005), a Hottentot Khoisan woman from the Eastern Cape of South Africa, is a well-documented example of the sexual exploitation of Black women's bodies for entertainment. The story of Baartman, who was coerced to travel to Europe and then later sold to a circus, is one example that illustrates how Black bodies were used as commodities and for entertainment. Baartman's body was depicted as primitive, grotesque, lascivious, unfeminine, and obscene (Ashley, 2021; Neeto, 2005; Parkinson, 2016), and her rounded buttocks became a symbol of deviant womanhood that fostered a negative attitude towards the body shape of Black women and promoted the current version of fetishizing Black women's buttocks (Ashley, 2021).

The Jezebel stereotype is still associated with many negative implications for Black women. Misogynoir, a term coined by Bailey (2014), describes hatred of Black women, and this is apt in discussions of the Jezebel trope. Misogynoir is especially toxic in the visual violence against Black women portrayed in popular culture (Bailey & Trudy, 2018). Adverse sexual health has been linked to the controlling image of Black womanhood portrayed in the media, particularly in rap music videos (Jerald et al., 2017; Peterson et al., 2007). College-aged and younger Black girls exposed to rap music are particularly vulnerable to experiencing negative body image and greater internalization of sexual stereotypes because of their developing sense of self (Duvall et al., 2013). They report an increased likelihood of engaging in risky sexual behavior, having multiple sexual partners, abusing substances, or testing positive for a sexually transmitted disease (STD). Black women have few media role models depicting healthy Black sexuality. They are primarily confronted with images that distort Black female sexuality by overemphasizing physical appearance and normalizing risky sexual behavior and substance use (Rebollo-Gil & Moras, 2012).

Endorsement of the Jezebel stereotype continues to support the dehumanization and sexual objectification of Black women and the justification of sexual and intimate partner violence (Cheeseborough et at., 2020). The idea that Black women are innately overly sexualized and possess an animalistic sexual appetite has been associated with greater chances of sexual assault and rationalization of the sexual assault, with few legal or social sanctions (Alderden & Ullman, 2012). Although all women face a risk of sexual assault, Black women experience a greater likelihood of sexual assault and aggravated sexual assault compared to a survey of all women. Furthermore, this controlling stereotype means that Black women often lack credibility as victims of assault and, upon disclosure of the assault, may receive limited support (Tillman et al., 2010; Jacques-Tiura et al., 2010).

Angry Black Woman (Sapphire)

The Angry Black Woman stereotype, also known as the Sapphire, was popularized by the minstrel television show in the 1940s 'Amos' n Andy' (Lorts, 2013), and depicts Black women as domineering, loud, angry, and emasculating. Contemporary media portrayals of the Angry Black Woman depict a woman who lacks compassionate or gentle attributes and is aggressive, angry, and emasculating. This stereotypical portrayal of Black women is often associated with seemingly irrational and unfounded displays of public anger. Physically, the Sapphire is depicted as a large, but not obese, domineering Black woman who can quickly demonstrate animated anger.

Because historical preference for acceptable femininity has endorsed a quiet or demure display of temperament for women, displays of anger and assertive behavior are discouraged even for white women, contributing to chronic stress, anxiety, somatic conditions, and depression (West, 2008). Black women face a dilemma regarding emotional expression. First, they feel pressure to demonstrate strength; second, they must endure without needing support (Nelson et al., 2016). Not surprisingly, Black women are disproportionately represented in stress disorders, including anxiety, depression, and post-traumatic stress, and face greater risk from the lack of treatment for these disorders (Williams & Lewis, 2019; Wright Lewis, (2020).

Furthermore, Black women face microaggressions due to race and gender (Moody & Lewis, 2019). Microaggressions are subtle and daily environmental racial and gendered slights and injuries that present as verbal attacks and insults leading to the silencing and marginalization of the victim (Pierce, 1970; Sue et al., 2008). Repeated exposure to microaggressions, combined with historical and ongoing oppression, is associated with increased internalization of anger in Black women and subsequent explosive rage (Ashley, 2014). Unfortunately, Black women face backlash from the dominant society for their displays of anger in the face of adversity and discrimination, which further exacerbates their mistreatment or prevents support (West, 2008).

Increasingly, Black women admit a desire to distance themselves from this stereotype by adopting a non-threatening stance. Black women disclose preoccupation with representing themselves differently by using impression management strategies, such as code-switching, in settings where different races are represented (Ashley, 2014; Harris-Perry, 2011). Code-switching, altering behavioral and physical appearances to gain respectability and fit into the dominant culture, can involve changing speech patterns or adopting whiter attributes to appear less "ghetto" in white spaces. This self-silencing is associated with racial battle fatigue, a descriptor for the emotional exhaustion experienced by racially minoritized people due to repeated exposure to racism. It impacts psychological, physical, and emotional well-being (Harris-Perry, 2011; Corbin et al., 2018).

Therapeutic Considerations

To heal the ongoing damage of these tropes in the lives of Black women clients, clinicians must gain knowledge and awareness of the psychological, emotional, and physical impact of internalizing these controlling stereotypes. Increased awareness promotes improved assessment and treatment of Black women in therapy.

There are overarching skills of culturally competent counseling needed for addressing all stereotypes when counseling Black women clients. Culturally competent clinicians must address the impact of race-based stereotypes on Black women with cultural humility and compassion (Bryant-Davis & Ocampo, 2005). Assessment and intervention require clinicians to create a safe therapeutic environment that facilitates Black women's disclosure of racist experiences. Therapists are responsible for broaching (Day-Vines et al., 2020) the subject of the client's race, without minimizing or avoiding the topic, as early as the first session with a Black client.

While Black women may be exposed to any of these tropes, and culturally responsive counseling is helpful in all scenarios, each stereotype presents specific and often distinct aspects of discrimination. Black women suffer identifiable harms related to each. Accordingly, therapists must tailor treatment to address the implications of each stereotype.

Therapeutic Implications of the Mammy Stereotype

Clinical areas of focus associated with the Mammy stereotype include assessing for stress-related disorders, chronic fatigue, emotional dysregulation, and disordered eating. When dealing with the Mammy stereotype, clinicians must also consider the implications for Black women clients regarding skin color and body size. When mental health professionals engage in cultural humility and examine their and the client's internalized bias associated with skin color and beauty standards, they are better equipped to address the effects on Black women's well-being. They can acknowledge that skin color and hair texture preference are crucial elements in therapy with Black women. Further, therapists can support clients in identifying the role of colorism in their life and the internalized messages and experiences based on standards of beauty rooted in an idealization of white femininity.

For therapists to deal effectively with Black women's body dissatisfaction, they need to examine culturally salient variables, such as a preference for lighter skin tone, straight hair texture, and a curvier body (Awad et al., 2015; Overstreet et al., 2010; Watson et al., 2015; 2019). Notably, a strong ethnic identity is a protective factor for a positive body image for Black women (Walker, 2021). Accordingly, counselors must explore ethnic and cultural identification and connection to promote buffering against white beauty ideals. Further, Black women can benefit from therapies incorporating intuitive eating principles, trusting the body to make healthy food choices for nourishment rather than being size or diet driven. It also involves therapists supporting clients as they learn to distinguish between emotional and physical hunger signals. The goal is to develop a healthier relationship with food and the body while challenging the diet culture.

Therapeutically, it is also crucial for clinicians to explore Black women's relationship with their hair and to open up discussions about discriminatory and traumatic experiences Black women may have experienced regarding their hair. Therapists must remember that Black hair in its natural state has historically been shamed and stigmatized; dreadlocks were so named because Black hair was considered dreadful, for example.

In 2019, California was the first state to pass the Crown (Create a Respectful Open World for Natural Hair) Act, which identified and addressed the prevalent discrimination against Black hair. It provided a much-needed prohibition to prevent discrimination in employment, housing, and public accommodation based on natural hair style and texture, including protective hairstyles like braids, cornrows, and twists. Unfortunately, to date, not all states have enacted this legislation. Therapists must be aware of the CROWN Act and seek opportunities to ensure it is enacted in their states.

Further, therapists can provide strategies for a healthy and affirming relationship with hair, including dispelling the myth about Black hair as distasteful in its natural state and affirming a Black woman's right to wear her hair in any way she chooses without consequence to her employment, housing, or other areas.

Therapeutic Implications of the Strong Black Woman Stereotype

Therapists can support clients to challenge the Strong Black Woman ideal of selflessness and explore reasonable expectations and boundaries in their relationships with others. Culturally responsive clinicians are aware of the demands on Black women to serve as tireless and self-sufficient caretakers. Clinicians should explore the paradox for Black women of being expected to be nurturing and feminine while also being strong. They must examine the emotional toll this exerts, mainly reflected in disorders such as depression, anxiety, disordered eating and sleeping, and punishing perfectionism (Abrams & Maxwell, 2019; Jones et al., 2021; Watson & Hunter, 2016).

Clinicians must recognize Black women's internalized pressure to be the pillar of strength for others and invite them to reimagine their own self-care as equally important (Watson & Hunter, 2015). Supportive relationships with other Black women improve the emotional well-being of Black women and address related health concerns (Somerville et al., 2023). Therapists can empower Black women by identifying supportive resources emphasizing collective coping as a clinical intervention (Liao & Yin, 2020). An example is the Sister Circle model, a fictive kin network designed to support Black women and build on a communal connection that predates slavery for people of African descent (Ibe et al., 2021; Neal-Barnett et al., 2011; Somerville et al., 2023).

Because of the relentless demands associated with selflessly caring for others and the resulting self-neglect, clinicians must assess maladaptive coping strategies Black women use to manage stressful emotions (Harrington et al., 2010). Therapists can provide a non-judgmental and supportive space to allow Black women to let their guard down. They can encourage clients to focus on emotional regulation skills, including mindfulness-based strategies, learning to identify and share emotions, demonstrate vulnerability, and release the pressure to be a pillar of strength to others. Dance movement can also be suggested as a healing opportunity for Black women (Kerney et al., 2023).

Crucially, Black women can reframe rest as a necessary part of mental health maintenance and see rest and restoration as a form of liberation and resistance to systemic racism (Hersey, 2022). Going back to slavery, Black women's value was linked to their work, and Black women suffering from the internalized Strong Black Woman trope continue to carry the burden of believing they must work twice as hard as everyone else to prove their worth. Rest and restoration are the required remedy for disrupting this perverse notion, and therapists can normalize and infuse rest as part of treatment.

Therapeutic Implications of the Welfare Queen

Clinicians can challenge the Welfare Queen trope by helping clients, particularly Black single mothers, question presumptions of laziness and greed that underlie such destructive labeling. In therapy, Black women benefit from creating a balanced view of motherhood and reducing the stigma of single parenthood. Clinicians can also validate clients' struggles, deal with their internalized shame, provide strategies for coping, and legitimize their efforts to seek the necessary support.

Clinicians must be aware that the stigmatization of poverty and class prejudice underlies the Welfare Queen trope. Poor individuals are blamed for their circumstances due to an entrenched idea that when people are successful, they worked hard, so the converse must also apply (Bonilla-Silva, 2007). Racialization of welfare is based on the idea that welfare recipients are visualized as inherently lazy Black people who violate the Protestant work ethic in preferring public benefits to work (Brown-Iannuzzi et al., 2017). The prevalent and supported view punishes poor mothers and sees them as taking advantage of the system. Welfare reform and restrictions often require single mothers to return to work as a condition of aid eligibility (Gilman, 2013). In reality, single Black mothers are faced with an impossible choice because they largely lack the education to earn more than minimum wage as unskilled labor; taking a job means losing food allowance, health insurance, and other government benefits while incurring childcare costs they cannot afford.

Structural racism lies at the core of the Welfare Queen stereotype. This complex issue involves significant implications for distressed neighborhoods, from food insecurity, criminalization, and unemployment, to limited access to housing, healthcare, and supportive resources. Further, long-standing welfare policies perpetuate poverty and racial inequities. To illustrate, racial biases inherent in Child Protective Services villainize Black mothers, resulting in discriminatory oversight, increased surveillance, and associated parenting stress from multiple systems (Merritt, 2020). Similarly, antipathy towards poor, single Black mothers more often justifies the removal of their children, with 53% of Black children being subject to maltreatment reports compared to 37% of white children in the United States (Kim et al., 2017).

Therapists treating Black women clients struggling with the Welfare Queen archetype must understand the trope as resulting from racism and generational poverty. They recognize the pervasive social justice associated with this trope and must be willing to disrupt the systemic power dynamics involved. Clinicians should also familiarize themselves with Race-Based Traumatic Stress (Carter, 2007), an emotional injury resulting from repeated exposure to interpersonal or institutional racism. This leads to the affected individuals' reduced ability to cope. The link between racial discrimination, poverty, and trauma is well-documented. For instance, higher levels of neighborhood poverty in Black neighborhoods result in more severe PTSD symptoms and reduced access to healthcare affords fewer treatment options (Ravi et al., 2023).

Therapists need to know that empowering Black communities and leveraging family and community strengths also leads to healing outcomes for individual Black women. Additionally, counselors can join organizations to disrupt the maternal health crisis and advance Black women's health outcomes through policy reforms. Black Mamas Matter Alliance is one of many such resources available to uplift and provide holistic care for Black mothers (Black Mamas Matter Alliance, 2018).

Therapeutic Implications of the Jezebel Stereotype

Therapy with Black women may involve confronting the sexually charged Jezebel trope. A therapist must explore the historical and modern implications of internalizing or rejecting the Jezebel stereotype to understand better Black women's self-perception and the impact of embracing or rejecting the stereotype. This discussion can be centered around disrupting assumptions regarding promiscuity, slut-shaming, and objectification (Smith et al., 2019). Therapists can support Black women in developing and maintaining healthy relationships and boundaries, selecting appropriate partners, and interrogating relationship difficulties between Black men and women.

Endorsing the Jezebel image of Black women can contribute to misidentification and inadequate treatment of sexual dysfunctions and sexual trauma. Therefore, therapists and clients benefit from exploring their own and the client's sexual stereotypes to understand the impact of the client's sexuality. For instance, in dating relationships, the Jezebel image can contribute to internalized sexual anxiety and sexual dysfunction (Leath et al., 2020) by either robbing Black women of the chance to be sexually inexperienced or promoting the view that they are always ready for sexual activity or welcome sexual violence When self-esteem is tied to sexuality, Black women may rely on early sexual activity to maintain self-esteem and receive love and attention. Alternatively, women may reject the Jezebel image by repressing their sexuality.

Endorsement of a healthy view of Black womanhood can promote therapeutic dialogue surrounding self-esteem and allows the therapist to provide a framework for healthy sexuality (Leath et al., 2021). Clinicians must disrupt misogynoir by addressing the Jezebel stereotype's external and internal implications. They must interrogate the external media popularized images that Black women welcome sexual violence. Further, they must support Black women who have internalized the Jezebel trope to explore a healthier version of sexuality to mitigate sexually risky behavior.

Black women who endorse the Jezebel stereotype face a greater likelihood of sexual assault (Anderson et al., 2018; Cheeseborough et al., 2020), and they often choose not to disclose assault due to the social repercussions. Thus, clinicians must initiate discussion of sexual violence and challenge the historical myth of the sexually insatiable Black woman as deserving of sexual assault to liberate clients from shame and promote greater disclosure in the future.

Factor and colleagues (2011) highlight the importance of understanding how the history of exploitation and discrimination contributes to risky health behaviors in Black women. As a result of the history of medical mistreatment perpetrated in communities of color in various forms, including forced sterilization, experimentation without consent, and withholding medical treatment, there is an ingrained lack of trust in health professionals and the medical system. Therefore, experiences with discrimination may result in resistance and rejection of medical advice as a form of activism against the dominant white norms (Factor et al., 2011). Resistance may include rejecting medical advice about high-risk factors or healthy sexual behaviors (Factor et al., 2011). When clinicians understand how historical discrimination about Black women's sexuality influences high-risk sexual behavior and acknowledge how racial stereotypes affect health, they identify and incorporate effective interventions to reduce their influence on risky behavior. Therapeutic Implications of the Sapphire (Angry Black Woman) Stereotype Challenging the Sapphire/Angry Black Woman trope is similarly critical for clinicians treating Black women clients. The Angry Black Woman stereotype is particularly damaging for Black women in leadership at work. The impression that Black women are innately angry impacts the perception that they are not capable or stable leaders, resulting in negative promotion and financial outcomes. They get penalized with lower evaluations and are forced to self-silence to reduce the impression of being aggressive. However, internalized and externalized anger expressions have serious consequences. Both are associated with racial trauma and epigenetic age acceleration (Motro et al., 2022; McKenna et al., 2021).

Additionally, it is relevant to know that conflicting aspects of masculinity and femininity are embedded in the Angry Black Woman archetype, and this juxtaposition has been associated with increased tension in heterosexual romantic relationships for Black women and unhealthy relationship dynamics. The conflict involves multiple layered issues of lack of protection and powerlessness that lead to expressions of anger. Therapists can provide strategies to help Black Women explore interpersonal and intra-personal anger that arise from the complexity of concerns for safety and protection. Middlemass, K. M. (2019).

Black women benefit when therapists can conceptualize anger as associated with generational, historical, and ongoing trauma, and those who help them examine how stereotypes related to the expression of anger and pain are projected as irrational anger (Greene, 2020). Clinicians can encourage Black women to process their anger and learn skills to regulate their emotions to prevent damaging professional and intimate relationships. These skills would help Black women effectively express and advocate for themselves without resorting to self-silencing. Black women also benefit from support groups with other Black women to develop emotional expression, problem-solving, and distress-tolerance strategies (Bryant-Davis et al., 2021).

Conclusion

Five controlling stereotypes about Black womanhood, the Mammy, Strong Black Woman, the Welfare Queen, the Jezebel, and the Sapphire/Angry Black Woman, reach back historically to slavery and continue to have profoundly detrimental effects on Black women. The Mammy is associated with a desire to extend help to others without consideration of the detriment to self-care and is associated with stress, depression, poor emotional regulation, and disordered eating (Peterson et al., 2007). The Strong Black Woman developed initially as a positive response by Black women to counteract the negative portrayal of Black femininity. However, the Strong Black Woman notion had the unintended consequence of setting up Black women to be perceived as superhumans who could ignore their own needs as the pillars of the Black community. Ironically, the Strong Black Woman trope overlaps with the Mammy stereotype in that Black women are still regarded as always helpful and available to the point of ignoring their own needs in service to others. The Welfare Queen archetype represents a poor and deceitful Black woman who scams government benefits to support a materialistic and immoral lifestyle. This representation stigmatizes single motherhood and portrays Black matriarchs as aberrant. The Jezebel image is associated with sexual objectification and victimization (Townsend et al., 2010). The Sapphire or Angry Black Woman stereotype is linked with seemingly inappropriate displays of rage despite negative social and emotional consequences. Internalizing these stereotypes, or making ineffective efforts to nullify them, can lead to emotional stress and trauma in Black women (Carter, 2007).

To counter the negative consequences of these stereotypes, therapists treating Black women are encouraged to adopt a culturally informed and antiracist stance in their clinical work by understanding, validating, and centering the experience of racism in clients' lives (Comas-Diaz, 2016; Comas-Diaz et al., 2019). Clinicians accomplished this by increasing their knowledge and awareness about the prevailing stereotypes of Black womanhood and their portrayal in media and the general society. Further, it is clinically impactful to broach issues of race and ethnicity with Black women regarding the impact of misogynoir in their own lives and to assess the types of specific racial influences for each woman. Clinicians must adopt a humble stance (Davis et al., 2011) that respects the intersectional nature of Black women's experiences related to racial identity development, socioeconomic status, educational attainment, and family history (Collins, 2004).

Clinicians must create a safe and trusting therapeutic relationship with Black women, including exploring the history of mistrust of clinical and health services (Bryant-Davis, 2019), including the past and present impact of racism. Furthermore, with race-based trauma treatment strategies, practitioners working with Black women should address self-care (Adkins-

Jackson et al., 2019), internalized grief, shame, and anger, and provide tools for coping and healing.

References

Abrams, J. A., Hill, A., & Maxwell, M. (2019). Underneath the mask of the strong Black woman schema: Disentangling influences of strength and self-silencing on depressive symptoms among US Black women. *Sex roles*, pp. 80, 517–526.

Adkins-Jackson, P. B., Turner-Musa, J., & Chester, C. (2019). The path to better health for Black women: Predicting self-care and exploring its mediating effects on stress and health. Inquiry: A Journal of Health Care Organization, Provision, and Financing, 56(8), 1–8. https://doi.org/10.1177/0046958019870968

Alderden, M. A., & Ullman, S. E. (2012). Creating a more complete and current picture: Examining police and prosecutor decision-making when processing sexual assault cases. Violence against women, 18(5), 525-551.

Allen, A. M., Thomas, M. D., Michaels, E. K., Reeves, A. N., Okoye, U., Price, M. M., Hasson, R. E., Syme, S. L., & Chae, D. H. (2019). Racial discrimination, educational attainment, and biological dysregulation among midlife African American women. *Psychoneuroendocrinology*, 99, 225–235.

Anderson, J. R., Holland, E., Heldreth, C., & Johnson, S. P. (2018). Revisiting the Jezebel stereotype: The impact of target race on sexual objectification. *Psychology of Women Quarterly*, *42*(4), 461-476.

Ashley, W. (2014). The angry black woman: The impact of pejorative stereotypes on psychotherapy with Black women. *Social work in public health*, *29*(1), 27–34.

Awad, G. H., Norwood, C., Taylor, D. S., Martinez, M., McClain, S., Jones, B., Holman, A. & Chapman-Hilliard, C. (2015). Beauty and body image concerns among African American college women. *Journal of Black Psychology*, *41*(6), 540–564.

Bailey, M., & Trudy. (2018). On misogynoir: Citation, erasure, and plagiarism. *Feminist Media Studies*,1 8(4), 762–768.

Bailey, M. (2014). More on the Origin of Misogynoir. Retrieved from Moyazb. tumblr. Com website:http://moyazb.tumblr.com/post/84048113369/more-on-the-origin-of-misogynoir.

Beauboeuf-Lafontant, T. (2003). Strong and large Black women? Exploring relationships between deviant womanhood and weight. *Gender and Society,* 17, 111–121.

Beauboeuf-Lafontant, T. (2007). You have to show strength: An exploration of gender, race, and depression. *Gender and Society,* 21, 28–51.

Beauboeuf-Lafontant, T. (2009). *Behind the mask of the strong Black woman: Voice and the embodiment of a costly performance.* Temple University Press.

Beauboeuf-Lafontant, T. (2016). Our plates are full: Black women and the weight of being strong. In *Doing Nutrition Differently* (pp. 59-78). Routledge.

Berger, M., & Sarnyai, Z. (2015). "More than skin deep": stress neurobiology and mental health consequences of racial discrimination. *Stress*, *18*(1), 1-10.

Bellinger, W. (2007). Why African American women try to obtain good hair. *Sociological Viewpoints. 23,* 233-72.

Black Mamas Matter Alliance. (2018). Setting the standard for holistic care of and for Black women. http://blackmamasmatter.org/wp-content/uploads/2018/04/BMMA_BlackPaper_April-2018.pdf

Blake, J. (2012). *Return of the welfare queen.* CNN Politics.

Bonilla-Silva, E. (2015). The structure of racism in color-blind, "postracial" America. *American Behavioral Scientist,* 59, 1358–1376. doi:10.1177/0002764215586826.

Brown-Iannuzzi, J. L., Dotsch, R., Cooley, E., & Payne, B. K. (2017). The relationship between mental representations of welfare recipients and attitudes toward welfare. *Psychological science,* 28(1), 92-103.

Bryant-Davis, T. (2019). The cultural context of trauma recovery: Considering the posttraumatic stress disorder practice guideline and intersectionality. *Psychotherapy, 56*(3), 400.

Bryant-Davis., Fasalojo, B., Arounian, A., Jackson, K. L., & Leithman, E. (2021). Resist and rise: A trauma-informed womanist model for group therapy. Women & Therapy, 1-24.

Bryant-Davis, T., & Ocampo, C. (2005). The trauma of racism: Implications for counseling, research, and education. The Counseling Psychologist, 33(4), 574-578.

Byrd, A., & Tharps, L. (2014). *Hair story: Untangling the roots of Black hair in America.* Macmillan.

Cain, M. C. (2008). The Art and Politics of Looking White: Beauty Practice among White Women in Antebellum America. *Winterthur Portfolio, 42*(1), 27–50.

Carter, R. T. (2007). Racism and psychological and emotional injury: Recognizing and assessing race-based traumatic stress. *The Counseling Psychologist, 35*(1), 13–105.

Cash, T. F., Morrow, J. A., Hrabosky, J. I., & Perry, A. A. (2004). How has body image changed? A cross-sectional investigation of college women and men from 1983 to 2001. *Journal of consulting and clinical psychology, 72*(6), 1081.

Cheeseborough, T., Overstreet, N., & Ward, L. M. (2020). Interpersonal sexual objectification, Jezebel stereotype endorsement and justification of intimate partner violence toward women. *Psychology of women quarterly, 44*(2), 203–216.

Chinn, J., Martin, I., & Redmond, N. (2021). Health equity among Black women in the United States. *Journal of Women's Health,*30(2), 212–219. https://doi.org/10.1089/jwh.2020.8868

Cobb, R. J., Thomas, C. S., Pirtle, W. N. L., & Darity Jr, W. A. (2016). Self-identified race, socially assigned skin tone, and adult physiological dysregulation: assessing multiple dimensions of "race" in health disparities research. *SSM-population health, 2,* 595–602.

Collins, P. H. (1990). Toward an Afrocentric feminist epistemology. In P. H. Collins (Ed.), *Black feminist thought* (pp. 201–220). Unwin Hyman.

Collins, P.H. (1991). Controlling images and Black women's oppression. Seeing ourselves: *Classic, contemporary, and cross-cultural readings in sociology*, 4, 266-273.

Collins, P. H. (2000). Gender, black feminism, and black political economy. *The Annals of the American Academy of Political and Social Science, 568*(1), 41–53.

Collins, P. H. (2002). *Black feminist thought: Knowledge, consciousness, and the politics of empowerment.* Routledge.

Collins, P. H. (2005). *Black sexual politics: African Americans, gender, and the new racism.* Routledge.

Comas-Díaz, L. (2016). Racial trauma recovery: A race-informed therapeutic approach to racial wounds. In A. N. Alvarez, C. T. H. Liang, & H. A. Neville (Eds.), *The cost of racism to people of color: Contextualizing experiences of discrimination* (pp. 341-375). American Psychological Association.

Comas-Díaz, L., Hall, G. N., & Neville, H. A. (2019). Racial trauma: Theory, research, and healing: Introduction to the special issue. *American Psychologist,* 74(1), 1-5. https://doi.org/10.1037/amp0000442

Corbin, N. A., Smith, W. A., & Garcia, J. R. (2018). Trapped between justified anger and being the strong Black woman: Black college women coping with racial battle fatigue at historically and predominantly White institutions. International Journal of Qualitative Studies in Education, 31(7), 626–643. https://doi.org/10.1080/09518398.2018.1468045

Creanga, A. A., Syverson, C., Seed, K., & Callaghan, W. M. (2017). Pregnancy-related mortality in the United States, 2011–2013. *Obstetrics and Gynecology, 130*(2), 366.

Crenshaw, K. (1989). Demarginalizing the intersection of race and sex: A black feminist critique of antidiscrimination doctrine, feminist theory, and antiracist politics. *u. Chi. Legal f.*, 139.

Crenshaw, K. (1990). Mapping the margins: Intersectionality, identity politics, and violence against women of color. *Stan. L. Rev., 43,* 1241.

Cronin, M. (2020). Anarcha, Betsey, Lucy, and the women whose names were not recorded: The legacy of J Marion Sims. *Anaesthesia and Intensive Care*, 48(3_suppl), 6-13.

CROWN Act of 2019, 116 USC §§ 3-6 CROWN Act of 2019, Cal. Education Code § 212.1 Crown Coalition. (2019). The official campaign of the CROWN Act. https://www.thecrownact.com

Davis, D. E., Hook, J. N., Worthington, E. L., Jr., Van Tongeren, D. R., Gartner, A. L., Jennings, D. J., II., & Emmons, R. A. (2011). Relational humility: Conceptualizing and measuring humility as a personality judgment. *Journal of Personality Assessment,* 93, 225–234. doi:10.1080/ 00223891.2011.558871.

Day-Vines, N. L., Cluxton-Keller, F., Agorsor, C., Gubara, S., & Otabil, N. A. A. (2020). The multidimensional model of broaching behavior. *Journal of Counseling & Development, 98*(1), 107–118.

DeVon, H. A., Burke, L. A., Nelson, H., Zerwic, J. J., & Riley, B. (2014). Disparities in patients presenting to the emergency department with potential acute coronary syndrome: It matters if you are Black or White. *Heart & Lung, 43*(4), 270-277.

Donovan, R. A., & West, L. M. (2015). Stress and mental health: Moderating role of the strong Black woman stereotype. *Journal of Black Psychology, 41*(4), 384-396.

Dow, D. M. (2015). Negotiating "the welfare queen" and "the strong Black woman" African American middle-class mothers' work and family perspectives. *Sociological Perspectives, 58*(1), 36-55.

Dunn, C. E., Hood, K. B., & Owens, B. D. (2019). Loving myself through thick and thin: Appearance contingent self-worth, gendered racial microaggressions, and African American women's body appreciation. *Body image*, *30*, 121–126.

Duru, O. K., Harawa, N. T., Kermah, D., & Norris, K. C. (2012). Allostatic load burden and racial disparities in mortality. *Journal of the National Medical Association*, *104*(1-2), 89-95.

Duvall, J. L., Oser, C. B., Mooney, J., Staton-Tindall, M., Havens, J. R., & Leukefeld, C. G. (2013). Feeling good in your own skin: The influence of complementary sexual stereotypes on risky sexual attitudes and behaviors in a community sample of African American women. *Women and Health*, 53, 1–19. doi:10.1080/03630242.2012.750260.

Ely, D. M., & Driscoll, A. K. (2019). *Infant mortality in the United States*, 2017: data from the period linked birth/infant death file.

Factor, R., Kawachi, I., & Williams, D. R. (2011). Understanding high-risk behavior among non-dominant minorities: A social resistance framework. *Social science & medicine*, *73*(9), 1292-1301.

Flowers, K. C., Levesque, M. J., & Fischer, S. (2012). The relationship between maladaptive eating behaviors and racial identity among African American women in college. *Journal of Black Psychology,* 38(3), 290-312.

Gilman, M. E. (2013). The return of the welfare queen. Am. UJ Gender Soc. Pol'y & L., 22, 247.

Glenn, E. N. (1992). From servitude to service work: Historical continuities in the racial division of paid reproductive labor. Signs: *Journal of women in culture and society,* 18(1), 1- 43.

Gordon, K. H., Castro, Y., Sitnikov, L., & Holm-Denoma, J. M. (2010). Cultural body shape ideals and eating disorder symptoms among White, Latina, and Black college women. *Cultural Diversity and Ethnic Minority Psychology,* 16(2), 135.

Greene, N. (2020). Misdiagnosing Generational Trauma and Grief: I Am Not Angry; I Am Triggered and Grief Stricken. In *Narratives of Hope and Grief in Higher Education* (pp. 139-152). Palgrave Macmillan.

Griffin, C. (2018). The Celia doctrine: A new defense against the criminalization of rape victims. *J. Legal Prof.*, *43*, 251.

Guidi, J., Lucente, M., Sonino, N., & Fava, G. A. (2020). Allostatic load and its impact on health: a systematic review. *Psychotherapy and psychosomatics,* 90(1), 11-27.

Hall, J. C. (2017). No longer invisible: Understanding the psychosocial impact of skin color stratification in the lives of African American women. *Health & Social Work,* 42(2), 71-78.

Hancock, A. M. (2004). *The politics of disgust: The public identity of the welfare queen*. NYU Press.

Hannon, J., & DeFina, R. (2014). Just skin deep? The impact of interviewer race on the assessment of African American respondent skin tone. *Race and Social Problems,* 6, 356–364.

Harrington, E. F., Crowther, J. H., & Shipherd, J. C. (2010). Trauma, binge eating, and the "strong Black woman." *Journal of consulting and clinical psychology*, *78*(4), 469-479.

Harris-Perry, M. V. (2011). *Sister citizen: Shame, stereotypes, and Black women in America*. Yale University Press.

Hersey, T. (2022). Rest is Resistance: A Manifesto. Hachette UK.

Hicken, M. T., Lee, H., Ailshire, J., Burgard, S. A., & Williams, D. R. (2013). "Every shut eye, ain't sleep": The role of racism-related vigilance in racial/ethnic disparities in sleep difficulty. *Race and social problems*, *5*(2), 100-112.

Hill, L., Artiga, S., & Ranji, U. (2022). Racial disparities in maternal and infant health: Current status and efforts to address them. Kaiser Family Foundation, 1.

Hirschmann, N. J., & Liebert, U. (Eds.). (2001). *Women and welfare: Theory and practice in the United States and Europe*. Rutgers University Press.

Howell, E. A. (2018). Reducing disparities in severe maternal morbidity and mortality. *Clinical obstetrics and gynecology*, *61*(2), 387-399.

Ibe, C. A., Haywood, D. R., Creighton, C., Cao, Y., Gabriel, A., Zare, H., Jones, W. & Gaskin, D. J. (2021). Study protocol of a randomized controlled trial evaluating the Prime Time Sister Circles (PTSC) program's impact on hypertension among midlife African American women. *BMC public health*, 21, 1-10.

Jacques-Tiura, A. J., Tkatch, R., Abbey, A., & Wegner, R. (2010). Disclosure of sexual assault: Characteristics and implications for posttraumatic stress symptoms among African American and Caucasian survivors. *Journal of Trauma & Dissociation*, *11*(2), 174-192.

Jeffries, R. B., & Jeffries, D. (2014). Reclaiming our roots: The influences of media curriculum on the natural hair movement. *Multicultural Perspectives,* 16(3), 160-165.

Jerald, M. C., Cole, E. R., Ward, L. M., & Avery, L. R. (2017). Controlling images: How awareness of group stereotypes affects Black women's wellbeing. *Journal of Counseling Psychology*, *64*(5), 487.

Jerald, M. C., Ward, L. M., Moss, L., Thomas, K., & Fletcher, K. D. (2017). Subordinates, sex objects, or sapphires? Investigating contributions of media use to Black students' femininity ideologies and stereotypes about Black women. *Journal of Black Psychology*, *43*(6), 608-635.

Johnson, E. R., Affuso, O., Levitan, E. B., Carson, T. L., & Baskin, M. L. (2019). Body image and dissatisfaction among rural Deep South African American women in a weight loss intervention. *Journal of health psychology*, *24*(9), 1167-1177.

Johnson, T. A., & Bankhead, T. (2014). Hair it is: Examining the experiences of Black women with natural hair. *Open Journal of Social Sciences,* 2, 86–100. doi:10.4236/jss.2014.21010

Jones, J. (2009). *Labor of love, labor of sorrow: Black women, work, and the family, from slavery to the present.* Basic Books.

Jones, M. K., Hill-Jarrett, T. G., Latimer, K., Reynolds, A., Garrett, N., Harris, I., Joseph, S. & Jones, A. (2021). The role of coping in the relationship between endorsement of the strong Black woman schema and depressive symptoms among Black women. *Journal of Black Psychology*, 47(7), 578-592.

Jordan, W. D. (2014). Historical origins of the one-drop racial rule in the United States. *Journal of Critical Mixed Race Studies,* 1(1), 98–132.

Kerney, M. A., Malone, N., Jackman, K. B., & Hargons, C. N. (2023). Dance movement therapy for Black womxn: A content analysis. *The Arts in Psychotherapy,* 85, 102058.

Kim, H., Wildeman, C., Jonson-Reid, M., & Drake, B. (2017). Lifetime prevalence of investigating child maltreatment among US children. *American journal of public health,* 107(2), 274-280.

Kite, M. E., Whitley Jr, B. E., & Wagner, L. S. (2022). *Psychology of prejudice and discrimination.* Taylor & Francis.

Kohler-Hausmann, J. (2007). The crime of survival": Fraud prosecutions, community surveillance, and the original" welfare queen. *Journal of Social History*, 329-354.

Kohler-Hausmann, J. (2015). Welfare crises, penal solutions, and the origins of the "welfare queen". *Journal of Urban History,* 41(5), 756-771.

Landor, A. M., & Halpern, C. T. (2016). The enduring significance of skin tone: Linking skin tone, attitudes toward marriage and cohabitation, and sexual behavior. *Journal of youth and adolescence*, *45*(5), 986-1002.

Landor, A. M., Simons, L. G., Simons, R. L., Brody, G. H., Bryant, C. M., Gibbons, F. X., Granberg, E. M. & Melby, J. N. (2013). Exploring the impact of skin tone on family dynamics and race-related outcomes. *Journal of Family Psychology*, *27*(5), 817–826.

Leath, S., Jones, M., Jerald, M. C., & Perkins, T. R. (2020). An investigation of Jezebel stereotype awareness gendered racial identity, and sexual beliefs and behaviors among Black adult women. *Culture, Health & Sexuality*, 1–18.

Leath, S., Jerald, M. C., Perkins, T., & Jones, M. K. (2021). A qualitative exploration of Jezebel stereotype endorsement and sexual behaviors among Black college women. *Journal of Black Psychology,* 47(4-5), 244-283.

Liao, K. Y. H., Wei, M., & Yin, M. (2020). The misunderstood schema of the strong Black woman: Exploring its mental health consequences and coping responses among African American women. *Psychology of Women Quarterly,* 44(1), 84-104.

Lorts, J. T. (2013). The NAACP Boycott of the Amos' n'Andy Show. In *The Economic Civil Rights Movement* (pp. 81–94). Routledge.

Lowy, A. S., Rodgers, R. F., Franko, D. L., Pluhar, E., & Webb, J. B. (2021). Body image and internalization of appearance ideals in Black women: An update and call for culturally sensitive research. *Body Image,* 39, 313-327.

MacDorman, M. F., Declercq, E., Cabral, H., & Morton, C. (2016). Is the United States maternal mortality rate increasing? Disentangling trends from measurement issues short title: US maternal mortality trends. *Obstetrics and Gynecology,* 128(3), 447.

Markin, R. D., & Coleman, M. N. (2023). Intersections of gendered racial trauma and childbirth trauma: Clinical interventions for Black women. *Psychotherapy,* 60(1), 27.

Mathews, T. J., & Johnson, G. S. (2015). Skin complexion in the twenty-first century: The impact of colorism on African American women. *Race, Gender & Class*, *22*(1-2), 248-274.

Major, B., Mendes, W. B., & Dovidio, J. F. (2013). Intergroup relations and health disparities: a social psychological perspective. *Health Psychology*, *32*(5), 514-524.

McCleary-Gaddy, A. T., & James, D. (2022). Skin tone, life satisfaction, and psychological distress among African Americans: The mediating effect of stigma consciousness. *Journal of health psychology,* 27(2), 422-431.

McKenna, B. G., Mekawi, Y., Katrinli, S., Carter, S., Stevens, J. S., Powers, A., Smith, A.K. & Michopoulos, V. (2021). When Anger Remains Unspoken: Anger and Accelerated Epigenetic Aging Among Stress-Exposed Black Americans. *Psychosomatic Medicine,* 83(9), 949-958.

McLaurin, M. A. (1991). *Celia, a slave* (Vol. 5). University of Georgia Press.

McSweeney, J. C., O'Sullivan, P., Cleves, M. A., Lefler, L. L., Cody, M., Moser, D. K., Dunn, K., Kovacs, M., Crane, P. B., Ramer, L., Messmer, P. R., Garvin, B. J., & Zhao, W. (2010). Racial differences in women's prodromal and acute symptoms of myocardial infarction. *American journal of critical care: an official publication, American Association of Critical-Care Nurses, 19*(1), 63–73. https://doi.org/10.4037/ajcc2010372.

Medina, C. (2011). An Alternative Strategy: Sex Scripts, and Women of Color. *Social Work and Public Health, (*26), 260–277.

Merritt, D. H. (2020). How do families experience and interact with CPS?. The ANNALS of the American Academy of Political and Social Science, 692(1), 203-226.

Middlemass, K. M. (2019). Black women excluded from protection and criminalized for their existence. *In Prisoner Reentry in the 21st Century* (pp. 145-156). Routledge.

Motro, D., Evans, J. B., Ellis, A. P., & Benson III, L. (2021). Race and reactions to women's expressions of anger at work: Examining the effects of the "angry Black woman" stereotype. *Journal of Applied Psychology.*

Monk Jr, E. P. (2021). The unceasing significance of colorism: Skin tone stratification in the United States. *Daedalus,* 150(2), 76-90.

Moody, A. T., & Lewis, J. A. (2019). Gendered racial microaggressions and traumatic stress symptoms among Black women. *Psychology of Women Quarterly*, 43(2), 201-214.

Motro, D., Evans, J. B., Ellis, A. P., & Benson III, L. (2022). Race and reactions to women's expressions of anger at work: Examining the effects of the "angry Black woman" stereotype. *Journal of Applied Psychology,* 107(1), 142.

Moynihan, D. P. the U.S. Department of Labor, Office of Policy Planning and Research. 1965. *The Negro Family: The Case for National Action*.

National Center for Health Statistics (U.S. (2012). Health, United States, 2011: With special feature on socio-economic status and health.

Neal-Barnett, A., Stadulis, R., Murray, M., Payne, M. R., Thomas, A., & Salley, B. B. (2011). Sister circles as a culturally relevant intervention for anxious Black women. *Clinical Psychology: Science and Practice,* 18(3), 266.

Obeng-Gyasi, S., Tarver, W., Carlos, R. C., & Andersen, B. L. (2021). Allostatic load: a framework to understand breast cancer outcomes in Black women. *NPJ Breast Cancer*, *7*(1), 1-4.

Overstreet, N. M., Quinn, D. M., & Agocha, V. B. (2010). Beyond thinness: The influence of a curvaceous body ideal on body dissatisfaction in Black and White women. *Sex roles*, *63*(1), 91-103.

Netto, P. (2005). Reclaiming the Body of the 'Hottentot' The Vision and Visuality of the Body Speaking with Vengeance in Venus Hottentot 2000. European *Journal of Women's Studies,* 12(2), 149-163.

Parkinson, J. (2016). The Significance of Sarah Baartman. *BBC News Magazine*, 7.

Peek, M. K., Cutchin, M. P., Salinas, J. J., Sheffield, K. M., Eschbach, K., Stowe, R. P., & Goodwin, J. S. (2010). Allostatic load among non-Hispanic Whites, non-Hispanic Blacks, and people of Mexican origin: effects of ethnicity, nativity, and acculturation. *American journal of public health, 100*(5), 940-946.

Peterson, S. H., Wingood, G. M., DiClemente, R. J., Harrington, K., & Davies, S. (2007). Images of sexual stereotypes in rap videos and the health of African American female adolescents. *Journal of Women's Health, 16*(8), 1157–1164.

Pierce, C. (1970). Offensive mechanisms. In C. Pierce & F. B.Barbour (Eds.), *The Black seventies: An extending horizon book* (pp. 265–282). Porter Sargent Publisher.

Randle, B. A. (2015). I am not my hair: African American women and their struggles with embracing natural hair! *Race, Gender & Class, 22*(1-2), 114-121.

Ravi, M., Mekawi, Y., Blevins, J., Michopoulos, V., & Stevens, J. (2023). Intersections of oppression: Examining the interactive effect of racial discrimination and neighborhood poverty on PTSD symptoms in Black women. *Journal of Psychopathology and Clinical Science,* 132(5),567–576.

Rebollo-Gil, G., & Moras, A. (2012). Black women and black men in hip hop music: misogyny, violence and the negotiation of (white-owned) space. *The Journal of Popular Culture, 45*(1), 118-132.

Reece, R. L. (2021). The gender of colorism: Understanding the intersection of skin tone and gender inequality. *Journal of Economics, Race, and Policy,* 4, 47-55.

Robinson, C. L. (2011). "Hair as Race: Why "Good Hair" may be Bad for Black Females." *The Howard Journal of Communications*, 22(4), 358–376.

Rosenthal, L., & Lobel, M. (2016). Stereotypes of Black American women related to sexuality and motherhood. *Psychology of women quarterly, 40*(3), 414–427.

Rosenthal, L., & Overstreet, N. (2016). Stereotyping. In H. S. Friedman (Ed.), *Encyclopedia of mental health* (2nd ed., Vol. 3, pp. 318–329). Academic Press. doi:10.1016/B978- 0-12-397045-9.00164-6.

Rucker III, C. E., & Cash, T. F. (1992). Body images, body-size perceptions, and eating behaviors among African-American and white college women. *International journal of eating disorders,* 12(3), 291-299.

Russell, K., Wilson, M., & Hall, R. (2013). *The color complex (revised): The politics of skin color in a new millennium.* Anchor.

Saperstein, A., & Penner, A. (2012). Racial fluidity and inequality in the United States. *American Journal of Sociology,* 118, 676–727.

Seeman, T., Epel, E., Gruenewald, T., Karlamangla, A., & McEwen, B. S. (2010). Socio-economic differentials in peripheral biology: Cumulative allostatic load. *Annals of the New York Academy of Sciences, 1186*(1), 223-239.

Siegel, R. L., Miller, K. D., Fuchs, H. E., & Jemal, A. (2021). Cancer statistics, 2021. *CA: a cancer journal for clinicians, 71*(1), 7-33.

Slaughter-Acey, J. C., Sneed, D., Parker, L., Keith, V. M., Lee, N. L., & Misra, D. P. (2019). Skin tone matters: Racial microaggressions and delayed prenatal care. *American journal of preventive medicine, 57*(3), 321–329.

Smith, D., Caruthers, L., & Fowler, S. (2019). *Womanish Black girls: Women resisting the contradictions of silence and voice.* Myers Education Press.

Somerville, K., Rowell, T., Stadulis, R., Bell, D., & Neal-Barnett, A. (2023). An evaluation of the feasibility and acceptability of sister circles as an anxiety intervention for pregnant Black women. *Women's Health,* 19, 17455057231185405.

Stein, G. (2013). Where Are All the Couch Potatoes and Welfare Queens? HuffPost Live: The Huffington Post.

Stephens, D. P., & Phillips, L. D. 2003. Freaks, gold diggers, divas, and dykes: The sociohistorical development of adolescent African American women's sexual scripts. *Sexuality & Culture,* 7, 3–47.

Sublette, N., & Sublette, C. (2015). *The American slave coast: A history of the slave-breeding industry.* Lawrence Hill Books.

Sue, D. W., Nadal, K. L., Capodilupo, C. M., Lin, A. I., Torino,G. C., & Rivera, D. P. (2008). Racial microaggressions against Black Americans: Implications for counseling. *Journal of Counseling & Development,* 86(3), 330–338.

Somerville, K., Rowell, T., Stadulis, R., Bell, D., & Neal-Barnett, A. (2023). An evaluation of the feasibility and acceptability of sister circles as an anxiety intervention for pregnant Black women. *Women's Health,* 19, 17455057231185405.

Thompson, C. (2009). Black women, beauty, and hair as a matter of being. *Women's Studies,* 38(8), 831-856.

Tikkanen R., Gunja M., FitzGerald M., Zephyrin L. (2020). *Maternal mortality maternity care U.S. compared 10 other countries.* Commonwealth Fund.

Tillman, S., Bryant-Davis, T., Smith, K., & Marks, A. (2010). Shattering silence: Exploring barriers to disclosure for African American sexual assault survivors. *Trauma, violence, & abuse, 11*(2), 59-70.

Townsend, T. G., Neilands, T. B., Thomas, A. J., & Jackson, T. R. (2010). I'm no Jezebel; I am young, gifted, and Black: Identity, sexuality, and Black girls. *Psychology of Women Quarterly,* 34(3), 273-285.

Turner, J. S. (2011). Sex and the spectacle of music videos: An examination of the portrayal of race and sexuality in music videos. *Sex Roles,* 64, 173–191.

Xing, C. Y., Doose, M., Qin, B., Lin, Y., Plascak, J. J., Omene, C., He, C., Demissie, K., Hong, C. C., Bandera, E. V. & Llanos, A. A. (2020). Prediagnostic allostatic load as a predictor of poorly differentiated and larger-sized breast cancers among Black women in the Women's Circle of Health Follow-Up Study. *Cancer Epidemiology and Prevention Biomarkers, 29*(1), 216-224.

Walker, A. (1983). *The color purple.* Women's Press Limited.

Walker Gautier, S. (2021). Black beauty: Womanist consciousness as a protective factor in Black women's body image satisfaction. *Journal of Black Psychology,* 47(8), 631-656.

Watson, N. N., & Hunter, C. D. (2016). "I had to be strong" tensions in the strong Black woman schema. *Journal of Black Psychology, 42*(5), 424–452.

Watson, L. B., Lewis, J. A., & Moody, A. T. (2019). A sociocultural examination of body image among Black women. *Body image, 31*, 280–287.

Watson, L. B., Robinson, D., Dispenza, F., & Nazari, N. (2012). African American women's sexual objectification experiences: A qualitative study. *Psychology of Women Quarterly,* 36, 458–475. doi:10.1177/0361684312454724.

West, C. M. (2008). *Mammy, Jezebel, Sapphire, and their Homegirls: Developing an" oppositional" gaze toward the images of Black women.* McGraw-Hill.

Whites, L. (1993). Celia: A Slave. *Civil War History*, *39*(1), 88-90.

Wilder, J., & Cain, C. (2011). Teaching and learning color consciousness in Black families: Exploring family processes and women's experiences with colorism. *Journal of family issues*, *32*(5), 577–604.

Williams, M. G., & Lewis, J. A. (2019). Gendered racial microaggressions and depressive symptoms among black women: A moderated mediation model. *Psychology of Women Quarterly,* 43(3), 368–380. https://doi.org/10.1177/0361684319832511

Williams, D. R., & Mohammed, S. A. (2013). Racism and health I: Pathways and scientific evidence. *American behavioral scientist*, *57*(8), 1152–1173.

Williams, D. R., Lawrence, J. A., & Davis, B. A. (2019). Racism and health: evidence and needed research. *Annual review of public health*, *40*, 105–125.

Windsor, L., Dunlap, E., and Golub, A. 2011. Challenging Controlling Images, Oppression, Poverty, and Other Structural Constraints: Survival Strategies Among African–American Women in Distressed Households. *Journal of African American Studies,* 15, 290–306.

Wright, L. N., & Lewis, J. A. (2020). Is physical activity a buffer? Gendered racial microaggressions and anxiety among African American women. *Journal of Black Psychology,* 46(2–3), 122–143. https://doi.org/10.1177/0095798420929112

Woods-Giscombé, C. L. (2010). Superwoman schema: African American women's views on stress, strength, and health. *Qualitative Health Research*, 20, 668-683.

Chapter 6

Untangling Black Hair: Black Women's Eternal Search for Self and Beauty

Katrina E. Pinkney*
Department of Counseling, University of the Cumberlands, Williamsburg, Kentucky, USA

Abstract

This chapter explores the interrelation of Black women's natural hair expression, identity development, and gendered racial trauma. A brief historical overview will explore inter and intraracial discrimination to stigmatize Black women's natural hair and hairstyles. The chapter will critically examine the negative impact of gendered racism and discrimination on Black women's identity development, self-esteem, and mental and emotional well-being. It will discuss painful and physically harmful hair care methods and hazardous ethnic hair products to meet white beauty standards. An exploration of hair discrimination in the workplace for Black women regarding their natural hair expression will further illuminate the negative impact on identity development and the suppression of authenticity. Additionally, the chapter will highlight the Black natural hair movement of the 1960s and early 1970s, a form of political and social activism to empower Black women to redefine Black femininity and reject discriminatory power structures.

Keywords: Black, African American, African, mulatto, Black hair, kinky hair, natural hair, hair extension, Black femininity

* Corresponding Author's Email: kpinkney10835@ucumberlands.edu.

In: How Did We Survive?
Editor: Tina Marie Glover
ISBN: 979-8-88697-918-3

In 2019, Black consumers spent $1.4 trillion in the United States. The total dollars spent had significantly increased by 48 percent since 2010. Their buying power exceeded whites by 40 percent and 43 percent of the total population (The Nielson Company, 2020). In 2017, the ethnic hair care and beauty industry were worth an estimated $4.2 billion. According to the Nielson Company (2018), Black consumers comprised 86 percent of the total dollars spent on hair and beauty. They exclusively spent $473 million on hair care products (The Nielson Company, 2018). These figures do not comprise the wig and hair extension market, another billion-dollar industry with predominantly Black female consumers (Chang, 2020).

The relationship between the Black community and their natural hair is intergenerational, complex, and profitable. The history of African Americans and their kinky curls, specifically with Black women, has been physically and emotionally traumatic. The ethnic hair care and beauty industry economically exploits Black women's beauty insecurities and continuous pursuit of social acceptance. Intraracial and interracial capitalists reinforce Black women's beauty ideals based on white cultural norms. Power structures founded in white supremacy devalue, dominate, and monetize Black women's bodies disregarding their physical and emotional well-being.

Africans and Hair Significance: A Way of Language

During the 15th century, the hairstyles of West African tribes were a form of language. A single hairstyle communicates age, marital status, religion, ethnic identity, wealth, hierarchy, geographical location, or mental health status. Africans held pride in their hair styling and grooming practices. Hair designs included braids, plaits, shells, flowers, beads, strips of material weaved into the hair, and shaved patterns (Byrd & Tharps, 2014; White & White, 1995). Young unmarried women in the Wolof community of Senegal partially shaved their heads. The more elaborate styles were worn by royalty, for example, in the Ijebu tribe of Guinea.

The maintenance and upkeep of healthy hair were significant. Unkempt hair signified an unhealthy mental and physical health state. It was acceptable for a widowed female to have unkempt hair for an extended time to grieve. Otherwise, individuals with messy hair were considered unwell, dirty, indecent, and could face ostracization. These West African tribes admired long, thick, full hair. Healthy, thick tresses symbolized power, life, prosperity in the family, and fertility. Hair was powerful. It was used spiritually to cast spells and was believed to increase medicine's potency (Byrd & Tharps, 2014).

The Indoctrination of African Slaves in America

The Transatlantic Slave Trade

Europeans started to explore the coast of Africa around 1444 (Byrd & Tharps, 2014). The transatlantic slave trade occurred continuously from 1501 to 1900 (Eltis & Richardson, 2010). The capture and enslavement of about 12.5 million Africans were cheap labor for producing and exporting commodities (e.g., sugar, rum, rice, tobacco, coffee, cotton, indigo, valuable metals, and other goods). The Brazilians, Spaniards, Portuguese, Dutch, British, Danes, French, Swedes, and North Americans bought African men, women, and children (Byrd & Tharps, 2014; Eltis & Richardson, 2010). Many did not survive the voyages, with 10.7 million documented as arriving in the Americas (Eltis & Richardson, 2010). Most of the enslaved were between 10 to 24 years old (Byrd & Tharps, 2014). The Africans imported to the Americas originated from various ethnolinguistic groups, mainly from the West Central Africa coastal region. Ethnic groups within this region included Aduma, Bobangi, Pende, Zombo, Yaka, Mbundu, Chokwe, and Ovambo (Eltis & Richardson, 2010).

Eltis and Richardson (2010) acknowledge that African captives may have been smuggled upon Christopher Columbus's third voyage to America in 1498. Documentation of the first African slaves indicated their arrival to British North America in 1619. Dutch traders sold about 20 Africans in Jamestown, Virginia. These Africans became indentured servants. They worked alongside white indentured servants from England, Scotland, and Ireland (Byrd & Tharps, 2014; Finkelman, 2012). By 1640, legal records in Virginia exhibited inconsistent sentences toward runaway African and white indentured servants. Some runaway Africans received a lifelong servitude sentence. Whereas white servants never received a lifelong sentence (Finkelman, 2012). From 1664 to 1671, about 1500 white servants were imported to Virginia yearly. About 6,000 white servants and 2,000 African slaves were indentured servants by 1671 (Horowitz, 1973).

The Lawful Foundation for the Institution of Slavery

After becoming eligible for freedom after years of servitude, African and white indentured servants purchased their sovereignty (Byrd & Tharps, 2014; Finkelman, 2012). Some of the freed African women coupled with free white men to have multiethnic children. These children of interracial couples (i.e., mulattos) were free. As offspring of indentured parents, these children and their families were living in poverty and were uneducated (Horowitz, 1973).

The fear of a growing free class of educated multiethnic people caused Virginia lawmakers to rethink English law. At the time, any child would inherit the status of their father. Under legal obligation, mulatto children were to receive an education and financial support from their fathers. Virginia legislators decided to adopt a Roman law. This law applied to the offspring of domestic livestock and animals. The offspring of a domestic animal was property to the owner of the female who gave birth (Finkelman, 2012). In 1662, Virginia legislators passed a law to designate that any children of an Englishmen and a negro enslaved woman would inherit the status of the mother (Finkelman, 2012, p. 112). This law set a precedent for the institution of slavery. Enslaved African women were property to have no control over their bodies and children. There would be no legal persecution for slave owners and other white men who sexually violated enslaved African women. Their offspring were property, and a means to increase wealth (Finkelman, 2012).

African Women in the New World and Hair Maintenance

In the North American colonies, slavery flourished after 1730 (Eltis & Richardson, 2010). Demand increased in mid-Atlantic southern states. Upon capture, it was common for the slave traders to shave the head of the Africans for sanitary purposes. The shaving of their hair also severed ties to the slaves' African identities, native land, and culture and diminished their self-worth (Byrd & Tharps, 2014). It temporarily silenced communication between tribes who spoke different languages and shared different cultures. Once arriving at plantations, white owners whittled away at the self-esteem and self-worth of their captives. African hair was a common attribute for ridicule by white slave owners.

Female slaves who worked in the fields in the hot and humid sun for hours traditionally wore head wraps and scarves. There needed to be more time for haircare maintenance. The hair may have been unhealthy (i.e., matted, tangled, patchy, or significantly damaged). It was not uncommon for problematic scalp infections such as ringworm and lice (Byrd & Tharps, 2014). The scarf or headwrap also acted as protection for the hair. It preserved protective styles, for example, braids, cornrows, and threading (White & White, 1995).

Slaves who worked in the house were always to look presentable. Female slaves wore their hair in braids, plaits, and cornrows (Byrd & Tharps, 2014). During the 18th century, wigs were popular amongst European men. Slaves of the wealthy wore wigs or styled their hair to resemble the wig styles (White & White, 1995). Whether neat or unkempt, Africans' hair was called wool and labeled ugly and unattractive (Byrd & Tharps, 2014; White & White, 1995). The verbal and emotional abuse of African slaves was daily. There were constant disparaging reminders that their physical features were not meeting the dominant culture's ideal beauty standards. With the increase of American-born slaves, intricate hairstyles with African origins dwindled toward the end of the 18th century (White & White, 1995).

Homemade Hair Care Remedies and Straighteners

In 1807, the United States abolished the transatlantic slave trade for the law to become effective the following year. However, the African slave trade continued into the late 19th century (Eltis & Richardson, 2010). Due to the outlawing of the transatlantic slave trade, there was an emphasis on the longevity of the domestic slave (Byrd & Tharps, 2014). Many slave owners were judged by their peers on the appearance and health of their slaves (Bellinger, 2007). On Sundays, more slave owners allowed their slaves to rest and attend church. Slaves took this day to participate in personal grooming and hair care maintenance (Byrd & Tharps, 2014; White & White, 1995).

Straight hair was the European ideal beauty standard. African and African-American female slaves were to adopt this hair maintenance and style standard. Slaves established creative methods to straighten their curly tresses. The least damaging straightening method was wrapping or threading. Wrapping the hair was common practice as early as infancy. This method trained the hair to loosen its curl pattern. A heated cloth was warmed and wrapped around the greased hair. Hair was also separated into small sections and wrapped with strings, strips of fabric, eel skin, or cotton to stretch the hair. Female slaves then protected the style by covering their hair with a headscarf or bandana (Byrd & Tharps, 2014; White & White, 1995).

Moderate to severe hair manipulations consisted of straightening with a heated butter knife or applying a creamy lye mixture. Slaves applied bacon grease, goose grease, or butter in a thick layer to the hair in preparation for straightening. They then used a heated butter knife, pulling it over sections of the hair. After straightening, the hair had a soft sheen. The most severe method was the use of lye. The creamy mixture of lye and potatoes was spread onto the hair and washed out after a tingling sensation. If the mixture stayed on the hair for too long, third-degree burns on the scalp and hair loss were possible (Byrd & Tharps, 2014).

Mulatto Slaves with Light Skin and Long, Straight Hair

Consensual and non-consensual sexual relations between owners and slaves produced mulatto offspring (Finkelman, 2012). Due to the law, the children were inevitably slaves and belonged to the slave owner (Finkelman, 2012; Byrd & Tharps, 2014). These children had light skin, sometimes to be white-passing. The hair was long to have a looser curl pattern. The straighter the hair, the greater the value associated with the slave. At slave auctions, light-skinned, straighter hair slaves sold five times more than slaves with dark skin and kinkier curls (Byrd & Tharps, 2014). The institution of slavery created an intraracial hierarchy amongst the African and African-American slaves (Byrd & Tharps, 2014; Hunter, 2007).

Colorism denied darker-skinned African Americans access to privileges and resources afforded to the lighter-skinned (Hunter, 2007). Dark-skinned slaves had bad hair. Slaves who were light-skinned had good hair (Byrd & Tharps, 2014, p. 34). Light-skinned slaves with straighter hair could work in the home (Byrd & Tharps, 2014; Hunter, 2007). They learned trade skills, received informal education, and had more opportunities to come and go from the plantation than darker complexion slaves (Reece, 2018). Despite the preferential treatment, the abuse of house slaves was common.

The owner and wife sexually, physically, and emotionally abused female house slaves. The mutilation of African-American female slaves' hair was a punishment enacted by the slave owner's wife. The wife was immensely jealous of multiethnic female slaves, especially if their hair was long and straight to resemble a white woman. She chopped the hair of the slave to ensure the slave did not sexually seduce her husband (White & White, 1995).

The Rise of the Elite Mulatto and the Black High Society

In 1860, about 40 percent of the free southern African-American population was mulatto. Of those enslaved, mulattos comprised only 10 percent (Berlin, 1974; Horowitz, 1973). In the deep South, free mulattos were around 75 percent (Berlin, 1974). The Emancipation Proclamation in 1863 and the abolishment of slavery two years later influenced the establishment of an elite social class of Blacks, the Black aristocracy (Byrd & Tharps, 2014; Finkelman, 2012; Gatewood, 2000; Horowtiz, 1973). The elite group was considered superior to freed African Americans and mulatto slaves to be the wealthiest of the Black social class (Byrd & Tharps, 2014; Gatewood, 2000; Horowitz, 1973). The aristocrats were free pre–Civil War to be one or two generations removed from slave-slave owner transgressions (Gatewood, 2000).

The criteria to be a member of the Black high society included a light skin tone, position in the church, possession of wealth or real estate, freedom at birth, marriage to whites or light-skinned Blacks, and work in a profession. Geographical location determines the emphasis on criteria for membership. The mulatto elite, Blacks with light skin and straight hair, a group researched extensively in Charleston, South Carolina (e.g., Harris, 1981), had a notoriety for strict membership standards, practiced discrimination based on skin color, and practiced extreme bias toward lower-class African Americans (Byrd & Tharps, 2014, p. 36; Gatewood, 2000). This group adopted the white dominant culture's values such as property ownership, servants, and obtaining formal education (Gatewood, 2000; Horowtiz, 1973). They were the bona fide free Blacks compared to the sot free (Byrd & Tharps, 2014, p. 37). Their social and economic privileges resulted from their assimilation into white cultural standards (Horowitz, 1973; Hunter, 2007).

The mulatto elite reinforced segregation and unequal status amongst African Americans. Some were outspoken about forming a third racial class (i.e., whites, Blacks, and Mulattos). Whites considered mulattos more intelligent, well-mannered, civilized, and respectable than African Americans. Mulattos were afforded more job opportunities and socialized with whites. In Charleston, the mulatto elite established schools, hospitals, churches, businesses, and civic organizations to exclude dark complexion African Americans (Gatewood, 2000). Byrd and Tharps (2014) identified the fine-tooth comb test to assess for kinkiness of hair and the brown paper bag test to measure the lightness of skin as methods used to exclude Blacks. The tension between elite mulattos and African Americans continued to grow. The conflict appeared in political races, educational and church matters, and social relationships (Gatewood, 2000).

The Black Hair Care Business Then and Now

With the abolishment of slavery, African Americans remained unequal to white Americans. In the early 19th century, many African Americans remained in the agricultural industry as sharecroppers in the Southern states (Weems, 1998). The racist ideologies established within slavery and systemic racism in America's judicial, political, educational, and socioeconomic structures identified African Americans as powerless and inferior regardless of free status (Weems, 1998). White Americans' overt behaviors to demonstrate hate for African Americans were irrational, violent, deadly (e.g., lynching), aggressive, and ongoing. Freed African Americans learned they remained unsafe and separate from whites in America.

Meanwhile, African Americans tried to assimilate into the white culture for survival. Black hair was a badge of slavery, where it reminded and was used to remind the now free person of their former status (Powell, 2018, p. 933). Hair was the primary identifier of race to have a ranking above skin color. Hair texture and skin tone determined class. Straight hair was associated with the middle and upper classes (Byrd & Tharps, 2014). In 20th century America, the quest for straight hair continued with female African Americans seeking social acceptance, worth, and economic mobility.

The Black Hair Care Business and Entrepreneurs of the Early 20th Century

During the Great Migration, about 1.7 million southern African Americans migrated to northern and western states between 1900 and 1940 (Weems, 1998, p. 7). They sought gainful employment opportunities to be prompted by World War I. African Americans also migrated to southern cities in significant numbers from rural America. The United States Census (1920) indicated that a growing number of African-American women obtained employment in the domestic and personal service industry. Within this industry, occupations included hairdressers and manicurists. Most African-American women in these positions were aged 25 to 44.

Before the Great Migration, white businesses disregarded African Americans as potential consumers due to their low-paying jobs and lack of disposable income. Advertisements from white business owners demeaned African Americans by featuring caricatures making fun of their physical features, offensive stereotypes, and the word nigger (Weems, 1998, p. 8). After the migration, white and Black-owned businesses saw profit in the African-American market. Beauty advertisements to target female African-American consumers in Black and white-owned newspapers had competing messages. White companies marketed the concept of whiteness to African-American consumers, from skin lighteners to hair straighteners (Gatewood, 2000; Trawick, 2011; Weems, 1998). Black businesses attempted to reframe white beauty ideals for African-American women by marketing hair straighteners and other hair care products. Four African-American entrepreneurs were successful in the beauty and hair care business, Annie Turnbo Malone with Poro College, Madam C. J. Walker with Leila College, Anthony Overton, and Sarah Spencer (Trawick, 2011).

There was more at stake for Black entrepreneurs in the haircare and beauty business than mere profit. They promoted empowerment, self-worth and esteem, financial independence, and economic mobility among African Americans. Annie Turnbo Malone and Madam C. J. Walker are well-renowned for becoming self-made millionaires. Once a sales agent of Poro products, Madam C. J. Walker was second to Malone to acquire this achievement. In the early 19th century, these accomplished Black entrepreneurs were fierce competitors in the profitable haircare market.

Annie Turnbo Malone and Madam C. J. Walker Dominate the Black Market

Madam C. J. Walker marketed the shampoo press and curl of the early 1900s. This straightening method used a hot comb, a metal comb heated on a range-top stove or burner. The comb is pulled through the hair to straighten it. Madame C. J. Walker sold the French-invented hot comb with her haircare products. The Madame C. J. Walker method and comb directly competed with Malone's puller instrument to straighten the hair. Walker argued that Malone's method would thin the hair with prolonged usage (Byrd & Tharps, 2014).

From 1915 to 1930, Malone and Walker paid for advertisements in the Black-owned St. Louis *Argus* newspaper. Less than a handful of Walker's advertising headlines exploited Black stereotypes for increased sales. A headline for a Walker advertisement in September 1922 read, When…But…Now…Madam CJ Walker's Wonderful Hair Grower, Tan-Off—A Safe Scientific Bleach (Trawick, 2011, p. 116). The headline for another Walker advertisement in February 1926 used phrasing such as Black women not wanting bad hair and ugly skin (Trawick, 2011, p. 188). In contrast, Malone did not use Black stereotypes or highlight competing products in her advertisements. Poro products endorsed hair and skin care products and encouraged entrepreneurship amongst the African-American community.

Both women commonly used beauty and beauty in advertisements to promote pride among African-American women (Trawick, 2011). Interestingly, no product advertisements ever condemned or downplayed the significance of straight hair and a light-skinned complexion. They emphasized a need for Black women to groom and style their hair to look presentable (Walker, 2000). Both women wore their hair straightened and curled to reinforce the ideology that natural hair was unacceptable (Byrd & Tharps, 2014; Walker, 2000).

Besides their million-dollar beauty enterprises, Malone and Walker grew educational and entrepreneurial opportunities for African-American women by opening colleges dedicated to training hairstylists and sales agents. These colleges also functioned as company headquarters and manufacturing facilities. Both opened civic organizations to cultivate Blacks' socialization and made considerable charitable contributions to support African Americans (Byrd & Tharps, 2014; Trawick, 2011).

The Rise of the Wig and Hair Extension Industry (1960s-1990s)

In the early 1960s, wigs and hairpieces were in high demand in the United States. European suppliers needed more supplies for U.S. manufacturers to outsource from China. In 1965, the U.S. Treasury Department banned the import of hair from China due to communism. It allowed hair import from Korean suppliers. The Korean wig market became significantly profitable, with wigs becoming a substantial export from South Korea in the late 1960s. In the U.S., the import of wigs from South Korea dominated the market throughout the decade. The Korean Exchange Bank opened a branch in Los Angeles to offer capital to Korean-owned businesses. Most of the banks' investments supported wig businesses. In 1965, Kanekan, a Japanese conglomerate, invented Kanekalon, a synthetic fiber to be an inexpensive substitute for human hair (Chang, 2020, p. 29). This cheap substitute helped South Korea expand from solely a human hair supplier to manufacturing wigs using Kanekalon.

During the 1970s, Korean-owned wig businesses expanded nationally. When white businesses left predominantly Black communities, Koreans purchased storefronts for low prices in these underdeveloped and low-income areas (Chang, 2020; Sapong, 2017). Korean immigrants and Korean Americans worked together to keep the wig industry operating within their community. In the late 1960s and early 1970s, beauty standards shifted to natural hair (i.e., the afro) during the Civil Rights and Black Power era (Chang, 2020; Walker, 2000). The expectation of long, straight hair returned in the mid-1970s. Sales for synthetic wigs skyrocketed as an inexpensive and versatile straight hair option. Black women comprised 40 percent of the spending market for wigs in the United States. In the 1970s and 1980s, Korean-owned hair and beauty supply businesses in the United States continued to grow (Chang, 2020).

During the late 1980s and early 1990s, the Black hair market shifted once again for hair extensions to be in high demand (Sapong, 2017). Shake-N-Go, a Korean manufacturer established in 1991, substantially grew during this time. Today, it is the largest manufacturer of hair extensions, wigs, hairpieces, and hair accessories globally (Sapong, 2017; Shake-N-Go, n.d.). Hair extensions accounted for at least half of the national sales in beauty supply stores. The hair and beauty supply industry continued to be relatively exclusive to Korean Americans, with African Americans encountering several barriers to sustaining a business. Examples of barriers include Korean wholesalers not providing products to African-American retailers and African-American manufactured beauty products not being carried by Korean American retailers.

African-American hair and beauty supply owners are less likely to be offered credit options, installment plans, and lower prices by Korean wholesalers (Chang, 2020). In the past two decades, a few African-American female entrepreneurs broke through barriers to maintain their beauty supply businesses (Chang, 2020; Sapong, 2017). They utilize suppliers in India and China, and owners produce custom-made wigs by hand (Sapong, 2017). Today, Korean Americans operate about 70 percent of the 10,000 beauty supply stores in the United States. The wig and hair extension industry has an estimated value of $6 billion (Sapong, 2017).

The Symbolization of the Afro (1960s to 1970s)

African-American women wore their natural hair to challenge dominant cultural norms, standards, and oppressive power structures in the late 1960s and early 1970s. The afro symbolized power and pride during the Black Power movement. For African-American women, rejecting white beauty standards and social norms was a personal and political decision. In the late 1950s, a small percentage of African-American women wore natural hair. Primarily African-American men, artists, intellectuals, and elite urban trendsetters wore natural hairstyles (Walker, 2000, p. 538). During this time, African-American women continued to wear their hair straightened and curled with the fear of social stigma and rejection if wearing their natural curls. African-American women who took the risk before the afro's popularity received disapproval and rejection from family, friends, and communities.

During the 1960s, the popularity of the afro continued to grow amongst the African-American community, and capitalists took notice. African-American women began to wear their natural hair supporting the Civil Rights movement (Walker, 2000). The styles were common among artists, activists, and those not members of the middle class. The afro was a direct rejection and challenge to negative stereotypes associated with African-American women (e.g., wearing their natural curls meant they were promiscuous) to originate from slavery and continued into the Jim Crow era. The media and fashion industry considered the afro a fad or fashion statement (Walker, 2000). By the late 1960s, the afro was common among Civil Rights activists, college students, actors, musicians, and some professionals.

Black nationalists encouraged African Americans to embrace their kinky curls as a form of Black liberation (Walker, 2000). During this time, there was also the establishment and activism of the Black Panther Party and movement. Black liberation ideology influenced the Black Panther Movement, which challenged sexism and patriarchy and reconceptualized gender roles (Spencer, 2008). African-American women who joined the Black Panther Party wore their natural hair in an afro to symbolize racial consciousness and resistance and redefined Black femininity (Spencer, 2008).

The afro became a divisive political symbol (Donahoo, 2021, p. 22). Black liberation ideology and the Black Panther Party encouraged African-American women to feel beautiful, attractive, and proud of their Blackness (Spencer, 2008; Walker, 2000). Whereas, in American society, the strong, Black woman was a villain. The afro's connection with the women of The Black Panther Party designated the natural hairstyle as threatening, rebellious, disruptive, and anti-white (Donahoo, 2021, p. 22). The Black Panther Party rejected the vilification associated with a Black woman's strength and natural hair. Women of the Black Panther Party personified power in the media and their organization's marketing. They wore afros, carried firearms, engaged in self-defense tactics, were outspoken, and protected the Black community alongside men (Spencer, 2008).

In 1969, the Black beauty industry recorded a 20 to 35 percent decline in sales. The more considerable decline occurred in urban areas such as New York, Chicago, and Los Angeles. The Black beauty industry noticed the afro's profitability in producing afro-specific hair care, styling products, and advertisements for the Black community (Walker, 2000). Black hairstylists soon devised a marketing plan to promote afro hair care and maintenance. The afro still needed grooming and maintenance with products and hairstylists. In the early 1970s, natural hair was young, hip, and trendy (Walker, 2000, p. 551). By the mid-1970s, the popularity of the afro had diminished, and long, straight hair became the new trend (Chang, 2020). There was increased accessibility to chemical straightening products due to lower costs. The societal perceptions and limitations to wearing an afro pressured African-American women to straighten their kinky curls once again. Long, straight hair was attractive, a way to conform, and created opportunities for economic mobility (Donahoo, 2021).

The Natural Haircare Movement in the Early 2000s

The Black haircare market became more lucrative in the 1990s and early 2000s by introducing natural hair care products for African-American women. Before this time, the constant rotation of hair straightening products and wigs to achieve a straight look was in demand. The wig industry was popular into the 1970s and 1980s amongst women of color (Chang, 2020). In the early 1990s, a small group of Black entrepreneurs crafted pioneering products to meet African-American women's growing natural hair care needs—this small group of entrepreneurs of color primarily derived from New York.

Miko and Titi Branch, sisters and cofounders of Miss Jessie's, spent time in their kitchen perfecting their signature product, Curly Pudding, in Brooklyn, New York. Inspiration came from their paternal grandmother's hair care recipes (Easter, 2017; Miss Jessie's Originals, 2021, para 2). In 2004, Miss Jessie's hair care products were on store shelves (Miss Jessie's Originals, 2021, para 1). Lisa Price also established Carol's Daughter in Brooklyn by honing her beauty products in her home. She opened her first Carol's Daughter boutique in 1999 (Carol's Daughter, 2021, para 1).

Between 1991 to 1992, Richelieu Dennis launched a beauty business that would become a million-dollar hair care business. He crafted shea butter products with his mother and close friend in his New York apartment using his African grandmother's hair care and skin recipes (Douglas, 2018; Finley,

2017; Payne & Duster, 2017). An immigrant from Liberia, he sold the initial Shea Moisture products on the streets of New York City (Payne & Duster, 2017). In 2007, his hair care products first appeared at mass retailers. Ten years later, Sundial Brands estimated worth was $700 million (Easter, 2017). With a purpose to empower people to live more beautiful lives, Sundial Brands became the largest Black-owned personal care products company in the United States (Douglas, 2018, para. 4; Finley, 2017). Sundial Brands' hair products included Nubian Heritage, Madame C.J. Walker, and Nyakio. Unilever North America, a global consumer goods company, acquired Sundial Brands in December 2017. With the acquisition, Richelieu Dennis remained the CEO and Executive Chairman. He also ensured the allocation of funding for the New Voices Fund, a fund dedicated to investing in the business ventures of women of color (Finley, 2017).

Between 2011 and 2016, African-American women's purchase of hair relaxers decreased by 30.8 percent (Mintel, as cited in Easter, 2017). Beauty brands known to target white consumers acquired or developed their natural hair care lines to target African-American women. In 1998, L'Oréal purchased the Softsheen product line from Carson Products (Grigsby-Bates, 2014). In 2010, an Indian wellness company, Dubur, purchased Namaste Laboratories, which sold the Organic Root Stimulator products at $100 million. AB Brands created Cantu in 2014 and sold it to PDC Brands in 2015. In 2013, L'Oréal launched Au Naturale and bought Carol's Daughter in 2014 (Easter, 2017; Jerkins, 2017).

Rebranding and Advertisements to Alienate the Black Community

In the past decade, African-American female consumers' distrust of the Shea Moisture and Carol's Daughter brands worsened due to new marketing tactics appealing to whiteness and white consumers (Jerkins, 2017). In 2017, Shea Moisture's #EverybodyGetsLove campaign received national attention due to the backlash from its loyal customers. African-American women were livid to see mostly racially ambiguous women in advertisements. Many customers considered the advertisements offensive, a rejection, and a form of whitewashing. The company officially pulled the advertisements in April 2017 for Richelieu Dennis, CEO, and founder of Shea Moisture and Sundial Brands, to issue a public apology. He emphasized that Shea Moisture products were inclusive to benefit all women. He was transparent about the company's goal to remain successful in a competitive natural hair care market (Payne & Duster, 2017).

Before this public debacle, Shea Moisture was already scrutinized for a Twitter post in 2015. The controversial post featured a white child marketing the Shea Moisture brand. Many of Shea Moisture's African-American female consumers voiced their disapproval and disappointment with the post. A statement released by the company downplayed the post and denied it was an advertisement (Patrice, 2015). A few years before, Carol's Daughter found itself in a similar marketing controversy.

In 2011, Carol's Daughter introduced a new marketing campaign and advertisement to feature several multiethnic celebrities. African-American female consumers were vocal about their dissatisfaction with the ad and questioned the redirection of the brand. Steven Stoute, a Carol's Daughter investor at the time, spoke publicly in support of targeting multiethnic women. We believe we have put together a shoot that celebrates many different ethnicities, to become a mirror of what America's really becoming… They will serve as cultural ambassadors in bringing forth this acceptance that the definition of beauty is now colorless (Jerkins, 2017, para 8). By 2016, Carol's Daughter had grown its distribution with the new brand direction (Jerkins, 2017).

Adverse Health Associated with Black Hair Care Products, Practices, and Hairstyles

Endocrine-Disrupting Chemicals (EDCs) and Hair Care Products

Within the last two decades, a growing body of research (Gaston et al., 2020; Giulivo et al., 2016) has associated endocrine-disrupting chemicals (EDCs) found in hair care products with adverse hormonal processes and mutation (e.g., Evarts & Brown, 1980; Rojanapo et al., 1986). EDCs are mostly man-made, found in various materials such as pesticides, metals, additives or contaminants in food, and personal care products (Monneret, 2017, p. 403). EDCs (e.g., parabens, phenols, and phthalates) harm the body's endocrine system. The endocrine system releases hormones in precise amounts and at critical times to regulate growth, development, reproduction, metabolism, immunity, and mood (Monneret, 2017).

In the United States, African-American women have a higher prevalence of hormonal-related medical conditions and asthma than white women (Helm et al., 2018). The increased exposure to EDCs in hair products may contribute to this health disparity. EDCs are associated with an increased risk of breast cancer (Brinton et al., 2018; Giulivo et al., 2016; Llanos et al., 2017; McDonald et al., 2018), higher incidence of uterine fibroids (Wise et al., 2012), early menarche (James-Todd et al., 2011), obesity, type 2 diabetes (Giulivo et al., 2016), and adverse reproductive health outcomes (Engel et al., 2010; Giulivo et al., 2016; Sathyanarayana et al., 2013; Swan et al., 2005) amongst African-American women. Although, there are studies that do not support the association with uterine fibroids (Pollack et al., 2015; Weuve et al., 2010).

African-American women are more susceptible to exposure to these active chemicals with their significant usage of specific hair products than other racial and ethnic women. African-American women more frequently use hair relaxers, root stimulators, hair oil, and deep hair conditioners (James-Todd et al., 2012; Lewallen et al., 2015; Llanos et al., 2017; Wise et al., 2012). Exposure to these chemicals can occur through absorption in the skin and inhalation (Helm et al., 2018). It can also be transferable in-utero to a fetus (Monneret, 2017).

These chemicals are in hair care products for adults and children. James-Todd et al., (2012) uncovered that 69 percent of the 16 hair products assessed in their study contained placenta or a form of an EDC. Helm et al., (2018) tested 16 hair care products for 66 EDC or asthma-associated chemicals. The products contained 45 chemicals. Hair relaxers, hair lotions, and root stimulators contained nonylphenols, parabens, and fragrances. A fragrance commonly consists of diethyl phthalate (DEP), the most frequent chemical with the highest concentration levels. Hair relaxers for children comprised five chemicals prohibited by EU cosmetics regulators. Additionally, many discovered chemicals were not on the products' labels.

Chemical Straighteners/Hair Relaxers

Sishi et al., (2019) compared the pH levels of adult and children's hair relaxers. Hair relaxers differing in types (e.g., lye versus no lye) and strengths (e.g., regular versus super) shared similar pH levels. Relaxers containing sodium hydroxide had the highest pH levels. Chemicals with high pH levels increase the risk of severe skin and scalp burns, infection, hair breakage, and loss, and deprive the skin and scalp of keratin (i.e., protein) (Sedik et al., 2020; Sishi et al., 2019). A concentration of 0.5 percent sodium hydroxide can irritate the skin and be corrosive at 1 percent. Lithium hydroxide is an active ingredient in children's relaxers, marketed as a safer option, and can irritate the skin at a pH of 9.00 (Sishi et al., 2019).

The relaxers' final pH level, including the petrolatum in the relaxer kits to protect the scalp and skin, was more than 12.00. Compared to household cleaning products, bleach has a pH of about 11.00, and oven and drain cleaners range from 12.00 to 13.00 (Sishi et al., 2019). The literature shows that a healthy skin pH ranges from 4.00 to 6.00 (Proksch, 2018; Sishi et al., 2019). Darker-pigmented individuals, for example, African Americans, can have a lower pH compared to lighter-pigmented people (Proksch, 2018). A neutralizing shampoo is essential in the chemical hair straightening process to lower hair and skin pH levels to a healthier range.

In the study, 84 percent of the sodium hydroxide relaxers and 52 percent of the lithium hydroxide relaxers for adults did not include a neutralizing shampoo. Over a quarter of the children's relaxers did not contain the neutralizer shampoo. Of the relaxers to contain the shampoo, the amount of shampoo was insufficient to wash the hair according to the relaxer's instructions (Sishi et al., 2019). A neutralizing shampoo, which is slightly acidic, is used to close the hair shaft's cuticles after the straightening process. The shampoo has several purposes: maintaining the new formation of the hair fiber, decreasing the scalp's vulnerability to infection, reducing scalp inflammation, and restoring the hair and scalp's natural pH levels (Proksch, 2018; Sedik et al., 2020). According to the Occupational Safety and Health Act (OSHA) standards, all relaxers tested in the study were hazardous and corrosive (Sishi et al., 2019).

Traction Alopecia

Traction Alopecia (TA) is hair loss caused by prolonged hair shaft and follicle tension. The tension can result in permanent loss and damage. This condition impacts about one-third of African-American women and adolescents. The three types of traction alopecia are anterior, ophiasis, and patchy. The anterior is located at the front temporal hairline and is most prevalent among African-American women. For peripheral hairs to remain, an ophiasis pattern is along the posterior and parietal scalp. Everyday hairstyles associated with anterior and ophiasis patterns are up-dos (e.g., buns, ponytails, braids). A patchy pattern is ill-defined areas of decreased density throughout the scalp (Mayo & Callender, 2021, p. 177). Hairstyles, such as locs and specific braid patterns, can cause continuous tension in the same area. The frequent use of hair care products (e.g., hair rollers, clips, and other hair accessories) can also contribute to the problem.

The risk becomes more considerable with relaxed hair (Mayo & Callender, 2021). Relaxed hair has a weakened hair shaft due to the chemical straightener breaking the hair disulfide bond to straighten the strand. Unbeknownst to many, relaxed hair is more fragile than natural hair (Sishi et al., 2019). Natural hair is more prone to dryness and brittleness (Mayo & Callender, 2021). African-American women's repetitive wear of high-tension styles with relaxed hair increases the risk for hair loss and damage. Early warning signs of traction alopecia are pain, redness/irritation of the skin, folliculitis (i.e., braid bumps), or serum crust (i.e., the dried pus when a puss-filled bump ruptures). These early symptoms are reversible. Treatments include topical ointments, antibiotics, or intralesional corticosteroids. Protective and preventative hairstyles are natural and loose, with the recommendation of wigs as a versatile option (Mayo & Callender, 2021).

A Barrier to Physical Activity

African-American women's hairstyles act as a barrier to physical activity. African-American women wearing natural hair are more likely to participate in physical activity (Blackshear & Kilmon, 2020; Hall et al., 2013). Comparably, Joseph et al., (2018) learned that African-American women avoided physical activity related to hair-related concerns. Participants in the study expressed not wanting to sweat to maintain straightened or relaxed hairstyles to prevent the need for restyling. Concerns focused on the cost of restyling the hair and the time to do so. There was also mention of maintaining hairstyles appropriate for work environments. Women felt uncomfortable wearing curly or natural hair. They described their hair texture and hairstyles as a focal point of other racial and ethnic groups to receive unsolicited remarks in the workplace. Some participants felt that straight hairstyles upheld an appropriate image (Joseph et al., 2018).

Hair Discrimination in the 21st-Century Workplace

In the past 40 years, the federal courts have ruled in favor of employers' termination of African-American women for wearing their natural hair in ethnic hairstyles besides the afro (Powell, 2018). Title VII of the Civil Rights Act of 1964 prohibits discrimination based on individual characteristics, including race and gender (U.S. Equal Employment Opportunity Commission, n.d.-b). The U.S. Equal Employment Opportunity Commission (n.d.-a) website states, Race discrimination involves treating someone (an applicant or employee) unfavorably because he/she is of a certain race or because of personal characteristics associated with race (such as hair texture, skin color, or certain facial features) (para 1). Despite this statement, federal courts do not recognize when African-American women are discriminated against for hairstyles and hair textures besides afros, such as braids, twists, locs, and knots (Donahoo, 2021; Powell, 2018).

Hairism is discrimination based on hair. This form of discrimination promotes long, straight, and silky hair to reinforce white beauty standards. Different textures and hairstyles face rejection and scorn in the workplace (Donahoo, 2021). Opie and Phillips (2015) found hairstyle and hair texture more significant than race in determining professionalism and likelihood of success in corporate America for African-American women. Afrocentric hairstyles, such as the afro and locs worn by African-American women, were more frequently perceived as less professional. The individual was also considered less likely to succeed in corporate America. There were no significant differences in perception of professionalism and likelihood of success for white and African-American women with long, straight hair. African Americans were also significantly more critical of African-American women with Afrocentric hairstyles than whites (Opie & Phillips, 2015).

African-American women are more regulated in corporate workplace settings than women of other racial/ethnic groups. African-American women receive the workplace's formal grooming policies more often than white women. African-American women are 3.4 times more likely to have their hair considered unprofessional. Due to hair bias, African-American women are 1.5 times more likely to be sent home from work for hair-related issues. In a recent study, 80 percent of African-American women disclosed changing their hair to fit in at work (The Joy Collective, 2019). The Title VII of the Civil Rights Act of 1964 does not protect African-American women against gendered racial discrimination based on the intersection of their gender and racial constructs, as demonstrated by hairism (Powell, 2018). Kimberlé Crenshaw coined intersectionality to recognize that gender and race were not mutually exclusive. She also found that an intersection of race and gender influenced an African-American woman's experience of antidiscrimination law. . These laws overlooked their experiences with continued marginalization to not protect them (Crenshaw, 1989). The federal courts' failure to recognize hair discrimination sets a precedent for national standards (Powell, 2018).

In 2019, Dove and The Crown coalition, in partnership with Senator Holly J. Mitchell – CA, established The Creating a Respectful and Open World for Natural Hair (CROWN) Act to protect against discrimination based on race-based hairstyles (The Crown Act, n.d.-a, para. 1).

The following states have passed the Crown Act, Arkansas, California, Colorado, Connecticut, Delaware, New York, New Jersey, Maine, Maryland, Massachusetts, Michigan, Minnesota, Virginia, and Washington. Legislation inspired by the Crown Act has passed in the states of Alaska, Illinois, Louisiana, Oregon, New Mexico, Nevada, Nebraska, and Tennessee, (The Crown Act, n.d.-b). The Crown Act provides legal protection for African-American women against implicit bias from employers and work colleagues to create unwelcome and hostile work environments to result in economic loss (Donahoo, 2021).

Conclusion

African-American women's relationship with their kinky curls is one of complexity and survival. Their natural hair texture and expression continue to be policed by societal systems of power to act as a means of bodily control and censorship of authenticity. The intersection of gender and race for African-American women increases their vulnerability to victimization, impacting their physical, mental, and emotional well-being and accumulated wealth. The internalized, deep-rooted guilt and shame associated with the expression of kinky curls are valid and slow to demystify. There is hope with an increasing number of African-American women who reject and reframe stereotypes of Black femininity by wearing their natural curls—additionally, legislation such as The Crown Act combats racism, social injustice, and hair discrimination.

References

Bellinger, W. (2007). Why African-American women try to obtain good hair. *Sociological Viewpoints, 23*, 63-72. https://citeseerx.ist.psu.edu/viewdoc/download?doi=10.1.1.473.1938&rep=rep1&type=pdf.

Berlin, I. (1974). *Slaves without masters: The Free Negro in the antebellum South*. The New Press.

Blackshear, T. B., & Kilmon, K. (2020). Natural hair: A vital component to Black women's health. *Journal of Racial and Ethnic Health Disparities*. https://doi.org/10.1007/s40615-020-00922-4.

Brinton, L. A., Figueroa, J. D., Ansong, D., Nyarko, K. M., Wiae, S., Yarney, J., Biritwum, R., Brotzman, M., Thistle, J. E., Adjei, E., Aitpillah, F., Dedey, F., Edusei, L., Titiloye, N., Awuah, B., Clegg-Lamptey, J. N., Wiafe-Addai, B., & Vanderpuye, V. (2018). Skin lighteners and hair relaxers as risk factors for breast cancer: Results from the Ghana breast health study. *Carcinogenesis, 39*(4), 571-579. https://doi.org/10.1093/carcin/bgy002.

Byrd, A. D., & Tharps, L. L. (2014). *Hair story: Untangling the roots of Black hair in America* [Ebook]. St. Martin's Griffin. (Original work published 2002).

Carol's Daughter (2021). *About us*. https://www.carolsdaughter.com/about-us.html.

Chang, F. B. (2020). *Ethnically segmented markets*. University of Cincinnati College of Law Scholarship and Publications. https://scholarship.law.uc.edu/cgi/viewcontent.cgi?article=1407&context=fac_pubs.

Crenshaw, K. (1989). Demarginalizing the intersection of race and sex: A Black feminist critique of antidiscrimination doctrine, feminist theory, and antiracist politics. *University of Chicago Legal Forum, 1989*(1), 139–167. http://chicagounbound.uchicago.edu/uclf/vol1989/iss1/8.

Donahoo, S. (2021). Why we need a national crown act. *Laws, 10*(2), 1–22. https://doi.org/10.3390/laws10020026.

Douglas, N. (2018). *I'm Richelieu Dennis, owner of Essence and Sundial Brands, and this is how I work.* https://lifehacker.com/im-richelieu-dennis-owner-of-essence-and-sundial-brand-1826418739.

Easter, M. (2017, August 17). Money flowing into the natural hair industry is a blessing and curse for those who built it up. *Los Angeles Times*. https://www.latimes.com/business/la-fi-natural-hair-industry-20170809-htmlstory.html.

Eltis, D., & Richardson, D. (Eds.). (2010). *Atlas of the transatlantic slave trade*. Yale University Press.

Engel, S. M., Miodovnik, A., Canfield, R. L., Zhu, C., Silva, M. J., Calafat, A. M., & Wolff, M. S. (2010). Prenatal phthalate exposure is associated with childhood behavior and executive functioning. *Environmental Health Perspectives, 118*(4), 565-571. https://doi.org/10.1289/ehp.0901470.

Evarts, R. P., & Brown, C. A. (1980). 2,4-diaminoanisole sulfate: Early effect on thyroid gland morphology and late effect on glandular tissue of Fischer 344 rats. *JNCI: Journal of the National Cancer Institute, 65*(7), 197-204. https://doi.org/10.1093/jnci/65.1.197.

Finkelman, P. (2012). Slavery in the United States: Persons or property. In J. Allain (Ed.), *The legal understanding of slavery: From the historical to the contemporary* (pp. 105-134). https://scholarship.law.duke.edu/faculty_scholarship/2709/

Finley, T. (2017, November 28). Unilever to acquire Sundial Brands, the parent company of Shea Moisture. *The Huffington Post*. https://www.huffpost.com/entry/unilever-acquires-sundial-brands-shea-moistures-parent-company_n_5a1d872be4b0714 03b294f6e.

Gaston, S. A., James-Todd, T., Harmon, Q., Taylor, K. W., Baird, D., & Jackson, C. L. (2020). Chemical/straightening and other hair product usage during childhood, adolescence, and adulthood among African-American women: Potential implications for health. *Journal of Exposure Science and Environmental Epidemiology, 30*, 86-96. https://doi.org/10.1038/s41370-019-0186-6.

Gatewood, W. B. (2000). *Aristocrats of color: The Black elite, 1880-1920.* University of Arkansas Press. (Original work published 1991).

Giulivo, M., de Alda, M. L., Capri, E., & Barceló, D. (2016). Human exposure to endocrine disrupting compounds: Their role in reproductive systems, metabolic syndrome, and breast cancer: A review. *Environmental Research, 151*, 251-264. http://dx.doi.org/10.1016/j.envres.2016.07.011.

Grigsby-Bates, K. (2014, October 24). A Black cosmetic company sells or sells out? *NPR: Morning Edition.* https://www.npr.org/sections/codeswitch/2014/10/24/358263731/a-black-cosmetic-company-sells-or-sells-out.

Hall, R. R., Francis, S., Whitt-Glover, M., Loftin-Bell, K., Swett, K., & McMichael, A. J. (2013). Haircare practices as a barrier to physical activity in African-American women. *JAMA Dermatol, 149*(3), 310-314. https://doi.org/10.1001/jamadermatol.2013.1946.

Harris, R. L., Jr. (1981). Charleston's elite and Afro-American elite: The brown fellowship society and the human brotherhood. *The South Carolina Historical Magazine, 82*(4), 289-310. https://www.jstor.org/stable/27567708.

Helm, J. S., Nishioka, M., Green Brody, J., Rudel, R. A., & Dodson, R. E. (2018). Measurement of endocrine disrupting and asthma-associated chemicals in hair products used by Black women. *Environmental Research, 165*, 448–458. https://doi.org/10.1016/j.envres.2018.03.030.

Horowitz, D. L. (1973). Color differentiation in the American system of slavery. *The Journal of Interdisciplinary History, 3*(3), 509-541. https://doi.org/10.2307/202552.

Hunter, M. (2007). The persistent problem of colorism: Skin tone, status, and inequality. *Sociology Compass, 1*(1), 237-254. https://doi.org/10.1111/j.1751-9020.2007.00006.x.

James-Todd, T., Senie, R., & Terry, M. B. (2012). Racial/ethnic differences in hormonally-active hair product use: A plausible risk factor for health disparities. *Journal of Immigrant and Minority Health, 14*, 506–511. https://doi.org/10.1007/s10903-011-9482-5.

James-Todd, T., Terry M. B., Rich-Edwards, J., Deierlein, A., & Senie, R. (2011). Childhood hair product use and earlier age at menarche in a racially diverse study population: A pilot study. *Annals of Epidemiology, 21*(6), 461-465. https://doi.org/10.1016/j.annepidem.2011.01.009.

Jerkins, M. (2017, April 5). The whitewashing of natural hair care lines. *Racked.* https://www.racked.com/2017/4/5/15189534/whitewashing-natural-hair-care-carols-daughter-shea-moisture.

Joseph, R. P., Coe, K., Ainsworth, B. E., Hooker, S. P., Mathis, L., & Keller, C. (2018). Hair as a barrier to physical activity among African-American women: A qualitative exploration. *Frontiers in Public Health, 5*, 1–8. https://doi.org/10.3389/Fpubh.2017.00367.

Lewallen, R., Francis, S., Fisher, B., Richards, J., Li, J., Dawson, T., Swett, K., & McMichael, A. (2015). Haircare practices and structural evaluation of scalp and hair shaft parameters in African American and Caucasian women. *Journal of Cosmetic Dermatology, 14*, 216-223. https://doi.org/10.1111/jocd.12157.

Llanos, A. A. M., Rabkin, A., Bandera, E. V., Zirpoli, G., Gonzalez, B. D., Zing, C. Y., Qin, B., Lin, Y., Hong, C. C., Demissie, K., & Ambrosone, C. B. (2017). Hair product use and breast cancer risk among African American and White women. *Carcinogenesis, 38*(9), 883-892. https://doi.org/10.1093/carcin/bgx060.

Mayo, T. T., & Callender, V. D. (2021). The art of prevention: It's too tight-loosen up and let your hair down. *International Journal of Women's Dermatology, 7*(2), 174–179. https://doi.org/10.1016/j.ijwd.2021.01.019.

McDonald, J. A., Tehranifar, P., Flom, J. D., Terry, M. B., & James-Todd, T. (2018). Hair product use, age at menarche, and mammographic breast density in multiethnic urban women. Environmental Health, 17(1), 1–8. https://doi.org/10.1186/s12940-017-0345-y.

Miss Jessie's Originals (2021). *Who we are.* https://missjessies.com/pages/our-story.

Monneret, C. (2017). What is an endocrine disruptor? *Comptes Rendus Biologies, 340*(9-10), 403–305. https://doi.org/10.1016/j.crvi.2017.07.004.

Opie, T. R., & Phillips, K. W. (2015). Hair penalties: The negative influence of Afrocentric hair on ratings of Black women's dominance and professionalism. *Frontiers in Psychology, 6*, 1–14. https://doi.org/10.3399/fpsyg.2015.01311.

Patrice, C. (2015, February 24). Shea Moisture faces backlash over use of White children in online ad. *BGLH Marketplace*. https://bglh-marketplace.com/2015/02/shea-moisture-faces-backlash-over-use-of-white-children-in-online-ads/.

Payne, A., & Duster, C. R. (2017, April 25). Shea Moisture ad falls flat under back backlash. *NBCBLK.* https://www.nbcnews.com/news/nbcblk/shea-moisture-ad-falls-flat-after-backlash-n750421.

Pollack, A. Z., Buck-Louis, G. M., Chen, Z., Sun, L., Trabert, B., Guo, Y., & Kannan, K. (2015). Bisphenol A, benzophenone-type ultraviolet filters, and phthalates in relation to uterine leiomyoma. *Environmental Research, 137*, 101–107. https://doi.org/10.1016/j.envres.2014.06.028.

Powell, C. (2018). Bias employment discrimination and Black women's hair: Another way forward. *BYU Law Review, 2018*(4), 933–967. https://digitalcommons.law.byu.edu/lawreview/vol2018/iss4/7.

Proksch, E. (2018). pH in nature, humans, and skin. *The Journal of Dermatology, 45*(9), 1044-1052. https://doi.org/10.1111/1346-8138.14489.

Reece, R. L. (2018). Genesis of U.S. colorism and skin tone stratification: Slavery, freedom, and Mulatto-Black occupational inequality in the late 19th century. *The Review of Black Political Economy, 45*(1), 3-21. https://doi.org/10.1177/0034644618770761.

Rojanapo, W., Kupradinum, P., Tepsuwan, A., Chutimataewin, S., & Tanyakaset, M. (1986). Carcinogenicity of oxidation product of p-phenylenediamine. *Carcinogenesis, 7*(12), 1997-2002. https://doi.org/10.1093/carcin/7.12.1997.

Sapong, E. (2017, April 25). Roots of tension: Race, hair, competition, and Black beauty stores. *Minnesota Public Radio.* https://www.mprnews.org/story/2017/04/25/black-beauty-shops-korean-suppliers-roots-of-tension-mn.

Sathyanarayana, S., Barrett, E., Butts, S. F., & Wang, C. W. (2013). Phthalate exposure and reproductive hormone concentrations in pregnancy. *Reproduction, 147*(4), 401–409. http://dx.doi.org/10.1530/REP-13-0415.

Sedik, H. M., Gheida, S. F., Ibrahim, W. M., & Doghaim, N. N. (2020). Effect of hair straightening treatment on porosity and cysteic acid content of hair. *Journal of Advances in Medicine and Medical Research, 32*(18), 91-97. https://doi.org/10.9734/JAMMR/2020/v32i1830661.

Shake-N-Go (n.d.) *About us.* https://www.snghair.com/about-us.

Sishi, V. N., Van-Wyk, J. C., & Khumalo, N. P. (2019). The pH of lye and no-lye hair relaxers, including those advertised for children, is at levels that are corrosive to the skin. *The South African Medical Journal., 109*(12), 941–946. https://doi.org/10.7196/SAMJ.2019.v109i12.14010.

Spencer, R. C. (2008). Engendering the Black freedom struggle: Revolutionary Black womanhood and the Black Panther Party in the bay area, California. *Journal of Women's History, 20*(1), 90–113. https://doi.org/10.1353/jowh.2008.0006.

Swan, S. H., Main, K. M., Liu, F., Stewart, S. L., Kruse, R. L., Calafat, A. M., Mao, C. S., Redmon, J. B., Ternand, C. L., Sullivan, S., & Teague, J. L. (2005). Decrease in anogenital distance among male infants with prenatal phthalates exposure. *Environmental Health Perspectives, 113*(8), 1056–1061. https://doi.org/10.1289/ehp.8100.

The Crown Act (n.d.-a). *Creating a respectful and open world for natural hair.* https://www.thecrownact.com/.

The Crown Act (n.d.-b). *Creating a respectful and open world for natural hair.* https://www.thecrownact.com/about.

The Joy Collective. (2019). Dove: The crown research study. https://static1.squarespace.com/static/5edc69fd622c36173f56651f/t/5edeaa2fe5ddef345e087361/1591650865168/Dove_research_brochure2020_FINAL3.pdf.

The Nielson Company. (2018). *Black impact: Consumer categories where African Americans move markets.* https://www.nielsen.com/us/en/insights/article/2018/black-impact-consumer-categories-where-african-americans-move-markets/.

The Nielson Company. (2020). *Power of the Black community from moment to movement: The African American diverse intelligence series 2020.* https://www.nielsen.com/us/en/insights/report/2020/the-power-of-black-community-from-moment-to-movement/#popupForm.

Trawick, C. V. (2011). *Annie Malone and Poro College: Building an empire of beauty in St. Louis, Missouri, from 1915 to 1950* [Doctoral dissertation, University of Missouri]. University of Missouri Digital Archive. https://doi.org/10.32469/10355/14502.

United States Census Bureau. (1920). *Volume 4. population, 1920. occupations* (41084484v4ch04) [Data set]. United States Census Bureau. http://www2.census.gov/prod2/decennial/documents/41084484v4.zip.

U.S. Equal Employment Opportunity Commission. (n.d.-a). *Race/color discrimination.* https://www.eeoc.gov/racecolor-discrimination.

U.S. Equal Employment Opportunity Commission. (n.d.-b). *Title VII of the Civil Rights Act of 1964.* https://www.eeoc.gov/statutes/title-vii-civil-rights-act-1964h.

Walker, S. (2000). Black is profitable: The commodification of the afro, 1960-1975. *Enterprise & Society, 1*(3), 536-564. https://www.jstor.org/stable/23699596.

Weems, R. E., Jr. (1998). *Desegregating the dollar: African American consumerism in the twentieth century.* New York University Press.

Weuve, J., Hauser, R., Calafat, A. M., Missmer, S. A., & Wise, L. A. (2010). Association of exposure to phthalates with endometriosis and uterine leiomyomata: Findings from NHANES, 1999-2004. 9*Environmental Health Perspectives, 118*(6), 825-832. https://doi.org/10.1289/ehp.0901543.

White, S. L., & White, G. (1995). Slave hair and African American culture in the eighteenth and nineteenth centuries. *The Journal of Southern History, 61*(1), 45-76 https://www.jstor.org/stable/2211360.

Wise, L. A., Palmer, J. R., Reich, D., Cozier, Y. C., & Rosenberg, L. (2012). Hair relaxer use and risk of uterine leiomyomata in African-American women. *American Journal of Epidemiology, 175*(5), 432-440. https://doi.org/10.1093/aje/kwr351.

Part 3. Diagnosing and Treatment Practices

Chapter 7

Mindfulness-Based Stress Reduction as a Treatment for Traumatic Stress for African-American Women

Tiffany R. Williams[1,*]
Paigean Jones[2]
and Chomba Muwele[3]
[1]Psychology, Tennessee State University, Nashville, Tennessee, USA
[2]Social Work, Howard University, Washington, DC, USA
[3]Psychology, Tennessee State University, Nashville, Tennessee, USA

Abstract

Posttraumatic Stress Disorder (PSTD) is highest for African Americans, and African American women are at a higher risk of experiencing at least one traumatic event in their lifetime. African American women are more likely than other women to suffer childhood sexual abuse by a family member (US Department of Justice, 2015). Maternal mortality is highest among African American women, as they are three times more likely to die and two times more likely to experience morbidity than the White woman. With risk factors such as childhood trauma, exposure to violence, and mortality it is imperative for professionals to look at alternatives to stress reduction such as mindfulness-based treatment for post-traumatic stress disorder. This chapter looks at the current statistics and application of mindfulness in treatment.

Keywords: African American women, Black women, trauma, etiology of trauma, mental health, posttraumatic stress disorder, mindfulness

---

* Corresponding Author's Email: twill278@tnstate.edu.

In: How Did We Survive?
Editor: Tina Marie Glover
ISBN: 979-8-88697-918-3

The lifetime prevalence of Posttraumatic Stress Disorder (PSTD) is highest for African Americans, reported at 8.7% compared to 7.0% for Hispanics, 7.4% for Whites, and 4.0% for Asians (Roberts et al., 2011). African American women are at a potentially high risk of experiencing at least one trauma in their lifetime (Meshberg-Cohen et al., 2016). There are several factors that increase African American women's vulnerability to experiencing trauma and to generating a traumatic stress response (Alim et al., 2006;8, 2002; Lacey et al., 2021). As compared to White women, African American women are twice as likely to experience domestic violence, especially women who are between the ages of 20-37 (Green, 2017; Lacey et al., 2021). African American women are more likely than other women to suffer childhood sexual abuse by a family member (US Department of Justice, 2015). Maternal mortality is highest among African American women, as they are three times more likely to die and two times more likely to experience morbidity than White women (Melillo, 2020).

Stigma, cultural mistrust, and other systemic barriers reduce the likelihood that African American women will seek mental health treatment, let alone treatment for trauma (Alvidrez et al., 2008; Roberts et al., 2011). Culturally appropriate and responsive treatments are needed to encourage radical healing (Helms et al., 2012). As there are few practitioners who identify as women of color (5%) and even less psychologists who identify as African American (4%), culturally competent practitioners are essential and needed to foster posttraumatic growth for these women (Richards, n.d.; Woods-Giscombe et al., 2016). Mindfulness-Based Stress Reduction (MBSR) is an evidence-based intervention shown to reduce perceived stress for African Americans (Khoury et al., 2015; Woods-Giscombé et al., 2019). This chapter will begin with a description of the prevalence of trauma, identify risk factors that increase vulnerability to experiencing traumatic stress, highlight common treatments for trauma, and present MBSR as a culturally informed treatment for traumatic stress for African American women.

African American Women and Trauma

The Diagnostic and Statistical Manual of Mental Disorders 5th Edition (DSM-5) specifies the criteria for a diagnosis of PTSD include "exposure to actual or threatened death, serious injury, or sexual violence," physiological reactions, continual distress, emotional and cognitive fluctuations, and avoidance and arousal (American Psychiatric Association, 2013, pp. 271-272). Among

African American women, the prevalence of exposure to violence and history of violence makes these women more susceptible to developing PTSD as well as other comorbid psychological (e.g., depression, substance abuse) or health conditions (e.g., reproductive health, traumatic brain injury; Cimino et al., 2019; Jackson et al., 2017; Sabri & Gielen, 2019). The prevalence of PTSD with the comorbidity of major depressive disorder is reported as higher for African American women than men (Alim et al., 2006).

Risk Factors

Research indicates several risk factors associated with increased vulnerability to traumatic stress for African American women. These factors include, but are not limited to, early childhood trauma, exposure to violence, and racial and gender discrimination. Although discussed separately, the following risk factors are inextricably linked, especially to understanding how they contextually and oppressively impact the overall health and well-being of African American women. Therefore, this section will provide greater insight into describing and highlighting relevant social and systemic issues that inform African American women's experience of trauma and comorbid mental health and health conditions.

Childhood Trauma

Child maltreatment is reported as highest, about 15.3%, for African American children (Roberts et al., 2011). As compared to other racial or minority groups, African American children are twice as likely to experience maltreatment in childhood, girls are more likely than boys to experience sexual assault, and these girls often develop into women who continue to experience higher rates of sexual assault (CDC, 2020). Childhood maltreatment increases risk of experiencing trauma in adulthood (CDC, 2020).

Adverse childhood experiences (ACEs) increase the risk of experiencing trauma in later adulthood (McLaughlin et al., 2017). According to the Centers for Disease Control and Prevention (CDC; 2020), more than half of the adult population experienced at least one ACE in their lifetime, with one-third of those exposed to multiple kinds of ACEs. Girls and various racial and ethnic minority groups are also at greater risk of exposure to ACEs than their counterparts (CDC, 2020). Furthermore, several types of childhood adversities are associated with the increased likelihood of post-traumatic stress development, including physical and sexual abuse, neglect, and parent psychopathology (McLaughlin et al., 2017). These findings support the notion that childhood adversities can cause trauma reactions in children and adolescents and increase their likelihood of experiencing trauma in adulthood.

Childhood maltreatment also includes sexual abuse and assault. One of the more common types of childhood maltreatment experienced by African American children is sexual assault. One in four African American girls is sexually assaulted before the age of 18, with African American girls being more likely to experience sexual assault than boys (DuMonthier et al., 2020). Research further found that the revictimization rates are higher among African American women, suggesting that many of those who experience childhood sexual assault are more likely to be sexually revictimized in adulthood (Orcutt et al., 2005; Relyea & Ullman, 2017; West et al., 2000). Thus, childhood maltreatment is a risk factor that increases African American women's susceptibility to traumatic stress.

Exposure to Violence

The US Department of Justice (2015) report the highest rates of hate crimes (62.7%) are committed toward African Americans. In 2019, 48.5% of African American victims were subjected to hate crimes by perpetrators with Anti-Black or African-American bias (Federal Bureau of Investigation Crime Reporting Program, 2019). Expectedly, African American women experience disproportionately higher levels of violence as compared to women in other racial groups (DuMonthier et al., 2020; Sabri & Gielen, 2019). The violence these women experience occurs in multiple contexts, such as home, school, workplace, and in their neighborhoods. The most common types of violence African American women experience include race-related crimes, intimate partner mistreatment, rape or sexual abuse, and homicide (Cimino et al., 2019). Violence is also experienced systemically, and in the community, through racial profiling, police brutality, and being filtered through the criminal justice system (Jenkins, 2008). African American girls are more likely to be imprisoned in response to school-related incidents (DuMonthier et al., 2020). African American women are twice as likely to be imprisoned as compared to their White counterparts (DuMonthier et al., 2020).

The magnitude of violence African American women experience is tragic and abhorrent. These women experience the highest rates of sexual violence with more than 20% reported being raped in their lifetime (Green, 2017). Four in ten indicate experiencing physical violence, while women of all other racial groups report less (Green, 2017). More than 40% of African American women report victimization from intimate partner violence, which is also more than all other women (DuMonthier et al., 2020). They were almost 3.5 times more likely to be murdered by men than White women in 2018 (Violence Policy Center, 2020). Furthermore, African American women are more likely to be killed by a significant other, spouse, or family member as compared to African American men (Violence Policy Center, 2020). Not only are African American women more likely to be killed by a male who is known to them, but most often the death of the woman follows an argument, and a firearm is used (Violence Policy Center, 2020).

With the highest rates of violence experienced among African American women, there most certainly is an elevated risk of incurring mental health problems (Anderson et al., 2015; Cimino et al., 2019). African American women experience a higher risk of internalizing the psychological consequences of "humiliation, insults, name-calling, and coercive control" resulting from experience of violence (Green, 2017, pp. 1). Exposure to violence generates physical, psychological, and emotional wounds that create a stress response. The manifestation of stress produces a variety of outcomes including traumatic stress, anxiety, depression, and difficulty with focus to name a few (Cimino et al., 2019; Lacey et al., 2021). Furthermore, the effects of direct experiences of violence in conjunction with systemic or community violence, such as the victimization of police brutality on African American women (e.g., advocacy efforts made for the death of Breonna Taylor versus George Floyd) or being inundated with images of racialized violence or sociopolitical messages through technological devices, news outlets, and social media, can generate collective trauma (Donovan & Williams, 2013; Hirschberger 2018). Collective trauma refers to catastrophic events that occur in a society that produce a shared psychological reaction and traumatic memory for a group, or collective (Hirschberger 2018). Experience of multiple types of violence (e.g., intimate partner violence, rape) in conjunction with other oppressive risk factors (e.g., ACES, racial and gender discrimination) increases the risk of comorbid anxiety, mood, and substance disorders as well as physical health complications (e.g., traumatic brain injuries) (Donovan & Williams, 2013; Lacey et al., 2020).

Racial and Gender Discrimination

African American women experience unique stressors associated with the intersectionality and dual stigmatization of their race, gender, and other salient social identities. The mistreatment of African American women is rooted in systemic attitudes and beliefs such as sexism, classism, heterosexism, and racism (Awad et al., 2015). Furthermore, a unique form of oppression experienced by African American women, navigating contexts where the intersection of racism and sexism is prevalent is known as gendered racism (Essed, 1991; Moody & Lewis, 2019; Szymanski & Lewis, 2016; Thomas et al., 2008). African American women endure repeated occurrences of gendered racism, such as gendered racial microaggressions, through the daily demeaning societal messages, prejudices of members within the dominant culture, and racialized and stereotypical gendered images (e.g., Jezebel, Sapphire; Jones & Shorter-Gooden, 2003; Lewis & Neville, 2015).

Gendered racial microaggressions have a positive relationship with traumatic stress (Moody & Lewis, 2019). Though African American women learn to cope with overt and covert micro-and macro-aggressions they experience (Donovan et al., 2012; Sue et al., 2007), these experiences are associated with adverse mental health and several psychological outcomes for African American women. Psychological outcomes associated with gendered racism experienced by African American women include higher levels of psychological distress (King, 2003; Lewis & Neville, 2015; Thomas et al., 2008), depression (Banks et al., 2006; Klonoff et al., 1999), anxiety (Neville & Wright, 2020; Pieterse et al., 2012;), alcohol-related consequences (Blume et al., 2012), and psychiatric symptoms (Klonoff et al., 1999; Pieterse et al., 2012). African American women may also experience higher post-traumatic stress symptoms related to experiences of gendered racial microaggressions (Holder et al., 2009). Therefore, there is a positive correlation between gendered racial microaggressions and traumatic stress for African American women (Moody & Lewis, 2019).

Treatment of Trauma

More than half of all individuals living in the United States are adversely impacted by traumatic events (Powers et al., 2021). Among the most significantly impacted are African Americans, who report up to an 88%

exposure rate to traumatic experiences throughout the course of their lifetime (Blakey & Grocher, 2020; Powers et al., 2021; Stevens-Watkins et al., 2014). African Americans are more likely than their white counterparts to be exposed to traumatic events throughout the course of their lifetime (Blakey & Grocher, 2020; Powers et al., 2021), and experience a 9.1% overall prevalence rate of Posttraumatic Stress Disorder (Williams et al., 2014). African American women, who report up to a 51% lifetime exposure rate to interpersonal traumas such as intimate partner violence, sexual assault, and childhood trauma, are disproportionately impacted by traumatic experiences when compared to other demographics (Blakey & Grocher, 2020; Meshberg-Cohen et al., 2016; Stevens-Watkins et al., 2014).

Research centered on the traumatic experiences of women is limited (Izadi et al., 2020). Studies show that women were less likely to report experiences of trauma, and further, were more likely to minimize traumatic experiences (Izadi et al., 2020). Research on the trauma treatment and experiences of African American women is even further limited, as studies show that African American women are less likely than their white counterparts to seek out mental health services to cope with the impact of traumatic experiences (D. M. Johnson & Zlotnick, 2007; Stevens-Watkins et al., 2014). Culturally relevant treatment modalities are needed to foster radical healing and posttraumatic growth.

Exposure to trauma can contribute to a variety of adverse health outcomes including, but not limited to, depression, anxiety, PTSD, disordered eating, neurological disorders, and increased risk of substance use (Dailey et al., 2011; Harrington et al., 2010; Stevens-Watkins et al., 2014). Additionally, chronic exposure to trauma can contribute to cardiovascular disease, diabetes, and certain cancers, which disproportionately impact African American populations, and African American women in particular (Armour-Burton & Etland, 2020; Blount et al., 2020; Chinn et al., 2021; Cortés & Breathett, 2021; Cummings et al., 2017; Dixon et al., 2020; Stevens-Watkins et al., 2014).

To date, there is not yet research that demonstrates the efficacy of Mindfulness-Based Stress Reduction (MBSR) with African American women exposed to trauma. However, there is some research that demonstrates the utility of MBSR as a culturally responsive evidence-based treatment for African American women. We argue that radical healing and posttraumatic growth can be fostered for these women with a) a strong, affirming, and safe therapeutic alliance, b) a culturally appropriate and comprehensive assessment of their trauma experiences and racial narratives, and c) participation in a structured MBSR program.

Common Treatments

Treatment of trauma for African American women must begin with the practitioner establishing a strong therapeutic alliance that fosters authenticity, affirmation, and openness (Bryant-Davis, 2006; Comas-Díaz, 2016). Practitioners must operate from a culturally competent and sensitive approach when assessing African American women's trauma experiences and stories (Helms et al., 2012). For example, operating from a race-informed trauma approach could empower these women, provide a space for them to share their trauma stories, and inspire critical consciousness, which facilitates radical healing and posttraumatic growth (Comas-Díaz, 2016). A comprehensive assessment must follow to include assessing across five domains: perceived discrimination, sexual abuse histories, family adversity, intimate partner violence, and trauma history (Helms et al., 2012). After assessing and conceptualizing the effects of trauma, the practitioner must utilize culturally appropriate treatments to build and strengthen self-healing capacities, promote self-regulation, and offer trauma symptom relief (Bryant-Davis & Ocampo, 2005; Comas-Díaz, 2016; Helms et al., 2012).

There are a host of evidence-based treatments for trauma including Cognitive Processing Therapy (CPT; Asmundson et al., 2019; Holliday et al., 2017; Schnyder & Cloitre, 2015), Eye Movement Desensitization and Reprocessing (EMDR; Lipscomb & Ashley, 2021; Schnyder & Cloitre, 2015; Solomon et al., 2009), Narrative Exposure Therapy (NET; Mørkved et al., 2014; Schnyder & Cloitre, 2015; Siehl et al., 2021), Brief Eclectic Psychotherapy (de la Rie et al., 2021; Schnyder & Cloitre, 2015), Prolonged Exposure Therapy (Williams et al., 2014), and Complicated Grief Treatment (CGT; Schnyder & Cloitre, 2015; Shear & Gribbin Bloom, 2017). However, there is limited data that addresses the specific ways in which culture, race, and ethnicity may impact the efficacy of these treatment approaches across diverse populations (Lipscomb & Ashley, 2021; McClendon et al., 2020). Evidence suggests that African Americans are less likely to experience a significant reduction in trauma-related symptoms, even when engaging in evidence-based treatment approaches that showed significant reduction in trauma-related symptoms for other demographics (Williams et al., 2014).

Mindfulness-Based Stress Reduction

Mindfulness-Based Stress Reduction (MBSR) is an evidence-based approach developed in 1979, by researcher and mindfulness practitioner, Jon Kabat-Zinn, PhD (Brazier, 2016; Hazlett-Stevens, 2020; Khoury et al., 2015; Pascoe et al., 2017). Rooted in the spiritual teachings of Buddha (Shonin et al., 2016; Van Gordon et al., 2015), MBSR was initially developed as a treatment approach to assist chronic pain patients in cultivating mindfulness-based skills to cope with stressors related to chronic pain and illness (Hazlett-Stevens, 2020).

Traditional MBSR programs are structured as an eight-week intensive course, consisting of approximately 30 hours of instruction time (Hazlett-Stevens, 2020; Khoury et al., 2015; Kilpatrick et al., 2011). Over the course of eight weeks, participants attend weekly sessions, which can last up to 150 minutes per session, where they are taught, and engage, in mindfulness-based skills such as meditation, breathwork, body scans, and yoga postures (Duncan & Bardacke, 2010; Pascoe et al., 2017). Additionally, participants engage in weekly homework assignments to continue to cultivate a personal formal, and informal mindfulness-based practice (Duncan & Bardacke, 2010).

Mindfulness-based interventions have been shown to be effective in the treatment of a variety of conditions, including chronic stress, anxiety, and depression (Brooks et al., 2021; Pascoe et al., 2017; Perlini et al., 2020; Shonin et al., 2016), as well as substance abuse, eating disorders, diabetes, binge eating, insomnia, cancer, arthritis, and heart disease, etc. (Cifu et al., 2018; C. C. Johnson et al., 2018; Rosenbaum, 2014; Woods-Giscombé & Black, 2010). Emerging research also indicates that mindfulness may be effective in restructuring the brain, physically and chemically, in order to alleviate symptoms caused by chronic stress, depression, and anxiety (Grecucci et al., 2015; Jinich-Diamant et al., 2020; Kilpatrick et al., 2011).

Studies that have incorporated mindfulness interventions with African American populations have been limited (Berger, 2018; Park et al., 2015; Tenfelde et al., 2018). This research is even further limited when seeking studies centered on African American women. According to the literature on the coping skills of African American women, African American women are likely to engage in Africultural Coping Strategies (ACS) as a first line of defense for stress management (Morrison & Hopkins, 2019; Watson-Singleton et al., 2020). ACS include behaviors such as seeking social support from friends, relatives, and church communities, etc. (Donovan & Williams, 2013; Graham, 2016), collective coping, such as engaging in social activism, joining community and raced based organizations, and engaging in policy-making activities (Graham, 2016; Liao et al., 2020), engaging in avoidance oriented strategies, such as ignoring the stressor or choosing not to respond to stressors (Hall, 2018; Jones et al., 2020; Lewis et al., 2017), and most significantly, engaging in religious and spiritual coping strategies, such as attending church, prayer, meditation, and engaging in collective coping with church family (Lewis et al., 2017; Spates et al., 2020; Stevens-Watkins et al., 2014).

Spirituality and religious coping skills practiced by African American women can be characterized as mindfulness techniques (Graham, 2016; Stevens-Watkins et al., 2014). Spiritual and religious practices include the creation of rituals, meditation, prayer, internalization of personal values, acceptance of the present moment, and resilience in the face of adversity, through spiritual teaching (Stevens-Watkins et al., 2014). Spirituality and religion are associated with improved overall well-being, as well as a reduction in symptoms of depression, anxiety, and PTSD (Spates et al., 2020; Stevens-Watkins et al., 2014), and these results are typical in mindfulness-based studies. African American participants in prior mindfulness-based studies noted that a barrier to participation in mindfulness was a lack of cultural relevance (Tenfelde et al., 2018; Zhang, 2013). Researchers and clinicians may foster cultural competence and relevance in mindfulness by appealing to the present spiritual and religious practices of African American women, through the incorporation of prayer, scripture, and other religious rituals into traditional mindfulness-based practices (Tenfelde et al., 2018).

In conclusion, African American women are at a particularly high risk of experiencing traumatic stress. Risk factors identified that increase their vulnerability to traumatic stress include child maltreatment, exposure to and victimization to violence, and racial and gender discrimination as well as other oppressive factors not mentioned. Comorbidity of mental health (e.g., anxiety, depression) and health (e.g., traumatic brain injury) conditions further complicate these women's quality of life. African American women are less inclined to seek help and when they do they face barriers (e.g., cultural mistrust, stigma, gendered racism) that hinder their healing and treatment progress. It is vital that clinicians are culturally competent and sensitive. They must provide safe, validating, and affirming therapeutic spaces and need to be comfortable with encouraging African American women to share their trauma events and racial narratives. A thorough assessment of trauma experiences, racial stories, systemic barriers, experiences of violence, and these factors' connection to mental health outcomes is necessary. Additionally, culturally appropriate interventions, such as MBSR, can be used to foster radical healing and encourage posttraumatic growth for African American women experiencing traumatic stress.

References

Alim, T. N., Charney, D. S., & Mellman, T. A. (2006). An overview of Posttraumatic Stress Disorder in African Americans. *Journal of Clinical Psychology, 62*(7), 801-813. https://doi.org/10.1002/jclp.20280.

Alvidrez, J., Snowden, L. R., & Kaiser, D. M. (2008). The experience of stigma among Black mental health consumers. *Journal of Health Care Poor Underserved, 19*(3), 874-893. https://doi.org/10.1353/hpu.0.0058.

Armour-Burton, T. & Etland, C. (2020). Black feminist thought: A paradigm to examine breast cancer disparities. *Nursing Research, 69*(4), 272-279. https://doi.org/10.1097/NNR.0000000000000426.

Asmundson, G. J. G., Thorisdottir, A. S., Roden-Foreman, J. W., Baird, S. O., Witcraft, S. M., Stein, A. T., Smits, J. A. J., & Powers, M. B. (2019). A meta-analytic review of cognitive processing therapy for adults with posttraumatic stress disorder. *Cognitive Behaviour Therapy*, *48*(1), 1–14. https://doi.org/10.1080/16506073.2018.1522371.

Awad, G. H., Norwood, C., Taylor, D. S., Martinez, M., McClain, S., Jones, B., Holman, A., & Chapman-Hilliard, C. (2015). Beauty and Body Image Concerns Among African American College Women. *The Journal of Black Psychology, 41*(6), 540–564. https://doi.org/10.1177/0095798414550864.

Barlow, J. N. (2020, February). Black women, the forgotten survivors of sexual assault. African American women are at disproportionate risk of sexual violence. Here's how you can help. *American Psychological Association: Public Interest.* http://www.apa.org/pi/about/newsletter/2020/02/black-women-sexual-assault.

Berger, M. T. (2018). I do practice yoga! Controlling images and recovering the Black female body in 'skinny White girl' yoga culture. *UC Berkeley: Race & Yoga, 3*(1), 31-49. https://doi.org/10.5070/R331034199.

Blakey, J. M. & Grocher, K. B. (2020). "Keeping it real": The relational effects of trauma among African American women and their substance abuse treatment counselors. *Journal of Interpersonal Violence*, *35*(17–18), 3405–3436. https://doi.org/10.1177/0886260517708403.

Blount, L., Boyd, T., Owens, S., & Revelle, J. (2020, October). Black women vote: National health policy agenda 2020-2021. *Black Women's Health Imperative.* https://3hqwxl1mqiah5r73r2q7zll1-wpengine.netdna-ssl.com/wp-content/uploads/2021/01/BWHI_NHPA_2020-21.pdf.

Brazier, D. (2016). Mindfulness: Traditional and Utilitarian. In R. E. Purser, D. Forbes, & A. Burke (Eds.), *Handbook of mindfulness* (pp. 63–74). Oakland, CA: Springer International Publishing. https://doi.org/10.1007/978-3-319-44019-4_5.

Brooks, J. R., Lebeaut, A., Zegel, M., Walker, R. L., & Vujanovic, A. A. (2021). Anxiety sensitivity and suicide risk: Mindfulness as a psychological buffer for Black adults.

Journal of Affective Disorders, *289*(15), 74–80. https://doi.org/10.1016/j.jad.2021.04.012.

Centers for Disease Control and Prevention (2019). *Preventing Adverse Childhood Experiences: Leveraging the Best Available Evidence.* Atlanta, GA: National Center for Injury Prevention and Control, Centers for Disease Control and Prevention https://www.cdc.gov/violenceprevention/pdf/preventingACES.pdf.

Chinn, J. J., Martin, I. K., & Redmond, N. (2021). Health equity among Black women in the United States. *Journal of Women's Health*, *30*(2), 212–219. https://doi.org/10.1089/jwh.2020.8868.

Cifu, G., Power, M. C., Shomstein, S., & Arem, H. (2018). Mindfulness-based interventions and cognitive function among breast cancer survivors: A systematic review. *BMC Cancer*, *18*(1), 1163. https://doi.org/10.1186/s12885-018-5065-3.

Cimino, A. N., Yi, G., Patch, M., Alter, Y., Campbell, J. C., Gundersen, K. K., Tang, J. T., Tsuyuki K., & Stockman, J. K. (2019). The effect of intimate partner violence and probable traumatic brain injury on mental health outcomes for Black women. *Journal of Aggression, Maltreatment, & Trauma, 28*(6), 714-731. https://doi.org/10.1080/10926771.2019.1587657.

Cortés, Y. I., & Breathett, K. (2021). Addressing inequities in cardiovascular disease and maternal health in Black women. *Circulation: Cardiovascular Quality and Outcomes*, *14*(2). https://doi.org/10.1161/CIRCOUTCOMES.121.007742.

Cummings, D. M., Lutes, L. D., Littlewood, K., Solar, C., Hambidge, B., & Gatlin, P. (2017). Impact of distress reduction on behavioral correlates and a1c in African American women with uncontrolled type 2 diabetes: Results from EMPOWER. *Ethnicity & Disease*, *27*(2), 155-160. https://doi.org/10.18865/ed.27.2.155.

Dailey, D. E., Humphreys, J. C., Rankin, S. H., & Lee, K. A. (2011). An exploration of lifetime trauma exposure in pregnant low-income African American women. *Maternal & Child Health Journal*, *15*(3), 410–418. https://doi.org/10.1007/s10995-008-0315-7.

de la Rie, S. M., van Sint Fiet, A., Bos, J. B. A., Mooren, N., Smid, G., & Gersons, B. P. R. (2021). Brief Eclectic Psychotherapy for Moral Trauma (BEP-MT): Treatment protocol description and a case study. *European Journal of Psychotraumatology*, *12*(1), 1929026. https://doi.org/10.1080/20008198.2021.1929026.

Dixon, H. D., Michopoulos, V., Gluck, R. L., Mendoza, H., Munoz, A. P., Wilson, J. G., Powers, A., Schwartz, A. C., Umpierrez, G. E., & Gillespie, C. F. (2020). Trauma exposure and stress-related disorders in African-American women with diabetes mellitus. *Endocrinology, Diabetes & Metabolism*, *3*(2), e00111. https://doi.org/10.1002/edm2.111.

Donovan, R. & Williams, M. (2013). Living at the intersection: The effects of racism and sexism on Black rape survivors. In C. M. West (Eds.), *Violence in the lives of Black women: Battered, black, and blue*. New York, NY: Routledge.

DuMonthier, A., Childers, C., Milli, J. (2020). *The status of Black women in the United States: Executive Summary.* https://iwpr.org/iwpr-issues/race-ethnicity-gender-and-economy/the-status-of-black-women-in-the-united-states/.

Duncan, L. G., & Bardacke, N. (2010). Mindfulness-based childbirth and parenting education: Promoting family mindfulness during the perinatal period. *Journal of Child and Family Studies*, *19*(2), 190–202. https://doi.org/10.1007/s10826-009-9313-7.

Essed, P. (1991). *Understanding everyday racism: An interdisciplinary theory*. Thousand Oaks, CA: Sage.

Federal Bureau of Investigation Uniform Crime Reporting. (2019). *Hate Crimes Statistics*. https://ucr.fbi.gov/hate-crime/2019.

Federal Bureau of Investigation Uniform Crime Reporting. (2015). *Hate Crimes Statistics*. https://ucr.fbi.gov/hate-crime/2015.

Graham, A. (2016). Womanist preservation: An analysis of Black Women 's spiritual coping. *International Journal of Transpersonal Studies*, *35*(1), 106–117. https://doi.org/10.24972/ijts.2016.35.1.106.

Green, S. (2017, July 13). *Violence against Black women, many types, far reaching effects*. https://iwpr.org/iwpr-issues/race-ethnicity-gender-and-economy/violence-against-black-women-many-types-far-reaching-effects/.

Grecucci, A., Pappaianni, E., Siugzdaite, R., Theuninck, A., & Job, R. (2015). Mindful emotion regulation: Exploring the neurocognitive mechanisms behind mindfulness. *BioMed Research International*, *2015*, 1–9. https://doi.org/10.1155/2015/670724.

Hall, J. C. (2018). It is tough being a Black woman: Intergenerational stress and coping. *Journal of Black Studies*, *49*(5), 481–501. https://doi.org/10.1177/0021934718766817.

Harrington, E. F., Crowther, J. H., & Shipherd, J. C. (2010). Trauma, binge eating, and the "Strong Black woman." *Journal of Consulting and Clinical Psychology*, *78*(4), 469–479. https://doi.org/10.1037/a0019174.

Hazlett-Stevens, H. (2020). Mindfulness-based stress reduction for health care staff: Expanding holistic nursing paradigms to the whole system. *Holistic Nursing Practice*, *34*(5), 301-305. https://doi.org/10.1097/HNP.0000000000000404.

Hirschberger, G. (2018). Collective trauma and social construction of meaning. *Frontiers in Psychology, 9,* 1-14. https://doi.org/10.3389/fpsyg.2018.01441.

Holliday, R. P., Holder, N. D., Williamson, M. L. C., & Surís, A. (2017). Therapeutic response to Cognitive Processing Therapy in White and Black female veterans with military sexual trauma-related PTSD. *Cognitive Behaviour Therapy*, *46*(5), 432–446. https://doi.org/10.1080/16506073.2017.1312511.

Jenkins, E. J. (2008). Black women and community violence: Trauma, grief, and coping. *Women & Therapy, 25*(3-4), 29-44. https://doi.org/10.1300/J015v25n03_03.

Jinich-Diamant, A., Garland, E., Baumgartner, J., Gonzalez, N., Riegner, G., Birenbaum, J., Case, L., & Zeidan, F. (2020). Neurophysiological mechanisms supporting mindfulness meditation–based pain relief: An updated review. *Current Pain and Headache Reports*, *24*(10), 56. https://doi.org/10.1007/s11916-020-00890-8.

Johnson, C. C., Sheffield, K. M., & Brown, R. E. (2018). Mind-body therapies for African American women at risk for cardiometabolic disease: A systematic review. *Evidence Based Complementary and Alternative Medicine*, *2018*, 1–11. https://doi.org/10.1155/2018/5123217.

Johnson, D. M. & Zlotnick, C. (2007). Utilization of mental health treatment and other services by battered women in shelters. *Psychiatric Services*, *58*(12), 1595-1597.

Jones, S. C. T., Anderson, R. E., Gaskin-Wasson, A. L., Sawyer, B. A., Applewhite, K., &Metzger, I. W. (2020). From "crib to coffin": Navigating coping from racism-related stress throughout the lifespan of Black Americans. *American Journal of Orthopsychiatry, 90*(2), 267–282. https://doi.org/10.1037/ort0000430.

Jones, C., Shorter-Gooden, K. (2003). *Shifting: The double lives of Black women in America.* New York, NY: HarperCollins.

Khoury, B., Sharma, M., Rush, S. E., & Fournier, C. (2015). Mindfulness-based stress reduction or healthy individuals: A meta-analysis. *Journal of Psychosomatic Research, 78*(6), 519-528. https://doi.org/10.1016/j.jpsychores.2015.03.009.

Kilpatrick, L. A., Suyenobu, B. Y., Smith, S. R., Bueller, J. A., Goodman, T., Creswell, J. D., Tillisch, K., Mayer, E. A., & Naliboff, B. D. (2011). Impact of mindfulness-based stress reduction training on intrinsic brain connectivity. *NeuroImage, 56*(1), 290–298. https://doi.org/10.1016/j.neuroimage.2011.02.034.

King, K. R. (2003). Racism or sexism? Attributional ambiguity and simultaneous membership inmultiple oppressed groups. *Journal of Applied Social Psychology, 33*(2), 223–247. https://doi.org/10.1111/j.1559-1816.2003.tb01894.x.

Lacey, K. K., Mouzon, D. M., Parnell, R. N. & Lawson, T. (2021). Severe intimate partner violence, sources of stress and the mental health of U.S. Black women. *Journal of Women's Health, 30*(1), 17-28. https://doi.org/10.1089/jwh.2019.8215.

Lewis, J. A., Williams, M. G., Peppers, E. J., & Gadson, C. A. (2017). Applying intersectionality to explore the relations between gendered racism and health among Black women. *Journal of Counseling Psychology, 64*(5), 475–486. https://doi.org/10.1037/cou0000231.

Lewis, J. A., Neville, H. A. (2015). Construction and initial validation of the Gendered Racial Microaggressions Scale for Black women. *Journal of Counseling Psychology, 62*(2), 289-302. doi:10.1037/cou0000062.

Liao, K. Y.-H., Wei, M., & Yin, M. (2020). the misunderstood schema of the Strong Black Woman: Exploring its mental health consequences and coping responses among African American women. *Psychology of Women Quarterly, 44*(1), 84–104. https://doi.org/10.1177/0361684319883198.

Lipscomb, A., & Ashley, W. (2021). A critical analysis of the Utilization of Eye Movement Desensitization and Reprocessing (EMDR) psychotherapy with *African American clients. Journal of Human Services: Training, Research, and Practice, 7*(1). Article 3. https://scholarworks.sfasu.edu/jhstrp/vol7/iss1/37, 17.

McClendon, J., Dean, K. E., & Galovski, T. (2020). Addressing diversity in PTSD treatment: disparities in treatment engagement and outcome among patients of color. *Current Treatment Options in Psychiatry, 7*(3), 275–290. https://doi.org/10.1007/s40501-020-00212-0.

McLaughlin, K., Koenen, K., Bromet, E., Karam, E., Liu, H., Petukhova, M., ... Kessler, R. (2017). Childhood adversities and post-traumatic stress disorder: Evidence for stress sensitization in the World Mental Health Surveys. *British Journal of Psychiatry, 21*(5), 280-288. doi:10.1192/bjp.bp.116.197640.

Melillo, G. (2020). Racial disparities persist in maternal morbidity, mortality and infant health. *American Journal of Managed Care.* https://www.ajmc.com/view/racial-disparities-persist-in-maternal-morbidity-mortality-and-infant-health.

Meshberg-Cohen, S., Presseau, C., Thacker, L. R., Hefner, K., & Svikis, D. (2016). Posttraumatic Stress Disorder, health problems, and depression among African

American women in residential substance use treatment. *Journal of Women's Health, 25*(7), 729-737. https://doi.org/10.1089/jwh.2015.5328.

Mørkved, N., Hartmann, K., Aarsheim, L. M., Holen, D., Milde, A. M., Bomyea, J., & Thorp, S. R. (2014). A comparison of Narrative Exposure therapy and Prolonged Exposure therapy for PTSD. *Clinical Psychology Review, 34*(6), 453–467. https://doi.org/10.1016/j.cpr.2014.06.005.

Moody, A. T., & Lewis, J. A. (2019). Gendered Racial Microaggressions and traumatic stress symptoms among Black women. *Psychology of Women Quarterly, 43*(2), 201–214. https://doi.org/10.1177/0361684319828288.

Morrison, K. S., & Hopkins, R. (2019). Cultural identity, africultural coping strategies, anddepression as predictors of suicidal ideations and attempts among African American female college students. *Journal of Black Psychology, 45*(1), 3–25. https://doi.org/10.1177/0095798418813511.

Orcutt, H. K., Cooper, M. L., & Garcia, M. (2005). Use of sexual intercourse to reduce negative affect as a prospective mediator of sexual revictimization. *Journal of traumatic stress, 18*(6), 729–739. https://doi.org/10.1002/jts.20081.

Park, C. L., Braun, T., & Siegel, T. (2015). Who practices yoga? A systematic review of emographic, health-related, and psychosocial factors associated with yoga practice. *Journal of Behavioral Medicine, 38*(3), 460–471. https://doi.org/10.1007/s10865-015-9618-5.

Pascoe, M. C., Thompson, D. R., & Ski, C. F. (2017). Yoga, mindfulness-based stress reduction and stress-related physiological measures: A meta-analysis. *Psychoneuroendocrinology, 86,* 152–168. https://doi.org/10.1016/j.psyneuen.2017.08.008.

Perlini, C., Bellani, M., Rossetti, M. G., Rossin, G., Zovetti, N., Rossi, A., Bressi, C., Piccolo, L. D., & Brambilla, P. (2020). Mindfulness-based interventions in the early phase of affective and non-affective psychoses. *Journal of Affective Disorders, 263,* 747–753. https://doi.org/10.1016/j.jad.2019.10.011.

Powers, A., Mekawi, Y., Fickenwirth, M., Nugent, N. R., Dixon, H. D., Minton, S., Kim, Y. J., Gluck, R., Carter, S., Fani, N., Schwartz, A. C., Bradley, B., Umpierrez, G. E., Pace, T. W. W., Jovanovic, T., Michopoulos, V., & Gillespie, C. F. (2021). Emotion dysregulation and dissociation contribute to decreased heart rate variability to an acute psychosocial stressor in trauma-exposed Black women. *Journal of Psychiatric Research, 142*, 125-131. https://doi.org/10.1016/j.jpsychires.2021.07.032.

Relyea, M., & Ullman, S. E. (2017). Predicting sexual assault revictimization in a longitudinal sample of women survivors: Variation by type of assault. *Violence Against Women, 23*(12), 1462–1483. https://doi.org/10.1177/1077801216661035.

Richards, E. M. (n.d.). *Mental health among African American women.* https://www.hopkinsmedicine.org/health/wellness-and-prevention/mental-health-among-african-american-women.

Roberts, A. L., Gilman, S. E., Breslau, J., Breslau, N., & Koenen, K. C. (2011). Race/ethnic differences in exposure to traumatic events, development of post-traumatic stress disorder, and treatment-seeking for post-traumatic stress disorder in the United States. *Psychological Medicine, 41*(1), 71–83. https://doi.org/10.1017/S0033291710000401.

Rosenbaum, E. (2014). Mindfulness--Based Stress Reduction and social work. In *Mindfulness and acceptance in social work: Evidence-based interventions and emerging applications* (p. 26). Augusta, GA: Context Press.

Sabri, B. & Gielen, A. (2019). Integrated multicomponent interventions for safety and health risks among Black female survivors of violence: A systematic review. *Trauma Violence Abuse, 20*(5), 720-731. https://doi.org/10.1177/1524838017730647.

Schnyder, U., & Cloitre, M. (Eds.). (2015). *Evidence Based Treatments for Trauma-Related Psychological Disorders: A practical guide for clinicians*. New York, NY: Springer International Publishing. https://doi.org/10.1007/978-3-319-07109-1.

Shear, M. K., & Gribbin Bloom, C. (2017). Complicated Grief Treatment: An Evidence-Based Approach to Grief Therapy. *Journal of Rational-Emotive & Cognitive-Behavior Therapy, 35*(1), 6–25. https://doi.org/10.1007/s10942-016-0242-2.

Shonin, E., Van Gordon, W., & Singh, N. N. (2015). *Buddhist foundations of mindfulness* (1st ed.). Oakland, CA: Springer International Publishing.

Siehl, S., Robjant, K., & Crombach, A. (2021). Systematic review and meta-analyses of the long-term efficacy of narrative exposure therapy for adults, children and perpetrators. *Psychotherapy Research, 31*(6), 695–710. https://doi.org/10.1080/10503307.2020.1847345.

Solomon, E. P., Solomon, R. M., & Heide, K. M. (2009). EMDR: An evidence-based treatment for victims of trauma. *Victims & Offenders, 4*(4), 391–397. https://doi.org/10.1080/15564880903227495.

Spates, K., Evans, N. M., Watts, B. C., Abubakar, N., & James, T. (2020). Keeping ourselves sane: a qualitative exploration of Black women's coping strategies for gendered racism. *Sex Roles, 82*(9–10), 513–524. https://doi.org/10.1007/s11199-019-01077-1.

Stevens-Watkins, D., Sharma, S., Knighton, J. S., Oser, C. B., & Leukefeld, C. G. (2014). Examining cultural correlates of active coping among African American female trauma survivors. *Psychological Trauma: Theory, Research, Practice, and Policy, 6*(4), 328-336. https://doi.org/10.1037/a0034116.

Szymanski, D. M., & Lewis, J. A. (2016). Gendered racism, coping, identity centrality, and African American college women's psychological distress. *Psychology of Women Quarterly, 40*(2), 229–243. https://doi.org/10.1177/0361684315616113.

Pieterse, A. L., Todd, N. R., Neville, H. A., Carter, R. T. (2012). Perceived racism and mental health among Black American adults: A meta-analytic review. *Journal of Counseling Psychology, 59*(1), 1–9. doi:10.1037/a0026208.

Sue, D. W., Capodilupo, C. M., Torino, G. C., Bucceri, J. M., Holder, A. M., Nadal, K. L., & Esquilin, M. (2007). Racial microaggressions in everyday life: implications for clinical practice. *The American Psychologist, 62*(4), 271–286. https://doi.org/10.1037/0003-066X.62.4.271.

Tenfelde, S. M., Hatchett, L., & Saban, K. L. (2018). "Maybe Black girls do yoga": A focus group study with predominantly low-income African-American women. *Complementary Therapies in Medicine, 40*, 230–235. https://doi.org/10.1016/j.ctim.2017.11.017.

Thomas, A. J., Witherspoon, K. M., Speight, S. L. (2008). Gendered racism, psychological distress, and coping styles of African American women. *Cultural Diversity & Ethnic Minority Psychology, 14*(4), 307–314. doi:10.1037/1099-9809.14.4.307.

Van Gordon, W., Shonin, E., Griffiths, M. D., & Singh, N. N. (2015). Mindfulness and the Four Noble Truths. In E. Shonin, W. Van Gordon, & N. N. Singh (Eds.), *Buddhist Foundations of Mindfulness* (pp. 9–27). Oakland, CA: Springer International Publishing. https://doi.org/10.1007/978-3-319-18591-0_2.

Violence Policy Center (2020). *When men murder women: An analysis of 2018 homicide data*. https://vpc.org.

Watson-Singleton, N. N., LoParo, D., Mekawi, Y., Hampton-Anderson, J. N., & Kaslow, N. J. (2020). Africultural Coping Systems Inventory: Psychometrics in a clinical sample of African American women. *Journal of Black Psychology*, *46*(6–7), 457–481. https://doi.org/10.1177/0095798420957503.

West, C. M., Williams, L. M., & Siegel, J. A. (2000). Adult sexual revictimization among black women sexually abused in childhood: A prospective examination of serious consequences of abuse. *Child Maltreatment, 5*(1), 49–57. https://doi.org/10.1177/1077559500005001006.

Williams, M., Malcoun, E., Sawyer, B., Davis, D., Nouri, L., & Bruce, S. (2014). Cultural adaptations of Prolonged Exposure Therapy for treatment and prevention of Posttraumatic Stress Disorder in African Americans. *Behavioral Sciences*, *4*(2), 102–124. https://doi.org/10.3390/bs4020102.

Woods-Giscombé, C. L., & Black, A. R. (2010). Mind-body interventions to reduce risk for health disparities related to stress and strength among African American women: The potential of mindfulness-based stress reduction, loving-kindness, and the NTU therapeutic framework. *Complementary Health Practice Review, 15*(3), 115–131. https://doi.org/10.1177/1533210110386776.

Woods, K. C., Buchanan, N. T., Settles, I. H. (2009). Sexual harassment across the color line: Experiences and outcomes of cross versus intraracial sexual harassment among Blackwomen. *Cultural Diversity & Ethnic Minority Psychology, 15*(1), 67–76. https://doi.org/10.1037/a0013541.

Zhang, H., & Emory. (2015). A Mindfulness-based intervention for pregnant African American women. *Mindfulness, 6,* 663–674. https://doi.org/10.1007/s12671-014-0304-4.

Chapter 8

Misdiagnosing and Underdiagnosing African-American Women: Implications for Trauma-Informed Care

Theresa Libios*
Doctoral Candidate, Walden University, Minneapolis, Minnesota, USA

Abstract

This chapter aims to shed light on misdiagnosing and underdiagnosing African American women. This is not a new phenomenon though it is understudied and unchallenged. Research suggests that mental health disparities exist with little success in closing the disparity gap. Mechanisms to close the disparity in understanding the attributing factors that influence barriers and causation of misdiagnosing and underdiagnosing (McGuire & Miranda, 2008). Clinician stereotyping impels minimizing symptoms and an inability to perceive the effects of the intersectionality of gender, race, and trauma. Because the unique symptomatology of African American women's interventions should resemble a trauma-informed approach focused on cultural experiences and Adverse Childhood Experiences (ACEs; CDC, 2021a). ACEs explore the longitudinal effects of childhood trauma impacting adults' mental and physical health. Hunn and Craig (2009) argued that challenging life events impact psychological health leading to depression in African American women, and the absence of culturally sensitive assessments contributes to misdiagnoses and underdiagnosing implications. This chapter further proposes best practices for assessing and gauging the mental health of African American women by conceptualizing historical, sociocultural, and individual traumatic experiences.

* Corresponding Author's Email: theresalibios@gmail.com.

In: How Did We Survive?
Editor: Tina Marie Glover
ISBN: 979-8-88697-918-3

Keywords: African American women, Black women, trauma, mental health, counseling, underdiagnosed

Assertive Black Women: Shouldering the World

To understand the phenomena, we must take a step back to view the origins and contributing factors of misdiagnosing and underdiagnosing African American women. Historically the role of African American women has been complicated by unrealistic stereotypes. The colloquial phrase "Strong Black Woman" alludes to power, strength, and endurance. The characterization that African American women shoulder the world implies independence and emotionlessness. African American women are seen as strong black women, holding them to perfection with unwavering strength. The "strong black woman" persona holds everyone up, takes the caregiver role for family, community, and friends, and supports social change efforts (Liao et al., 2020). This stereotype leaves no room for weakness, illness, or self-care. The responsibility of such a schema is compounded with gender, racism, and the conceptualization that African American women are void of mental illnesses, needing help, and feeling pain. Where did this "perceived indestructible nature" originate?

Historical Beginnings

Historical doctrine offers a glimpse of how African American women were devalued as slave shows yet valued as strongly as their African American male counterparts. Distinguished as physically more robust and psychologically more tenacious than White women endorsed the rationalization for their treatment (Harris-Lacewell, 2001). Treatment has spiraled from generation to generation. African American women have shouldered child-rearing for their slave owners while witnessing their children and family being sold, never to see them again. When allegations of misalignments were perceived, African American women received punitive assaults just as their male counterparts. There was no room for displaced heartache or spaces for voiced opinions or felt feelings. Sexual violation, in multiple forms, was expected and deemed a right of action for slave owners (Talty, 2003). Sexual assaults were meant to dominate and demean those once valued attributes of strength yet still required in certain circumstances. These are just a few historical parameters African American women endured to pass those experiences onto their daughters and prepare them for these mirrored encounters. How does a mother prepare her offspring for the brutality of pain she knows firsthand and then mentally and physically carry on with her daily responsibilities? They shouldered the world by giving, caring, and accepting without complaint.

The post-slavery era brought Jim Crow laws, emerging incarcerations, and lynchings of African American males. Along with these the debilitate seemingly hardships African American women continued to shoulder the family system. In the 21st Century, African American women were freed yet shackled by racism, stereotyping, sexual subjectivity, limited opportunities, unleveraged salaries, and health disparities. Such disproportionate social-economic status (SES) influences Adverse Childhood Experiences and a means of survival. Survival that culturally resonates with an atmosphere of a "strong black woman" where there is no space for failure, giving up, or giving in to the struggle. To survive, she must cope. The coping strategies of African American women resemble silence and perseverance. Silence to keep it all together still carries the schema of a "strong black woman" holding on to the responsibilities of the community, responsibilities of family hardships, and working inside and outside the home (Broussard, 2013). With fragmented homes, African American women represent many single-parent homes, whereas an average of 51% of black children live in single-mother households (Abrams et al., 2014). Managing family and community responsibilities renders little time for personal care or attending to mental health symptomatology. Those are the hidden vulnerabilities of African American women resulting in independence and creative survival mechanisms resembling maladaptive coping skills. Hence the "Strong Black Women" persona. It is not a persona born of arrogance but one of resilience, strength, nurturing, and a selfless approach to caregiving. These behaviors have been modeled and passed from generation to generation, carrying the same qualities, survival instincts, codes of honor, and endurance with the expectation of being strong yet silent.

Challenges and Issues in Mental Health

Silence comes at an unmeasurable price, as does the unyielding "Strong Black Women" persona. The intersectionality of being a woman, an African American woman, and generational trauma confounds the conceptualization of strength, which impedes mental health. As mental health professionals, we were taught to perform intake sessions to gather clients' histories. If we do so, are we intently and intensely listening to their narratives, historically and contemporarily? Is the experience of African American women being conceptualized in a manner that represents their unique experiences? To capture the African American woman's experience means taking the time to analyze generational traumas, and transference and discern the intersectionality of race, gender, the role of the position, and the responsibility of what it means to survive as an African American woman. Viewing the totality of generational trauma and its historical maladaptive psychological effects that continue to influence the mental health of African American women. The effects are seen in how care is perceived and conceived by those requiring care and clinicians responsible for providing mental health services.

In 2006, Hunn and Craig (2009) asserted the necessity for clinicians to conceptualize the unique experiences of African American women. The unique experiences are complex as they intersect with gender, race, generational trauma, discrimination, and cultural responsibilities. However, in 2021 this approach is still being argued while the disparity gap is not being decreased. Research illustrates disparity gaps and highlights barriers to mental health services without discussing or investigating the effects of prolonged, unbridged action steps. African American women are at an increased risk of mental illness because of socioeconomic status (SES), race-related stressors, and their unique lived experiences. Yet, mental health services are not utilized within the same proportions as Caucasian women (APA, 2017).

Multiple factors contribute to the challenges and issues that are evidenced in the underutilization of mental health services. The literature review revealed limited studies investigating African American women's mental health pathologies and symptomologies. Limited studies discussed challenges and issues about barriers that lead to mental health disparity gaps and highlighted statistics as visual evidence (APA, 2017). Common barriers cited are limited access, stigma, trust factors, and lack of culturally competent clinicians (APA, 2017; Hunn & Craig, 2009). The challenges and issues equal misdiagnosing and underdiagnosing, increasing the mental health disparity gap. Focus has implied barriers and identified barriers, challenges, and concerns. However, limited dedicated research studies have eluded concrete efforts to decrease disparity gaps that lead to misdiagnosing and underdiagnosing of African American women.

African American women are less likely to be diagnosed with a mood disorder yet are at higher risk of being misdiagnosed with schizophrenia

(APA, 2017). An added depth to the disparity gap is that those with a mental illness are more inclined to be incarcerated than members of the Caucasian population (APA, 2017). Misdiagnosing and underdiagnosing are challenges that enumerate how the client and clinician perceive mental health. Barriers are the roadblocks that affect how some clinicians approach the mental health care of African American women. In turn, those identical barriers affect African American women's health-seeking behaviors. Communication differences and clinician perceptions are additional strains that increase misdiagnosing and underdiagnosing of the mental health of African American women. For further exploration of the misdiagnosis of African Americans with mental issues, see Bell et al., (2015a), Bell et al., (2015b), and Suite et al., (2007).

Defining the Layers and Types of Traumas

In the sections above, multiple situations are described. Each of these situations can cause stress, and over time, this stress causes damage to the body and brain and may surface as mental and/or physical health symptoms. The types of stress are described below. Also, the following sections will define and describe trauma, complex trauma, developmental trauma, adverse childhood experiences, intergenerational trauma, historical trauma, and race-based traumatic stress. In the end, the hopes are for readers to understand how all may be applied to Black women's experiences and how each's complexities might lead to misdiagnosis or underdiagnosis. The life-long effects of each may present as symptoms of other disorders.

Stress Leads to Trauma

At some point in their life, it is reasonable to say that everyone experience stress. Changes in one's day-to-day life and/or unexpected events cause stress. However, in these situations, the stress is short-lived and can be easily changed by making changes, modifying what we can control, and coping. When stress and stressful situations cannot be easily mediated or moderated, stress levels build, and stress begins to have longer-lasting effects. Stress becomes toxic. The Center for the Developing Child at Harvard University (n.d.) defines three types of stress responses: (a) positive stress, which is considered a normal part of day-to-day life and characterized by short-term increases in heart rate and stress hormones; (b) tolerable stress, which is related to more significant and/or longer-lasting events, more significantly triggers the body's alert system, but is buffered by supportive relationships that prevent long-term effects of the stress response; and (c) toxic stress, which is connected to frequent and/or long-term adversities and is a long-term triggering of the stress response system that can disrupt the development and functioning of the brain architecture. Toxic stress is described in many research articles as stress that becomes traumatic. Bremmer (2006, p. 446, para. 4) notes

> Symptoms of PTSD are hypothesized to represent the behavioral manifestation of stress-induced changes in brain structure and function. Stress results in acute and chronic changes in neurochemical systems and specific brain regions, which result in long-term changes in brain "circuits" involved in the stress response.

Stress becomes traumatic when the intensity of the frightening events becomes unmanageable to the point of threatening physical and psychological integrity (Lieberman & van Horn, 2008).

Trauma

A review of research and writing will yield multiple definitions of trauma and types of traumas. In the following section, definitions will be established. The Substance Abuse and Mental Health Services Administration (SAMHSA, 2014, p. 7) describes trauma as:

> Trauma results from an event, series of events, or set of circumstances experienced by an individual as physically or emotionally harmful or threatening and has lasting adverse effects on the individual's functioning and physical, social, emotional, or spiritual well-being.

In the definition above, note that the definition is generic and describes single and repeated experiences. This definition of trauma does not help conceptualize and separate those who have experienced a single event from those who have experienced multiple or repeated events. In the past, single instances of trauma have been defined as Type I trauma. Those who have experienced multiple or repeated events have been defined as Type II trauma.

In current literature, the term complex trauma is more appropriate for conceptualizing those who have experienced multiple or repeated events.

Complex Trauma

As readers review research, they will find many definitions for complex trauma. In the past, it might have been referred to as Type II Trauma, and in many cases, it is referred to as Complex Posttraumatic Stress Disorder (PTSD). Readers might also notice that in many cases, the definition includes reference to children because most conceptualize complex trauma as traumatic experiences occurring over a lifetime that often begins in childhood. The National Child Traumatic Stress Network (NCTSN) offers the most widely used definition; however, this definition includes the term *children* in it. This is not to say that the NCTSN definition is accurate. Instead, it is to say that if one is looking for a definition that can be applied across the lifespan, one needs to search further. To find a definition that is not specific to children, the most comprehensive definition comes from the Blue Knot Foundation. The Blue Knot Foundation's (2021, para. 1) definition of complex trauma is as follows:

> Complex trauma (a) is usually interpersonal (i.e., occurs between people); (b) involves 'being or feeling' trapped; (c) is often planned, extreme, ongoing, and/or repeated, (d) often has more severe, persistent and cumulative impacts; (e) involves challenges with shame, trust, self-esteem, identity and regulating emotions; (f) has different coping strategies (i.e., these include alcohol and drug use, self-harm, over- or under-eating, over-work etc.; and (g) affects emotional and physical health, wellbeing, relationships, and daily functioning. (**Note**: this definition has been reformatted for presentation, yet nothing has been removed or paraphrased).

For validating a working definition of complex trauma, see Wamser and Vandenberg (2013). This article offers empirical evidence for the definition of complex trauma.

Developmental Trauma and ACEs

van der Kolk (2005) described experiencing repeated traumatic events during childhood as developmental trauma. The duration and intensity of the traumatic experiences and the age of onset of these experiences can determine the outcome of both complex and developmental trauma. Courtois (2004, as cited in Sar, 2010, p. 2) describes developmental trauma as "a type of stressful event that occurs repeatedly and cumulatively, usually over some time, and within specific relationships and contexts."

ACEs may be traumatic in nature and occur during childhood and adolescence (CDC, 2021b). The term was coined by and described in the landmark study, "Relationship of Childhood Abuse and Household Dysfunction to Many of the Leading Causes of Death in Adults: The Adverse Childhood Experiences (ACE) Study" (Felitti et al., 1998). Multiple researchers have connected ACEs to developmental and complex trauma (Oral et al., 2016; van der Kolk, 2005).

Historical Trauma

Mohatt et al., (2014) state that historical trauma was initially associated with children who had survived the Holocaust, but in recent decades has been further applied to other groups. As with other trauma types, multiple definitions exist. For conceptualization, a comprehensive definition and description comes from the Administration for Children and Families, a department within the U.S. Department of Health and Human Services (n.d., para. 1)

> Historical trauma is multigenerational trauma experienced by a specific cultural, racial, or ethnic group. It is related to significant events that oppressed a particular group of people because of their status as oppressed, such as slavery, the Holocaust, forced migration, and the violent colonization of Native Americans. While many in such a group will experience no effects of the historical trauma, others may experience poor overall physical and behavioral health, including low self-esteem, depression, self-destructive behavior, marked propensity for violent or aggressive behavior, substance misuse and addiction, and high rates of suicide and cardiovascular disease. Acute problems of domestic violence or alcohol misuse that are not directly linked to historical trauma may be exacerbated by living in a community with unaddressed grief and behavioral health needs.

Mohatt et al., (2014) and Sotero (2006) note that understanding the concept of historical trauma can illuminate how it impacts the health of racial and ethnic populations and how it can provide direction for reducing health disparities.

Intergenerational Trauma

The term intergeneration trauma refers to how one generation's traumatic experiences impact future generations' mental and physical health. James (2019, para. 2) describes intergenerational trauma as "a concept developed to help explain years of generational challenges within families. It is the transmission (or sending down to younger generations) of the oppressive or traumatic effects of a historical event." Intergenerational trauma has been studied, and there is evidence of an epigenetic mechanism for this transmission (Anda et al., 2006; Jiang et al., 2019; Yehuda & Lehrner, 2018). In this sense, the epigenetic outcomes are alterations in genes and what is genetically passed down to future generations.

Race-Based Traumatic Stress

In a 2006 issue of *Psychiatric Times*, researcher Robert T. Carter defines and describes race-based traumatic stress as

> Race-based traumatic stress injury can be a consequence of emotional pain that a person may feel after encounters with racism, which can be understood in terms of specific types of acts (as distinct types: racial harassment or hostility, racial discrimination, or avoidance, and/or discriminatory harassment, aversive hostility). How encounters with racism are experienced depends on many factors associated with an individual's background, health, and cognitive processing. Thus, the person who interprets and appraises his racial encounter as extremely harmful (emotionally painful), sudden, and uncontrollable may exhibit signs and symptoms associated with the stress and possible trauma of racism. (Carter, 2006, para. 6)

Helms et al., (2010), in an article about racism and ethnoviolence, further describes the meaning or race-based trauma, as Carter et al., (2013) in their development of the Race-Based Traumatic Stress Symptom Scale and Carter et al., (2017), in their article about race-based Traumatic stress. For a further exploration of racial trauma, see Nadal et al., (2019), Ortega-Williams et al., (2021) and Prather et al., (2018).

Factors and Situations Associated with the Development of Complex Trauma

An individual's demographic variables may act as preexisting attributes or risk factors for developing complex trauma. These include being female, younger when the trauma occurs, having minority/ethnic status, lower socioeconomic status, and having lower levels of education/lower intelligence (Brewin et al., 2000; King et al., 2004). Preexisting mental health issues may also predispose an individual to develop complex trauma (Brewin et al., 2000; Ozer et al., 2003). Adverse childhood experiences (family instability, low-income family functioning, and lack of support) have also been linked to the development of complex and potentially complex trauma (Lauterbauch et al., 2007).

Courtois (n.d., pp. 2-3) offered an explanation and extensive list of other factors and situations that may lead to the development of complex trauma when she stated:

Cumulative adversities faced by many persons, communities, ethnocultural, religious, political, and sexual minority groups, and societies around the globe can also constitute forms of complex trauma. Some occur over the life course beginning in childhood and have some of the same developmental impacts described above. Others, occurring later in life, are often traumatic or potentially traumatic and can worsen the impact of early life complex trauma and cause the development of complex traumatic stress reactions. These adversities can include but are not limited to:

- Poverty and ongoing economic challenges, and lack of essentials or other resources
- Community violence and the inability to escape/re-locate
- Homelessness
- Disenfranchised ethno-racial, religious, and/or sexual minority status and repercussions
- Incarceration and residential placement and ongoing threat and assault
- Ongoing sexual and physical re-victimization and re-traumatization in the family or other contexts, including prostitution and sexual slavery
- Human rights violations, including political repression, genocide/ "ethnic cleansing," and torture
- Displacement, refugee status, and relocation

- War and combat involvement or exposure
- Developmental, intellectual, physical health, mental health/psychiatric, and age-related limitations, impairments, and challenges
- Exposure to death, dying, and the grotesque in emergency response work.

Many of the events and circumstances mentioned by Courtois can be reviewed in the research and writings of Brewin et al., (2000), Ford and Courtois (2009), King et al., (2004), and Vogt et al., (2007). For more reading that may shed light on the traumatic experiences of African American, see Kira (2010), Marsella (2010), Meshberg-Cohen et al., (2016), Nicolaidis et al., (2010), Powers et al., (2020), Sibrava et al., (2019), and Wrenn et al., (2011).

Assessment

Considering that assessment is a vital part of an accurate diagnosis as well as comprehensive case conceptualization, it should be a priority to find trauma assessments that have been culturally validated. Adams et al., (2016) noted that it is essential to screen individuals to determine their victimization type because most of those who experience repeated/ongoing emotional and/or physical traumas are conceptualized as poly-victims and may require a different level of treatment. Screening should also consider pre-trauma resilience, active support systems, and available resources. The U.S. Department of Veterans Affairs, National Center for PTSD (2021) provides a thorough summary list of assessment tools that may be used to screen for Posttraumatic Stress Disorder (PTSD). NCTSN (n.d.) provides a summary of assessment tools to assess for complex trauma, yet most of the tools mentioned are for use with children and adolescents. The International Society for Traumatic Stress Studies (ITSS; n.d.) lists a summary of assessment tools for child and adult trauma. When reviewing the assessments listed from any of these sources or selecting an assessment, it is essential to seek cultural validation of the assessment tool. Many tools have not been validated or deemed reliable across cultures, much less with Black women. To further demonstrate the dearth of culturally specific research into the validity and reliability of assessment tools, consider this: the Handbook of Test and

Measures for Black Populations (Jones, 1996) was published in 1996 and has not been updated since.

Of the assessment tools that have accomplished some cultural validation studies, most have yet to be mentioned by any national source. To develop a culturally valid and reliable assessment tool, race, ethnicity, and discrimination should be included. Below is a list of assessment tools that have cultural validity and reliability:

- Adverse Childhood Experiences International Questionnaire (ACES-IQ; WHO, 2018)
- Cultural Formulations Interview (CFI; Lewis-Fernández et al., 2014)
- Race-Based Traumatic Stress Symptom Scale (RBTSSS; Carter et al., 2013)
- Multiculturally Sensitive Mental Health Scale (MSMHS; Chao & Green, 2011)
- Stressful Life Events Screening Questionnaire (SLESQ; Goodman et al., 1998; Green et al., 2006)
- The UConn Racial/Ethnic Stress and Trauma Survey (UnRESTS; Williams, Metzher, et al., 2018)
- Trauma Symptoms of Discrimination Scale (TSDS; Williams, Printz, et al., 2018)

Finally, in a review article, Williams et al., (2021) offers a summary of research and assessments incorporating racial trauma into the conceptualization of PTSD. This article serves as a comprehensive and up-to-date resource.

Treatment of Complex Trauma

Multiple evidence-based practices can be used to treat complex trauma. When reviewing these practices, readers should see that all have similarities and are based on guiding principles derived from complex trauma research. Therefore, this section will describe a comprehensive list of suggestions that may be used as guidelines for treating complex trauma rather than summarize some of them.

Cloitre et al., (2012), as part of the International Society for Traumatic Stress Studies, and Kezelman and Stavropoulous (2019), as part of the Blue

Knot Foundation, offer comprehensive guidelines for the treatment of complex trauma. Cloitre et al., (2012) recommend a three-phased approach. Phase 1 establishes safety by reducing the clients' environmental factors that cause eth client to feel in danger. Phase 2 includes a review and reappraisal of trauma memories in the context of the safe environment achieved in Phase 1. Phase 3 involves transitioning out of therapy and increased engagement within the client's community.

Kezelman and Stavropoulous (2019) build on the work of Christine Courtois, Marylene Cloitre, and others with a recommendation for a three-phased approach. Their approach includes 44 guidelines for the implementation of the treatment, and the guidelines are connected to specific phases of the treatment. In their approach, Phase 1 is described as focused on establishing safety and stabilizing the client, Phase 2 is centered on processing the traumatic experiences, and Phase 3 is focused on integrating the experiences.

Other notable articles to consider when conceptualizing complex trauma treatment for adults exist. Briere and Scott (2015) describe the necessary component of complex trauma treatment in adolescents and adults. Lawson et al., (2013) describe complex trauma treatment for adults and include theoretical underpinnings, supportive research, and examples of od the dialogue that might go on between counselor and client. For trauma treatment specific to African American populations, see Davis et al., (2008), Graves et al., (2010), and Ortega-Williams et al., (2021).

Trauma-Informed Practices

Defined trauma-informed practices in mental health suggest a need to understand an individual's life experiences to provide them with the appropriate treatment. Because of an increased understanding of trauma and the necessary treatment components, trauma-informed care has garnered much attention and led to significant research and writing. Kimberg and Wheeler (2019) define principles of trauma-informed care and practical approaches for implementation. DeCandia and Guarino (2015) describe trauma-informed care from an ecological perspective. Ranjbar et al., (2020) describes cultural humility as a part of trauma-informed care. Grant (2008) describes the trauma-informed practice for African American women in alcohol and other drug treatment to improve treatment outcomes. Finally, Taha et al., (2015) report the results of a study about culturally informed treatment for abused, suicidal

African American women. The National Center for Trauma-Informed Care (NCTIC), as part of the U.S. Department of Justice, provides many resources for trauma-informed care. In support of what many of these articles describe, Graves et al., (2010, p. 41, para. 7), in an article about the need for culturally informed practices to address trauma, suicidal behavior, and overt aggression in African American adolescents, note, "...without accurate, culturally-informed research that is theory-driven, the components of any intervention may be ill-conceived."

Resolutions to Decrease Misdiagnosing and Underdiagnosing

One of the first steps clinicians should consider is applying The Pair of ACEs concept, which outlines Adverse Childhood Experiences and Adverse Community Environments (ACEs). The pair of ACEs explores negative childhood experiences and illustrates how those negative experiences lead to early mortality in adulthood (CDC, 2021a). The chart below lists categories of challenges that are impactful experiences that have lasting effects on developmental factors and decrease life span. Reviewing the chart from the bottom to the top, childhood experiences paired with community adversaries influence the trajectory of adulthood.

Adverse Childhood Experiences	Adverse Community Environments
Death	Short Life Span
Disease, Disability, and Social Problems	Poverty
Adoption of Health Risk Behavior	Systematic Racism
Social, Emotional, & Cognitive Impairment	Lack of Opportunity
Disrupted Neurodevelopment	Homelessness
Adverse Childhood Experiences	Limited Access to Care
Social Conditions/Local Context	Community Violence

The double negative challenges provide insight into the theory of conceptualizing individual lived experiences as a vital element to addressing the mental health treatment of African American women. This approach is not a collective suggestion however it is a culturally responsive approach that is individually client centered. Meaning to treat African American women and decrease misdiagnosing clinically and underdiagnosing, clinicians should consider their individual experiences. Lived experiences increase mental illnesses and position clients in predisposed categories of decreased emotional and physical health outcomes. Leading the trend for decreased emotional and physical health outcomes from four or more ACEs categories are minority females (CDC, 2021a).

A third layer added to ACEs is the consideration of generational trauma or historical trauma. These traumas are intergenerational/transgenerational and experienced collectively as a group (CDC, 2021a). They are collective in nature and affect multiple generations. The generational/historical trauma is foundational, passed from generation to generation, first-hand experience, experienced vicariously, and persists as a chronic syndrome. These traumas become ingrained into the family, taking root as a norm. The chart below illustrates examples of generational/historical traumas.

Generational Trauma/Historical Trauma
Death
Pandemics
Discrimination
Forced Displacements
Mass Incarcerations
Sexual Assaults
Family Disbursement
Slavery

These traumas oftentimes are collective and contribute to the psychological traumas of African American women. They influence identity, sense of belonging, and are instrumental in fortifying maladaptive behaviors strengthening the "Strong Black Woman" persona. Accumulated as transmissions and absorbed with the communities generational/historical traumas may present as stressors, post-traumatic stress, depression, and anxiety disorders. However, the effects of generational/historical traumas are rarely identified, discussed, or considered with respect to mental health.

Resolutions for decreasing misdiagnosing and underdiagnosing African American women is to first identify causation, barriers, and dismissive approaches. In an effort to appropriately conceptualize African American women best practices should include the totality of the individual experiences. The tree illustration below is an adaptation from the original Pair of ACEs concept with addition of historical experiences.

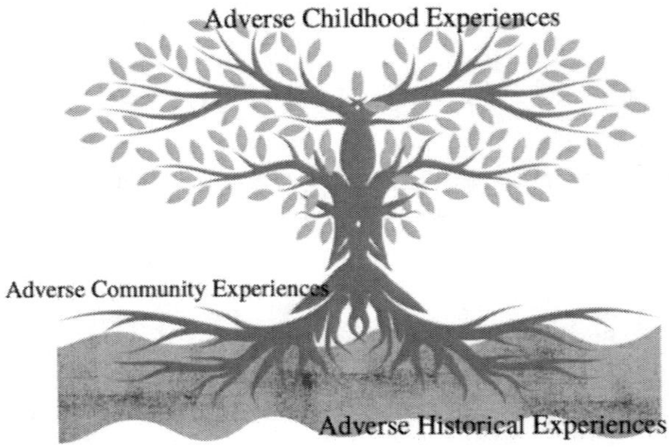

Drawing from the historical experiences of African American generational trauma are foundational; they feed the roots of individual experiences. One could argue that they are rooted and ingrained culturally giving momentum to the "Strong Black Woman" perception. They guide behaviors, actions, values, conscious, and unconscious dialogues. Historical experiences feed and nourish the community transmitting adverse elements that impact community and individual well-being. The branches extend from the community into the homes and lives of children where the leaves are representative of experiences. It is a system that cultivates, producing African American women that shoulder the world. The preponderance of the weight causes stressors that have direct linkage to the three layers of ACEs.

While ACEs originally illustrated the impact of adverse childhood experiences on development and life span it demonstrates structural factors that affect African American women. ACEs highlights the intersections and overlapping experiences of African American. The multitude of those common experiences are the driving forces that lead to prolonged adverse mental health symptoms that go untreated or dismissed. Broadening the scope of what clinicians view as individual experiences to the structural focus of historical events, current events, and the lived experiences of clients (Greer, 2011). The African American woman has multifaceted realms of adversities to navigate where intersectionality converges multiple times in the scope of twenty-four hours. That convergence is experienced as gender racism, sexual racism, and ethic racism creating oppression and disenfranchisement perpetuating increased mental health factors (Copeland & Butler, 2007).

These sociocultural factors are unique experiences that contribute to depression and other mental health disorders (Hunn & Craig 2009).

In an effort to diagnose and treat African American women for mental health disorders, it is essential to understanding and identifying mental health disorders for this special population that has unique experiences (Copeland & Butler, 2007; Liao et al., 2020). The symptoms of mental health disorder may present themselves different than other populations, therefore it may present issues in identifying mental disorders or narrowing the correct mental health disorder. This is why the whole context of the individual in relation to ACEs should be used as a collaborative measure to diagnose African American. In an effort to diagnose and treat African American women, sociocultural impact should be implemented as standard practices. By doing so this creates culturally responsive spaces for clients and decreases the opportunity for misdiagnosing and underdiagnosing African American women.

References

Abrams, J. A., Maxwell, M., Pope, M., & Belgrave, F. Z. (2014). Carrying the world with the grace of a lady and the grit of a warrior: Deepening our understanding of the "strong Black Woman" schema. *Psychology of Women Quarterly, 38*(4), 503-518. https://doi.org/10.1177/0361684314541418.

Adams, Z. W., Moreland, A., Cohen, J. R., Lee, R. C., Hanson, R. F., Danielson, C. K., Self-Brown, S., & Briggs, E. C. (2016). Polyvictimization: Latent profiles and mental health outcomes in a clinical sample of adolescents. *Psychology of Violence, 6*(1), 145-155. doi: 10.1037/a0039713. PMID: 26958417; PMCID: PMC4779364.

Administration for Children and Families, U.S. Department of Health, and Human Services. (n.d.) *What is historical trauma*. https://www.acf.hhs.gov/trauma-toolkit/trauma-concept.

American Psychiatric Association. (2017). *Mental health facts about African Americans*. https://www.psychiatry.org/psychiatrists/cultural-competency/education/mental-health-facts.

Anda, R. F., Felitti, V. J., Bremner, J. D., Walker, J. D., Whitfield, C., Perry, B. D., Dube, S. R., & Giles, W. H. (2006). The enduring effects of abuse and related adverse experiences in childhood. A convergence of evidence from neurobiology and epidemiology. *European Archives of Psychiatry and Clinical Neuroscience, 256*(3), 174-186. https://doi.org/10.1007/s00406-005-0624.

Bell, C. C., Jackson, W. M., & Bell, B. H. (2015a). Misdiagnosis of African Americans with psychiatric Issues - Part I. *Journal of the National Medical Association, 107*(3), 25-34. doi: 10.1016/S0027-9684(15)30048-1. PMID: 27282720.

Bell, C. C., Jackson, W. M., & Bell, B. H. (2015b). Misdiagnosis of African Americans with psychiatric issues - Part II. *Journal of the National Medical Association, 107*(3):35-41. doi: 10.1016/S0027-9684(15)30049-3. PMID: 27282721.

Blue Knot Foundation. (2012). *What is complex trauma?* https://www.blueknot.org.au/Resources/Information/Understanding-abuse-and-trauma/What-is-complex-trauma.

Bremner, J. D. (2006). Traumatic stress: Effects on the brain. *Dialogues in Clinical Neuroscience, 8*(4), 445-461. https://doi.org/10.31887/DCNS.2006.8.4/jbremner.

Brewin, C. R., Andrews, B., & Valentine, J. D. (2000). Meta-analysis of risk factors for posttraumatic stress disorder in trauma-exposed adults. *Journal of Consulting and Clinical Psychology, 68*(5), 748-766. https://doi.org/10.1037/0022-006X.68.5.748.

Briere, J, & Scott, C. (2015). Complex trauma in adolescents and adults: Effects and treatment. *Psychiatric Clinics of North America, 38*(3), 515-527. doi: 10.1016/j.psc.2015.05.004. PMID: 26300036.

Broussard, P. A. (2013). Black women's post-slavery silence syndrome: a twenty-first century remnant of slavery, Jim Crow, and systemic racism - who will tell her stories? *Journal of Gender, Race, and Justice, 16*(2), 373.

Carter, R. T. (2006). Race-based traumatic stress. *Psychiatric Times, 23*(14). https://www.psychiatrictimes.com/view/race-based-traumatic-stress.

Carter, R. T., Johnson, V. E., Roberson, K., Mazzula, S. L., Kirkinis, K., & Sant-Barket, S. (2017). Race-based traumatic stress, racial identity statuses, and psychological functioning: An exploratory investigation. *Professional Psychology: Research and Practice, 48*(1), 30-37. https://doi-org.umiss.idm.oclc.org/10.1037/pro0000116.

Carter, R. T., Mazzula, S., Victoria, R., Vazquez, R., Hall, S., Smith, S., Sant-Barket, S., Forsyth, J., Bazelais, K., & Williams, B. (2013). Initial development of the Race-Based Traumatic Stress Symptom Scale: Assessing the emotional impact of racism. *Psychological Trauma: Theory, Research, Practice, and Policy, 5*(1), 1-9. https://doi.org/10.1037/a0025911.

Centers for Disease Control and Prevention. (2021a). *About the CDC-Kaiser ACE study.* https://www.cdc.gov/violenceprevention/aces/about.html?CDC_AA_refVal=https%3A%2F%2Fwww.cdc.gov%2Fviolenceprevention%2Facestudy%2Fabout.html.

Center for Disease Control and Prevention. (2021b). *Preventing adverse childhood experiences.* https://www.cdc.gov/violenceprevention/aces/fastfact.html?CDC_AA_refVal=https%3A%2F%2Fwww.cdc.gov%2Fviolenceprevention%2Facestudy%2Ffastfact.html.

Center for the Developing Child (n.d.). *Toxic stress.* Harvard University. https://developingchild.harvard.edu/science/key-concepts/toxic-stress/.

Chao, R. C.-L., & Green, K. E. (2011). Multiculturally Sensitive Mental Health Scale (MSMHS): Development, factor analysis, reliability, and validity. *Psychological Assessment, 23*(4), 876-887. https://doi.org/10.1037/a0023710.

Cloitre, M., Courtois, C. A., Ford, J. D., Green, B. L., Alexander, P., Briere, J., Herman, J. L., Lanius, R., Stolbach, B. C., Spinazzola, J., Van der Kolk, B. A., & Van der Hart, O. (2012). The *ISTSS expert consensus treatment guidelines for complex PTSD in adults*. http:// www.istss.org.

Copeland, V. C., & Butler, J. (2007). Reconceptualizing access: A cultural competence approach to improving the mental health of African American women. *Social Work in Public Health, 23*(2/3), 35-58. doi: 10.1080/19371910802148263. PMID: 19306587.

Courtois, C. A. (n.d.). *Understanding complex trauma, complex reactions, and treatment approaches.* http://www.giftfromwithin.org/html/cptsd-understanding-treatment.html.

Davis, R. G., Ressler, K. J., Schwartz, A. C., Stephens, K. J., & Bradley, R. G. (2008). Treatment barriers for low-income, urban African Americans with undiagnosed posttraumatic stress disorder. *Journal of Traumatic Stress, 21*(2), 218-222. https://doi.org/10.1002/jts.20313.

Felitti, V. J., Anda, R. F., Nordenberg, D., Williamson, D. F., Spitz, A. M., Edwards, V., Koss, M. P., & Marks, J. S. (1998). Relationship of childhood abuse and household dysfunction to many of the leading causes of death in adults. The Adverse Childhood Experiences (ACE) Study. *American Journal of Preventative Medicine, 14*(4), 245-258. doi: 10.1016/s0749-3797(98)00017-8. PMID: 9635069.

Ford, J. D., & Courtois, C. A. (2009). Defining and understanding complex trauma and complex traumatic stress disorders. In C. A. Courtois & J. D. Ford (Eds.), *Treating complex traumatic stress disorders: An evidence-based guid*e (pp. 13-30). Guilford Press.

Goodman, L. A., Corcoran, C., Turner, K., Yuan, N., & Green, B. L. (1998). Assessing traumatic event exposure: General issues and preliminary findings for the Stressful Life Events Screening Questionnaire. *Journal of Trauma Stress,11*(3), 521-542. doi: 10.1023/A:1024456713321. PMID: 9690191.

Grant, G. (2008) *Using trauma-informed practices to improve AOD treatment outcomes for African women.* Ontrack Communications. http://citeseerx.ist.psu.edu/viewdoc/download?doi=10.1.1.454.6888&rep=rep1&type=pdf.

Graves, K. N., Kaslow, N. J., & Frabutt, J. M. (2010). A culturally informed approach to trauma, suicidal behavior, and overt aggression in African American adolescents. *Aggression and Violent Behavior,15*(1). 26-41. https://doi.org/10.1016/j.avb.2009.07.014.

Green, B., Chung, J., Daroowalla, A., Kaltman, S., & DeBenedictis, C. (2006). Evaluating the Cultural validity of the Stressful Life Events Screening Questionnaire. *Violence Against Women, 12*(12), 191-213. https://doi.org/10.1177/1077801206294534.

Greer, T. M. (2011). Coping strategies as moderators of the relation between individual race-related stress and mental health symptoms for African American women. *Psychology of Women Quarterly*, 35(2), 215-226. https://doi.org/10.1177/0361684311399388.

Harris-Lacewell, M. (2001). No place to rest: African American political attitudes and the myth of Black women's strength. *Women and Politics, 23*, 1-34. https://doi.org/10.1300/J014v23n03_01.

Helms, J. E., Nicolas, G., & Green, C. E. (2010). Racism and ethnoviolence as trauma: Enhancing professional training. *Traumatology, 16*(4), 53-62. https://doi.org/10.1177/1534765610396728.

Hunn, V. L., & Craig, C. D. (2009). Depression, sociocultural factors, and African American women. *Journal of Multicultural Counseling & Development, 37*(2), 83-93. https://doi.org/10.1002/j.2161-1912.2009.tb00093.x.

International Society for Traumatic Stress Studies. (n.d.) *Clinical resources.* https://istss.org/clinical-resources.

James, P. (2019). Inter-generational trauma: 6 ways its affects families. *Winter 2019 Newsletter.* Duke University, Office for Institutional Equity. https://oie.duke.edu/inter-generational-trauma-6-ways-it-affects-families.

Jiang, S., Postovit, L., Cattaneo, A., Binder, E. B., & Aitchison, K. J. (2019). Epigenetic modifications in stress response genes associated with childhood trauma. *Frontiers in Psychiatry, 10*, Article 808. https://doi.org/10.3389/fpsyt.2019.00808.

Jones, R. L. (1996). *Handbook of test and measures for Black populations.* Cobb & Henry.

Kezelman, C. A., & Stavropoulous, P. A. (2019). Practice guidelines for clinical treatment of complex trauma. *Blue Knot Foundation.* https://www.blueknot.org.au/Resources/Publications/Practice-Guidelines/Practice-Guidelines-2019.

Kimberg, L., & Wheeler, M. (2019). Trauma and trauma-informed care. In M. R. Gerber (Ed.), *Trauma-informed healthcare approaches: A guide for primary care* (Ch. 2). Springer.

King, D. W., Vogt, D. S., & King, L. A. (2004). Risk and resilience factors in the etiology of chronic posttraumatic stress disorder. In B. T. Litz (Ed.), *Early intervention for trauma and traumatic loss* (pp. 34-64). The Guilford Press.

Kira, I. A. (2010). Etiology and treatment of post-cumulative traumatic stress disorders in different cultures. *Traumatology, 16*(4), 128-141. https://doi.org/10.1177/1534765610365914.

Lauterbach, D., Koch, E. I., & Porter, K. (2007). The relationship between childhood support and later emergence of PTSD. *Journal of Traumatic Stress, 20*(5), 857-867. doi: 10.1002/jts.20249. PMID: 17955546.

Lawson, D. M., Davis, D., & Brandon, S. (2013). Treating complex trauma: Critical interventions with adults who experienced ongoing trauma in childhood. *Psychotherapy, 50*(3), 331-335. https://doi.org/10.1037/a0032677.

Lewis-Fernández, R., Aggarwal, N. K., Bäärnhielm, S., Rohlof, H., Kirmayer, L. J., Weiss, M. G., Jadhav, S., Hinton, L., Alarcón, R. D., Bhugra, D., Groen, S., van Dijk, R., Qureshi, A., Collazos, F., Rousseau, C., Caballero, L, Ramos, M., & Lu, F. (2014). Culture and psychiatric evaluation: Operationalizing cultural formulation for DSM-5. *Psychiatry, 77*(2), 130-154. doi: 10.1521/psyc.2014.77.2.130. PMID: 24865197; PMCID: PMC4331051.

Liao, K. Y. H., Wei, M., & Yin, M. (2020) The misunderstood schema of the strong Black woman: Exploring its mental health consequences and coping responses among African American women. *Psychology of Women Quarterly, 44*(1), 84-104. https://doi.org/10.1177/0361684319883198.

Lieberman, A., & Van Horn, P. (2008). *Psychotherapy with infants and young children: Repairing the effects of stress and trauma on early attachment.* The Guilford Press.

Marsella, A. J. (2010). Ethnocultural aspects of PTSD: An overview of concepts, issues, and treatments. *Traumatology, 16*(4), 17-26. https://doi.org/10.1177/1534765610388062.

McGuire, T. G., & Miranda, J. (2008). New evidence regarding racial and ethnic disparities in mental health: Policy implications. *Health Affairs (Project Hope), 27*(2), 393-403. https://doi.org/10.1377/hlthaff.27.2.393.

Meshberg-Cohen, S., Presseau, C., Thacker, L. R., Hefner, K., & Svikis, D. (2016). Posttraumatic stress disorder, health problems, and depression among African American women in residential substance use treatment. *Journal of Women's Health, 25*(7), 729-737. https://doi.org/10.1089/jwh.2015.5328.

Mohatt, N. V., Thompson, A. B., Thai, N. D., & Tebes, J. K. (2014). Historical trauma as public narrative: A conceptual review of how history impacts present-day health. *Social Science & Medicine* (1982), 106, 128-136. https://doi.org/10.1016/j.socscimed.2014.01.043.

Nadal, K. L., Erazo, T., & King, R. (2019). Challenging definitions of psychological trauma: Connecting racial microaggressions and traumatic stress. *Journal for Social Action in Counseling & Psychology, 11*(2), 2-16. https://doi.org/10.33043/JSACP.11.2.2-16.

National Center for Trauma-Informed Care (NCTIC), National Institute of Corrections. (n.d.). *U.S. Department of Justice*. https://nicic.gov/sources/national-center-trauma-informed-care-nctic-alexandria-va.

National Child Traumatic Stress Network (n.d.). *Measures review*. https://www.nctsn.org/treatments-and-practices/screening-and-assessments/measure-reviews.

Nicolaidis, C., Timmons, V., Thomas, M. J., Waters, A. S., Wahab, S., Mejia, A., & Mitchell, S. R. (2010). "You don't go tell White people nothing": African American women's perspectives on the influence of violence and race on depression and depression care. *American Journal of Public Health, 100*(8), 1470-1476. https://doi.org/10.2105/AJPH.2009.161950.

Oral, R., Ramirez, M., Coohey, C., Nakada, S., Walz, A., Kuntz, A., Benoit, J., & Peek-Asa, C., (2016). Adverse childhood experiences and trauma informed care: The future of health care. *Pediatric Research, 79*(1), 227-233. https://doi.org/10.1038/pr.2015.197.

Ortega-Williams, A., Crutchfield, J., & Hall, J. C. (2021). The colorist-historical trauma framework: Implications for culturally responsive practice with African Americans. *Journal of Social Work, 21*(3), 294-309. ttps://doi.org/10.1177/1468017319890083.

Ozer, E. J., Best, S. R., Lipsey, T. L., & Weiss, D. S. (2003). Predictors of posttraumatic stress disorder and symptoms in adults: A meta-analysis. *Psychological Bulletin, 129*(1), 52-73. https://doi.org/10.1037/0033-2909.129.1.52.

Powers, A., Woods-Jaeger, B., Stevens, J. S., Bradley, B., Patel, M. B., Joyner, A., Smith, A. K., Jamieson, D. J., Kaslow, N., & Michopoulos, V. (2020). Trauma, psychiatric disorders, and treatment history among pregnant African American women. *Psychological Trauma: Theory, Research, Practice, and Policy, 12*(2), 138-146. https://doi.org/10.1037/tra0000507.

Prather, C., Fuller, T. R., Jeffries, W. L., 4th, Marshall, K. J., Howell, A. V., Belyue-Umole, A., & King, W. (2018). Racism, African American women, and their sexual and reproductive health: A review of historical and contemporary evidence and implications for health equity. *Health Equity, 2*(1), 249-259. https://doi.org/10.1089/heq.2017.0045.

Ranjbar, N., Erb, M., Mohammad, O., & Moreno, F. A. (2020). Trauma-informed care and cultural humility in the mental health care of people from minoritized communities. *Focus: The Journal of Lifelong Learning in Psychiatry, 18*(1), 8-15. https://doi.org/10.1176/appi.focus.20190027.

Sar, V. (2011). Developmental trauma, complex PTSD, and the current proposal of DSM-5. Eur *Journal of Psychotraumatology, 2*, 1-9. doi: 10.3402/ejpt.v2i0.5622. PMID: 22893823; PMCID: PMC3402152.

Sibrava, N. J., Bjornsson, A. S., Pérez Benítez, A., Moitra, E., Weisberg, R. B., & Keller, M. B. (2019). Posttraumatic stress disorder in African American and Latinx adults: Clinical course and the role of racial and ethnic discrimination. *The American Psychologist, 74*(1), 101-116. https://doi.org/10.1037/amp0000339.

Sotero M. (2006). A conceptual model of historical trauma: Implications for public health practice and research. *Journal of Health Disparities Research and Practice, 1*(1), 93-108.

Substance Abuse and Mental Health Services Administration. (2014). *SAMHSA's concept of trauma and guidance for a trauma-informed Approach.* HHS Publication No. (SMA) 14-4884. Substance Abuse and Mental Health Services Administration.

Suite, D. H., La Bril, R., Primm, A., & Harrison-Ross, P. (2007). Beyond misdiagnosis, misunderstanding, and mistrust: Relevance of the historical perspective in the medical and mental health treatment of people of color. *Journal of the National Medical Association, 99*(8), 879-885. PMCID: PMC2574307. PMID: 17722664.

Taha, F., Zhang, H., Snead, K., Jones, A. D., Blackmon, B., Bryant, R. J., Siegelman, A. E., & Kaslow, N. J. (2015). Effects of a culturally informed intervention on abused, suicidal African American women. *Cultural Diversity & Ethnic Minority Psychology, 21*(4), 560-570. https://doi.org/10.1037/cdp0000018.

Talty, S. (2004). *Mulatto America: At the crossroads of Black and White culture: A social history.* HarperCollins.

United States Department of Veterans Affairs, National Center for PTSD. (2021). *List of measures.* https://www.ptsd.va.gov/professional/assessment/list_measures.asp.

van der Kolk, B. A. (2005). Developmental Trauma Disorder: Toward a rational diagnosis for children with complex trauma histories. *Psychiatric Annals, 35*(5), 401-408. https://doi.org/10.3928/00485713-20050501-06.

Vogt, D. S., King, D. W., & King, L. A. (2007). Risk pathways for PTSD: Making sense of the literature. In M. J. Friedman, T. M. Keane, & P. A. Resick (Eds.), *Handbook of PTSD: Science and practice* (pp. 99-115). The Guilford Press.

Wamser, N. R., & Vandenberg, B. R. (2013). Empirical support for the definition of a complex trauma event in children and adolescents. *Journal of Traumatic Stress, 26*(6), 671-678. doi: 10.1002/jts.21857.

Williams, M. T., Haeny, A. M., & Holmes, S. C. (2021). *Posttraumatic Stress Disorder and racial trauma. PTSD Research Quarterly, 32*(1), 1-9. ISSN: 1050-1835. https://www.ptsd.va.gov/publications/rq_docs/V32N1.pdf.

Williams, M. T., Metzger, I. W., Leins, C., & DeLapp, C. (2018). Assessing racial trauma within a DSM-5 framework: The UConn Racial/Ethnic Stress and Trauma Survey. *Practice Innovations, 3*(4), 242-260. https://doi.org/10.1037/pri0000076.

Williams, M. T., Printz, D. M. B., & DeLapp, R. C. T. (2018). Assessing racial trauma with the Trauma Symptoms of Discrimination Scale. *Psychology of Violence, 8*(6), 735-747. doi:10.1037/vio0000212.

World Health Organization. (2018). *Adverse Childhood Experiences International Questionnaire.* https://www.who.int/publications/m/item/adverse-childhood-experiences-international-questionnaire-(ace-iq).

Wrenn, G. L., Wingo, A. P., Moore, R., Pelletier, T., Gutman, A. R., Bradley, B., & Ressler, K. J. (2011). The effect of resilience on posttraumatic stress disorder in trauma-exposed inner-city primary care patients. *Journal of the National Medical Association, 103*(7), 560-566. https://doi.org/10.1016/s0027-9684(15)30381-3.

Yehuda, R., & Lehrner, A. (2018). Intergenerational transmission of trauma effects: Putative role of epigenetic mechanisms. *World Psychiatry: Official Journal of the World Psychiatric Association (WPA), 17*(3), 243-257. https://doi.org/10.1002/wps.20568.

Chapter 9

Openness and Depth: Gender and Racially Sensitive Clinical Practices Through the Lens of Afrocentricity, Black Feminism and Transformative Trauma-Informed Care Approaches

Lauren Downey*, EdD, LPCC-S, ACS and Ariel Dew†, MA, LPCC

The Trauma-Informed Counseling Center, Lexington, Kentucky, USA

Abstract

Many researchers and educators would argue that the historical struggles of Black women are well documented. And yet, at the macro level, well-informed, racially sensitive, gender-sensitive, and trauma-sensitive clinical practices exclusively designed to treat the multidimensional mental health needs of Black women remain limited. Paradoxically, there are a plethora of Black feminist theoretical perspectives that aim to encompass and capture the multifaceted nature of the marginalized experiences of Black women (Evans, Bell, & Burton, 2017). Even so, the question remains, is this enough? Jones and Guy-Sheftall (2017) argued the point that "The field of mental health is faced with the critical task of providing culturally relevant services that meet the complex psychological needs of Black women (pg. 201)." Furthermore, Jones and Guy-Shetfall (2017) highlighted the use of a specific theoretical paradigm (i.e., the BREATHE model) based upon Black feminist ideals

* Corresponding Author's E-mail: ldowney@theticcoflexington.com.

† Corresponding Author's E-mail: ariel.dew@gmail.com.

In: How Did We Survive?
Editor: Tina Marie Glover
ISBN: 979-8-88697-918-3

but are such frameworks widespread enough to become the standardized clinical treatment approach utilized to treat Black women's mental health needs? When will the mental health profession move beyond theory in order to actively employ an inclusive mental health treatment model that can be utilized to identify and employ detailed clinical approaches that encompass policies and clinical practices for Black women? "The challenge in the twenty-first century is to put Black feminist theory into action in mental health practice" (Jones & Guy-Sheftall, 2017). This book chapter will aim to identify and explore how specific aspects of three identified theoretical frameworks can be applied practically and clinically with Black women to employ counseling practices and approaches that are racial-, gender-, and trauma-informed.

Keywords: African American women, black women, trauma, etiology of trauma, mental health, counseling

Words of Fire: An Anthology of African American Feminist Thought. Sister Outsider: Essays and Speeches. All the Women Are White, All the Blacks Are Men, But Some of Us Are Brave: Black Women's Studies. The Black Woman: Anthology. Home Girls: A Black Feminist Anthology. Black Feminist Thought: Knowledge, Consciousness, and the Politics of Empowerment.

These groundbreaking literary works are the foremothers of this chapter. Many researchers and educators would argue that the historical struggles of Black women are well documented and yet, at the macro level, well-informed and structurally sound racial-, gender-, and trauma-sensitive clinical practices to treat the multidimensional mental health needs of Black women remain nonexistent (Brown et al., 2020; Jones & Harris, 2019). Effective counseling for Black women requires vigilant attention to both race and gender (Sanchez-Hucles, 2016), as marginalization with multiple cultural identities presents an array of challenging experiences. The Black identity particularly offers opportunities for one to develop adverse mental health outcomes, which can be insufficiently addressed in standard treatment practices developed for middle-class White Americans (Brown et al., 2020; Sanchez-Hules, 2016). Even in the realm of multicultural and social justice counseling models, there are many limitations regarding synthesizing multiple cultural and social identities (Williams, 2005). Paradoxically, a plethora of Black feminist theoretical perspectives aim to encompass and speak to the multifaceted, marginalized, and oppressive experiences of Black women (Evans et al., 2017). Theoretical frameworks that reflect the lived experiences of marginalized groups have certainly improved over the last 15 to 20 years (Abrams et al., 2014; Fulani, 2014). From trailblazing foundational research by Patricia Hill Collins, Kimberlé Crenshaw, and Beverly Guy-Sheftall, empowering and insightful theoretical frameworks have been developed to inform researchers, educators, and clinical practitioners on conceptualizing best the everchanging and multifaceted lived experiences of Black women (Lindsay-Dennis, 2015).

The question remains: What next steps are required for the field? Jones and Guy-Sheftall (2017) argued that culturally relevant services are needed in the field of mental health to meet the complex needs of Black women. Furthermore, Jones and Guy-Sheftall highlighted using a specific theoretical paradigm (i.e., the BREATHE model) based on the theoretical framework of Black feminism. Nevertheless, the question remains, are such frameworks widespread enough to become the standardized clinical treatment approach for treating Black women's mental health needs?

To quote Malcolm X, "The most disrespected person in America is the Black woman. The most unprotected person in America is the Black woman. The most neglected person in America is the Black woman" (Emba, 2019, para. 1). Now is the time for the clinical counseling profession to move beyond theory and actively employ inclusive and specific mental health treatment incorporating clinical approaches that encompass multidimensional and individualized clinical care for Black women. Per Jones and Guy-Sheftall (2017), "The challenge in the twenty-first century is to put Black feminist theory into action in mental health practice" (p. 201). In the context of these statements lies a great deal of truth for how Black women are perceived in the context of society's sociopolitical underpinnings. The statistics on Black women's overall health compared to White women are significantly higher due mainly to the various inequalities. Black women face (Chinn et al., 2021). Chinn et al. (2021) stated that

> No discussion of health equity among Black women is complete unless it considers the impacts of institutional- and individual-level forms of racism and discrimination against Black people. Nor is a review of health equity among Black women complete without understanding the intersectionality of gender and race and the historical contexts that have accumulated to influence Black women's health in the United States. (p. 212)

This quote indicates the significance that race and gender play in Black women's overall health and well-being, as Black women are at higher risk of experiencing adverse physical and psychological conditions than White women. Black women comprise 7% of the U.S. population and 13.6% of all U.S. women (National Center for Health Statistics, 2018). Black women are younger (36.1 years) than U.S. women overall (39.6 years; National Center for Health Statistics, 2018). However, many health conditions, including heart disease, stroke, cancers, diabetes, maternal morbidities, obesity, and mental health issues, are more prevalent among Black women. National epidemiological systems, like the Center for Disease Control (CDC) that aim to capture information on health risk factors and access to mental health, possess notable limitations regarding gathering health information on Black women (Brown et al., 2020; Chinn et al., 2021). Moreover, research findings on race and gender across mental health-related studies vary greatly. As a result of these variations, there is a dearth of research on effective clinical counseling approaches for Black women (Chinn et al., 2021).

Within the realm of clinical counseling and counselor education, concerns regarding multicultural humility, awareness, and competence have led the profession to examine the importance of clinical practitioners employing skills that highlight and incorporate necessary critical and culturally relevant counseling approaches for Black people (Brinkman & Donohue, 2020; Brown et al., 2020; Mosley et al., 2021). Black culture manifests from African ideals that commonly use spirituality, expressiveness, and perseverance to combat hardships. Healing from trauma involves vulnerability and courage. Specifically, Black women benefit from theoretical frameworks reflecting familiarity with their Black experience and culture. Such frameworks provide comfort and understanding in the healing journey.

This chapter's overarching theme is that the complex and elaborate lived experiences of Black women's lives significantly impact their mental health and well-being in a society that does not highlight or give space to their daily experiences. Black women must combat societal stressors and pressures related to sexism, classism, racism, and heterosexism (Grote et al., 2007; Jones & Guy-Sheftall, 2015; Kwate et al., 2003; Thomas et al., 2008). Black women report experiences of isolation, alienation, and denigration related to the "isms" they experience (Boyd-Franklin, 1991; Jones & Warner, 2011; Williams, 2005; Woods-Giscombé & Black, 2010). Recognizing the multilayered intricacies of Black women's lives, as documented in this chapter, clinical practitioners can adopt and employ clinical counseling practices that focus on constructs such as Black feminism, Afrocentricity, and trauma-informed care.

This chapter aims to provide an overview and detail-oriented praxises on how clinical practitioners can meet the needs of Black women who present with mental health symptoms related to trauma and their social identities in society. This chapter also explores aspirational clinical approaches practitioners can infuse into their counseling practices when working with Black women. Specifically, two clinical exercises that are aspirational in nature outline how practitioners can infuse the concepts of self-love and self-compassion into clinical practice with Black women. These clinical exercises have been crafted to embody specific culturally relevant theoretical orientations that are racial, gender, and trauma informed. The authors feel that such aspirational counseling approaches can help Black women feel understood, empowered, and resilient. Such tenets may improve Black women's mental and emotional well-being (Brown et al., 2020; Jones & Harris, 2019).

Black Feminism

The concept of Black feminism derives from the groundbreaking work of Patricia Hill Collins. As Jones and Guy-Sheftall (2015) noted, "Collins's (1990) landmark book *Black Feminist Thought* identified the fusion of activism and theory as its distinguishing characteristic" (p. 345). The core themes of Black feminist thought are (a) the interlocking of race, class, and gender oppression in Black women's personal, domestic, and work lives; (b) the necessity of recreating positive self-definitions and rejecting denigrating, stereotypical, and externally imposed controlling images (mammy, matriarch, welfare mother, whore), both in and outside of the Black community; and (c) the need for active struggle to resist oppression and realize individual and group empowerment (Collins, 1990).

A critical component of Black feminism is its ability to address the gaps and life concerns that other theoretical frameworks and paradigms do not incorporate and address (Jones & Guy-Sheftall, 2015). The Black feminist paradigm requires "taking an intersectional approach, attending to the different positioning of people based on their social identities, to explore and explain oppression and liberation processes" (Mosley et al., 2021, p. 2). It is important to note that such critical components of Black feminism can be employed throughout the counseling process.

Based on Mosley et al. (2021), fostering and creating counseling spaces that employ paradigms centered on individualism and multiculturalism can empower and best support Black women and their experiences of racial/gender oppression, marginalization, and trauma. Similarly, Brickman and Donohue (2020) stated that clinical practitioners should infuse multiculturalism and social justice components into initial counseling sessions when working with Black women, specifically, psychoeducation that reflects intersectionality and the Superwoman schema. The Superwoman schema reflects the benefits and liabilities of Black women engaging in multiple roles in their lives and how the intensity and stress of these roles have implications for their physical health (Woods-Giscombé, 2010).

Afrocentricity

Afrocentricity is a paradigm combining theory and application, consisting of social movement, research, cultural implementation, and lifestyle practices (Khokholkova, 2016). Molefi Kete Asante, a scholar, philosopher, and activist who founded Afrocentric theory, defined Afrocentricity as a paradigm positing that African people should reassert a sense of agency to achieve sanity (Asante, 2009). This paradigm is a revolutionary shift in thinking, proposed as a constructional adjustment to Black disorientation, de-centeredness, and lack of agency for studying ideas, concepts, events, personalities, and political and economic processes from the standpoint of Black people as subjects and not as objects (Asante, 2009).

Widely recognized for his work, Asante advanced the philosophy and methodological foundations of Afrocentricity as a theory for change (Chawane, 2016), specifically, that people of African descent should embrace African roots and debunk White culture. Khokholkova (2016) noted that Asante developed Afrocentricity to examine why Black people are disoriented. Further, his work framing Afrocentric theory addresses the impediments and impairments grounded in a Black woman's life and hardships due to the impacts of oppressive Eurocentric viewpoints.

Pellebon (2007) stated that in terms of action, Afrocentricity is a continuous process of rejecting Eurocentric social reality while embracing all aspects of Afrocentric reality amid a racist society. Afrocentrists assertively challenge Eurocentric perspectives as applied to or experienced by African people. Asante (2003) wrote that the

> Afrocentrist . . . studies every thought, action, behavior, and value, and if it is contradictory to [African] culture or our history, it is dispensed with

> quickly . . . Our problems come when we lose sight of ourselves, accept false doctrines, false gods, mistaken notions of what is genuinely in our history, and assume an individualistic, anti-humanistic, and autocratic posture. (p. 10)

Asante's quote highlights the influence of White culture in creating race-related stressors and generational trauma for Black women due to oppressive Eurocentric fallacies defaming African American historical experiences.

A longstanding history of overcoming trials and tribulations with exceptional strength enriches the Black experience. Originating from African roots, Black women possess innate perseverance and resilience in overcoming stressors and trauma. Further, following years of slavery and colonization, Black people were adversely subjected to Eurocentric values and cultural ideals (Chawane, 2016). Ongoing oppression resulting from unjust systems in the United States and living in a Eurocentric culture create barriers to advancement for Black women, significantly when these women are impacted by trauma. Asante's work framing Afrocentric theory addresses the impediments and impairments in Black women's lives and the hardships caused by the impact of oppressive Eurocentric viewpoints.

Critical Consciousness and Transformative Trauma-Informed Care

Trauma for Black women is multidimensional; therefore, clinical practitioners must address this dimensionality throughout the counseling process and give space to Black women who wish to explore and become consciously aware of how their lived experiences of race and other forms of trauma impact their mental health and well-being (Abrams et al., 2014; Mosley et al., 2021). *Critical consciousness* is broadly defined as "an intervention to mitigate, prevent, and resist racial trauma" (Mosley et al., 2021, p. 4). More specifically, when a racially minoritized woman becomes aware of her lived experiences of racism, her critical reflections are defined as essential consciousness in response to this realization and awareness (Mosley et al., 2021). Most importantly, the critical ideological paradigm as it relates to critical consciousness is subjective and individualized. When providing clinical counseling to Black women, the clinical practitioner's role is also to be mindful and cognizant of the notion that Black women's worldviews can be best illuminated through the critical consciousness paradigm (Brinkman & Donohue, 2020).

Trauma-informed clinical counseling practices are of great importance when treating women because of trauma's high impact on women's mental health. Women experience fewer traumatic events than men; however, the kinds of traumatic events women experience are typically associated with a higher risk for post-traumatic stress disorder (Vogt, 2019). Such susceptibility to adverse psychological outcomes for women results from chronic traumas such as interpersonal violence, sexual violence, and gendered social roles (Pemberton & Loeb, 2020; Vogt, 2019). Racial trauma's effects can create maladaptive symptomologies that cause significant distress and negative views of the world. Black women exposed to such trauma may also develop negative belief systems and trauma-related symptoms affecting their self-esteem and self-worth (Williams, 2018).

Clinical practitioners seek to provide a safe healing space; introducing critical consciousness as an intervention related to race-based trauma-informed care is fundamental to providing a safe space. Clinical practitioners must also use constructivist grounded theoretical methods to provide a space for reflection, exploration, and meaning making of Black women's multifaceted lived experiences and amplify the voices of Black women who have experienced racial trauma.

Clinical practitioners who begin the clinical counseling process with Black women by providing psychoeducation on critical consciousness can build more inclusive, meaningful, and safer spaces in which Black women can explore how they view themselves in relation to the world around them. Finally, practitioners can also explore how societal perceptions of Black women impact their everyday lives (Wallace, 2009). From a culturally relevant clinical lens, such an exploration requires administering trauma- and racially-informed assessment tools.

Diagnosing and Assessing Trauma in Black Women

Appropriate assessment of a Black woman's trauma requires using tools sensitive to her multifaceted presentation. The Posttraumatic Stress Disorder Checklist (PCL-5) and the Race-Based Traumatic Stress Symptom Scale (RBTSS) are two tools that can capture the racially sensitive makeup of a Black woman's trauma exposure and its impact. The PCL-5 is a 20-item self-report measure that assesses posttraumatic stress disorder symptoms in the fifth edition of the *Diagnostic and Statistical Manual of Mental Disorders* (*DSM-5*; Blevins et al., 2015). Trauma symptoms are commonly misdiagnosed for Black women due to uninformed clinical practitioners assessing from a narrow, westernized societal definition of trauma and overlooking and not incorporating present symptomologies. Using the PCL-5 when assessing a Black woman for trauma can help clinical practitioners identify and monitor trauma-related symptom changes during and following treatment (Blevins et al., 2015). Further, self-report measures can prevent misdiagnosing as they allow Black women to define their presenting challenges in accordance with *DSM-5* criteria.

The RBTSS is an instrument specifically designed to assess race-based trauma stressors. This tool was designed to evaluate the historical lacking appropriate cultural sensitivity to trauma-related stressors of racial discrimination, racism, stereotypes, and systematic oppression impacting the mental health of minorities (Carter & Pieterse, 2020). Administered by the clinical practitioner, the assessment consists of open-ended questions on specific incidents and racially related stressors that can impact emotional reactions (Carter & Pieterse, 2020). Using the PCL-5 and the RBTSS when assessing a Black woman's trauma history and how trauma has impacted her psychologically will provide a more significant conceptualization of clinical needs with appropriate considerations of race-based stressors and trauma-presenting symptomatology.

Six Guiding Principles for Trauma-Informed Healing

Exposure to trauma and managing its symptoms requires using trauma-informed care and counseling. Providing safe and empowering support in a counseling setting is crucial in the healing process for a Black woman's trauma. The Substance Abuse and Mental Health Services Administration's (SAMHSA) six key principles of a trauma-informed approach are foundational in treating trauma (Pemberton & Loeb, 2020). Each principle provides trauma-sensitive methods that direct a clinical practitioner to create and promote a safe and supportive environment following the aftermath of trauma (SAMHSA, 2014). These principles are the following:

1. Safety consists of providing the client with a sense of physical and psychological safety as a priority.
2. Trustworthiness is established through the clinical practitioner using transparency to build and maintain trust.

3. Peer support is encouraged by clinical practitioners by building trust, establishing safety, and empowerment.
4. Collaboration and mutuality are established by the clinical practitioner recognizing that healing occurs through relationships and sharing of power and decision-making. Further, the clinical practitioner recognizes that everyone plays a role in trauma-informed approaches.
5. Empowerment, voice, and choice driven by the clinical practitioner acknowledging that each person's experience is unique and requires an individualized approach.
6. Cultural, historical, and gender issues are addressed by the clinical practitioner actively moving past cultural stereotypes and biases while offering culturally responsive treatment that leverages the healing value of traditional cultural connections and recognizes and addresses historical trauma (SAMHSA, 2014).

Using these approaches can foster a trusting and empathetic space with validation for Black women who have experienced various types of traumas. The pure essence of Black women possessing a deeper, richer, and more vulnerable conceptualization of the underpinnings of a society that negatively impacts various aspects of their mental health and well-being allows room for establishing and identifying new ways in which these women can not only survive but thrive.

Implementing Black Cultural Values in Practice

Black women, the matriarchs of Black culture, often express managing hardships through instilling faith and strength in their lives. Further, engaging in gatherings, commemorating religion and spirituality, and embracing family are historical coping methods in Black culture. Despite these generationally used cultural practices, Black values and rituals are commonly absent in traditional clinical practices. Supplementing Afrocentricity in a Black woman's healing process allows transformation in multiple dimensions as the theory's methods affect psychological, political, social, cultural, and economic change (Asante, 2009). Pellebon (2007) and Khokholkova (2016) characterized the goals of Afrocentric theory as exposing and actively resisting White racial domination while empowering Black people to return to their center and oppose White America's racist-developed society dominated by

Eurocentric culture. The goals consist of facilitating Black people's connection to the African cultural system by raising collective consciousness; transforming Black people toward their cultural center; and converting ideologies of values, spirituality and rituals, and disciplines to an Afrocentric perspective (Pellebon, 2007).

In practice, Afrocentric models allow for spirituality, communalism, fluidity of time, emotional expressiveness, harmony with nature, interdependence, and allegiance to African cultural ideals to protect against the vicissitudes of racism (Sanchez-Hucles, 2016). Such principles in the model are common cultural traditions in the Black culture that are important for clinical practitioners to empower their Black women clients. Asante (2009) described the meaning for clients to embody cultural traditions as *Nija*, or "The Way," defined as a collective expression of an Afrocentric worldview representing the African spirit and spiritual survival grounded in Black woman traditions (Pellebon, 2007). Afrocentrist clinical practitioners exhibit Nija by bringing Black cultural rituals, gatherings, language, and values into sessions. Language, in particular, is used by greeting with borrowed African words such as *Habri gani*, meaning What is the news? Umoja, meaning unity. Additionally, Black cultural vernacular is reflected by words such as *brotha* and *sista* as other means to greet and embrace the African spirit (Khokholkova, 2016).

Using these cultural traditions in the clinical setting can bring comfort to a Black woman's mental health journey and allow her to incorporate African spirit and strength as aids in overcoming trauma. Further, establishing cultural presentation in clinical practice provides the opportunity for a Black woman to be understood and validated, in contrast to the barriers she faces in society.

From an Afrocentric Lens : The Process of Healing

The innateness of a Black woman's strength and the journey can be empowered and propelled through the lens of Afrocentric theory. Traditional psychotherapy theories were created based on White cultural norms and beliefs. Afrocentric theory, in contrast, is a framework that allows people of African descent to be viewed and treated guided by their own cultural worldviews instead of following colonized perceptions of European America. Embracing Afrocentric values embedded in the Black identity is critical in treating a Black woman's trauma. Clinical practitioners using such lenses must adopt the perspective that Afrocentricity is a theoretical framework based on the belief that people of African descent heal through reasserting a sense of agency to achieve sanity (Khokholkova, 2016). Khokholkova (2016) also stated that Black women could not heal without recognizing their true cultural identity and roots, which originated before their experiences of trauma. Further, Black women will struggle to thrive unless they recognize that American society is based on the White perspective that invalidates African culture (Khokholkova, 2016). In employing appropriate therapeutic practices with Black women, addressing their racial identity is not only necessary for cultural competency as a clinical practitioner, but essential.

Clinical practitioners who lack an understanding of the Afrocentric theoretical framework will lack empathy toward Black identity and culture. Lacking such an understanding can impede clinical practitioners' abilities to effectively and holistically treat Black women's trauma experiences (Gregory & Harper, 2001). Framed with rich African influence and cultural considerations, Afrocentric theory must be utilized by encompassing Afrocentrist principles. Identifying as an Afrocentrist, a clinical practitioner must understand that an accurate presentation of the Black collective experience for self-determination has to be adopted as the Eurocentric misrepresentation of African history psychologically dislocates Black people (Pellebon, 2007).

From a Black Feminist Lens: The Process of Healing

When Black women reach crisis points, they are more likely to withdraw or delay treatment because their ethnic, gender, and cultural needs go unrecognized or mistreated in most clinical settings (Jones & Guy-Sheftall, 2015). Culturally congruent, positive mental health paradigms that stress client strengths and recognize the deficits in their environments are essential when providing mental health services to Black women (Jones & Warner, 2011; Thomas et al., 2008; Woods-Giscombé & Black, 2010). Jones and Guy-Sheftall (2015) stated that

> Therapeutic interventions developed from a black feminist perspective must help black women recognize how the internalization of stereotypes and negative notions of black womanhood contribute to their negative psychological symptoms (for example, depression, anxiousness, low self-esteem, and decreased sense of mastery and control). (p. 347)

Culturally congruent mental health practices can positively impact the counseling experience (Jones & Harris, 2019). The profession of clinical counseling must work to adopt a structured approach and framework designed to meet the mental health needs of Black women accurately. To meaningfully employ clinical counseling practices from a Black feminist lens, clinical practitioners must have an understanding of intersectionality as a foundational praxis and incorporate it in their practice in order to best conceptualize Black women's complex and multilayered identities and struggles. The following sections explore original clinical practices developed by the authors of this chapter. Clinical practitioners can use these practices to ensure that Black women are heard, seen, and understood throughout the counseling process. The authors challenge and encourage current and future clinical practitioners to encompass the following tools derived from a Black feminist lens to help empower Black women.

The Importance of Cultivating Internalized Empowerment

A foundational definition of internalized empowerment is needed before exploring empowerment more in-depth. Internalize is defined as "To incorporate (values, patterns of culture, etc.) within the self as conscious or subconscious guiding principles through learning or socialization" (Merriam-Webster, n.d.-b, para. 1). Merriam-Webster Online (n.d.-a) defines empowerment as giving official authority or legal power to or as promoting the self-actualization of influence of an individual. From a mental health perspective, Chamberlin and Schene (1997) defined empowerment as "a complex, multidimensional concept designed to describe a process rather than an event" (p. 44). Therefore, the authors of this chapter conceptualize internalized empowerment as "Actively taking control of, learning about, and developing complex multidimensional attitudes and/or behaviors regarding one's life."

With such definitions in mind, it is essential that clinical practitioners who seek to understand Black women's worldviews and how societal predispositions centered around a Black woman as her "self" include ideals based on the belief that all Black women are strong and can handle anything. Practitioners can help Black women reframe negative societal predispositions and how they can impact their mental health; therefore, this chapter recommends that clinical practitioners use a Black feminist lens to help Black women dismantle preexisting societal predispositions and establish new ones.

Clinical practitioners can use two foundational counseling skills to help Black women foster internalized empowerment: the deep-rooted and intrinsic concepts of self-love and self-compassion. Per the growing body of research on the concepts of self-love and self-compassion, such concepts can help individuals redefine what it can look like to love oneself and show compassion and grace to oneself (Woods-Giscombé & Black, 2010). The following sections suggest approaches clinical practitioners can use to help Black women cultivate internalized empowerment. They reflect therapeutic counseling strategies derived from a Black feminist lens and center on the concepts of self-care and self-compassion.

Fostering Spirituality and Harmony in Clinical Counseling Settings

Ntu psychotherapy is an Afrocentric and spiritually based therapeutic approach to healing Black people to their cultural center. Deriving from the Bantu concept of essence, the Ntu model empowers therapeutic interactions as created vibrations composed of energy, authenticity, focus, and harmonious healing (Gregory & Harper, 2001). Ntu derives from an "Africentric" understanding of the world in practice, guiding Black people through their cultural principles of spirituality, family-focused, maintaining cultural competency, and using holistic systems and values (Gregory & Harper, 2001). When implemented in practice, clinical practitioners conduct sessions in circulatory phases, giving clients the ability to move through the healing process by reprocessing their beliefs (Gregory & Harper, 2001; Tovar-Murray, 2011). Using Ntu psychotherapy with Black women can promote transformative trauma healing, creating relief from self-blame and guilt.

Ntu psychotherapy has five phases: harmony, awareness, alignment, actualization, and synthesis. The following details on these phases are based on Tovar-Murray's (2011) and Gregory and Harper's 2001 work, highlighting the use of Ntu with a Black woman.

- Phase 1: Harmony, a state in which a Black woman is in tune with herself and her environment. Clinical practitioners can drive harmony by establishing an in-sync spiritual therapeutic relationship through techniques such as Black rituals, humor, libations, genograms, and self-disclosure.

- Phase 2: Awareness, the ability of a Black woman to know herself and others. Clinical practitioners assist the Black woman in developing greater awareness by identifying thoughts, feelings, and behaviors that do not align with her spirit or ancestors. Techniques in discovering self-awareness include identifying rigid negative beliefs, the empty chair, guided imagery, mediation, and creative visualization.
- Phase 3: Alignment, the Black woman's process of confronting her underlying dynamics and shifting perspectives. Clinical practitioners assist in discovering and challenging discrepancies, reframing negative cognitions, providing relaxation methods, raising spiritual awareness, and confronting fears.
- Phase 4: Actualization, prepping a Black woman for the steps into trauma healing with new behaviors through practice and planning. Clinical practitioners assist in providing homework assignments, role and behavior rehearsals, empowering affirmations, and building new skills.
- Phase 5: Synthesis, a place of reflection for a Black woman to evaluate the healing process and effectiveness of the therapeutic process to determine where she is and what she will continue to go through. Clinical practitioners assist Black women in moving past difficulties and creating new strength-based systems with effective and healthy problem-solving skills.

Exercises for Cultivating Self-Compassion in Clinical Counseling

Cultivating the concept of self-compassion in the beginning stages of the counseling process allows Black women a safe space to explore and intrinsically conceptualize the importance of lending grace and understanding to themselves, for themselves. By creating the space for Black women to explore and conceptualize what it means and looks like to extend self-compassion to themselves, a more vulnerable level of internalized empowerment can be fostered to allow a deeper exploration. Clinical practitioners can use a Black feminist paradigm to incorporate self-compassion exercises in session from a culturally informed perspective. The following aspirational self-compassion counseling approach is designed for the clinical practitioner to introduce as a cognitive skill-building approach that can help Black women increase their compassion and understanding of themselves on a deeper level.

Step 1: The practitioner can provide the client with psychoeducation about self-compassion.

Step 2: Following the exploration and definition of self-compassion, the clinical practitioner can then invite the client to explore and discuss the multifaceted layers of their social identities. The practitioner can encourage the client to explore at least two aspects of her social identity and invite the client to openly express her thoughts and feelings as they relate to the identities.

Step 3: As the client and practitioner begin to unpack how the client's identities interact with one another, the practitioner can begin to identify and recognize areas where the client can employ self-compassion toward herself. The practitioner can assist the client by using examples of applying a culturally relevant self-compassionate approach to viewing multiple social identities based on the tenets of Black feminism. For example, the clinical practitioner can ask the client, "In understanding how the three social identities we have discussed impact your daily life, what would it look like to reconfigure or reframe these identities from a place of compassion?"

Step 4: To help the client foster and better conceptualize how she can possess self-compassion for herself, the clinical practitioner can also choose to pose questions or make statements specifically on recognizing and validating the complexity of possessing multiple social identities and how this existence in itself requires strength. For example, the clinical practitioner may make statements like, "In exploring more in-depth the multidimensional aspects of your identity and how it impacts you emotionally, your everyday life is complex, and because it is so complex, I think it is important that you honor how strong you are for navigating this complexity day by day."

By infusing Black feminist epistemology with self-compassion, the hope is that Black women can feel more understood, seen, and empowered throughout the counseling process. Culturally relevant counseling practices may lead to positive cognitive and behavioral growth.

Creating a Safe Space with Self-Love Exercises

Self-love in the counseling process is often not viewed as a skill set per se. However, in actuality, loving one's self wholly and unconditionally does require a skill. Incorporating and understanding how the notions of power and oppression are viewed from the subjective perspective of Black women's lived experiences expands once the clinical practitioner introduces the strategy and skill of loving oneself without fear, judgment, and prejudice. Per Alinia (2015), one must strive to fully comprehend the importance of understanding a Black woman's reality on her terms. Clinical practitioners can combine Black feminist epistemology with clinical skills (Brinkman & Donohue, 2020) centered on self-love by introducing foundational concepts on how the Black woman views herself.

The following self-love journal exercises are designed to elicit information on three concepts: how Black women define self-love, what actions Black women take to love themselves, and how Black women can begin to love themselves more intentionally.

- Journal Prompt 1: Explore your very first memory of loving yourself or struggling with how to do so as a Black woman. What emotions and thoughts come to mind? Who taught you what you know about loving your blackness and loving your path as a woman?
- Journal Prompt 2: Often, people ask what inner self-love is. Essentially, inner self-love can be whatever you want it to be, but ideally, inner self-love is love that is derived and focused on how and what you love about yourself on the *inside and not the outside* (external or physical traits). Please explore how you can begin to dismantle and disseminate the false sense of self-love derived from external sources. How can you begin to reposition and shift your thinking and perception to consider the importance of interior/inner self-love versus exterior self-love? Identify two traits/characteristics that speak to your inner self-love and make you feel strong and safe. Furthermore, how willing are you to be vulnerable, open, and raw about your inner self-love or lack thereof?
- Journal Prompt 3: Upon reflection and conceptualizing what it means to become more connected to your inner self and how to love yourself more internally, the following three questions are designed to

highlight more specifically how you can prompt more internal self-love.

1. What is one step that you can initiate to align the exterior and interior characteristics that you love about yourself as a Black woman?
2. Intentionality is a must when focusing on self-love, as is listening to the body mentally, emotionally, and spiritually. As a Black woman, how can you begin to listen to your body from one of these areas of focus?
3. With the two internal traits/characteristics that you established last session that you love about yourself, upon exploring more in-depth, what other meaningful internal traits can be added to the list as you begin to subjectively find and redefine the internal characteristics that reflect and represent the love you have for yourself?

The self-love journal exercises encourage Black women to intentionally explore and cultivate empowering ways to love and view themselves free of judgment, stereotypes, and criticism from society. Based on the developed theories from Collins, Crenshaw, and Guy-Sheftall, it is essential to employ concepts that seek to understand and shed light on the Black lived experience. Employing these concepts helps to center the counseling process on racial and gender consciousness that attempt to make the lived experience of Black women the focal point of the counseling process. By centering the counseling process on the Black woman's worldview and view of herself, such viewpoints can inform the clinical practitioner on what the development of meaningful and individualized treatment plans and personalized goals for counseling should look like for Black women throughout treatment (Jones, 2015; Jones & Harris, 2019).

Directions for Future Research on Black Women's Mental Health

As previously noted, this chapter aims to provide aspirational guiding principles and counseling exercises that the authors have deemed appropriate in the mental health treatment of Black women. The theoretical orientations explored throughout this chapter speak to the importance of addressing, exploring, and attending to Black women's multifaceted lived experiences. Culturally aware clinical practitioners who wish to provide empowering and culturally sound counseling services to Black women can use the theories and aspirational counseling approaches discussed throughout the chapter to do so. Moreover, culturally responsive treatment approaches can help Black women grow and heal (Williams, 2005). Developing evidence-based counseling frameworks that clinical practitioners can use to provide efficacious and meaningful treatment to Black women is a necessity. It is currently required in mental health counseling and beyond.

Afrocentric theory and Black feminist theory give voice to the intricate cultural and trauma-sensitive needs of Black women. Newer developed theories, such as the womanist theory, present promising approaches to treating the multifaceted challenges Black women face. Principles of the womanist theory are grounded on viewing women of color as equal to all other women and men, embracing spirituality and strength, using humor and emotional expressions, and using connectedness and culture to heal Black women and empower them as free from societal oppressions (Sanchez-Hucles, 2016). Like Afrocentric theory and Black feminist theory, the womanist theory presents a holistic view of the Black woman. However, similar to Black feminist and Afrocentric theories, womanist theories are not widely used in clinical settings. Continued research and implementation of racial-, gender-, and trauma-informed theoretical orientations from a clinical counseling lens and paradigm remain critical. In years to come, continued development of evidence-based treatment modalities that encompass the tenets of culturally responsive theoretical frameworks designed to address the multifaceted and marginalized lived experiences of Black women is of great importance.

References

Abrams, J. A., Maxwell, M., Pope, M., & Belgrave, F. Z. (2014). Carrying the world with the grace of a lady and the grit of a warrior: Deepening our understanding of the "strong Black woman" schema. *Psychology of Women Quarterly*, *38*(4), 503–518. https://doi.org/10.1177/0361684314541418

Alinia, M. (2015). On Black feminist thought: Thinking oppression and resistance through intersectional paradigm. *Ethnic and Racial Studies*, *38*(13), 2334–2340. https://doi.org/10.1080/01419870.2015.1058492

Asante, M. (2003). *Afrocentricity: The theory of social change*. African American Images.

Asante, M. (2009, April 13). *Afrocentricity.* http://www.asante.net/articles/1/afrocentricity/

Blevins, C. A., Weathers, F. W., Davis, M. T., Witte, T. K., & Domino, J. L. (2015). The Posttraumatic Stress Disorder Checklist for DSM-5 (PCL-5): Development and initial psychometric evaluation. *Journal of Traumatic Stress*, *28*(6), 489–498. https://doi.org/10.1002/jts.22059

Boyd-Franklin, N. (1991). Recurrent themes in the treatment of African American women in group psychotherapy. *Women & Therapy*, *11*(2), 25–40. https://doi.org/10.1300/J015V11N02_04

Brinkman, B., & Donohue, P. (2020). Doing intersectionality in social justice-oriented clinical training. *Training and Education in Professional Psychology*, *14*(2), 109–115. https://doi.org/10.1037/tep0000274

Brown, D. L., Blackmon, S., Griffin-Fennell, F., Darden, T., & Bannerman, D. (2020). Intersectional perspectives of Black women's mental health: Strategies for clinical training. *Women & Therapy*, *43*(3–4), 330–347. https://doi.org/10.1080/02703149.2020.1729467

Carter, R., & Pieterse, A. (2020). *Measuring the effects of racism: Guidelines for the assessment and treatment of race-based traumatic stress injury*. Columbia University Press.

Chamberlin, J. (1997). A working definition of empowerment. *Psychiatric Rehabilitation Journal*, *20*(4), 43–46. https://www.mainstreamliving.org/media/articles/PBS_Training_Topic__A_Working_Defin_F1E8FC666B220.PDF

Chawane, M. (2016). The development of Afrocentricity: A historical survey. *Yesterday and Today*, (16), 78–99. https://doi.org/10.17159/2223-0386/2016/n16a5

Chinn, J. J., Martin, K. I., & Redmond, N. (2021). Health equity among Black women in the United States. *Journal of Women's Health*, *30*(2), 212–219. https://doi.org/10.1089/jwh.2020.8868

Collins, P. H. (2000). *Black feminist thought: Knowledge, consciousness, and the politics of empowerment*. Routledge.

Emba, C. (2019, January 9). Opinion: Black women deserve better. *The Washington Post*. https://www.washingtonpost.com/opinions/black-women-deserve-better-will-2019-be-the-year-of-change/2019/01/09/fc40e842-1439-11e9-803c-4ef28312c8b9_story.html

Evans, S. Y., Bell, K., & Burton, N. K. (2017). *Black women's mental health: Balancing strength and vulnerability*. SUNY Press.

Fulani, L. (2014). All power to the people! In L. Fulani (Ed.), *The psychopathology of everyday racism and sexism* (pp. xi–xix). Psychology Press.

Gregory, W. H., & Harper, K. W. (2001). The Ntu approach to health and healing. *Journal of Black Psychology*, *27*(3), 304–320. https://doi.org/10.1177/0095798401027003004

Grote, N. K., Bledsoe, S. E., Wellman, J., & Brown, C. (2007). Depression in African American and White women with low incomes: The role of chronic stress. *Social Work in Public Health*, *23*(2–3), 59–88. https://doi.org/10.1080/19371910802148511

Jones, L. V. (2015). Black feminisms: Renewing sacred healing spaces. *AFILIA: Journal of Women and Social Work*, *30*(2), 246–252. https://doi.org/10.1177/0886109914551356

Jones, L. V., & Guy-Sheftall, B. (2015). Conquering the Black girl blues. *Social Work, 60*(4), 343–350. https://doi.org/10.1093/sw/swv032

Jones, L. V., & Harris, M. A. (2019). Developing a Black feminist analysis for mental health practice: From theory to praxis. *Women & Therapy, 42*(3–4), 251–264. https://doi.org/10.1080/02703149.2019.1622908

Jones, L. V., & Warner, L. A. (2011). Evaluating culturally responsive group work with Black women. *Research on Social Work Practice, 21*(6), 737–746. doi:10.1177/1049731511411488

Khokholkova, N. (2016). Afrocentricity: The evolution of the theory in the context of American history. *Social Evolution & History, 15*(1), 111–125. https://www.sociostudies.org/journal/files/seh/2016_1/111-125.pdf

Kwate, N. O. A., Valdimarsdottir, H. B., Guevarra, J. S., & Bovbjerg, D. H. (2003). Experiences of racist events are associated with negative health consequences for African American women. *Journal of the National Medical Association, 95*(6), 450–460. https://www.ncbi.nlm.nih.gov/pmc/articles/PMC2594553/pdf/jnma00310-0068.pdf

Lindsay-Dennis, L. (2015). Black feminist-womanist research paradigm: Toward a culturally relevant research model focused on African American girls. *Journal of Black Studies, 46*(5), 506–520. https://doi.org/10.1177/0021934715583664

Merriam-Webster. (n.d-.a). *Empower.* Retrieved August 28, 2021, from https://www.merriam-webster.com/dictionary/empower

Merriam-Webster. (n.d.-b). *Internalize.* Retrieved August 28, 2021, https://www.merriam-webster.com/dictionary/internalize

Mosley, D. V., Hargons, C. N., Meiller, C., Angyal, B., Wheeler, P., Davis, C., & Stevens-Watkins, D. (2021). Critical consciousness of anti-Black racism: A practical model to prevent and resist racial trauma. *Journal of Counseling Psychology,* 68(1), 1–16. https://doi.org/10.1037/cou0000430

National Center for Health Statistics. (2018). *Health, United States 2018.* U.S. Department of Health and Human Services, Centers for Disease Control and Prevention. https://www.cdc.gov/nchs/data/hus/hus18.pdf

Pellebon, D. (2007). An analysis of Afrocentricity as theory for social work practice. *Advances in Social Work, 8*(1). https://doi.org/10.18060/139

Pemberton, J. V., & Loeb, T. B. (2020). Impact of sexual and interpersonal violence and trauma on women: Trauma-informed practice and feminist theory. *Journal of Feminist Family Therapy, 32*(1–2), 115–131. https://doi.org/10.1080/08952833.2020.1793564

Sanchez-Hucles, J. V. (2016). Womanist therapy with Black women. In T. Bryant-Davis & L. Comas-Díaz (Eds.), *Womanist and mujerista psychologies: Voices of fire, acts of courage* (pp. 69–92). American Psychological Association. https://doi.org/10.1037/14937-004

Thomas, A. J., Witherspoon, K. M., & Speight, S. L. (2008). Gendered racism, psychological distress, and coping styles of African American women. *Cultural Diversity and Ethnic Minority Psychology, 14*(4), 307. https://doi.org/10.1037/1099-9809.14.4.307

Tovar-Murray, D. (2011). Ntu psychotherapy framework with African American clients: An Afrocentric theoretical and spiritual model. *Journal of Counseling in Illinois, 1*(1), 11–20. https://cdn.ymaws.com/www.ilcounseling.org/resource/resmgr/publications/jci_compiled-final_version.pdf

Vogt, D. (2019). *Research on women, trauma and PTSD.* U.S. Department of Veterans Affairs, National Center for PTSD. https://www.ptsd.va.gov/professional/treat/specific/ptsd_research_women.asp

Wallace, G. (2009). A research brief: Exploring Black feminist consciousness in the lives of fifteen African American women. *Race, Gender & Class, 16*(1/2), 282–288.

Williams, C. B. (2005). Counseling African American women: Multiple identities—multiple constraints. *Journal of Counseling & Development, 83*(3), 278–283. https://doi.org/10.1002/j.1556-6678.2005.tb00343.x

Woods-Giscombé, C. L. (2010). Superwoman schema: African American women's views on stress, strength, and health. *Qualitative Health Research, 20*(5), 668–683. https://doi.org/10.1177/1049732310361892

Woods-Giscombé, C. L., & Black, A. R. (2010). Mind-body interventions to reduce risk for health disparities related to stress and strength among African American women: The potential of mindfulness-based stress reduction, loving-kindness, and the Ntu therapeutic framework. *Complementary Health Practice Review, 15*(3), 115–131. https://doi.org/10.1177/1533210110386776

Part 4. The Healing Process

Chapter 10

Let the Healing Begin: Black Women's Spirituality in Times of Trauma

Awa Jangha[1,*]
and Latoya Moss[2]
[1]Seminary of The Southwest, Austin, Texas
[2]Independent Researcher/Scholar

Abstract

What do we do when we face experiences of trauma? Where do we turn in times of prolonged stress? For many Black women, we call on what is sacred, what we deem a source of power and strength, and we engage the spirit within ourselves and each other to survive and thrive. This chapter will explore how Black women utilize spirituality to cope with trauma. In the Black community, music and lyrics play an integral part in how we process and cope (kinesthetically, auditorily, and somatically), especially in the Black church. As such, the information covered in this chapter is guided by lyrics that help organize the content supported by reflection questions throughout the work. Topics in this chapter include an overview of spirituality and religion, the interplay of trauma and spirituality, followed by a case example of a Black woman engaging her spirituality in the context of a traumatic experience with infertility. Won't you come with us on this sacred journey? Let the healing begin.

Keywords: African-American women, Black women, trauma, etiology of trauma

---

* Corresponding Author's Email: awa.jangha@ssw.edu.

In: How Did We Survive?
Editor: Tina Marie Glover
ISBN: 979-8-88697-918-3

Introduction

> *"Sing a song full of the faith that the dark past has taught us*
> *Sing a song full of the hope that the present has brought us*
> *Facing the rising sun of our new day begun*
> *Let us march on till victory is won"* (Johnson, 2001)

What do we do when we face experiences of trauma? Where do we turn in times of prolonged stress? People turn to sources of support and inspiration in times of stress, struggle, and trials. For many Black women, we call on what is sacred, what we deem a source of power and strength, and we engage the spirit within ourselves and each other to survive and thrive. For many, that source is their spiritual belief, which can include a community of like-minded believers or a personalized relationship with whatever one deems to be spiritual.

This chapter explores how Black women utilize spirituality to cope with trauma. More specifically, it considers the interplay of spirituality and religion with trauma and the variety of ways that they work together or against each other. Through the Black female experience lens, spirituality, religion, and trauma are explored, and reflection questions are provided to encourage further personal application. The authors, two Black female counselors, begin with a fictional case example (based on a compilation of real-life experiences) of a Black woman's engagement with spirituality when faced with a traumatic experience of infertility. The chapter also includes an overview of spirituality and religion (providing definitions and descriptions of each from a general perspective and a Black female perspective). Lastly, the authors explore the interplay of trauma and spirituality (defining trauma and stress and exploring the use of spirituality as a coping skill).

The reader will note how the use of music and lyrics are woven throughout to connect one means of healing (the power of music) to the understanding of spirituality and trauma for Black women. In the Black community, music and lyrics play an integral part in how we process and cope (kinesthetically, auditorily, and somatically), especially in the Black church. As such, the information covered in this chapter is guided by lyrics that help to organize the content. The lyrics that open this chapter are from the Black National Anthem, *Lift Every Voice and Sing*, written in 1900 by James Weldon Johnson (2001). This song is a powerful call to the Black community and serves as a source of inspiration for Black people facing the unique oppression that exists today. The themes of finding one's song, working together, acknowledging our hurt and oppression, and prevailing with faith gave ample encouragement and comfort. It reminds us that no matter what, we still have a song we can sing, a song rooted in spirituality that we can sing together as we march on and push forward.

Ella's Story

Ella is a 34-year-old Black woman. She grew up in a Christian home with both parents and is the oldest of three siblings. Ella describes her extended family as large and tight-knit. She has a niece and nephew from two of her siblings, eight aunts and uncles from both sides of her family, and more than 40 first cousins.

Having experience as a babysitter for her siblings and cousins, Ella stated she has always wanted to be a mom. After several failed relationships in her late teens and early twenties, Ella was excited to finally meet someone in Chris, who shared her passion for life and learning and had similar goals and values. Two of the shared values and goals of Ella and Chris were based on the two wanting to honor God with their sexuality and eventually having their own small but tight knit family. Ella and Chris dated for almost two years before they got married.

Ella was excited to begin trying to grow her family within her first year of marriage. However, that excitement soon led to disappointment after months and months of trying but not conceiving. She continued rationalizing her empty womb to herself and the family members (who kept asking about when she and Chris would have a baby) as God gave her and her husband more time to solidify their relationship and prepare for parenthood. Ella and Chris kept trying and praying. They felt rewarded when halfway into year two, Ella got pregnant.

The pregnancy seemed to be going well despite nausea and vomiting. However, Ella began experiencing increased pelvic pain and light vaginal bleeding around weeks 5 and 6. The visit to her doctor revealed an ectopic pregnancy (outside of the central uterine cavity) that would need to be monitored to see if it would resolve itself before invasive treatment. Ella began praying earnestly, petitioning God for the fertilized egg to shift in her body. She had a few trusted family and friends lifting her in prayer while she made positive declarations about herself and the baby. However, pelvic and abdominal pain increased along with the vaginal bleeding. In week 7 of the pregnancy, Ella had a spontaneous abortion, also known as a miscarriage. Ella and Chris were devastated. Her family and friends rallied around her, providing support and encouragement during the difficult time.

> *"I just can't give up now. I've come too far from where I started from.*
> *Nobody told me that the road would be easy.*
> *And, I don't believe He's brought me this far to leave me"*
> (Mary Mary, 2000)

Ella did some research on her own and found that couples are more likely to have better outcomes if they are able to conceive within three months of a miscarriage than those who wait long periods of time. Ella and Chris were determined not to give up. Five months after the first pregnancy loss, Ella conceived again. There was no pain or bleeding this time, and the fetus was properly placed. All seemed to be going well. However, again at 7 weeks, the pregnancy was lost. Ella cried out to the Lord, asking why. She questioned whether or not she had done something wrong and was being punished. The sadness surrounded her like a cloud.

Month after month, Ella continued to read scripture and talk to God about her desire to be a mom. She candidly told him of her want to be one of the women whose "children rise and call her blessed" (*English Standard Version Bible*, 2001, Prov. 31:28) and of the accounts of Hannah and Elizabeth from Old and New Testament scripture who both cried out to him for their wombs to be opened. In her quiet times of communion with God, Ella reminded him that he heard the prayers of those women and allowed them to give birth to Samuel and John the Baptist; she reminded him that he had heard the prayers of other women not in the Bible and had answered those in the affirmative. She was looking for him to do the same for her.

As Ella continued to pray, she also sought medical advice from an infertility specialist. Based on Ella's age and history of early pregnancy loss, the specialist talked with Ella about several options. One of those options was to supplement the progesterone made by Ella's body. This could be done by the use of steroid hormones called progestogens. Ella discussed with Chris the suggested plan of the steroid shots and how they have been found to help lower the risk of early pregnancy loss in the first trimester. Chris was on board.

Ella disliked injecting her body with steroids or having Chris give her the shot. However, she pushed through, reminding herself that if injections were what it would take to realize her dream, she would do it. She continued to pray and listen to music to uplift and encourage herself and relieve some of the symptoms of anxiety and depression. Ella watched her diet, engaged in light yoga for pregnant women, and worked to keep her stress levels low. This time, Ella made it past the first trimester. There was cautious optimism.

Ella researched on the internet what to expect during each week of pregnancy and what was happening developmentally with her growing baby. The cautious optimism began to grow. Ella learned that at 16 weeks, she should be able to see a tiny yet fully formed image, including arms, legs, fingers, and other distinct body parts. Ella's doctor could also tell her the sex of her baby. Ella was excited. Her research found that some abnormalities could also be seen if present. A little fear rose within Ella, and she hoped she and her baby would not be in that number.

Ready to learn the gender of her baby at the ultrasound and see the baby's outline on screen, Ella and Chris were both nervous yet excited about the appointment with the doctor. There was excitement as the image appeared on the monitor. The tech moved the instrument around, but there was no sound. Those feelings of excitement were short-lived. Ella listened intently for the "swooshing" that she read indicated heartbeat, but it did not come. Ella felt like a failure. She zoned out, held tightly to Chris's hand, and allowed the tears to fall as her doctor spoke to the couple about what Ella already knew happened to her baby.

Unfortunately, some version of Ella's experience has been shocking for many women worldwide. A part of the data from the National Survey of Family Growth (Chandra et al., 2002) reported that 12% or 7.3 million women between the ages of 15-44 experienced decreased ability to reproduce, also known as impaired fecundity (p. 14). The researchers further reported that after certain factors were accounted for, an estimated 2.1 million or 7.4% of married women were classified as infertile, with Black women ranging higher than their counterparts (p. 14). The above statistics can create many questions for the readers where answers may or may not exist. The survey highlights that infertility is not solely the inability to reproduce but also the challenges associated with conceiving and carrying a child to term.

There are a plethora of reasons, including some unknown to medical science, that 1 to 5 percent of women will lose their baby before week 20 in the second trimester (March of Dimes, 2017). Ella found herself in this number on three occasions. Frost et al. (2007) suggest that these early miscarriages are traumatic life events that can impact and possibly redefine a woman's sense of self. Further, based on their participant's responses, Frost et al. described the experience as "the loss of dreams, aspirations, expectations, and possibilities" (2007, p. 11). It is no wonder, then, that for women for whom this is a part of their lived experience, the need for an outlet is great on so many levels in order to quell or make sense of the guilt, sadness, anxiety, shame, deep longing, or times of questioning. Based on their research, Zukerman et al. (2016) reported that "women are more likely than men to endorse negative appraisals about themselves and the world, as well as blame themselves for the negative consequences of the traumatic event" (p. 328). Very similarly, when the case of Ella is considered, we see Ella question herself and her role in the trauma. Her ability to cope extended to other people and other areas.

Before, during, and after each pregnancy, Ella engaged her physical and spiritual support system in the form of her husband, Chris, and other family members and friends. However, she relied heavily on a different form of spirituality and religion as means of coping with the trauma associated with her experiences. Specifically, Ella continuously used communion with the God of her understanding through prayer, sacred text, and music to assist her during dark moments of uncertainty. She had a clear sense of her personal meaning of spirituality and religion, but these concepts are not so easily defined in a broader context. It raises the question, how are spirituality and religion defined?

Spirituality and Religion

> *"God of our weary years*
> *God of our silent tears*
> *Thou who has brought us thus far on the way*
> *Thou who has by Thy might Led us into the light*
> *Keep us forever in the path; we pray"* (Johnson, 2001)

The final verse of Lift Every Voice and Sing begins with the lyrics above. It is a call to remember the spiritual source from which many Black American families have been rooted. It is a reminder of not being alone and there being spiritual comfort and support that can provide hope during dark times. Within the context of these lyrics, spirituality is connected to a belief in God, and while this is true for some people, it is not true for everyone.

The terms spirituality and religion have a variety of meanings. It can be challenging to find a standard definition depending on one's context. Due to the very personal and numinous nature of spirituality and religion, these concepts are difficult to define, and settling on one agreed-upon definition has yet to take place in counseling research (Stewart-Sicking et al., 2020; Young

& Cashwell, 2020). As a result, a variety of definitions for spirituality and religion can be found in research (Bohecker et al., 2017; Pargament, 2007; Robert & Kelly, 2015). Beyond the world of research, spirituality and religion are both culturally specific. Depending on one's culture, the definition of each term will vary. Moreover, within each cultural context, it is important to recognize that, like Ella, every individual will have their own particular definition of these terms based on their life experience.

Spirituality Defined

"Every time I feel the spirit, moving in my heart I will pray" (Negro spiritual)

Spirituality is often perceived as being a personal and individual experience. It has been defined as "the search for what is sacred" (Pargament, 2007, p. 32), creating the opportunity to develop a personalized understanding of what brings meaning to life and what is sacred. This simple and concise definition is broad enough to encompass various beliefs. Some may connect their spirituality with God (or deities), while others connect their spirituality with other aspects of their life that are sacred to them (such as nature, family, energy, etc.). This definition of spirituality creates space for the variety that can be found within the spectrum of belief.

Additional definitions include descriptions that provide a more specific explanation, such as: "a universal human capacity to experience self-transcendence and awareness of sacred immanence, with resulting increases in greater self—other compassion and love" (Cashwell & Young, 2020, p. 12). The Association of Spiritual Ethical and Religious Values in Counseling (ASERVIC, n.d.) describes spirituality as the "drawing out and infusion of spirit in one's life" (para. 1) and "a personal affirmation of a transcendent connectedness in the universe" (Kelly, 1995, p. 4). Lastly, Bohecker et al. (2017) describe spirituality as including various outlooks on life, such as atheism and agnosticism (p. 128), and define it as "a way of being in the world that acknowledges the existence of a transcendent or unknown dimension in life that is intrinsically found within all human beings... internal and individual, and it goes beyond religious or cultural boundaries" (p. 129). These definitions describe a dimension of life that grounds and centers many people, similar to Ella.

Religion Defined

"He's got the whole world in his hands" (author unknown)

Religion is often viewed as having more structure, practices, rituals, and set beliefs shared by a group of people. It has been defined as "a belief that is associated with a world religion or specific philosophy… and is outwardly manifested by organized practices and sacred texts" (Robert & Kelly, 2015, p. xiii). Religion has also been described within ASERVIC's White Paper as "the codified, institutionalized, and ritualized expressions of peoples' communal connections to the Ultimate" (Kelly, 1995, p. 5) and as "an integrated system of belief, lifestyle, ritual activities, and institutions by which individuals give meaning to (or find meaning in) their lives by orienting them to what is taken to be sacred, holy, or the highest value" (Corbett, 1990, p. 2). The definitions of religion capture common characteristics across world religions that bring people together under a set structure and vision to articulate and make space for one's spiritual life. Religion is not always static either, as one may begin in the religion of one's family and shift away to explore and make one's own choice with the religion that best fits their life as an adult. While some might not change their affiliation or level of participation, others might become more involved and shift into more profound spiritual growth. Some have had no religious upbringing and might find that their religious path introduces them to various traditions. Here an eclectic approach is taken where they engage in a combination of religious practices that fit best for them.

Varieties of Spiritual and Religious Engagement

ASERVIC describes religion and spirituality as different concepts, even though religion can be a part of one's spirituality. This distinction is often seen in counseling research, where spirituality and religion require separate definitions because some people identify with one and not the other. In her study of how Black women define spirituality and religion, Mattis (2000) found that her participants associated religion with organized worship and the path of one's sacred journey; spirituality was associated with relationships, internalized positive values, and the outcomes of one's sacred journey. The 2014 PEW Religious Landscape Study found that 76.5% of Americans identify as religious, 22.8% as unaffiliated, and 0.6% as unsure (not knowing how they identify). Of those identifying as religious, 70.6% stated they were

Christian, 1.9% Jewish, 0.9% Muslim, 0.7% as Hindu, 0.7% as Buddhist, and 1.8% other faiths/religions. Of those identifying as Unaffiliated, 15.8% stated that they were nothing in particular, 3.1% as Atheist (where there is no belief in God or a Higher Power; Wiggins & Gutierrez, 2020), and 4% as Agnostic (where the belief is that nothing is known or can be known about God or a Higher Power; Wiggins & Guitierrez, 2020).

More specifically, Mohamed et al. (2021), in their survey of over 8,000 Black adults, found that 97% believe in God or a Higher Power, and more specifically: 78% were affiliated with a religion, 18% with nothing in particular, 2% with being Agnostic, and 1% with being Atheist. Across the general population and those, specifically Black American, there has been an increase in those who identify as religiously unaffiliated or Religious Nones (Agnostic, Atheist, and Nothing in Particular).

The engagement with spirituality and religion varies for each person. Furthermore, each individual's life experiences can impact the amount of time and energy given to these areas. There may be moments in our lives when we find ourselves devout, attending a religious service, or engaging in a personal spiritual practice with high self-discipline and commitment. However, we also recognize that there may be other times when life is so busy, or things are going so well that we may not remember to utilize our spiritual and religious resources with the same zeal. There also may be times in our lives when challenges and stressors overwhelm us and a) leave us no energy to tap into our spiritual supports or b) bring us to our knees with questions and struggle with our beliefs. To some degree, the latter is what we saw in Ella; she pressed into her spirituality more ardently- replete with questions. Giving ourselves grace during this time is essential as we experience spirituality as a strength and a struggle.

Spirituality and Religion as a Strength and as a Struggle

"Precious Lord, take my hand" (Thomas Dorsey, 1932)

The lyrics to the song, *Precious Lord* by Thomas Dorsey, can help to further our understanding of the interplay of spirituality in trauma through a reflection on oral history. Many have recounted that Thomas Dorsey was away from his pregnant wife when she went into labor prematurely. Before he could return to her, she and the infant son died in childbirth. In response to the grief and significant loss he experienced, Dorsey penned the words to *Precious Lord.*

When the lyrics are reviewed, there is an urgency, weight, and heaviness in the petition: "...hear my cry, hear my call, hold my hand lest I fall...I am tired, I am weak, and I am worn." Traumatic experiences require an outlet as appraisals of events are conducted.

For some, spirituality is a strength that is a part of their self-care, an anchor in challenging times, and a foundation for guidance in navigating one's journey. For others, spirituality is a struggle where one feels rejected, abandoned, shamed, or 'not enough' for not meeting standards/expectations of personal or communal spiritual/religious beliefs. A person might fluctuate between spirituality being a strength and a struggle throughout their life. The hope is that as one spiritually develops and matures, they can decrease the amount of experienced struggle and increase their experiences of spirituality as strength.

Spirituality can manifest as a strength physically and emotionally and be central to the healing process when experiencing hurt. Physically persons who are spiritually and religiously active have had lower rates of mortality and healthier lifestyles which could be attributed to a spiritual community's discouragement of engaging in risky behavior, inherent social support, and spiritual coping skills such as prayer (Masters & Hooker, 2012). Spirituality and religion have also been associated with greater experiences of happiness, well-being, and life satisfaction along with posttraumatic growth, which is the ability to grow from and improve after the experience of trauma (Park & Slattery, 2013; Werdel & Wicks, 2012). In addition, spirituality and religion have offered ways for people to navigate forgiveness, have guidelines for living, engage with social support with spiritually like-minded persons, explore meaning and purpose, ponder and understand life after death, and regulate emotions through meditative practices (Park & Slattery, 2013). We saw Ella engage her spirituality as a support through her support system and use of sacred text to explore the meaning of her experience.

Spirituality as a struggle can manifest in varying ways. Persons might experience a spiritual crisis when they question their faith and spiritual values, feel abandoned or punished by God, are running away from their values or calling, or have been hurt by persons or practices of their religion (Murray-Swank & Murray-Swank, 2012). Differences in spiritual beliefs can also cause interpersonal conflict or struggle and make some relationships more challenging (Stewart-Sicking et al., 2020). In addition, working through the grief process may spark the experience of spirituality as a struggle, especially within an American society where spiritual and religious platitudes are often said to comfort mourners when a death has occurred. For instance, "She's in a better place… or, It was God's will" can bring anger, confusion, and spiritual questioning to persons in the midst of grief (depending on where they are in their process). In Ella's case, she experienced a spiritual crisis in her questioning and her grief.

During these times of spiritual struggle, it is important to have a support system in place to walk with you as you process the experience, normalize feelings that come up, and discern the next steps needed for your own well-being (Murray-Swank & Murray-Swank, 2012). Knowing you are not alone in navigating your spirituality during times of struggle can be a comfort. For some Black women, making it through these experiences results in a deeper, stronger faith. If Ella had been a part of a spiritually based support group for women struggling with infertility, this might have helped navigate her experience.

Experiences of Spirituality and Religion for Black Women

"I had a praying grandmother" (Helen Baylor, 1995)

In Helen Baylor's song, 'Helen's Testimony,' she speaks her truth, sharing her life experiences of navigating the world and traumatic experiences. Periodically she shifts from talking about her story to singing from the depths of her soul. One line that repeats throughout shines as an example of the power of spiritual support for Black women during challenging times. She sings repeatedly, "But I had a praying grandmother," crediting her grandmother's prayer, spirituality, and faith as a lifeline that brought her through her experiences and back to her own spiritual support system. This is just one example of how Black women experience spirituality and religion.

Historically, spirituality has been a source of strength and comfort for the African-American community, especially in the Black Church. The spiritual and religious beliefs of generations of Black people have sustained us through experiences of trial, challenge, and unimaginable trauma. Even when deliverance, freedom, and justice did not manifest in the life of our ancestors, the stability of Black spirituality (in all its variety) has made space for support, questioning, transformation, and rededication.

Everyday spiritual experiences for Black women include the connection of spirituality and cultural identity, communal support, and interconnectedness of body and spirit. Dr. Reeda Walker describes a Black female perspective of spirituality that acknowledges that "though some traditions are fading, a lot of your understanding about who you are and whom Black people are beginning in the Black church" (2020, p. 119). She acknowledges the groundedness of Black culture that can be found in the spiritual experiences of Black people, where our spiritual values and beliefs shape how we behave and engage with life challenges and unjust systemic oppression.

There are also shared experiences of the power of believing in and seeking prayer from family and of finding new meaning in words from sacred texts that apply specifically to your life's circumstances (bringing emotional and spiritual healing). This was evident in Ella's use of scripture that reminded her of God's grace and in her family's support via prayer. Dr. Walker states that,

> As someone who endures the highs and lows of Black womanhood, I know that your faith in God has impacted how you have managed to sustain the psychological fortitude that you have... your foremother brought her spirituality with her from West Africa. She went through the most trying of times. Her humanity was denied, but she somehow believed that God and her ancestors would get her through. This powerful spirituality, along with enormous creativity and the instinct to survive, was passed on to you... Though we may refer to the Spirit by different names, at the core of our beliefs is a faith in that which cannot be seen. (Walker, 2020, p. 120-121)

Experiences of the Spirit vary across spiritual and religious beliefs for Black women, but often there is a developmental journey in one's spiritual life. In exploring the connection between body and soul, Patton (2017) interviewed three Black women and found that healing took place in the journey and development of their holistic self (including mind, body, and spirit). Each had varied paths to finding this integration of the physical and spiritual. One utilized yoga with nutrition, another combined dance with wellness, and the last integrated social consciousness with an embrace of African religious traditions. Honoring the body through a spiritual lens was a natural progression of valuing the physical vehicle that allows us to achieve our spiritual purpose. Ella's struggle to conceive exemplifies how the physical (her body) and the spiritual (her beliefs and values) were intertwined. As the previous examples have shown, spirituality and religion have strong, rich roots within the Black experience and can be a resource when facing challenging times and traumatic experiences. Let us now explore and define trauma.

The Interplay of Trauma and Spirituality

"I'm a survivor, I'm not gon' give up
I'm not gon' stop, I'm gon' work harder
I'm a survivor, I'm gonna make it
I will survive, keep on survivin'' (Destiny's Child, 2001)

Trauma and Stress

Understanding the meanings of stress and trauma helps determine how to cope. Stress is defined by the DSM-5 (*Diagnostic and Statistical Manual of Mental Disorders- 5th edition*; one of the primary classification tools used for diagnosing mental disorders) as "the pattern of specific and nonspecific responses a person makes to stimulus events that disturb his or her equilibrium and tax or exceed his or her ability to cope" (American Psychiatric Association, 2013, p. 829). Here stress is described by the times when life knocks us off balance and makes it harder for us to function or cope normally. We might find ourselves engaging in intentional self-care, reaching out to our support system, and turning our faith in what we deem sacred when responding productively to stress. Ella dealt with stress with each experience of trying and becoming pregnant, and she utilized her spirituality and support system when experiencing that stress. We also might find our daily life habits being impacted when we respond unproductively to stress (i.e., eating, sleeping, working too much or too little, or taking on too much as we try to be 'strong' and handle it all ourselves).

"I'm not your superwoman
I'm not the kind of girl that you can let down
And think that everything's okay
Boy, I am only human" (Karyn White, 1989)

Stereotypes of being the 'Strong Black Woman/Superwoman,' or being the 'Angry Black woman,' can reemphasize the expectations Black women navigate (Jacobs & Davis, 2017). These stereotypes can increase our stress. The Superwoman stereotype can make us feel like we have to live up to unrealistic responsibilities of taking care of everyone to neglect ourselves. It can also impose on us the constant mandate to be 'strong' and not show vulnerability or express any need for help. The Angry Black woman stereotype can put Black women into a box when we need to articulate our voices. However, any use of the assertive expression is deemed aggressive and, therefore, angry. To counter this expectation, some choose silence and only share portions of their voice or perspective in safe enough environments. Managing our own and others' expectations of us can certainly be stressful, and that stress can add to the challenge of coping when faced with trauma.

The Substance Abuse and Mental Health Services Association defines trauma as "an event, series of events, or set of circumstances that is experienced [or witnessed] by an individual as physically or emotionally harmful or life-threatening and that has lasting adverse effects on the individual's functioning and mental, physical, social, emotional, or spiritual well-being" (2019, para. 2). Trauma extends beyond the popular examples of war, violence, and sexual assault. Whether you experience or witness a large, one-time event or several smaller occurrences, the impact is one that negatively affects your ability to function across many levels (i.e., work, relationships, spirituality, emotional and physical health, etc.) over a lasting period of time. Ella's repeated devastation in experiencing miscarriages is a powerful and common example of infertility as a traumatic experience. Because this type of trauma is so personal and not often shared, many suffer in silence, unaware of the support available to cope with the lasting effects that impact multiple areas of life.

Black women, in comparison to white women, experience disproportionately higher rates of trauma (Blakely, 2016). The combination of individual traumatic experiences with ongoing racial/generational trauma (such as gendered racism) can lead to the experience of complex trauma, "a combination of early and late-onset, multiple, and sometimes highly invasive traumatic events, usually of an ongoing, interpersonal nature" (Blakely, 2016, p. 42). Experiences of systematic oppression (i.e., police brutality, lack of equitable maternal health care, working harder for less, etc.) can become so frequent that we may not even recognize it as trauma but as the everyday reality for Black women. Finding ways to cope is essential to working through trauma, and spirituality can be one of those coping mechanisms.

Spirituality and Religion as Means of Coping with Trauma and Stress

Among the findings of the 2012 Gallup Poll were two critical considerations for this current writing: (1) when compared to their counterparts, Blacks have been found to be a highly religious ethnic group, and (2) regarding gender, women appear to be more religious than their male counterparts. If these two data points were to be combined, then it is possible to deduce that Black women may be in a class all by themselves regarding being highly religious.

Fallot and Heckman (2005) studied religious and spiritual coping in women trauma survivors. While their study did not single out Black women, the researchers did find significant use of religion and spirituality to carry on in the midst of conditions related to mental health and substance use. On the other hand, Gregg (2011) did look specifically at religious and spiritual coping in Black women. Gregg's participants spoke of their faith and relationship with God, acting as an anchor during one of life's storms. Subsequently, they could experience a level of stillness and unmatched support.

Similar to some of the findings by Gregg (2011), this idea of using the relationship with the God of their understanding as a means of coping and commitment was discussed by Moss and Snodgrass (2017). Utilizing a subset of findings from a larger study, the authors looked at the trauma experience in clergywomen. Religion and spirituality were reportedly seen as "a double-edged sword that can both cut and yet aid in the healing process" (Moss & Snodgrass, 2017, p. 609). Moreover, healing, whether emotional, physical, and or spiritual, for trauma survivors is very important.

"Traumatic experiences are weighty and profound in the sense that they are life-altering" (Moss, 2014, p. 15). These experiences can cause an individual to question their life, meaning, purpose, and even their belief in God or a higher power. On the other hand, there is also the opportunity for the traumatic experience to help solidify the relationship or tie the individual to that supreme being as a means of coping: making it through the experience(s) and finding a way to eventually ascribe meaning and purpose to all that has been or is being endured.

Spates et al. (2019) found that the critical components of "prayer and spirituality" were instrumental in participants remaining hopeful and positive in times of stress and racial trauma experienced as Black women. "Their faith seemed particularly useful in helping them navigate issues outside their control" (Spates et al., 2019, p. 519). While not racially driven, the experience of multiple miscarriages was outside of Ella's control. Like the women in the Spates et al. study, prayer and spirituality helped to sustain Ella in the times she struggled with the most. However, when Ella incorporated the arts through music, she added another layer to her coping.

According to the American Music Therapy Association (AMTA) (2006), "music is a form of sensory stimulation" that has the power or ability to foster coping by providing individuals a way to "express difficult feelings and emotions," including those associated with trauma (p. 1). The type of music being used in times of stress and adversity has been found to have a great impact, whether positively or negatively, on an individual's coping (Ahmadi, 2013). While he looked at several classifications of music like nature and healing music, when speaking specifically of religious music, Ahmadi et al. described religious music as "a spiritual experience - a key that opens the door to a room where the patient can contact God" (2013, p. 158). So, suppose the thoughts of AMTA and Ahmadi et al. are coupled and extended. In that case, there is the sense that music (instrumental and lyrical components) are a way to either join with or convey secret -intimate messages that the individual may not have the vocabulary or language to express to the God of their understanding.

What is more, there is the opportunity for the lyrics to, in return, convey messages (from God) to the individual in a conversational manner. One of the participants in the study by Moss (2014) had a similar experience as she listened to music and engaged God in conversation. While singing and crying out, there was a moment, "... it was as if God said to me, 'let me do this'...that's what I felt ... God took it, and I could move on" (p. 104). Not only did the lyrics provide space for communion, but coping and healing also took place.

Like lyrics, there is power in instruments. As passed down through oral traditions, our ancestors used drums to convey and receive similar messages to and from the spirit(s). Ugobude (2020) reported on the importance of drums in African culture. One of the drums singled out was the Ngoma drum, whose rhythms were used to help lower the effects of stress and provide healing. What the above says to us is that music in its entirety - lyrics and instrumental- have been passed down throughout the generations to this specific population of Black women as a way to engage the spirit realm conveying messages and aiding in healing while living through experiences of stress and trauma. Before we wrap up, let us turn our attention once again to our case study.

Ella's Story Continued

> *"I'm not enough unless you come, Will you meet me here again ...Let your love rise above every fear"* (Elevation Worship)

Watson et al. (2018) purported that after a miscarriage, mothers generally face challenges as they live and move through the grieving process. Ella was no different. In the days and weeks after Ella and Chris left the doctor's office, she struggled to come to grips with what had happened. There were moments of tears, and doubt, coupled with moments of peace and assurance. Ella allowed herself the space to share with her closest girlfriend the pain she felt and received some of the support she needed. Ella and Chris were determined not to give up on their dream. They talked through their plan.

A year after that faithful visit that revealed Ella's third miscarriage, she found herself in the hospital room facing another monitor again. This time, at 37 weeks and 6 days, the "swooshing" sound could be heard. Even more to her delight, she saw a little girl - all the fingers and toes in place. Ella smiled. Upon further examination, the doctor turned to the woman on the table next to Ella and alerted the other woman that she was in early labor as her cervix was already 2cm dilated. They needed to prepare to head to the hospital. The baby was going to appear prior to the 40 weeks.

After 48 hours of labor, little Caroline (meaning joy) appeared. Ella and Chris became parents when a young mother chose them through an adoption agency. According to the surrogate, there was just something compelling about Ella and Chris's story, pictures, and recorded interview that drew her to them. She believed they could provide for the baby in ways she could not.

When Ella held Caroline (aka Carly) for the first time, tears streamed down her face. Ella recalled singing over her, "He is the God of the breakthrough, and anything is possible" (Bethel Music, 2020).

Conclusion

As presented throughout this writing, trauma can manifest itself in many ways. Specifically, this writing briefly touched on trauma in the form of the oppression of ancestors during slavery, the gendered racism of today, and various health challenges to name a few. In addition, spirituality and religion were discussed in their manifestations as strengths and struggles during challenging times. In Ella's case, she faced the traumatic experience of infertility by using both positive religious coping (i.e., use of scripture and spiritual songs) and negative religious coping (i.e., questioning God). This chapter explored how spirituality and trauma interact and utilized Ella's story to guide understanding of the concepts covered. Spirituality, religion, trauma, and stress were all explored from both a general lens and one specific to Black women. This chapter sought to normalize the common experience of trauma and stress and highlight how spirituality - inclusive of communion with a higher being and external supports- and the use of music can be present and most helpful while navigating through such experiences.

Processing/Reflection Questions

The following questions can help you personalize some of the content we have covered and highlight your unique experience of spirituality, trauma, and coping.

- How do you define spirituality and religion?
  - Are they the same for you or separate entities?
- When has spirituality been a strength in your life, and when has it been a struggle?
- What stands out to you when you reflect on spirituality over your lifespan?
  - How do you engage with what is sacred to you in the present?
- How do you differentiate between trauma and stress in your life?
- What have you found to be helpful in how you cope with trauma or stress?
- In what ways have what you hold sacred helped you during times of trauma or stress?
- What music inspires you and/or helps you during challenging times?
- Have you identified your safe space or inner circle with whom you can be your transparent and authentic self? How can you be that for someone else?

References

Ahmadi, F. (2013). Music as a method of coping with cancer: A qualitative study among cancer patients in Sweden. *Arts & Health*, 5(2), 152–165. https://doi.org/10.1080/17533015.2013.780087.

American Music Therapy Association (2006). Music therapy in response to crisis and trauma. https://www.musictherapy.org/assets/1/7/MT_Crisis_2006.pdf.

American Psychiatric Association. (2013). *Diagnostic and statistical manual of mental disorders (DSM)* (5th ed.). American Psychiatric Publishing.

Association for Spiritual, Ethical, and Religious Values in Counseling. (n.d). ASERVIC white paper. http://www.aservic.org/resources/aservic-white-paper-2/.

Baylor, H. (1995). Helen's Testimony [Song]. On *The Live Experience*. Nashville. Word Records.

Bethel Music. (2020). Anything is possible [Song]. *On Revival's in the Air.* Redding. Bethel Music.

Bohecker, L., Schellenberg, R., and Silvey, J. (2017). Spirituality and religion: The ninth CACREP core curriculum area. *Counseling and Values*, 62, 128-143. https://doi.org/10.1002/cvj.12055.

Blakely, J. M. (2016). The role of spirituality in helping African American women with histories of trauma and substance abuse heal and recover. *Social Work & Christianity*, 43(1), 40–59. https://psycnet.apa.org/record/2016-07636-004.

Chandra A, Martinez G. M., Mosher W. D., Abma J. C., and Jones J. (2005). Fertility, family planning, and reproductive health of U.S. women: Data from the 2002 National Survey of Family Growth. National Center for Health Statistics. *Vital Health Stat*, 23(25), 1-160. https://pubmed.ncbi.nlm.nih.gov/16532609/.

Corbett, J. M. (1990). *Religion in America.* Prentice-Hall.

Destiny's Child. (2001). Survivor [Song]. On *Survivor.* New York. Columbia Records.

Dorsey, T. (1932). Precious lord, take my hand [Song].

English Standard Version Bible. (2001). ESV Online. https://biblehub.com.

Elevation Worship (2018). Here again [Song]. On *Hallelujah Here Below.* Charlotte. Elevation Worship Records.

Fallot, R. D., and Heckman, J. P. (2005). Religious/spiritual coping among women trauma survivors with mental health and substance use disorders. *The Journal of Behavioral Health Services & Research*, 32(2), 215–226. https://doi.org/10.1007/BF02287268.

Frost, J., Bradley, H., Levitas, R., Smith, L., and Garcia, J. (2007). The loss of possibility: Scientisation of death and the special case of early miscarriage. *Sociology of Health & Illness*, 29(7), 1003–1022. https://doi.org/10.1111/j.1467-9566.2007.01019.x.

Gallup Poll (2012). Seven in 10 Americans are very or moderately religious, but Protestant population is shrinking as "unbranded religion grows." https://news.gallup.com/poll/159050/seven-americans-moderately-religious.aspx

Gregg (2011). I'm a Jesus girl: Coping stories of Black American women diagnosed with breast cancer. *Journal of Religion and Health*, 50, 1040-1053. https://doi.org/10.1007/s10943-010-9395-y.

Jacobs, S., and Davis, C. (2017). Challenging the myths of Black women- a short-term structured art experience group: Exploring the intersections of race, gender, and intergenerational trauma. *Smith College Studies in Social Work*, 87(2-3), 200-219. https://doi.org/10.1080/00377317.2017.1324091.

Johnson, J. W. (2001). Lift every voice and sing. In D. Carpenter & N.E. Williams (Eds.). *African American Heritage Hymnal.* (pp. 540). Gia Publications.

Kelly, E. W. (1995). *Spirituality and religion in counseling and psychotherapy: Diversity in theory and practice.* American Counseling Association.

March of Dimes (2017). Miscarriage. https://www.marchofdimes.org/ complications/ miscarriage.aspx.

Mary Mary. (2000). Can't Give Up Now. On *Thankful*. Columbia Records.

Masters, K. S., and Hooker, S. A. (2012). In J.G. Aten, K.A. O'Grady, & E.L. Worthington (Eds.), *The psychology of religion and spirituality for clinicians: Using research in your practice* (pp.357-385). Routledge.

Mattis, J. S. (2000). African-American women's definitions of spirituality and religion. *Journal of Black Psychology*, 26(1), 101-122. https://doi.org/10.1177/0095798400026001006.

Mohamed, B., Cox, K., Diamant, J., and Gecewicz, C. (2021, February 16). *Faith among Black Americans.* Pew Research Center. https://www.pewforum.org/2021/02/16/faith-among-black-americans/.

Moss, L. S. (2014). Survivors of personal and professional trauma: Exploring the lived experiences of female clergy diagnosed with cancer. [Doctoral Dissertation, Loyola University Maryland].

Moss, L. S., and Snodgrass, J. (2017). Called and committed: The lived experiences of female clergy cancer survivors. *Pastoral Psychology*, 69(5), 609–623. https://doi.org/10.1177%2F0091647119856938.

Murray-Swank, N. A., and Murray-Swank, A. B. (2012). Navigating the storm: Helping clients in the midst of spiritual struggles. In J.G. Aten, K.A. O'Grady, & E.L. Worthington (Eds.), *The psychology of religion and spirituality for clinicians: Using research in your practice* (pp. 217–244). Routledge.

Pargament, K. I. (2007). *Spiritually integrated psychotherapy: Understanding and addressing the sacred.* Guilford Press.

Park, C. L., and Slattery, J. M. (2013). Religion, spirituality, and mental health. In R.F. Paloutzian & C.L. Park (Eds.), *Handbook of the psychology of religion and spirituality* (2nd ed., pp. 540–559). Guilford Press.

Patton, R. (2017). My body is a vehicle: Narratives of Black women holistic healers on spiritual development, mental healing, and body nurturing. In S.Y. Evans, K. Bell, & N. K. Burton (Eds.). *Black Women's Mental Health: Balancing Strength and Vulnerability.* (pp. 141–159). SUNY Press.

Pew Research Center. (2014). Pew Religious Landscape Study. http://www.pewforum.org/religious-landscape-study/state/texas/.

Robert, T. E., and Kelly, V. A. (Eds.) (2015). *Critical incidents in integrating spirituality into counseling.* American Counseling Association.

Spates, K., Evans, N. M., Watts, B. C., Abubakar, N., and James, T. (2019). Keeping ourselves sane: A qualitative exploration of Black women's coping Strategies for gendered racism. *Sex Roles*, 82, 513–524. https://doi.org/10.1007/s11199-019-01077-1.

Stewart-Sicking, J. A., Fox, J., and Deal, P.J. (2020). *Bringing religion and spirituality into therapy: A process-based model for pluralistic practice*. Routledge.

Substance Abuse and Mental Health Services Association. (2019, August 2). *Trauma and violence*. U.S. Department of Health and Human Services. https://www.samhsa.gov/trauma-violence.

Ugobude, F. (2020). The importance of drums in African tradition. https://guardian.ng/life/the-importance-of-drums-in-african-tradition/.

Walker, R. (2020). *The unapologetic guide to Black mental health: Navigate an unequal system, learn tools for emotional wellness and get the help you deserve.* New Harbinger Publications.

Watson, M., Jewell, V., and Smith, S. (2018). Journey interrupted: A phenomenological exploration of miscarriage. *The Open Journal of Occupational Therapy*, *6*(3), 1-16. https://doi.org/10.15453/2168-6408.1439.

Werdel, M. B., and Wicks, R. J. (2012). *Primer on posttraumatic growth: An introduction and guide.* John Wiley & Sons, Inc.

White, K. (1989). Superwoman [Song]. On *Karyn White*. Los Angeles. Warner Brothers.

Wiggins, M. I., and Gutierrez, D. (2020). Culture and worldview. In C.S. Cashwell & J.S. Young (Eds.) *Integrating spirituality and religion into counseling: A guide to competent practice* (3rd ed; pp. 69-93). American Counseling Association.

Young, J. S., and Cashwell, C. S. (2020). Integrating spirituality and religion into counseling: An introduction. In C.S. Cashwell & J.S. Young (Eds.) *Integrating spirituality and religion into counseling: A guide to competent practice* (3rd ed., pp. 3-30). American Counseling Association.

Zukerman, G., Korn, L., and Fostick, L., (2016). Religious coping and posttraumatic stress symptoms following trauma: The moderating effects of gender. *Psychology of Religion and Spirituality*, 9(4), 328–336. https://doi.org/10.1037/rel0000075.

Chapter 11

Counseling African-American Women: A Person-Centered Spiritual Approach

Cerise D. Lewis*, PhD, LMFT, LPCC
Lewis Family Wellness Center, Brooklyn Park, Minnesota, USA

Abstract

Addressing the mental health of African American women is best approached from a culturally sensitive lens. Childhood for many African American women is peppered with physical, sexual, and emotional traumas that emerge in adulthood as anxiety, depression, mood disorders, and intrapersonal problems (Kapoor et al., 2018). As a collective group, African American women are often stereotyped and categorized as angry, welfare queens, or the strong Black woman (Dow, 2015). These biased, gendered racial microaggressions are encountered by Black women every day, compounding their adverse psychological and emotional distress (Lewis et al., 2016). African American women seek support from counselors that acknowledge, empathize, and appreciate their experiences. Research literature indicated that positive outcomes from therapy hinge on a solid relationship with a counselor (Kivlighan et al., 2014) and the application of culturally sensitive counseling (Frey, 2013). Thus, it is imperative to counsel African American women by recognizing their strengths, being aware of power differentials between client and counselor, and emphasizing the importance and value of their social and cultural experiences. Spending a significant amount of time joining and developing an authentic and trusting relationship is of the utmost importance. The application of practical and theoretical models is second to the development of the client-counselor relationship.

* Corresponding Author's Email: info@lewisfamilywellness.com.

In: How Did We Survive?
Editor: Tina Marie Glover
ISBN: 979-8-88697-918-3

Historically, therapeutic models were based on the dominant culture and adapted to multicultural clients, often minimizing the importance of culture, ethnicity, beliefs, and individual values (Quin, 2013). Due to multiple factors, person-centered models are proven evidence-based approaches for African American women. For example, the client is in control of the session; they are empowered to take charge of their lives, and clients develop self-acceptance, confidence, and understanding of themselves and their strengths (Quinn, 2013).

Keywords: African American women, Black women, trauma, microaggressions, spiritual, person centered

Introduction: What Is Trauma?

Merriam-Webster defines trauma as an emotional response to a deeply distressing or disturbing experience. There are three types of trauma acute, chronic, and complex (Courtois, 2008). Acute trauma is categorized as a single incident, such as surviving a natural disaster. Chronic trauma is a repeated and prolonged experience, such as reoccurring domestic abuse. Complex trauma is the concurrent exposure to various traumatic experiences that may be singular or repetitive events, such as a woman surviving a rape, emotional abuse from an intimate partner, homelessness, and the sudden loss of a child.

Trauma causes a physiological and emotional response that emerges during or after a traumatic experience (Van der Kolk, 2003). The severity of a traumatic experience determines the type of response that happens in the body and mind and mirrors the five stages of grief and loss. The five stages of grief and loss are denial, anger, bargaining, depression, and acceptance. Everyone experiences these stages differently (Schmelzer, 2018). Some will go through each stage several times randomly, whereas others progress through the stages one time, beginning with denial and ending with acceptance. After a traumatic experience, there may be sounds, smells, thoughts, and other triggers that arouse negative emotional responses making a person feel trapped and unable to function (Helsel, 2015). Living a *normal* life after experiencing trauma is a process.

Overcoming trauma is a healing journey best approached with the help of mental health professionals (Sue et al., 2019). Mental health professionals (licensed professional counselors, marriage and family therapists, social workers, and psychologists) help people navigate their traumatic experiences and work through the healing process. Effective mental health professionals leverage a client's strengths and utilize a person-centered approach when counseling clients overcoming trauma. Although people of all demographics experience traumas, African American women are a population that merits deeper exploration.

This chapter provides an overview of African American women's traumatic experiences from slavery to the present day. The overview includes a historical account of childhood abuses, stigmatizations, poverty, institutionalized racism, systemic oppression, and societal norms that promote inequalities. The remainder of the chapter focuses on a practical model to help women heal from trauma called the person-centered spirituality approach.

Sources of Trauma

Trauma can be classified as big events or small events. Big traumatic events include natural disasters, rape, serious car accidents, terminal illness, child loss, repetitive experiences like domestic violence or child abuse, war, being arrested, witness to a murder, and racism. In contrast, small traumas are not typically categorized as trauma by most people. However, small traumas include becoming overwhelmed by something that seems insignificant, emotions that arouse physiological sensations in the body and mind, holding beliefs that cause distress, unprocessed big traumas, loss of concentration and focus, causing one to question their capabilities, life purpose, and worth. If the trauma is big or small, the effects of the trauma can be debilitating. African American women have endured many types of traumas, from slavery (Longman-Mills & Abel, 2019) to today (Mosley et al., 2021).

American slavery was a legally organized labor model comprising enslaved peoples brought from Africa to the United States of America. The trauma began when Africans were taken from their families by force, chained, put on boats, and shipped across the Atlantic Ocean to arrive in an unknown new world (Longman-Mills & Abel, 2019). In America, the men and women were separated, sold, and sent to plantations all over the south, never seeing each other again. African women were brutalized by their captors and forced to do hard labor alongside their male counterparts. Then, beatings, psychological, sexual, and emotional abuse were inflicted to make them submit to their new way of living. Enslaved men and women were forced to copulate to produce offspring (more labor). Slave masters raped their male and female slaves for pleasure, often impregnating the females (Livesey, 2017). It was not uncommon for the slave master to murder the newborn child or give it to another plantation owner to avoid accountability for their crime.

These traumatic experiences are in the DNA of African American women and have been passed down through the generations (Grossi, 2020). Several centuries passed before slavery was abolished in the United States, including a civil war, lost lives, and a more significant divide of the United States North and South. Although the American laws changed, which abolished chattel slavery, the hearts and minds of many whites had not changed. The emergence of Jim Crow was a reboot of slavery without the plantations and slave masters. Like chattel slavery, African American men and women were targets of hatred, experiencing racial trauma every day in the communities where they lived and were never treated as equals. Police had the right to arrest and eventually kill unarmed African American men, further traumatizing the hearts and minds of their mothers and fathers. The killing of unarmed African American men was a common occurrence that did not become a priority for the American government until 2020 (Yang et al., 2021).

In 2020, an unarmed, nonviolent African American man, George Floyd, was arrested for a supposed fake $20 bill. A young African American woman recorded the murder on her phone and shared it with the world. It was only then that light was shined on America and its treatment of African American people. The institutionalized systemic oppression and discrimination of African Americans were finally being revealed and acknowledged (Smith & Oliver, 2021). The racist covering over corporations, businesses, community agencies, and schools was also being exposed.

African American women also experience significant amounts of discrimination and distress (Dickens et al., 2019). Many African American women have been overlooked for promotion; some believe African American women were hired to meet a quota since they fit into two demographics. Some people see them as holding positions because of affirmative action and not their skills and capabilities. African American women are also compared to other racial groups when considering gender discrimination (Johnson & Pietri, 2020).

It is common for people to think that the experiences of women are all the same. African American women's experiences from a gender perspective have similarities. However, the racial component of the African American women's experience is unlike any other demographic, as previously discussed. The racial aspect changes the purview for African American women due to the additional stressors.

There are three categories that African American women experience in workplaces and the community microaggressions, biases, and assumptions (Lewis et al., 2016). According to the Merriam-Webster dictionary, a microaggression is a subtle and everyday slight or insult; it can include insensitive comments based on an array of racial assumptions related to criminality, intelligence, cultural values, citizenship, it also minimizes or denies the racial experience of people of color. This definition is a broad way of looking at microaggressions and encompasses many things. Imagine, for a moment, the level of hurt and confusion that microaggressions may cause. For example, a woman described taking her five children to the doctor.

> When my children were all under 10, you know, it's easier to take them all at the same time, see the same doctor and do all the physicals during one visit, it might take a couple of hours, but you knock it all at one time. I took all of my kids into the doctor's office; we were sitting down. The nurse greets us by saying, 'Wow, are these all of your kids?' And I said, absolutely, they are all mine. Then she says, 'Do they all have the same father?' And I'm stunned. My mouth was wide open And I was shocked beyond measure that a person could ask such a question

The microaggression in this example suggests that as an African American woman with multiple children, it is not possible to have one father. This belief about African American women is insulting and demeaning.

Microaggressions show up in the workplace as subtle slights and insensitive comments about appearance (Dickens et al., 2019). African American women wear their hair in many different styles. Technology has advanced so much that you could have braids one day, and the next, you are rocking a 28" weave. African American women have short, medium, and long hair; some are just about bald with a tight fade. Others wear wigs, weaves, and microlinks. The reality is that their hair is versatile for most African American women and may look different every day.

One woman shared a story about her co-worker asking about braids. She said the woman asked her if the braids were "extensions." Extensions was a term used in the 80s and 90s entirely out of date and out of touch. When she asked to touch the hair, the woman said she felt insulted and embarrassed. Moreover, she reported feeling like she was on display. These two examples of microaggressions are overt. There are also overt examples that most African American women have experienced at one point in their lives.

Microaggressions may cause you to question your identity and who you are as a person (Lewis et al., 2016). Your identity is intrinsic and extrinsic factors like beliefs, qualities, personality, visual presentation, and expressions. When challenged by microaggressions, a person's thought process could make them question if they are good enough or accepted (Dickens et al., 2019). More subtle microaggressions happen too. For example, in the grocery store and receiving glances from other shoppers and workers as if you should not be there; being watched by a store clerk when trying on clothing in a department store, and when engaging with a group of friends, you laugh out loud and are asked by your white friend to be less animated and quiet down because you are too loud.

The belief that African American women are loud and angry is a stereotype (Dickens et al., 2019). Stereotypes are an oversimplification of an image or thought about a person or thing. Stereotypes are rooted in assumptions and bias. An assumption is something that is accepted as true or is certain to happen without proof. Some common assumptions about African American women include they are angry, they are domineering, many people believe that African American women are on welfare, they are combative and aggressive. The truth is that every person is unique, and assumptions should not be made about them, nor should we hold a bias toward African American women.

A bias is a tendency or an inclination, or prejudice toward or against something or someone (Kempf, 2020). A bias can be positive or negative. For example, a person may have a bias toward chocolate ice cream over any other flavor. It becomes harmful if we apply that same thinking process about biases to negative attitudes, feelings, or beliefs about people of certain ethnic or racial groups. Bias is encountered when people choose friends. They tend to choose friends that look like them or believe and think similarly.

Middle and high school are breeding grounds of trauma for African American girls. Too often, teachers compare African American girls to their white girl counterparts suggesting that African American girls are hypersexual, indicating that they are not as feminine as white girls (Carter Andrews et al., 2019). Likewise, there are higher rates of behavior problems in schools. Teachers and administrative staff feel that African American girls are more problematic than white girls. Thus, there are higher suspensions, increased referrals, and ultimately more African American girls find their way into the legal system. Teachers abuse their power and authority and attempt to silence African American girls preventing them from have a voice to speak up for themselves.

The research literature also showed that childhood for many African American women and girls is peppered with traumas like poverty and homelessness (Kapoor et al., 2018). Poverty plagues many African American women. If African American women cannot find adequate employment, they will struggle to find housing and a stable living situation. They may be forced to seek shelters, live with a family member, and possibly be homeless. Unstable living situations are breeding grounds for broken homes, single-parent households, and domestic violence. At the hands of their caregivers, African American girls experience physical, sexual, psychological, and emotional abuse.

Statistically speaking, in 2020, the American Psychological Association reported that one in four African American girls would be sexually abused before 18. Between 40 and 60% of African American women reported being subjected to sexual abuse before they were 18 years old. Also, African American girls compared to white girls under the age of 12 experienced a higher level of rape than any other person of color or white girls. Couple these statistics with the racial inequities happening in present-day America and the problems of the past; African American women are hurting, and they need healing.

The stressors experienced by African American women started with slavery, Jim Crow laws, and childhood experiences. For many, adulthood is riddled with physical, emotional, and sexual abuse that lies dormant in the body and mind (Long & Ullman, 2013). Untreated trauma can erupt at any moment from an array of triggers. The triggers elicit a negative response to trauma.

The negative response to trauma is a mental health condition that emerges in a variety of ways. Adverse responses include psychological and emotional problems, including anxiety, depression, mood disorders, feeling isolated, low self-esteem, and identity issues. African American women are said to be resilient and able to withstand just about anything. However, in a recent study, Erving et al. (2020) explored African American women and the impact of stress on their physical and mental health. The findings indicated that African American women are stressed and experience depression due to everyday discrimination, financial problems, and family issues. The study further showed that spirituality and looking to God were strengths that can reduce depressive symptoms. Addressing African American women's mental health and wellness is imperative to help them overcome the trauma and heal.

African American Women and Mental Health

It is well known that many African American women avoid counseling due to mistrust, cultural disparities, and stigma associated with healthcare (Fripp & Carlson, 2017; Harris, Nelson et al., 2020; Woods-Giscombe et al., 2016). A large body of research showed the brokenness of the medical and behavioral health system for African Americans due to the ugly history of African Women and men being treated like guinea pigs for various medical research (Vernon, 2020). Historically behavioral health was not designed to meet the cultural identifiers of African Americans.

The research literature indicated that theoretical models and approaches were adapted to African American women without considering their cultural identifiers and unique experiences (Danzer et al., 2016). The strong Black woman schema is an example of a cultural factor for African American women. The strong Black woman is a racial and gendered description of Black women rooted in a belief that Black women should go through life and turn a blind eye to their mental and emotional wellbeing (Dow, 2015).

Over the past several years, dismantling the strong Black woman schema has uncovered the reality of African American women who masked depression and anxiety to push through challenges and difficulties for their families, friends, and anyone else in need (Abrams et al., 2019). Conceptually, the strong Black woman schema places an unrealistic expectation on African American women to restrain emotions, be independent and take care of everyone connected to them at all costs (Abrams et al., 2019). Ignoring mental health is detrimental and dangerous to the overall wellbeing of African American women (Evans et al., 2017).

Attending to one's mental health must become a priority and commitment for a long high-quality life (Bartholomew et al., 2018). African American women need therapists and counselors who are skilled and culturally competent in assessing, conceptualizing, and integrating techniques and interventions to facilitate growth and healing. Most people look for a counselor who looks like them and is skilled and culturally competent. Generally, African American women want to see an African American clinician (Scharff et al., 2021). In the United States of America, only 4% of all counselors are African American. It is unrealistic to think that an African American therapist or counselor is available to every African American woman seeking counseling. Regardless of your ethnic or racial background, developing the skills and cultural competence to meet African American women's unique and individual needs is the priority.

Skilled and Culturally Competent Counselors

A skilled and culturally competent counselor is easy to identify. They are open-minded and respect cultural differences. (Scharff et al., 2021). Culturally competent and skilled counselors are committed to learning about differences, they are aware of their biases, they work to eliminate prejudices and discrimination. A skilled and culturally sensitive counselor will broach cultural topics by bringing up noticeable differences between the counselor and the client (King & Borders, 2019). They will acknowledge differences in ethnic backgrounds and ask their clients how they feel about working with them. They normalize conversations about culture and intentionally practice engaging clients about their cultural dynamics throughout the counseling process.

Addressing a client's specific cultural identifiers ensures a safe, nonjudgmental, and nurturing space; and fosters strong rapport between the client and counselor (King & Borders, 2019). The counselor values the unique experiences of their clients, creating holding spaces for their hurt, pain, and experiences. They offer clients a judgment-free atmosphere to explore, discover, and grow past their trauma to eventually flourish and become a new version of themselves.

Client-Counselor Relationships

Skilled and culturally competent counselors establish relationships built upon trust, authenticity, and honesty. As previously stated, the medical and behavioral health system was notorious for treating African Americans poorly (Fripp & Carlson, 2017). Many people developed a distrust and negative view of mental health and mental health practitioners. Thus, it is vital to begin all new counseling relationships by first establishing a strong therapeutic alliance. The counselor initiates a therapeutic alliance, which begins with honesty, empathy, active listening, and unconditional acceptance (Zilcha-Mano et al., 2016), ingredients for a strong connection.

Connection is the lifeblood of the therapeutic relationship. When a connection is strong, clients feel safe (Zilcha-Mano et al., 2016). Safety is the key to helping clients be vulnerable and open. Openness leads to acknowledgment and acceptance of past experiences. Acknowledgment and acceptance of one's life experiences open the door to growth, and growth sets the stage for healing.

Healing is a process of becoming whole again; it is a transformation of sorts that encompasses a redefinition of oneself, life, and life's meaning (Rhodes, 2015). Healing is the transcendence of past suffering and the arrival of a new beginning and place of wholeness where nothing is missing, nothing is lacking, and nothing is broken in the person's life. Healing the emotional and psychological wounds of African American women is best addressed from a person-centered spiritual approach.

Spirituality in Counseling

A predominant cultural identifier for African American women is spirituality (Reed & Neville, 2014). Spirituality is a personal relationship between a higher power and an individual that may include prayer, meditation, and diverse rituals and practices. According to a study led by Larissa Portnoff and published in a 2016 article called *Spirituality Cuts in Half the Relative Risk for Depression: Findings from The United States, China, And India*, spirituality is a known mitigating factor of depression, anxiety, and suicidal ideation, especially amongst African American women, resulting in positive mental health and wellness outcomes. Spirituality is often neglected in counseling due to the counselor's inexperience and discomfort with the topic (Scott et al., 2016). A counselor's discomfort often relates to a lack of education, training, and skill development. Counselors may believe that conversations about spirituality and faith should be with pastors and spiritual leaders. Although faith and spirituality should be addressed with clergy, counselors must learn to integrate spirituality into counseling sessions if the client desires it to ensure the best outcomes.

Counselors can integrate spirituality into the counseling process in several ways. First, including spirituality, faith, and religious questions in the biopsychosocial and intake forms provides a space for clients to identify specific practices, affiliations, and beliefs important to them (Butts & Gutierrez, 2018). Ask the client-specific questions about their desire for inclusion of their faith and spirituality, for example, "What are your spiritual or faith practices?" "What areas of your life have you seen your spirituality as a strength or limitation?" These questions help the counselor assess and conceptualize the client's case from a culturally sensitive lens. Second, broaching conversations about beliefs and spirituality and how they want to include them in counseling, for example, "How do you want your spiritual beliefs and values included in counseling." "What types of practices would you feel comfortable sharing and including in our sessions?" "How do you see me supporting your spirituality as your counselor?" These questions demonstrate the counselor's openness to the client's culture and values, a key component of person-centered counseling.

Person-Centered Theory

Counselors can create a setting that welcomes their client's cultural identifiers by aligning with theoretical models inclusive of multicultural factors like person-centered therapy (Quinn, 2013). Research literature indicated that historically, counseling theories were based on the dominant culture and adapted to people of color, often minimizing the importance of culture, ethnicity, and spiritual beliefs. Person-centered or client-centered counseling is an evidence-based approach and has proven effective with many racial and ethnic groups.

Carl Rogers developed Person-centered or client-centered therapy in the 1940s. He is well known as one of the most influential psychotherapists of the 20th century. He is also one of the founders of humanistic psychology (Rogers, 1959). Humanistic psychology focuses on a client's needs and helping them achieve their full potential and reach self-actualization or complete acceptance of themselves. Although it seems counterintuitive to apply a theory developed by a white man to African American women, the attributes of this theory are suitable and appropriate for this population.

Initially, Rogers' research was developed using the dominant group, white people. His work transitioned in the 70s and 80s, where his research was replicated across diverse cultural backgrounds (Quinn, 2013). The results indicated that a client-centered approach was effective in helping clients meet their therapeutic goals (Quinn, 2013). The fundamental belief of client-centered therapy was that people have the ability and capacity to grow and change by becoming self-actualized.

The person-centered model applied to African American women works well for several reasons. The client is in control of the session; the counselor receives them in a warm nonjudgmental space, is validated and empowered to take charge of their lives, and develops self-acceptance, confidence, and understanding about themselves and their strengths. Many counselors use a person-centered therapy model built upon empathy, congruence, and unconditional positive regard. Helping African American women reach self-actualization welcomes the experiences of Black women in a judgment-free space requires counselors to apply these attributes consistently.

A person-centered approach is nondirective (Rogers, 1959). The client is the expert and has full autonomy and decision-making power in the counseling process. The counselor does not tell the client what to do; they are a guide or an advisor. Moreover, the counselor creates an atmosphere of empathy. They step into the shoes of the client to see things through their vantage point. The counselor sets aside what they think about the client and their own experience and accepts their reality. The counselor positions themself to empower, encourage and support the client. They provide tools, recommendations, and suggestions for things that will help the client reach the level of growth and change that they seek. A client-centered counselor can motivate their client by being present. They will extend unconditional positive regard and compassion to ensure that growth and change happen.

Accepting oneself and reaching full potential (self-actualization) is the goal of therapy for many African American women overcoming trauma. In short, the common theme is that they want to move past guilt and shame and accept themselves. They want to discover their passions and purpose for life to achieve their full potential and live a happy and fulfilling life, their best life. A person-centered approach combined with spirituality can result in goal attainment and healing for African American women.

Spirituality & Healing

In this chapter, spirituality references are connected to Christianity and a belief in Jesus Christ. Spirituality is a transcendent relationship between a person and high power or supreme being, such as God. The relationship between the individual and God provides answers and direction through faith and purpose for life. Moreover, spirituality connects the individual to a belief system, an image of self, and how they interact with the world. Overall, the spiritual relationship with God should facilitate growth and ultimately healing. For the spiritual African American woman trying to overcome trauma, the relationship with God should lead them to a place of healing.

Healing is a significant benefit for those that believe in Jesus. A foundational principle of Christianity is that everyone who believes in Jesus and has faith can be healed. Many accounts in the Bible showed that each person's faith manifested their healing; several examples include the woman with the issue of blood (Matthew 9:22), the ten lepers (Luke 17:19), and a blind man (Mark 10:52). Not only did Jesus heal physical illnesses, but he healed psychological and emotional issues as well.

Psychological and emotional issues are spiritual issues. Some examples include but are not limited to fear, anger, anxiety, sadness, depression, behavioral disorders, and paranoia, all of which can emerge from a traumatic experience. Healing in a physical sense, such as a broken arm to its original state, is tangible or concrete, whereas healing the psychological and emotional aspects of a person are intangible or abstract. Healing a physical part of the body can be seen directly with the eyes, but healing a psychological or emotional issue is seen only by signs of behavioral changes and new responses to people and stimuli (e.g., places, situations, smells). A person knows that they are psychologically or emotionally healed when their response to people and stimuli no longer holds them back from living a whole and productive life. A person healed from trauma is free to live a life where nothing is missing, lacking, or broken.

Trauma is a form of captivity and loss. Healing brings freedom and restoration from the trauma. The scriptures tell us that Jesus came to heal people from mental and emotional traumas when he says, 'I have come to heal the brokenhearted and preach deliverance to the captives' (Luke 4:18). An excellent example of psychological healing is found in Matthew, where Jesus encounters a person described as a lunatic, a mentally ill person. Overall, God wants every person healed. Evidence of God's desire for people's healing is found in 3 John 2, which says, I wish above all things that you may prosper and be in health, even as your soul (mind, intellect, and emotions) prospers.

Overcoming trauma from a spiritual perspective requires an exchange. The exchange is a process of turning over the painful memories, the relationships, attachments, and thought processes that are reminders of the traumatic event for God's healing. A key scripture that illustrates the exchange says, cast every care on the Lord, for he cares for you (1 Peter 1:7). Sometimes people need help to navigate the exchange of trauma for healing. Therapists can guide clients to a place of healing using a person-centered spiritual approach.

A Person-Centered Spiritual Approach

A person-centered spiritual approach is a therapeutic concept that weaves together empathy, authenticity, unconditional positive regard with the client's faith and spirituality practices. Unconditional acceptance, warmth, empathy, and affection show clients that they are seen, heard, valued, and welcomed. The stage is set for them to begin working on themselves and begin to heal from the past.

Unconditional acceptance recognizes that all African American women are not the same, their experiences may look similar, but they are unique, just like their fingerprints. Ideally, clients should have the freedom to express their feelings, actions, motivations, and experiences. Moreover, clients should be themselves without any fear of judgment. The counselor's ears should be attentive to the client and ready to peel back the layers of trauma to expose the beauty of their client and their healed soul.

Being attentive to clients, counselors must remove the biases and assumptions discussed previously. Counselors must be willing to engage with African American women with fresh eyes and ears with each new client. The following are some specific things counselors can do to avoid putting African American women clients into a box. First, learn to respect African American women for who they are and not who you or society expects them to be. African American women are beautiful; it is the role of the counselor to help clients see their beauty inside and out.

Beauty in African American women is a diversity of experience, exterior color, and way of thinking; counselors must learn how to meet clients where they are in their healing journey and make that the starting point. Second, counselors must be patient with clients and not try to force change. The healing process takes time and lots of validation and encouragement to try things that may seem scary and unrealistic. Thus, integrating activities, techniques, and interventions that apply to African American women is critical. The person-centered spiritual approach keeps you focused on the client's faith and spirituality as a strength. Helping clients conceptualize their challenges and solutions from the lens of their faith and spirituality keeps them on track and moving toward their goals.

Third, counselors should be authentic with clients. Use client language but stick to a vernacular that aligns with you as a counselor. At the beginning of a new client relationship, you are both getting to know each other. As previously discussed, the therapeutic relationship is the most important component to reaching the client's goals. Thus, ensuring that you are your authentic self (self-awareness) positions you to do your best work as a counselor and welcomes the client to be their authentic self.

Fourth, learn how to eliminate judgment. When people finally come to counseling, countless people have judged them, and their new counselor should not add to this list. The art of active listening and unconditional positive regard are keys to success. We must dispel the myth that African American women are loud, angry, combative, and aggressive by encouraging them to talk about their experiences in a safe, nurturing, and nonjudgemental space. We must rewrite the notion of African American women that their passion is not aggression, and their drive is not domination. These characteristics are tied to resilience, motivation, and determination to be the very best.

Finally, counselors must accept and respect that trauma is real, especially racial trauma. Most people do not have a hard time believing that domestic violence, rape, child molestation, and emotional abuse occurred in a person's life. However, racial trauma is another story. Just because it did not happen to you is not evidence that racial trauma is not real. As counselors, we must avoid minimizing and dismissing racial traumas. We cannot afford to play devil's advocate suggesting that the experience was not "that bad" or suggesting that the client played a part in being racially traumatized. When we question the validity of a client's story, we can destroy the client-counselor relationship and void any attempt to help the client heal from the trauma.

The counselor's role is to first and foremost manage their biases and presumptions to protect the client-counselor relationship. Counselors must set aside their preconceived notions about the presenting problem and description of the experience. Then, allow the counseling process to naturally progress. Allow the client to be the expert and take the lead. In short, bite your tongue, listen to learn, and create a holding space for the stories to unfold.

Once the safe space is created, integrate their faith and spirituality as part of the case conceptualization. During the intake session, the counselor should initiate a conversation that asks about the client's faith and spirituality practices and how they should be included in the counseling process. Although it may be uncomfortable, it is necessary to promote healing from the trauma.

Clients and counselors may be uncomfortable with faith and spirituality. Most of the time, discomfort is due to the unknown components of the client's faith and spirituality and how they will be used in therapy. Broaching the topic helps to remove the discomfort and demonstrates empathy and understanding. Moreover, it helps the client and counselor collaborate on a plan for treatment and alignment on what is important to the client and how their faith and spirituality can facilitate healing.

Once a treatment plan is in place. Future sessions should include interventions that leverage the client's faith and spirituality. The following section will outline several effective interventions, including affirmations and faith confessions, mindfulness, bibliotherapy, art, music, and exploratory tasks.

Affirmations & Faith Confessions

Affirmations and faith confessions are tools that renew the mind. One of the challenges with trauma is the negative impression it leaves on the mind. To help clients change their thought processes about trauma, they need to learn new information; they need to change their understanding about who they are and who God designed them to be in this life. The trauma stole their previous way of thinking and caused them to conform to the negativity and pain of the experience. Now, applying scriptural confessions and affirmations can help the client overcome negative beliefs and thoughts.

What does a faith confession or affirmation sound like? The first step is helping clients identify scriptures based on their specific goals for therapy and their specific traumatic life event. If a client presents to therapy indicating that they have low self-esteem and a lack of worth, transform these scriptures into personal affirmations that the client recites out loud:

1. I am altogether beautiful; God loves me, there is no flaw in me. (Song of Solomon 4:7)
2. I praise you, for I am fearfully and wonderfully made. Wonderful are your works; my soul knows it very well. (Psalm 139:14)
3. God has numbered the hairs on my head; I have no fear; I am more valuable than many sparrows. (Luke 12:7)

Introducing scriptural affirmations develops an internal strength and empowerment that connects the client's faith with God's word. Scriptural affirmations are directly related to meditation and prayer. Incorporating meditation and prayer are mindfulness activities, another valuable intervention in the healing process.

Mindfulness

Mindfulness is an effective intervention to help African American women reduce the impact of trauma (Dutton et al., 2013). Mindfulness is a mental state where a person is focused and conscious of the present moment (Trammel, 2015). Further, the person is open and accepting of their feelings, thoughts, and senses. Rhodes (2015) discussed the benefits of yoga (useful in mindfulness practices) in helping African American women practice calmness and regulate emotions to be more self-aware and present. Like yoga, mindfulness practices help clients learn to be fully present as they practice prayer and meditation. These sacred times can help the client to rid themselves of painful memories from the past. Clients can learn how to live in the present through mindfulness practices and leave the past behind them. Clients can keep a gratitude journal, noting things they are grateful for and how their life is transforming. They can also track their progress and learn to release the past and move toward the future.

Bibliotherapy

Bibliotherapy is a psychoanalytic therapeutic intervention that uses literature to overcome issues with grief and trauma (Steward & Ames, 2014). The counselor may assign a specific sacred text, novel, or other self-help reference book to help clients address their presenting problem. In theory, the client will identify with a character in the literature. They can learn from the character how to manage their problems, overcome them, and eventually heal. Bibliotherapy is effective in helping clients develop problem-solving skills, increase self-awareness, and clarify identity.

Art and Music

Art and music are excellent ways to help clients express their emotions. Research literature indicated that expressive therapies such as art (Schouten et al., 2015), music (Landis-Shack et al., 2017), and writing are vehicles to help people heal from trauma (Glass et al., 2019). Art and music are cognitive tools to help clients elicit imagery and access deep emotions and feelings (Landis et al., 2017). Application of expressive art, music, and writing in counseling may include listening, reciting passages, singing, creating original works, playing instruments, and discussing the experience.

Exploratory Tasks

Exploratory tasks are homework assignments given by the counselor to the client. Conceptually, the counselor wants to help the client develop skills to understand their spiritual beliefs and values. Counselors may ask clients to find specific stories in the Bible that align with their life experiences. The client would be asked to reflect on the passages of scripture and what the passage means to them. During the subsequent counseling session, the client can share their reflection. The counselor may have additional questions and probe the client to go deeper to access emotions and feelings holding up their healing. The client will develop self-awareness, gain strength to overcome their past, and develop personal power to move forward.

Conclusion

Trauma for African American women began in slavery and continues to manifest in many ways today. Helping African American women heal from trauma requires culturally sensitive and person-centered counselors. Applying a person-centered spiritual approach for counseling is a theoretical concept that may help clients heal from traumas. Counselors can use affirmations and faith confessions, mindfulness, bibliotherapy, art, music, and exploratory tasks as interventions to help many African American women heal from childhood abuses, stigmatizations, poverty, institutionalized racism, systemic oppression, and societal norms that promote inequalities.

References

Abrams, J. A., Hill, A., & Maxwell, M. (2019). Underneath the mask of the strong Black woman schema: Disentangling influences of strength and self-silencing on depressive symptoms among US Black women. *Sex roles*, *80*(9), 517-526.

Avent, J. R., Cashwell, C. S., & Brown-Jeffy, S. (2015). African American pastors on mental health, coping, and help seeking. *Counseling & Values*, *60*(1), 32–47. https://doi.org/10.1002/j.2161-007X.2015.00059.x.

Bartholomew, M. W., Harris, A. N., & Maglalang, D. D. (2018). A call to healing: Black Lives Matter movement as a framework for addressing the health and wellness of Black women. *Community Psychology in Global Perspective*, *4*(2), 85-100.

Brewer-Smyth, K., & Koenig, H. G. (2014). Could spirituality and religion promote stress resilience in survivors of childhood trauma? *Issues in mental health nursing*, *35*(4), 251-256.

Carter Andrews, D. J., Brown, T., Castro, E., & Id-Deen, E. (2019). The impossibility of being perfect and white: Black girls' racialized and gendered schooling experiences. *American Educational Research Journal, 56*(6), 2531-2572.

Courtois, C. A. (2008). Complex trauma, complex reactions: Assessment and treatment. *Psychological Trauma: Theory, Research, Practice, and Policy, S*(1), 86-100. https://doi.org/10.1037/1942-9681.S.1.86.

Danzer, G., Rieger, S. M., Schubmehl, S., & Cort, D. (2016). White psychologists and African Americans' historical trauma: Implications for practice. *Journal of Aggression, Maltreatment & Trauma*, *25*(4), 351-370.

Dickens, D. D., Womack, V. Y., & Dimes, T. (2019). Managing hypervisibility: An exploration of theory and research on identity shifting strategies in the workplace among Black women. *Journal of Vocational Behavior*, *113*, 153-163.

Dutton, M. A., Bermudez, D., Matas, A., Majid, H., & Myers, N. L. (2013). Mindfulness-based stress reduction for low-income, predominantly African American women with PTSD and a history of intimate partner violence. *Cognitive and behavioral practice*, *20*(1), 23-32.

Erving, C. L., Satcher, L. A., & Chen, Y. (2021). Psychologically resilient, but physically vulnerable? Exploring the psychosocial determinants of African American women's mental and physical health. *Sociology of Race and Ethnicity*, *7*(1), 116-133.

Evans, S. Y., Bell, K., & Burton, N. K. (2017). *Black women's mental health: Balancing strength and vulnerability*. SUNY Press.

Fripp, J. A., & Carlson, R. G. (2017). Exploring the influence of attitude and stigma on participation of African American and Latino populations in mental health services. *Journal of Multicultural Counseling and Development*, *45*(2), 80–94. https://doi.org/10.1002/jmcd.12066.

Glass, O., Dreusicke, M., Evans, J., Bechard, E., & Wolever, R. Q. (2019). Expressive writing to improve resilience to trauma: A clinical feasibility trial. *Complementary therapies in clinical practice*, *34*, 240-246.

Grossi, É. (2020). New avenues in epigenetic research about race: Online activism around reparations for slavery in the United States. *Social Science Information*, *59*(1), 93-116.

Helsel, P. B. (2015). Witnessing the body's response to trauma: Resistance, ritual, and nervous system activation. *Pastoral Psychology*, *64*(5), 681-693.

Kapoor, S., Heather, K. D., Watson-Singleton, N., Are, F., Elmore, C. A., Crooks, C. L., . . . Kaslow, N. J. (2018). Childhood abuse, intrapersonal strength, and suicide resilience in African American females who attempted suicide. *Journal of Family Violence*, *33*(1), 53-64.

Kempf, A. (2020). If we are going to talk about implicit race bias, we need to talk about structural racism: Moving beyond ubiquity and inevitability in teaching and learning about race. *Taboo: The Journal of Culture and Education*, *19*(2), 115-132.

King, K. M., & Borders, L. D. (2019). An experimental investigation of white counselors broaching race and racism. *Journal of Counseling & Development*, *97*(4), 341-351.

Landis-Shack, N., Heinz, A. J., & Bonn-Miller, M. O. (2017). Music therapy for posttraumatic stress in adults: a theoretical review. *Psychomusicology: Music, Mind, and Brain*, *27*(4), 334-342.

Livesey, A. (2017). Conceived in violence: enslaved mothers and children born of rape in nineteenth-century Louisiana. *Slavery & Abolition*, *38*(2), 373-391.

Long, L., & Ullman, S. E. (2013). The impact of multiple traumatic victimization on disclosure and coping mechanisms for Black women. *Feminist Criminology*, *8*(4), 295-319.

Longman-Mills, S., Mitchell, C., & Abel, W. (2019). The Psychological Trauma of Slavery: The Jamaican Case Study. *Social and Economic Studies*, *68*(3/4), 79-264.

Mosley, D. V., Hargons, C. N., Miller, C., Angyal, B., Wheeler, P., Davis, C., & Stevens-Watkins, D. (2021). Critical consciousness of anti-Black racism: A practical model to prevent and resist racial trauma. *Journal of Counseling Psychology*, *68*(1), 1-16.

Nelson, T., Shahid, N. N., & Cardemil, E. V. (2020). Do I really need to go and see somebody? Black women's perceptions of help-seeking for depression. *Journal of Black Psychology*, *46*(4), 263-286.

Quinn, A. (2013). A person-centered approach to multicultural counseling competence. *Journal of Humanistic Psychology*, *53*(2), 202-251.

Reed, T. D., & Neville, H. A. (2014). The influence of religiosity and spirituality on psychological well-being among Black women. *Journal of Black Psychology*, *40*(4), 384-401.

Rhodes, A. M. (2015). Claiming peaceful embodiment through yoga in the aftermath of trauma. *Complementary therapies in clinical practice*, *21*(4), 247-256.

Rogers, C. R. (1959). Client-centered therapy. *American handbook of psychiatry*, *3*, 183-200.

Scharff, A., Roberson, K., Sutherland, M. E., & Boswell, J. F. (2021). Black therapists working with Black clients: Intervention use and caseload preferences. *Practice Innovations*, *6*(2), 77–88. https://doi.org/10.1037/pri0000147.

Schmelzer, G. L. (2018). *Journey through trauma: A trail guide to the 5-phase cycle of healing repeated trauma*. Penguin.

Schouten, K. A., de Niet, G. J., Knipscheer, J. W., Kleber, R. J., & Hutschemaekers, G. J. (2015). The effectiveness of art therapy in the treatment of traumatized adults: a systematic review on art therapy and trauma. *Trauma, Violence, & Abuse*, *16*(2), 220-228.

Scott, S. K., Sheperis, D. S., Simmons, R. T., Rush-Wilson, T., & Milo, L. A. (2016). Faith as a cultural variable: Implications for counselor training. *Counseling and Values*, *61*(2), 192–205. https://doi.org/10.1002/cvj.12037.

Smith, R. J., & Oliver, B. U. (2021). Advocating for Black lives—a call to dermatologists to dismantle institutionalized racism and address racial health inequities. *JAMA Dermatology*, *157*(2), 155-156.

Stewart, P. E., & Ames, G. P. (2014). Using culturally affirming, thematically appropriate bibliotherapy to cope with trauma. *Journal of Child & Adolescent Trauma*, *7*(4), 227-236.

Sue, D. W., Sue, D., Neville, H. A., & Smith, L. (2019). *Counseling the culturally diverse: Theory and practice*. John Wiley & Sons.

Trammel, R. C. (2015). Mindfulness as enhancing ethical decision-making and the Christian integration of mindful practice. *Social Work and Christianity*, *42*(2), 165-177.

Van der Kolk, B. A. (2003). *Psychological trauma*. American Psychiatric Pub.

Vernon, L. F. (2020). Tuskegee syphilis study, not America's only medical scandal: Chester M. Southam, MD, Henrietta Lacks, and the Sloan-Kettering research scandal. *Online Journal of Health Ethics*, *16*(2), 1-10.

Watson, N. N., & Hunter, C. D. (2015). Anxiety and depression among African American women: The costs of strength and negative attitudes toward psychological help-seeking. *Cultural Diversity and Ethnic Minority Psychology*, *21*(4), 604.

Woods-Giscombe, C., Robinson, M. N., Carthon, D., Devane-Johnson, S., & Corbie-Smith, G. (2016). Superwoman schema, stigma, spirituality, and culturally sensitive providers: Factors influencing African American women's use of mental health services. *Journal of Best Practices in Health Professions Diversity: Research, Education And Policy*, *9*(1), 1124.

Yang, N., Collins, J. W., & Burris, H. H. (2021). States with more killings of unarmed black people have more extensive black–white preterm birth disparities. *Journal of Perinatology*, *41*(2), 358-359.

Zilcha-Mano, S., Muran, J. C., Hungr, C., Eubanks, C. F., Safran, J. D., & Winston, A. (2016). The relationship between alliance and outcome: Analysis of a two-person perspective on alliance and session outcome. *Journal of Consulting and Clinical Psychology*, *84*(6), 484–496. https://doi.org/10.1037/ccp0000058.

Chapter 12

Black Women: Pregnancy and Trauma

Kimberley Dockery*, **PhD, LMFT**
Yorkville University, Toronto, Canada

Abstract

This book chapter will explore the experiences of Black women who experienced trauma before, during, or after their pregnancy and childbirth journeys. Black women may experience individual, cultural, historical, or even medical trauma throughout pregnancy. Exposure to these traumatic experiences during pregnancy and childbirth can cause additional emotional and physical responses. Evaluating how important maternal health disparities can change if there is adequate support for moms is important. The quality of prenatal and postpartum care can make a difference for Black women during this uncertain time. Connecting with a trauma-informed therapist and/or doula can help women identify and address specific experiences to journey well during and after pregnancy. Uncovering how trauma narratives usually ignored or dismissed impact women within our communities is imperative. Black women face barriers to postpartum mental health care, including a lack of access and stigma around mental health. However, it is essential to continue to build awareness and education for our Black mothers to seek care differently. For example, organizations like Black Mamas Matter Alliance are amplifying the voices of mothers to address the importance of introducing legislation that cultivates research, changes policy, and advances care for Black mamas. By closing the gaps, we improve maternal/maternal mental health quality and educate healthcare providers about implicit bias.

---

* Corresponding Author's Email: drkimberleydockery@gmail.com.

In: How Did We Survive?
Editor: Tina Marie Glover
ISBN: 979-8-88697-918-3

Keywords: pregnancy, Black women, postpartum mental health, medical trauma

Introduction

According to the Centers for Disease Control and Prevention, Black and indigenous women are three to four times more likely to die from pregnancy-related causes than white women. Throughout the United States, women continue to die while pregnant, during childbirth, and even a year after having their baby. However, our country's maternal mortality rate surpasses other developing countries worldwide. According to The American College of Obstetricians and Gynecologists (ACOG), people of color will represent most of the United States population in 2050. Yet, racial and health disparities persist in women's healthcare system. However, the health disparities that Black women face continue to be a complex problem. Black women are more likely not to have health insurance, face financial challenges that impact their ability to access women's wellness care and cannot even start prenatal care when they learn of their pregnancy. Women also experience more health conditions that can impact them and baby, including diabetes, hypertension, cardiovascular disease, and uterine fibroids. Our healthcare system needs to address multiple layers that include physical, psychological, and emotional health concerns for Black women across their lifespans. This chapter will address the history of Black women and pregnancy narratives and how we can advocate and offer more awareness to improve access to quality care.

Understanding the Impact of Pregnancy and Trauma

Black women may experience individual, cultural, historical, or even medical trauma throughout pregnancy. Exposure to these traumatic experiences during pregnancy and childbirth can cause additional emotional and physical responses. While birthing your child can be a wonderful and joyous experience for many women, for some Black women, it is a time of sadness and trauma. Studies show that new mothers of color have rates of postpartum depression soaring close to 38% compared with a 13-19% rate for all new mothers (Keefe, Brownstein-Evans, & Rouland Polmateer, 2016). This finding highlights that women of color are not screened for postpartum mood concerns or offered support from a therapist or postpartum doula. Consider the impact on the mother and her family if she isn't receiving the necessary medical treatment and therapeutic services. Research shows screening pregnant and postpartum women for depression can significantly reduce depressive symptoms. The U.S. Preventive Services Task Force (USPSTF) is an independent national expert panel that publishes evidence-based and preventative medicine research. In 2002 and 2009, the USPSTF stated that guidelines for all adults should screen for depression, but this excluded pregnant women citing a lack of evidence for this specific population. However, in 2014, The Task Force revisited their recommendations, and the American Psychological Association (APA) weighed in to address the need and screening benefits for pregnant and postpartum women. In addition to the above finding, researchers noted how perinatal depression is linked with pregnancy risks such as pre-eclampsia, preterm birth, and low birth weight. It also highlighted more alarming outcomes which can negatively affect children, including breastfeeding complications, family distress, abuse, and neglect of children (Brette et al., 2011). Exposure to trauma during pregnancy and childbirth can also cause additional emotional and physical responses in the mother and baby.

Our Personal Trauma Narratives

> "Our spirits have a way of dulling the traumatic, of blunting painful memories to lessen their ache."-Cicely Tyson.

My grandmother was known as a strong black woman who served as a midwife in her rural community in Mississippi. But her narrative of witnessing abuse as a small child, rape as a young teenager, and ongoing racism in her small town impacted this beautiful soul. Being affected by various aspects of trauma can impact anyone's ability to have healthy relationships, feel safe in school and work environments, and remain healthy physically and emotionally. My grandmother was often stern in her tone and behavior instead of what some would call loving. As one who understands more about her trauma history, Black women tend not to unpack their narratives. It is inherited why Black women seem disconnected within their mind and body connections; trauma is a key player in this experience.

Maya Angelou stated, "There is no agony like bearing an untold story inside of you." This quote summarizes how not having sacred space to begin to process traumatic lived experiences can deeply impact women for generations. As a Black woman working in a healthcare system and within the field of family therapy, I have been in many traumatic situations dominated by white providers that do not recognize how devalued and marginalized Black women's physical and emotional care is dismissed during pregnancy and beyond. In the book post-traumatic *slave Syndrome*, author DeGruy inquires, "Isn't it likely that many slaves were severely traumatized? Furthermore, did the trauma and the effects of such horrific abuse end with the abolition of slavery?" The trauma that my grandmother experienced not only lives in her body but is traced back decades within her ancestral lineage. Our culture must recognize that millions of black bodies have experienced centuries of trauma. For the healing process to shift, white Americans must imagine themselves in black, red, and brown bodies. In Resmaa Menakem's book *My Grandmother's Hands*, she asks, "If we don't address our ancient historical trauma, what will we pass down to our children and to their children and grandchildren?" The answer to this question is absolute. We cannot afford to turn our eyes away from the suffering Black women have experienced and how their experiences now are linked to broader histories.

Black Women and Maternal Mental Health

Historically, studies show that Black women are less likely to seek mental health support to stigma and cultural barriers around mental health. Many women of color who do seek help from a mental health provider are often seen as weak women. Our culture tends to silence our struggles, and Black women must take care of everyone else rather than themselves. Women lean into their faith to lessen their burden and to seek strength with adversity, especially when faced with oppression, racism, and socioeconomic stressors.

Racial bias in healthcare is vast and puts women of color at risk. Consider that the mortality rate for babies born to Black women with a doctorate or professional degree is higher than that for white women who never finished high school. According to Kozhimannil et al., 2011, racial and ethnic differences in the perception and treatment experiences of low-income women of color versus white women include limited access to healthcare services, a disconnection with providers, a lack of access to providers that look like them and unavailability of culturally linguistically appropriate services. Another study discovered that low-income mothers of color need more access to health screening and treatment options. In 2016, Keefe, Brownstein-Evans &

Rouland Polmateer found that access to services, flexibility, and community-based support was imperative to offer adequate support for expectant mothers.

Much attention has been given to postpartum mood disorders such as postpartum depression or postpartum anxiety but not all expectant and new moms who experience mental health concerns deal with postpartum depression. Other mood disorders within the postpartum period include postpartum post-traumatic stress disorder (P-PTSD). Postpartum PTSD is not discussed, but for new moms who experience it, the condition is very real and unsettling. This mood disorder can impact how you enter into motherhood and care for yourself and your new baby. Women tend to focus on staying healthy and, hopefully, during labor and delivery. However, not every mom's birthing experience is joyful.

According to the American College of Obstetricians and Gynecologists (ACOG), three to sixteen percent of recently delivered moms describe their birth as traumatic and express severe trauma stress responses during the postpartum period. A new mom who experiences P-PTSD all report that their childbirth experience triggered anxiety and pain. Trauma from severe morning sickness, fertility, and/or pregnancy complications varies during pregnancy and after birth. As a therapist in OB-GYN, women have reported trauma during childbirth if labor and delivery were long and painful if there was a severe tear, hemorrhage, or even an emergency C-section after planning to have a natural birth or even epidural. Trauma, including premature birth, can also impact the mom and baby's lived experience.

American Psychological Association (APA) emphasizes that sometimes practitioners do not correctly diagnose P-PTSD, especially when it is not included in standard screening for postpartum mood concerns. Many women with P-PTSD many exhibit depressive symptoms and are misdiagnosed with having postpartum depression. However, the conditions overlap, and Postpartum Depression can exacerbate P-PTSD; they are quite different.
P-PSTD happens due to the trauma or perceived trauma; white Postpartum Depression happens because of hormonal changes a woman experiences after delivery. It is important to note that there is a distinction between the two diagnoses. Understanding what effective treatment plans can offer women during this delicate time is imperative.

Any stress, anxiety, and/or trauma, racial factors, or even medical trauma can trigger P-PTSD. For example, a woman with fears about her safety in specific settings, direct exposure to racial abuse or discrimination, and medical professionals not taking their personal experiences seriously might exacerbate more trauma responses. Years ago, I recall reading a Time magazine article about Serena Williams and her postnatal care experience. Serene described how she had to convince medical staff to address her concerns after having her daughter, Olympia. Serena stated in that 2017 interview, "All of my status characteristics screamed 'competent,' but nothing could shut down what my Blackness screams when I walk into the room." Even in the world's wealthiest and most medically advanced nation, Black women continue to experience discrimination and lack of quality healthcare than white women. Medical providers are fully aware of these healthcare disparities; how are they addressing them? A global superstar athlete had to intervene directly with medical staff to advocate for necessary postnatal care. What does that say about an average Black women's treatment after birth and beyond?

Impact of Experiencing Trauma and Loss

Today, African-American women experience more infant loss, stillbirth, and miscarriage than white women in the United States. Yet the data does little to help us understand the experience of loss and trauma for Black women and their families. Culturally, Black women have called upon their past and, specifically, their ancestors' narratives of loss and trauma to share their embodied experiences. Our country's unfortunate yet repetitive narrative is the image of African-American women who is physically strong without enough vulnerability to warrant consideration. Black women are often seen as incompetent and not allowed to understand their trauma within the context of gender, race, class, and even hierarchy.

Through generational narratives and even songs, Black women have narrated a history within the African-American embodiment of physical and psychological pain, anxieties, and mourning. Trauma-informed care is a framework that considers past trauma's effect on current behavior and the ability to cope and hopefully minimize the experiences of reliving trauma again. There is a pressing need for perinatal clinicians, including physicians, nurses, midwives, doulas, and mental health providers, to support pregnant women and their families. As a behavioral health therapist specializing in perinatal mood, Black women have often expressed that their stories are often ignored or dismissed by their OB providers. Some women of color have reported feeling not cared for and powerless during their child-birthing and postnatal care encounters. A sense of safety for mother and baby is compromised. Not having a trauma-informed care provider to offer compassion and comfort can increase the risk factor of postpartum mental health concerns. Black women with postpartum symptoms often do not score high on the Edinburgh scale, a screening tool that inquiries about cognitive and affective symptoms experienced in the last seven days.

Importance of African-American Perinatal Mental Health Providers

As an African-American therapist, I often inquire about more somatic symptoms like headache or abdominal pain to gather a better understanding of postpartum mood shifts in mind and body. Often women of color are not forthcoming about underlying pain, trauma, or depressive, anxious symptoms. Some women have avoided vulnerability and seeking care because of the fear of child welfare services being involved. Reports from several states found that child welfare workers deem Black women unfit at higher rates than white women, even when examining factors like education and poverty.

Again, a sense of safety and certainty is imperative when offering trauma-informed care to women as a provider. Suppose you have past trauma of not feeling supported and heard by your OB provider. Why would one assume a new mother offering honesty about her experiences regarding her emotional health? No single change can reserve traumatic birth experiences for Black women in a system based on racism. I hope that after giving birth, more women of color will feel more comfortable seeking support from a midwife, doula, and/or therapist who is sensitive to holding space for sadness, irritability, and sudden crying that may arise. The strong Black women stereotype and cultural expectations of the role of the Black mother kept her from putting herself first. Like most narratives, women of color know how to care for everyone else because their family system has always been this way. However, there must come a point where women must honor that taking care of themselves does not compromise their abilities and capabilities as great mothers to their children. They must also model the importance of allowing others to fill the gap. Changing the narrative of Black women's tolerance of physical and emotional pain has to change.

With all this in mind, how can trauma-informed clinicians who look like us address the unique concerns and challenges that impact Black women during pregnancy and motherhood? What is necessary to move this conversation forward and create movement in this field? How can women that look like me remain empowered, given circumstances? We must look at culture and address how prejudice and discrimination impact the emotional health and well-being of women of color. Research is needed to address the different ways to adequately offer quality healthcare to birth persons of color. Black women experience perinatal depression, anxiety, psychosis, and even postpartum depression disorders. Research studies are far behind in offering more diverse populations and addressing adequate health disparities for women of color. There is also a call for studies to address perinatal screening tools. Addressing if somatic complaints are more commonly reported versus cognitive complaints, whether medications work, and what treatment modalities are better tailored and more effective for Black women.

What to Do Differently and Understanding Our Concerns

Many Black women share concerns about not trusting providers who are not culturally competent with their maternal mental health concerns. Women need to connect with providers that look like them. I had heard many stories from women who finally visited me who found the process quite burdensome, not connecting with a provider with similar racial or ethnic background. For women with limited resources, a national online directory called Therapy for Black Girls offers a search engine to find therapists in your area or, even more conveniently, online therapy sessions. Another option is called Fertility for Colored Girls. This online platform supports women of color who have experienced fertility and reproductive health concerns. Again, the virtual therapy options have broadened the ability for women to utilize services that would be more challenging to access. The hope is that more accessibility will offer more awareness and support for women to share their unique narratives.

African-American women tend to hold on to the trauma from infertility, miscarriage, infant loss, and stillbirth and lack the option to unpack those experiences as Black mothers and families. The silence that contributes to the demise of Black women and their babies can change. Often, I reflect on the psychological weight Black women carried throughout generations around childbirth. The history of women having to nurse their master's wives' babies and the impact of black mothers not having the privilege to nurse and bond with their babies. Black women had to force themselves not to fall in love with their newborns. The impact of this type of trauma and disconnection has been passed down for generations. Due to the trauma of wet nursing, breastfeeding during a women's postpartum period has since been negatively stigmatized in the Black Community.

In addition to that, Black bodies have been historically highly sexualized or degraded in the United States. The perception of a Black women's sexual health and rights have been negatively impacted which dampens the personal and intimate experience for the mother and baby. Advocacy around breastfeeding has been the primary narrative for white, cis-gendered women.

Organizational Change and Building Awareness

Statistics from the Centers for Disease Control and Prevention and the Department of Health and Human Services report that 69 percent of Black breastfeed from birth as opposed to 85 percent of white women. This is the lowest rate of all ethnic groups. Forty-four percent of Black women continue to breastfeed at six months as opposed to 62 percent of white women and 57 percent of women overall. This present-day health disparity in the Black community is impacting women during postpartum. One in four women returns to work ten days after having their baby. Black women are more likely to have jobs that do not provide flexibility and proper access to pumping upon their return to work.

Although the Patient Protection and Affordable Care Act (ACA) provisions require employers to provide break times and options for private locations for their employees to nurse, many companies fail to comply with this mandate. This issue is more prominent in low-wage jobs, which include more disproportionate numbers of Black women employees. In addition to the work stressors, Black women are more likely to live in food deserts, which means less access to quality nutrition to maintain an adequate milk supply.

The month of August is currently known as national breastfeeding month. The pause brings awareness, recognition, and celebration to uplift Black women who have been oppressed for generations around breastfeeding their babies. Feeding your child this way offers power and autonomy over Black women's minds and bodies. For many women, the advice they are given around breastfeeding comes in a healthcare setting, clinic, or hospital shortly after their delivery. Though advice and guidance from trusted family and friends are crucial, any problems or deficits are usually diagnosed by an OB provider, midwife, nurse, doula, or lactation specialist. For Black women, the probability that this medical professional will be a person of color is slim.

Author and birth equity advocate LaBrisa Williams stated, "Only 2.6 percent of the nation's doctors identify as Black or African American, and in 2020, these groups accounted for a mere 7.3 percent of students enrolled in medical school." I recall having a few conversations recently with women of color postpartum moms who expressed immense gratitude and joy for not having the daunting conversation with their OB providers to formula feed their newborns. It has been a reality in Black communities for women to be viewed as incompetent and not given the same support and education to work with a lactation specialty or doula to address any questions or past complications with breastfeeding. Continuing the dialogue around the power of sharing childbirth and postpartum narratives is essential.

With birth equity studies and initiatives, policymakers, academics, and healthcare officials hope the personal narratives they receive can help them understand the increase in maternal mortality and morbidity in Black women compared to women of other races. Organizations like National Birth Equity Collaborative, Black Mamas Alliance, Irth, and Black Girls Breastfeeding Club share the mission to create solutions to optimize Black maternal, infant, sexual and reproductive well-being. These organizational systems offer training, research, resources, policy, and training to improve the systems for women of color and help them thrive in various phases of their pregnancy journey.

For example, Black Mamas Alliance has held a conference for Black women, providers, advocates, clinicians, and other stakeholders working to improve Black maternal health through birth justice, reproductive justice, and human rights systems. This year, I attended the virtual conference. I found it created a vast platform for learning, in-depth conversations, and mobilization to generate not only support for one another but transform how we address Black maternal health concerns. The conference generated space for meaningful dialogue and education on existing reproductive and health equality. It was a powerful experience to witness Black Mamas Alliance offer such value within holistic care, clinical innovation, policy/advocacy, and research. To date, discussions about Black Maternal Health and Mental health are minimal. Black Mamas Alliance (BMMA) has created a space that centers around the voices and experiences of black mothers.

National Birth Equity Collaborative is another organization focused on the sexual and reproductive health and wellness of Black women. NBEC has become the leading expert and advocate for change in Black Maternal health and infant mortality crises. It was established by a black OB/GYN, Dr. Joia Crear-Perry, who experienced firsthand the healthcare and racial disparities. Black women endured these disparities during childbirth and the postnatal period. Dr. Crear-Perry understood the importance of creating a healthy and safe space for moms and their babies. A significant part of her life's work has been to include more awareness of this health crisis and to offer solutions. Her organization also trains clinicians and medical birthing facilities to provide more equitable care to women of color.

National Birth Equity Collaborative (NBEC) has also collaborated with Black Mamas Alliance for National Black Maternal Health Week in April. This weeklong national event brings awareness, advocacy, and community building for the lived experiences of black mothers and their families. The term "Black Mamas" represents the full diversity of our lived experiences that includes birthing persons (cis women, trans folks, and gender-nonconforming individuals) and all people of African descent across the diaspora."- The Black Mamas Matter Alliance.

Irth app was created by Kimberly Seals Allers, who had her first child after graduating with her master's degree from Columbia University. Who was single and only had access to student health insurance. Ms. Allers has shared her narrative about giving birth at New York City's best hospital but experiencing trauma, disrespect, and poor medical care. Her narrative might sound similar to others I have shared throughout this chapter. According to researchers at Stanford University, women have reported implicit bias that impacts their care and treatment received during childbirth and the postnatal period. Because of her personal experience, Allers has focused her life's work on writing, speaking, and advocating for equity in maternal and infant health.

In addition to publishing her fifth book, The Big Letdown-How Medicine Big Business, and Feminism Undermine Breastfeeding, Allers created a new project called Irth. It was created to change the narrative around how media and technology address health disparities. The cell phone application provides "Yelp-like" reviews and ratings for women of color to search for or leave reviews for maternal and pediatric clinicians and birthing hospitals in the United States. The mission is to generate more autonomy for Black women to be informed about whom they select for their and their baby's care. It also allows you to filter reviews by race, income, gender, and sexual orientation.

Black Girls' Breastfeeding Club was founded by a mother and public health researcher/scientist, Dr. Ayanna Robinson. Her organization aims to provide culturally relevant information and resources around decision-making about breastfeeding and infant feeding. Dr. Robinson's goal is to offer alternative narratives around positive breastfeeding for women of color while also holding space for the historical and social factors that have influenced decisions to breastfeed as Black women. By promoting education for women through online, social media, and community events, Dr. Robinson's goal is to highlight more positive narratives and inspire other women of color to share their journeys. Research suggests that breastfeeding mothers release less stress hormone responses in their bodies. The hope is that more shared experiences and imagery of Black women breastfeeding can re-story the narrative for generations to come.

Closing the Gap and Creating More Support Systems

The work of improving Black maternal health and mental health is not easy. It requires an ongoing commitment to individuals, families, and communities to understand the oppression and trauma of women of color. Becoming a mother and caring for your new baby is an indescribably rewarding yet unsettling experience for women of color. Pregnancy comes not only with a range of emotions and potential health challenges. It is normal for Black women to desire a sense of care and safety from their medical support system. Additionally, it is ideal for her social support network to include providers that include a behavioral health therapist, doula, or lactation specialist to look like her. When entering this transitional stage in your life, your medical care team must support the expectant mother fully. The endless statistics of racially related stressors and maternal mortality rates that come with pregnancy as a woman of color can change. Our responsibility is to create a significant shift in the physical and emotional well-being of expectant and postpartum mothers of color. As systemic thinkers, policymakers, and change agents, we are responsible for cultivating differences among the social isolation, mental health stigma, misinformation, and distrust within medical systems for Black women. Any woman of color who becomes pregnant should navigate through a healthcare system that offers support, respect, and space to maintain physical and emotional wellness.

Organizations like Black Mamas Alliance and Irth can generate more systems to address how anti-racism advocacy and training can offer space to eradicate racism in maternal health. Even with more awareness, policy, and strategies, our healthcare can look different, but it requires meaningful change. By offering more culturally and trauma-informed care providers, mothers can adjust to motherhood, breastfeed peacefully, care for their newborns, and lean into coping strategies to manage the normal changes and stressors that postpartum mothers face within this life-changing journey.

In 2019, Oklahoma State University Medical Centers and Hillcrest, started a pilot study to collaborate by addressing what historically has made it unlikely for clinicians to be heard and seen as Black mothers. The new program Team Birth was created to offer the expectant mom a voice in her childbirth care plan. The goal was to create a system that provides accountability for decisions about care between the mother and her medical care team. The model is built around a labor and delivery plan within a huddle framework magnifying the patient's voice in more shared decision-making to offer safer care for her and their baby. The outcome of the pilot highlighted the importance of how communication, experience, and a sense of dignity were essential aspects of this more collaborative labor and delivery framework. The program also offered an option to connect with an e-doula after delivery. Again, this is a minor shift but an example of how pregnancy can look different for future births.

Conclusion

As a woman of color and therapist, I often encourage my patients who are women of color to advocate for themselves and have a loved one or close friend help advocate on their behalf. It makes a difference when you are receiving support from someone who has a similar cultural or ethnic background to yourself. I encourage women of color to permit themselves to seek those supportive systems to start journeying differently through pregnancy. We all have work to do but we must work through our untold stories.

References

Beauregard J. L., Hamner H. C., Chen, J., Avila-Rodriguez, W., Elam-Evans L. D., Perrine, C.G., Racial Disparities in Breastfeeding Initiation and Duration Among U.S. Infants Born in 2015. MMWR Morbidity and Mortality Weekly Report 2019; 68:745–748. DOI: http://dx.doi.org/10.15585/mmwr.mm6834a3.

Gregory, S. "*Serena Williams Opens Up About Her Complicated Comeback, Motherhood, and Making Time to Be Selfish." Time,16,08,2018. https://time.com/5368858/serena-williams-comeback/.*

Hawkins S.S., Dow-Fleisner, S., Noble, A., Breastfeeding and the Affordable Care Act. *Pediatric Clinics of North America*. 2015;62(5):1071-1091. https://pubmed.ncbi.nlm.nih.gov/26318941/.

Henry J. Kaiser Family Foundation. Health coverage for the black population today and under the Affordable Care Act. Menlo Park (CA): KFF; 2013. Available at:http://kff.org/disparities-policy/fact-sheet/health-coverage-for-the-black-population-today-and-under-the-affordable-care-act.

Keefe, R. H., Brownstein-Evans, C., Rouland Polmanteer, R.S., (2016): Having our say: African American and Latina mothers provide recommendations to health and mental health providers working with new mothers living with postpartum depression, Social Work in Mental Health, doi: 10.1080/15332985.2016.1140699.

Kozhimannil K. B., Adams A. S., Soumerai S. B., Busch A. B., Huskamp, H., New Jersey's efforts to improve postpartum depression care did not change treatment patterns for women on Medicaid. Health Affairs. 2011; 30(2):293–301. http://doi.org/10.1377/hlthaff.2009.1075. [PubMed: 21289351].

Menakem, R., 2017. *My Grandmother's Hands*. Las Vegas, NV: Central Recovery Press.

Racial and ethnic disparities in obstetrics and gynecology. Committee Opinion No. 649. American College of Obstetricians and Gynecologists. Obstetrician Gynecology 2015;126: e130-4 US Preventive Services Task Force. Perinatal Depression: Preventive Interventions. 12,02,2019. https://www.uspreventiveservicestaskforce.org/uspstf/recommendation/perinatal-depression-preventive-interventions.

Williams D. R., & Rucker T. D., Understanding and addressing racial disparities in health care. *Health Care Financing Review*. 2000;21(4):75-90. https://www.ncbi.nlm.nih.gov/pmc/articles/PMC4194634/.

Chapter 13

"Reclaiming Connection": Interpersonal Healing in African-American Women Assailed by Relational Trauma

Ryan T. Wright*
Western Michigan University, Kalamazoo, Michigan, USA

Abstract

This paper argues for the validity and utility of using existential, person-centered, and interpersonal approaches when counseling Black Women harmed by trauma. Furthermore, the argument is made that these approaches allow Black women to heal on an intrapersonal and interpersonal level by addressing the core cognitive and affective wounds caused by trauma. Key aspects of these theoretical approaches: meaning-making (existential), unconditional positive regard (person-centered), and corrective emotional experience (interpersonal) are discussed; to offer a viewpoint on helping African-American women work through their trauma to feel emotionally safe in their ability to relate to others. Finally, the concept of relational depth will be explored to offer a guideline of a therapeutic encounter that can aid in Black women feeling heard, understood, and affirmed within their social-cultural context.

Keywords: relational depth, interpersonal, relational

---

* Corresponding Author's Email: ryan.t.wright@wmich.edu.

In: How Did We Survive?
Editor: Tina Marie Glover
ISBN: 979-8-88697-918-3

Relational Trauma and African-American Women

Trauma has become ubiquitous in lay and clinical settings due to its pervasive presence in society. The DSM-V (Diagnostic and Statistical Manual of Mental Disorders Fifth Edition) defines trauma as the following: any event (or events) that may cause or threaten death, serious injury, or sexual violence to an individual, a close family member or friend (American Psychiatric Association, 2013). Furthermore, trauma impedes our ability to feel safe, secure, and in control. Whether the traumatic event was acute (single event) or chronic (repetitive event), the remnants of feeling often endangered manifest as rigid behaviors designed to protect us from real or perceived harm.

One frequent source of trauma is destructive and exploitative relationships. Relational trauma has been defined as relationships with a profound violation of human connection (Schneider, 2018). Encompassed in relational trauma are baneful experiences of intimate partner violence, domestic violence, emotional/psychological abuse, neglect, grief, sexual abuse/exploitation, and any harmful event experienced by another person. The residual effects of relational trauma can leave individuals with shame, guilt, rage, and/or depression.

The interpersonal process of the change process (Teyber & Teyber, 2017), an integrative theoretical framework in psychotherapy emphasizing the intersection of relationships, thinking patterns, and attachment, explores how early relational trauma impacts functioning on an inter and intrapersonal level. As illustrated later, relational trauma causes one to become fixated and stuck in how they think, view themselves, and relate to others (Teyber & Teyber, 2017). Bright Quest, a leading residential therapy center on relational trauma, offered these sobering facts on its prevalence: 20% of women report being sexually assaulted at some point in their lives, 13% of children are physically bullied each year, and 33& emotionally bullied, 60% of adults suffered abuse and/or experienced other types of family difficulties ("Relational Trauma") n.d. These numbers capture a glimpse of how common relational trauma is and how it affects people across the developmental spectrum.

Relational trauma affects not only people in terms of age but also based on race. African-American women have and continue to face toxic stress based on systemic racism, poverty, and intimate partner violence (Warner, 2017). Recent police killings of unarmed African-American women such as Breonna Taylor, Sandra Bland, India Kager, Korryn Gaines, Michelle Cusseaux, and many others reinforce the notion that African-American women are not safe nor protected by those that claim to protect them. When harmed by being in relation to law enforcement, African-American women are assailed by the following stereotypes: promiscuous with no grounding in moral reasoning, and they are conditioned to violence based on their environment (Jacobs, 2017). These biased viewpoints underscore a more sobering belief about African American women harmed by police: it was their fault, and they inadvertently contributed to their violence. These messages can disempower and dissuade African American women from trusting institutions to care for their welfare.

Data in intimate partner violence research (IPV) show that more than 40% of African-American women experience IPV in their lifetime compared to 31.5 percent of the general population (DuMonthier, Childers, & Mili, n.d). It has also been noted that intimate partner violence is the leading cause of death among African-American woman ages 15-35 (Jones, 2014). Not feeling safe in intimate relationships can leave an indelible mark of shame, anger, and resentment. Sexual abuse usually accompanies intimate partner violence and is prevalent among African-American women. More sobering statistics speak to the need to be aware of the prevalence of sexual abuse in communities of African American women: 25% of African-American girls will be sexually abused before the age of 18, 46% of African-American women report being subjected to coercive sexual contact by the age of 18 (Barlow, 2020). African-American women are being harmed at an alarming rate in relationships and the larger society. The toxic stress of being harmed in relationships further perpetuates symptomatic behavior indicative of stress-related mental disorders. Suppose relationships are a central part of human existence. How do we best support society's vulnerable and often ignored group in feeling safe, connected, and empowered in their relationships?

The scope of this chapter is to explore pathways to the healing process in working with African-American women that have suffered relational trauma. Existential, Interpersonal, and person-centered approaches will be explored as they strongly emphasize the quality of the relationship as a vehicle of change. An argument will also be made that these process-based approaches facilitate a deep level of evolution by facilitating both a corrective emotional experience and relational depth (a heightened sense of transpersonal connection between two individuals) (Mearns & Cooper, 2017). Two fictional case vignettes will be illustrated to describe how these approaches can be applied to working with African-American women. Finally, social justice implications will be examined to further speak to advocacy efforts. The hope is that this chapter will reinforce the need to utilize process-oriented approaches to helping

African American woman reclaim their power and ability to reconnect in relationships.

The lived experiences of African-American women have been laden with trauma (Dailey, Humphreys, Rankin, & Lee, 2011; Yoder, 2005; Collins & Collins, 2005) related to many stressors that are environmental, systematic, and interpersonal. For example, a report published by the National Center on Violence Against Women in the Black Community in Washington, D.C., stated that 45% of Black women reported experiencing intimate partner violence in the 2010-2012 survey (Hargrove, 2018). More sobering was the data that Black women ages 25-29 were 11 times more likely than Caucasian women to be murdered while pregnant (Hargrove, 2018). Lastly, they reported that 1 in 5 or 20% of Black women experienced stalking in their lifetime. According to a report by the YWCA, 40% of Black women reported experiencing forced sexual contact by age 18 ("Girls of Color," n.d.). This data supports the view that women of color experience an abundance of trauma within intimate social spaces.

African-American women who have experienced relational trauma may turn to substance abuse to cope with feelings of loneliness and isolation. A sample of 104 African-American women receiving substance abuse treatment (Meshberg-Cohen, Pressau, Thacker, Hefner, and Svikis, 2016) found that 94.2% of consumers experienced at least one traumatic event. The most frequent traumatic event experienced was being incarcerated, followed by sexual assault. This research highlights the indelible mark that trauma leaves on African-American women in that, in some instances, substance use becomes the safe haven when there is a lack of social support and the ability to facilitate nurturing relationships with others.

Seeking help to work through and process relational trauma can be challenging for women of color. In examining opportunities and threats to healing from intimate partner violence, Finfgeld-Connet (2015) found that the following barriers prevent African-American women from obtaining help: the ambivalence of others, fear, mental health problems, and a pessimistic view of social services. These barriers will continue to maintain a sense of isolation and disconnection from others which can lead to rigid interpersonal coping styles (Teyber & Teyber, 2017) mentioned earlier.

Also equally harmful are the intrapersonal consequences of disconnection that can arrive from becoming emotionally cut off from meaningful social contact. In a practical sense, this can be reflected in African American women developing core beliefs that reflect the following themes and motifs in response to trauma experienced. "I am unlovable," " I do not need help from anyone," "It is my fault," "I am stupid," "I deserved it," If I do not do ______, then _____will not love me," "Boys do not cry," "I do not need an intimate partner," and or "why am I so sensitive/needy." Though, this list is not exhaustive. It highlights the criticism and negation of parts of the self. In analyzing these invalidating statements, we can see a deep polarization in which parts of the self become cut off. This can also present as low affection and emotional withdrawal towards children and other relationships. Another marker of the deep polarization of self is the overuse of the words "should" and "must." These two words signal conditional acceptance of self. Often, the goal of these rigid self-beliefs and expectations is not to make a "mistake" interpersonally that will cause them to re-experience the trauma.

Relationally, the term strong Black woman can be seen as both a source of strength and a hindrance to healing. The "strong Black woman" expectations are to nurture the family, support the male, raise the kids, and provide consistent emotional support and nurturance to others. What often happens is that this moniker is rigidly applied and made as an extension of one's identity. It is not uncommon to witness African-American women neglecting self-care, prioritizing the needs of others in place of self, and uncritically self-sacrificing (Liao, Wei, & Yin, 2020). Once again, we see how certain aspects of self are denied and repressed when rigidly adopting a fixed view of self. Furthermore, their study showed that the "strong Black woman" schema was associated with depression, loneliness, and anxiety when internalized (Liao et al., 2020).

Another intrapersonal consequence of trauma that can be witnessed in African-American women is a lack of self-compassion. The three components of self-compassion are self-kindness, common humanity, and mindfulness (Neff & Germer, 2018). Self-kindness refers to responding to ourselves in a non-critical way to nurture unconditional acceptance. Common humanity expresses the idea that our experiences, both positive and negative, are shared by others. This motivates us to seek help and assistance from others. The last component of self-compassion is mindfulness which entails being aware and introspective of one's emotions and intentions.

Relational Impact of Trauma

Often trauma evokes feelings of loneliness, anxiety, and psychosis that can lead to interpersonal conflicts, further maintaining disconnection from others and self. When analyzed from an interpersonal perspective, loneliness is a risk factor for depression. One reason is that being alone deprives a person of therapeutic human contact that can serve as social support. Another reason is that loneliness deprives a person of opportunities to learn about self in relation to others.

Trauma can also produce debilitating anxiety that causes avoidance of social interactions or behaviors that make unwanted reactions from others. Teyber and Teyber (2017) labeled these behaviors as inflexible interpersonal coping strategies. Exacting interpersonal coping processes help to protect and shield us from unresolved core emotions often related to the following emotions: shame, grief, loss, regret, inadequacy, low self-worth, anger, or any uncomfortable feeling that causes distress. Three distinct interpersonal styles or ways of relating to others often emerge as an attempt to get interpersonal needs met. Due to the rigidity of the interpersonal styles, partial satisfaction of emotional needs is met.

The three interpersonal styles that may emerge from persons assailed by trauma are moving toward, moving against, and moving away (Teyber & Teyber, 2017). Persons may attempt to get their emotional needs and manage their anxiety by appeasing others. In this way, they often overlook their stress by making others comfortable to avoid criticism and conflict. These clients are categorized as "moving towards" others to get close to others to fix their interpersonal problems. People that fall into this category are often thought of as the quintessential "people pleasers" that believe that the self is secondary to others. Victims of sexual trauma or emotional abuse may be susceptible to this interpersonal style (Collins & Collins, 2005) due to powerlessness and lack of safety. Though they achieve superficial relief by avoiding conflict, they do so at the expense of personal empowerment and agency.

Trauma can also be managed interpersonally by using aggression and force to ward off uncomfortable emotions. Some people who have experienced chronic trauma will protect against feelings of vulnerability by attempting to dominate others. Persons who employ this relating style believe they must obtain control by any means. Interpersonally, they may challenge others and engage in unbalanced power-wise relationships in their favor. Paradoxically they get power in their relationships but at the expense of developing emotional depth due to their inability to be emotionally open and vulnerable to others.

Lastly, others may cope with trauma interpersonally by employing a relational style defined by emotionally withdrawing from others. These are often individuals that display rigid self-reliance at all costs. Interpersonally they may limit their effect by intellectualizing their feelings and objectifying others. They often boast about how they can "cut people off" and be okay with being alone. Underneath their rigid self-reliance is usually an intense fear of rejection and hurt. Thus, their relationships are defined as transactional and lacking the affection needed to deepen their connection with others. The fear of being hurt emotionally often drives this interpersonal style. Loneliness, abandonment and a lack of appreciation characterize the developmental history of this style.

Psychosis and other forms of severe mental illness often have an interpersonal etiology. In their systematic review of analyzing the impact of interpersonal trauma on severe mental illness, Mauritz et al. (2013) found that psychosis was highly prevalent in women that experienced sexual trauma. Furthermore, their results showed that sexual abuse was prevalent in 44-64% of women with severe mental illness compared to 20-34% of men. This shows how interpersonal trauma can disrupt a person's intrapersonal functioning and ability to form a healthy identity. Relational experiences that consistently deprive a person of emotional stimulation and invalidate their sense of belonging can be detrimental to their psyche. To cope, individuals may retreat into an inner world to protect themselves from being emotionally hurt (Mearns & Cooper, 2018). Relationally, psychosis can be explained as an attempt to retain a semblance of self while engaging in a hostile world.

Thus far, we have explored the consequences of not being able to relate to others meaningfully and how trauma exacerbates disconnection from others. When applied to women, trauma has impacted the lives of all women at some point in their life. Specifically, sexual abuse and intimate partner violence have been traumatic experiences closely associated with trauma experienced by females. The Women's College Hospital based in Toronto, Canada, highlighted these facts about women and trauma: 14-20% of women will be raped at least once in their lifetime, 25-28% of women will experience intimate partner violence, someone will stalk 8-24% of women, and 25-35% of women will have experienced sexual abuse in their childhood ("What is interpersonal," n.d.). These numbers show that at least 1 in 4 women will experience some form of relational trauma throughout their lives.

Culturally, research has shown differences between racial/ethnic classes regarding their experience of trauma (Roberts, Gilman, Breslau, & Koenen, 2011). According to their data, Roberts et al. (2011) found that Post-traumatic stress disorder was highest amongst persons that identified as Black and lowest among persons that identified as Asian. Furthermore, they showed that Blacks and Hispanics were more likely to experience child abuse and other adverse childhood experiences. Lastly, their systematic literature review showed that compared to their white counterparts, persons identified as Black were less likely to seek treatment. This may be due to shame, guilt, embarrassment, or general mistrust of the mental health system. Black women experience high rates of stress related to interpersonal trauma compared to other groups, and the trauma experienced often originates during formative experiences. Poverty and economic and racial stress can lead to a dearth of nurturing therapeutic experiences with others that facilitate bonding, connection, and relatedness.

Process-Based Approaches and Relational Trauma

Several therapeutic approaches can aid African-American women in healing from relational trauma. Existential, Person-Centered, Relational Cultural Therapy and Interpersonal therapy all strongly emphasize the quality of the therapeutic relationship (Corey, 2017; Comstock et al., 2008). By focusing on the quality of the relationship, African-American women can experience a more reparative interpersonal interaction that serves as an exception to their previous harmful relationships. This dynamic is often a corrective emotional experience (Teyber & Teyber, 2017). The experience of being validated, understood, and empowered in a relationship can facilitate emotional safety while allowing African-American women to work through core emotional issues. The four therapeutic approaches will be discussed below to illustrate how they promote interpersonal healing in their unique way.

Relational Cultural Theory can assist African-American women in healing interpersonally by addressing how contextual factors impact their ability to connect with others (Comstock et al., 2008). The emphasis on the social context of relationships can help reconceptualize African Americans' relational challenges as rooted in oppression, intersectionality, and social injustice. By addressing these themes, a therapist can better understand African-American women holistically and the embeddedness of their trauma stemming from dysfunctional family systems, relationships, and systemic oppression. This approach could greatly benefit African-American women who have experienced direct racial trauma or acute marginalization stemming from being a female and a minority. Relational Cultural Theory advocates for the use of mutual empathy (Comstock et al., 2008). The narratives and diverse worldviews espoused by African American women can be invited and honored. This act in and of itself can be profoundly reparative and empowering.

Comprehensive and trans-theoretical in its approach to interpersonal therapy, both as a short-term intervention and framework, provides valuable resources to heal interpersonal trauma. Concepts such as the corrective emotional experience have been supported in the treatment planning process (Sperry & Sperry, 2020) as a time-limited treatment outcome. Interpersonal can aid African American women in gaining insight into their cyclical relationship patterns that stem from early maladaptive core beliefs or schemas. One issue that could be addressed within this approach is the strong Black woman. Within the framework of interpersonal theory, the "strong Black woman" identity could be analyzed within the family/cultural milieu to examine how it both helps and hinders relating to others. Building upon this insight, interpersonal therapy could address interpersonal deficits precipitated by relational trauma. Interpersonal therapists could assist African American women in developing greater flexibility in relationships by viewing problems as a case-by-case scenario and not an overgeneralization or continuation of past hurtful relationships.

Whereas interpersonal and relational-cultural therapy helps African-American women heal from the outside (focusing on the context of their relationships with others), person-centered and existential approaches can generate more in-depth intrapersonal healing in African-American women by focusing on subjective processes such as (congruence and meaning-making). Person-centered therapy can greatly assist African American women due to its non-directive and processes-oriented nature (Cory, 2017; Gehart, 2018). Interacting with a therapist and practitioner that communicates through words and actions an unconditional acceptance of the client is deeply rewarding. African-American women can experience feeling valued holistically and within their frame of reference. This can allow them to be emotionally freed to explore suppressed aspects of themselves within therapy.

Furthermore, they can develop greater trust in themselves and the ability to behave in ways congruent with their values and self-identity. Working with minorities within the African-American community, such as the LGBT or biracial communities that often face stigmatization and emotional abuse, person-centered therapists can help to fortify their sense of self and unique identity. This can increase their capacity to experience emotions and deepen their empathy for others.

Existential therapy can be applied to working with African-American women with viewed through the lenses of ACES (Adverse Childhood Experiences). Within an existential framework, the aim would be to assist women in recreating new meaning while expanding their capacity to engage with rather than avoid life. Relationally, existential therapy speaks to three forms of isolation that may present themselves in working with women African-American women—interpersonal, intrapersonal, and existential isolation (Yalom, 1980). Interpersonal isolation can be reflected by avoidance of others and socially withdrawing from interacting with people. Intrapersonal isolation is akin to dissociation in those victims of relational trauma who are cut off from experiencing their emotional selves (Yalom, 1980), and finally, existential isolation, whereby a person grapples with the loneliness of existence. As noted by (Zyromski et al., 2018), the application of presence, holding, caring, and challenging can be restorative in helping trauma victims regain their ability to feel emotionally safe and empowered within relationships. By strengthening the quality of the relationship between therapist and client and affirming the client's subjective experience, the therapist can restore disowned parts of their client's sense of self.

Fictional Case Illustration of Interpersonal Healing

A fictional case illustration will provide an example of how existential, interpersonal, person-centered, and relational cultural theory can help African American women heal interpersonally. The case illustrations will depict two fictional African-American women that have suffered relational trauma. Though these two cases do not fully capture the depth and complexity of relational trauma within the female African-American community, they represent a close approximation. The first case will reflect an African American female client presenting with depression stemming from sexual abuse. Reflect on a client suffering from years of domestic abuse and addiction. These two clients are born out of this writer's experience working with African American women in a community mental health center in a major city.

Sarah is a 29-year-old woman of African-American descent presenting in therapy for feelings of depression, loneliness, and anxiety. Sarah reports that she was raised in a middle-class family with her parents and two younger siblings. During her 7th grade year, Sarah was sexually assaulted by a male family friend, her godfather. Sarah attempted to tell her parents about the incident but was shunned and told not to tarnish the family name. Sarah has reported that since the incident, she has had difficulty trusting other and avoids physical and emotional intimacy altogether. Sarah reports that she wants to learn how to feel and become more emotionally connected to her feelings rather than suppress her emotions. Sarah expressed that she manages her fear of intimacy by avoiding sharing parts of herself with others and prematurely ending relationships once they become "too deep" or personal. Sarah maintains that her sexual abuse has rendered her unlovable and dirty. Sarah also blames her skin complexion as a reason for the abuse, citing that dark-skin Black girls are not valued as much as light-skinned girls.

In approaching working with Sarah, a therapist first could utilize tenets of relational cultural, and person-centered therapy to build a heightened sense of empathy. This could be accomplished by checking in and assessing her moment-to-moment experience of the therapeutic relationship. Deep honoring can be earned by attending to Sarah's experience in a non-judgmental manner. Culturally, exploring what it means to be a dark-skinned African-American female can allow Sarah to be understood within her frame of reference. This focus on existing and being with Sarah by deeply hearing her narrative helps her to reaffirm that her feelings and coping mechanisms are valid. Within establishing unconditional positive regard, the sharing and processing of emotions from both therapist and Sarah generate mutuality (Edelstein, 2015) in the relationship. When Sarah communicates and relives painful experiences from her past therapist provides an emotional container where her feelings are valued and engaged within the session. This communicates that whatever emotion is spontaneously expressed is not too intense for the therapist. This creates a safety net for emotional exploration.

Addressing external factors such as family dynamics and oppressive social systems can add valuable context to Sarah's behaviors. Sarah can start to view her challenges less as a personal deficit and more as an attempt to navigate hostile systems. This may negate the internalization of negative stereotypes of African American women as angry or masculine.

Sarah's avoidance of intimacy could be addressed by educating her on attachment theory and interpersonal coping styles. Sarah's presentation resembles that of an avoidant style. In working with Sarah, the therapist can recognize and maintain a deep commitment to Sarah despite her avoidance of trusting the therapist at times. Sarah's avoidance can be seen as an attempt to negotiate emotional safety and to see if the therapist unconditionally accepts her. This could move Sarah towards a corrective emotional experience.

Existentially, exploring how Sarah constructs the meaning of her experiences as a woman of color can reaffirm her sense of identity and well-being. In lieu of Sarah's sexual trauma, where she was not allowed to choose, the therapist's non-directive approach places the direction and control back toward her. Furthermore, utilizing tenets of Black Existentialism (Vereen et al., 2017), therapists could generate discourse on what it means to be irreducible. Here the therapist could explore the intersectionality of her multiple identities and how they interact to form a coherent whole in her life. Social-politically addressing racism, marginalization, and her ability to recreate meaning in her life should be emphasized to show an awareness of the harmful effects of microaggression and other forms of subtle racism. Lastly, the therapist could assist Sarah in clarifying what constitutes her authentic self both within and outside the Black community.

By attending to these various elements, Sarah could re-experience a more empathic, nurturing, and affirming relational experience. Sarah's ability to express her emotions and engage in emotional intimacy would be key markers to her ability to feel restored relationally. Sarah may also represent a more expansive and deepened knowledge regarding her identity as an African American woman.

Implications for Practice

The need for human connection has never been more critical than now. In the wake of a racial, medical, and political pandemic, Americans have become alienated and polarized. This deep polarization occurs on many levels and stymies our natural tendency towards human connection and relatedness. Research has consistently shown how infants engage in behaviors to elicit and sustain interactions with others (cite). Furthermore, studies on attachment theory show the indelible mark both positive and negative experiences with caregivers have on interpersonal and intrapersonal behavior (Teyber & Teyber, 2017). On the positive side, formative caregiver relationships can support common fear and anxiety in meeting one's emotional needs. It can also lead to self-efficacy in finding and maintaining relationships that facilitate reciprocal love and nurturance.

Implications for Practice

Though the scope of this chapter were African-American women healing from relational trauma, I acknowledge that women of color are constantly being harmed and dehumanized. Relational trauma assaults a person's sense of self and safety. According to (Williams, 2005), adequately working with African

Americans requires helpers to contextualize and validate the lived experiences of African American women in an oppressive society. This helps to shift the blame and burden from viewing the self as flawed to viewing the self as attempting to function in a harmful environment. The ability to nurture and sustain emotional contact with African-American women communicates a deep empathy and regard for their self-worth. It is essential to attend to the quality and process of the relationship via *tracking* (sharing awareness of client responses and bodily actions moment-moment) and to check in (asking questions regarding the subjective experience of the relationship between therapist and client) to ensure that mutuality is present.

On a deeper level, emotionally containing painful experiences through validating responses (I am beginning to understand better based on your history) and normalizing reactions take the need for defensiveness to persist. Lastly, it is essential to know that African-American women are irreducible. They encompass various roles, identities, and interests in society and within their families. Expanding their awareness of how they impact the world and the challenges they face; can empower them to see beyond their trauma and move toward their inherent strengths.

References

Annamma, S. A., Anyon, Y., & Joseph, M. N. (2016). *Black girls and school discipline: The Complexities of being overrepresented and understudied.* 54(2), 211-242. Retrieved from: https://doi.org/10.1177/0042085916646610.

Bremner, D. J. (2005). Effects of traumatic stress on brain structure and function: relevance to early responses to trauma. *Journal of Trauma & Dissociation*, (6)2, 51–68. Doi: 10.1300/J229V06N02_06.

Collins, B. G. & Collins, M. T. (2005). *Crisis and trauma developmental-ecological intervention* Brooks-Cole Publishing.

Collins, G. B. & Collins, M. T. (2005). *Crisis and trauma*. Belmont, CA: Brooks/Cole, Cengage Learning.

Comstock, D. L, Hammer, R. T., Strentzsch, J., Cannon, K., Parsons, J., & Salazar II, G. (2008). Relational-Cultural Theory: A framework for bridging relational, multicultural, and social justice competencies. *Journal of Counseling and Development* (86)1, pp. 279-287 retrieved from: https://doi.org/10/1002/j.1556-6678.2008.tb00510.x.

Corey, G. (2017). *Theory and practice of counseling and psychotherapy* (10th ed.) Cengage Learning.

Dailey, E. D., Humphreys, C. J., Rankin, H. S., & Lee, A. K. (2011). An exploration of lifetime trauma exposure in pregnant low-income African American women. *Maternal and Child Health Journal* (15) 410–418. Retrieved from https://doi.org/10.1007/s10995-008-0315-7.

Edelstein, B. (2015). Frames, attitudes, and skills of an existential-humanistic psychotherapist. In K. J. Schneider, J. F. Fraiser, & J. F. T. Bugental, *The handbook of humanistic psychology* (2nd ed. pp. 435-449). Sage Publishing.

Finfgeld-Connett, D. (2015). Intimate partner violence and its resolution among African American women. *Global qualitative nursing research*. Retrieved from: https://doi.org/10.1177/2333393614565182.

Gehart, D. (2016). *Theory and treatment planning in counseling and psychotherapy* (2nd ed). Cengage Learning.

Hargrove, S. (2018). *Intimate partner violence in the black community. The National Center On Violence Against Women in the Black Community*. Retrieved from: https://ujimacommunity.org/wp-content/uploads/2018/12/Intimate-Partner-Violence-IPV-v9.4.pdf.

Jacobs, M. S, (2017*). The violent state: black women's invisible struggle against police violence* In William and Mary Journal of Women and the Law: 2017 Special Issue: Enhancing Women's effect on Law Enforcement in the age of police and protest.

Jelicic, M & Merckelbach, H. (2004). Traumatic stress, brain changes, and memory deficits. A critical note. *Journal of Nervous and Mental Disease*, (192)8, 548-553 doi:10.1097/01.nmd.0000135494.20416.59.

Mauritz, M. W., Gossens, J. J. P., Draijjer. N., van Achterber, T (2013). Prevalence of interpersonal trauma exposure and trauma-related disorders in severe mental illness, *European Journal of Psycotramatology*, 4:1, DO1: 10.3402/ejpt.v4i0.19985.

Mearns, D & Cooper, M (2018). *Working at relational depth in counseling & psychotherapy* (2nd ed). Sage Publishing.

Meshberg-Cohen, S., Presseau, C. Thacker, L. R.., Hefner, K. & Syikis, D. (2016). Post-traumatic stress disorder, health problems, and depression among African American women in residential substance use treatment. *Journal of women's health*, 25(7), 729-737 retrieved from: https://doi.org/10.1089/wh.2015.5328.

Neff, K. & Germer, C. (2018). *The mindful self-compassion workbook: a proven way to accept yourself, build inner strength, and thrive*. New York, NY: Guilford Press.

Roberts, A., Gilman, S., Breslau, J., Breslau, N., & Koenen, K. (2011). Race/ethnic differences in exposure to traumatic events, development of post-traumatic stress disorder, and treatment-seeking for post-traumatic stress disorder in the United States. *Psychological Medicine*, 41(1), 71-83. Doi:10.1017/S0033291710000401.

Sperry, L., & Sperry, J. (2012). *Case conceptualization: mastering this competency with ease and confidence*. Rouledge/Taylor & Francis Group.

Teyber, E., & Teyber, F. H. (2017). *Interpersonal process in therapy: An integrative model (7th ed.)* Cengage Learning.

Tilman, S., Bryant-Davis, T., Smith, K., & Marks, A. (2010). Shattering silence: exploring barriers to disclosure for African American sexual assault survivors. *Trauma Violence Abuse* 11(2), 59–70. Doi: 10.1177/1524838010363717.

Vereen, L. G., Wines, A. L., Lemberger-Truelove, T., Hannon, M. D. & Burt, I. Black existentialism: extending the discourse on meaning and existence. *Journal of*

Humanistic Counseling (56) 1, pp. 72-84. Retrieved from: https://doi.org/10.1002/johc.12045.

Williams, C. B. (2011). Counseling African American women: multiple identities-multiple constraints. *Journal of Counseling & Development* (83)3, pp. 278–283. Retrieved from: https://doi.org/10.1002/j.1556-6678.2005.tb00343.x.

Yalom, I. (1980). *Existential psychotherapy*. Basic Books.

Yoder, C. (2005). *The little book of trauma healing*. Intercourse, PA: Good Books.

Zyromski, B., Dollarhide, C. T, Yahyahan, A., Geiger, S. Oehrtman, J. P., & Clarke, H. (2018) Beyond complex trauma: an existential view of adverse childhood experiences. *Journal of humanistic counseling* (57)3, pp. 156-171. DOI: 10.1002/JOHC.12080.

Part 5. Institutional and Systemic Trauma

Chapter 14

"I Want to Live!": Exploring the Inequities in the U.S. Healthcare System

Allison N. Hotz*, PhD
Robin Oatis-Ballew, PhD
and Esther Lynch, PhD
Tennessee State University, Nashville, Tennessee, USA

Abstract

Across the lifespan, Black women face consistent oppression due to their unique intersectionality. Institutionalized racism and its residual effects frequently result in outcomes that could have been prevented or routinely treated with appropriate medical care. The ramifications of this discrimination can negatively affect psychological and physical well-being.

This empirical research explored how institutionalized racism impacts the healthcare that early adulthood Black women access and receive. In early adulthood, Black women with medical conditions experience significant health disparities in reproductive, cancer, heart disease, and maternal health. Prior literature has given minor attention to capturing the voices of these Black women. This chapter will focus on Black women's perspective and experience with systemic racism in their medical treatment, with white providers, and interactions with the healthcare system. Specifically, notable themes that are a cause for concern will be discussed. These themes include systemic racism, discrimination, and invalidation - all of which negatively impacted psychological and physical well-being over an extended period.

* Corresponding Author's Email: ahotz2010@gmail.com.

In: How Did We Survive?
Editor: Tina Marie Glover
ISBN: 979-8-88697-918-3

Continuing to document the medical experiences of Black women could further the interdisciplinary movement toward creating strategic and realistic plans to acknowledge systemic flaws and resolve healthcare disparities. Black women in this study voiced probable solutions that could support well-being. Specifically, they shared their need and desire for advocacy in their medical care. If white providers worked towards allyship, this could be a foundational step towards closing the healthcare gap that plagues Black women and the Black community.

Keywords: African American Women, trauma, inequities, healthcare

Case Vignette

Gloria and Robert are an African American couple that has been married for 8 years and are child-free. They initially sought marital counseling for support following a miscarriage. It is evident that they have a lot of affection for one another, are mutually supportive, have fun together, and generally, get along well. Therapy proceeds smoothly; after several months, they are moving forward together in their grief and have learned new skills to improve their communication further. With regard to pregnancy and parenthood, they have decided that if it is meant to be, it will be. At the end of the counseling experience, they are reminded that they are welcome to return to counseling if they ever feel that it could be useful for them again.

Two years later, in the Spring of 2021, Robert and Gloria unexpectedly returned to counseling following a very upsetting OB-GYN appointment for Gloria. During the appointment, a white female doctor informed Gloria that she had Poly Cystic Ovarian Syndrome (PCOS), which can negatively affect fertility. This was confusing to Gloria as she did not believe that she had been assessed for that. When she questioned the physician, the doctor pushed back, stating that Gloria was assessed and informed of this during her previous appointment 1 year ago. However, due to the rapid emergence of COVID-19, Gloria canceled her annual appointment in the Spring of 2020. When Gloria stated this, she was informed that she was wrong. The doctor then left the room with the door open. After several minutes, Gloria realized that, apparently, the appointment was over. Gloria called Robert to tell him what had happened. However, she was crying so hard that Robert could not fully understand her. Then, the phone connection abruptly ended.

Introduction

This chapter will highlight how Black women can be adversely impacted by the healthcare system, as illustrated in the experience above. The chapter will also address how Black women, allies, and the medical and mental health communities can advocate for equitable treatment in medical care. The chapter will further integrate the case vignette, other healthcare experiences, and insights from African American women. They will be used to illustrate medical racism and identify potential ways to address health disparities using the concepts and solutions discussed throughout this chapter. The women whose stories and insights are shared in this chapter all had current or chronic medical diagnoses at the time of their interviews or therapy sessions.

Background

In April 2021, the Centers for Disease Control declared that racism is a serious threat to public health. It is a public health concern because many of the diseases and conditions that the population faces are preventable. Black women who seek treatment for their medical and psychological concerns are not consistently getting their immediate needs met (American Public Health Association, 2020). This is evidenced by the high volume of clients with chronic and untreated illness and stark premature mortality rates. Racism acts as a barrier to health equity and equality (American Public Health Association, 2020). The experience of trauma that is also related to medical racism has public health implications as well.

To understand Black women's experiences in the healthcare system, it is important to provide some brief historical as well as current context. Throughout United States history, medical racism has had an adverse impact on African Americans and led to health disparities. Historically, medical racism dates to slavery where the racial divide determined quality of care (Rowe, 2015). It also led to inhumane medical interventions and bias in medicine. For instance, J Marion Sims, who some consider as the 'Father of Gynecology,' famously conducted unethical experiments on enslaved Black women (Cooper-Owens, 2018). Further examples of medical bias are the persistent assumptions that minorities are either easily susceptible to or immune to diseases.

The healthcare disparities that Black women experience are associated with severe health consequences in an array of areas. These range from reproductive and cardiovascular issues to diabetes, cancer, and untreated psychological concerns. There is also current evidence that Black women and children are particularly impacted by inequities in the healthcare system and face disproportionate Black maternal mortality rates (Howell, 2018). Furthermore, racial and ethnic minorities from lower incomes are more likely to be diagnosed with or at risk of developing serious and chronic illnesses such as diabetes and hypertension, and face premature mortality (Goleman, 2019).

Healthcare disparity: Differences in the incidence, prevalence, mortality and burden of diseases and other adverse health conditions that exist among specific populations in the United States (NIH, 2011) Differences in health outcomes that are closely linked with social, economic and environmental disadvantage (Office of Minority Health, 2011).

When considering healthcare disparities for Black women, prior research has identified pervasive and detrimental outcomes (Baciu et al., 2017). Black women and the symptoms they experience are less likely to be taken into consideration when under examination or while receiving medical treatment. This is often due to common societal stereotypes associated with Black women like the *Strong Black Woman* (SBW) and the notion that Black women have a higher pain threshold than other groups (McClurg et al., 2020; VanNoy et al., 2020). Also, Black women are susceptible to an influx of psychological concerns related to residual trauma, untreated depression and anxiety, race-related stress, and racism (Lewis et al., 2017; Haynes 2017). Furthermore, microaggressions are known to be a factor that decreases interest in seeking healthcare treatment (Lewis et al., 2017). Essentially, systemic oppression increases physical distress and negatively impacts Black women's wellbeing.

To highlight the severity of medical racism and add to the existing literature, a qualitative study was conducted to investigate lived experiences in the patient-to-doctor interaction (Hotz, 2021). The research question guiding this exploration was: What are Black women's experiences with systemic racism in the healthcare system? The study recruited Cisgender Black women diagnosed with a physical health condition being treated by white medical providers. Each participant was asked eight interview questions from an original protocol. Here are a few examples from the protocol:

- Tell me, what have been your experiences with racism in the healthcare system as a patient, if any?
- What have been your experiences with your medical provider(s)?
- How do you mentally and physically feel before and after a visit with your medical provider?
- How has the "patient to doctor" relationship been for you?
- Describe an experience from your medical treatment that continues to stick with you or that you can't forget?
- What are the symptoms that you experience?
- Tell me, how do you think stereotypes entered into the healthcare system?
- How does our society inform how you interact with the healthcare system?

Several themes emerged from the analysis of the responses to the protocol. The themes are related to systemic racism, implicit bias, and invalidation and invisibility.

Systemic racism, which is also known as institutional racism, is defined as a form of racism that is immersed in a culture or organization via regulations and laws. It is under a system that embraces racist ideation where discrimination is more likely to occur to people because of their ethnic origin, culture, or skin color. Unlike individual racism, which is usually identifiable and overt in nature, systemic racism is subtle, covert, and not as noticeable. For example, a doctor stating they will only see white patients is an example of overt racism. On the other hand, a doctor telling a Black Woman that she is exaggerating her symptoms, should just go home, and rest is an example of covert racism. Covert racism leaves the individual feeling confused with mixed emotions about what just happened because there is no clear indication, they just experienced discrimination. Yet, they experience all of the emotions that come with being discriminated against.

Covert Racism: a socially accepted form of racial discrimination that is indirect, subtle, and disguised.

Overt Racism: a generally socially unaccepted form of racial discrimination that is obvious, direct, and perceivable.

As illustrated in the case vignette, Gloria's treatment was subpar compared to what the average person would expect. It does appear as if her provider did not take the time to confirm an accurate diagnosis or that she even had the correct chart. This clearly reflects concepts related to systemic racism and invalidation which will be discussed in the following paragraphs.

What's Going on in the Healthcare System

Systemic racism is a convoluted webbed-like structure that is challenging to dismantle because of its entanglement in healthcare, criminal, and educational systems. Specifically, racism's presence in the healthcare system leads to the transmission of implicit bias and prejudice against marginalized communities in the provision of managed care. Systemic racism leads to worsening healthcare disparities such as lack of access to providers, poor quality of care, neglect, unattended symptoms leading to chronic illness and premature mortality. Additionally, systemic racism in the healthcare system trickles down to graduate medical education and other professional healthcare training programs. This cycle continues the transmission of implicit bias. As a result, Black women are finding their own way of navigating the health system.

One of these ways is by ensuring they are seeing a Black doctor when possible. Black patients reported a decrease in discrimination, microaggressions, and even anxiety when seeing Black doctors as opposed to doctors of a difference race (Whaley, 2001). For Black pregnant women, some existing barriers are avoided or reduced by seeing Black Gynecologists and Black doulas. Research has confirmed a significantly higher survival rate for Black babies treated by Black doctors (Greenwood, Hardeman, Huang, & Sojourner, 2020). Below are some disclosures from Hotz's study (2021) pertaining to Black women's experiences with systemic racism in their medical care. The next part of this chapter will continue the discussion of Black women's experiences with discrimination in their medical care and the healthcare system.

> I wouldn't say like blatantly racism. I feel like I haven't necessarily experienced that. It's hard to tell sometimes to be honest. Definitely, more covert.
>
> As a Black woman, you can just really tell the difference in care. It's apparent. They see only a diagnosis. Racism in the healthcare system, in my personal experience, is being able to tell the difference in care that's

> provided. I recently had a miscarriage; about seven months ago. And it's just sad to say, because when you're in the hospital, white nurses and doctors will just let you die. Seriously, they will let you die. I felt close to death when I was in the ER. white healthcare providers do not treat you as they would treat their own if they were in your position with the same symptoms.
>
> The incision from my C-section infection didn't close until I was like four months postpartum probably, like early April. It was the worst pain that I've ever felt in my life. After the C-Section, my incision got infected. And before I knew it was infected I was telling the nurse practitioner, because my doctor was on vacation, that something was wrong then because I was in so much pain. They kept telling me like, "Oh, your pain should be better now." Um, like, you shouldn't be in any pain. "There's nothing wrong with your incision", and then she said like, "You can't get any more pain medication because there's nothing wrong with your incision." Implying that I was just there for pain meds (laughs). I was like, I do not want pain medication. I want you all to figure out what's wrong because I know something's wrong.

Implicit Bias

Within the healthcare system, discrimination of patients is often the result of healthcare professionals acting on the implicit biases they may have. Within the context of the healthcare system, *implicit bias* is defined as unconscious attitudes or stereotypes towards a person because of their gender, ethnicity, nationality, social status, race, and other differences. While it is undeniable that everyone, including healthcare professionals, has implicit bias; there is a justifiable cause for alarm when a provider with implicit biases decides on treatment choices that can be life changing. Research has found that health care providers specifically have negative attitudes towards people of color and positive attitudes towards whites (Hall et. al, 2015). Some providers demonstrate this bias deliberately while others do so inadvertently; both through verbal and non-verbal communication. A medical provider with high implicit bias is more likely to shorten the visit time and inquiry of the presenting concern with a Black patient (Penner et al., 2010). Additionally, conversations between medical providers with high implicit bias and Black patients are driven by the provider, leaving little time for patients to express their concerns. In the perspective of some white providers, they reported that their awareness of the distrust in the African American community towards them influences their need to talk more to appear competent (Hagiwara et al., 2013).

Discrimination is defined as the unjust or prejudicial treatment of people based on their race, age, or sex.

On the other hand, Black patients pick up on these biases and respond negatively, whether the provider was acting on the bias intentionally. All of these factors can affect whether a patient receives the correct diagnosis and treatment. Thus, it is crucial that biases are reduced and effectively managed or the effects will continue to have detrimental consequences on the doctor-patient relationship and, in turn, the health of Black women.

The Patient-Healthcare Professional Interaction

The manifestation of these race related attitudes by both the Black patient and white provider results in the perception that non-Black providers are not patient-centered or culturally competent (Penner, et al, 2016). For patients, the experience of these biases often results in feeling confused and anxious which leads to more difficulty recalling their providers recommendations, a lack of confidence in the provided treatment plans, and the belief that the provided treatment plans are not attainable (Penner et. al, 2016). In the end, it appears that what occurs within the appointments is a result of the interaction of the biases both the provider and patient carry. Unfortunately, it is these experiences that further complicate the patient-health professional relationship and it is these interactions that negatively affect the events that follow.

Invalidation and Invisibility

Invalidation and invisibility are other common experiences that Black women shared related to medical racism and implicit bias. The next part of this chapter will discuss Black women's experiences with these dynamics in their medical care and the healthcare system. Below are some disclosures about Black women's experiences with implicit bias and the resultant invalidation and discrimination in their medical care.

Invalidation is defined as a negative social interaction when a person's shared emotions and affective experiences are perceived as incorrect, invalid, or inappropriate (Zielinski, & Veilleux, 2018).

> But if this white girl my same age woulda' came in to the doctor's office with the same problems and symptoms I have, they would've prevented it or found a way to help her and stop her symptoms and pain! I feel like since I'm on like lower-income insurance, I just feel like they kinda match the quality of care with physicians to that.

> I had a lot of issues when I was pregnant, and they were constantly dismissed. I had a really bad UTI, and it was probably a week before I figured out what it was after going to the ER. I was roughly 20 weeks, and I had like this crazy pain in my side, and they kept telling me like, "It's just normal." "It's round ligament pain, like normal pregnancy pains". I kept telling them 'something is wrong' and they wouldn't let me talk to my doctor. Like they had this protocol where you had to call and talk to the OB nurses before you could speak to your doctor. The severity of my UTI could've been prevented if they would have taken action when I first told them I was having a problem.

As highlighted here, invalidation is one of the themes that emerged from the research interviews supporting this chapter. The women interviewed shared moments of disconnection and invisibility as well. One stated *"I feel like they don't hear me whenever I go into these appointments. No matter who I talk to."* This disconnection in the patient - doctor relationship could be improved with accessing allyship in the medical treatment that Black women receive. The Black women interviewed disclosed personal experiences with the invalidation of symptoms and distress when interacting with their medical providers. Stereotyping, microaggressions, and gaslighting occurred in their medical care, which led to the worsening of physical and psychological symptoms. For these Black women, invalidation represented invisibility and silence.

Invisibility was a shared feeling among Black women in their medical care appointments. The depreciation of fears and symptoms, feeling ignored, unnecessary use of medical jargon, and outright dismissal led to Black women feeling invisible and unheard. When gaslighted, Black women took on the responsibility and placed blame on themselves for their diagnoses and symptoms. The root cause of invalidation and the resultant invisibility was implicit bias, colorblindness, and an apparent disconnection in the patient-to-doctor relationship.

Invalidation led to an increased risk of emotional dysregulation for these Black women. When medical providers and their healthcare teams ignore socio determinants of health, minimize pain, and use stereotypes, this harms Black women. When faced with these interventions, Black women will adopt stereotypes such as the *Strong Black Woman* and believe that they carry a high pain tolerance. Often, Black women unknowingly lean into these beliefs and utilize them as protective strategies from future threats and harm. Lack of allyship in Black women's medical care is noticeable because of the disjunction in the patient to doctor relationship. Providers must work on their implicit biases and consult with culturally informed mentors who can support their transition to allyship in order to effectively meet Black women's healthcare needs. Below are some disclosures about Black women's experiences with invalidation in their medical care. Following the disclosures, the next part of this chapter will discuss potential solutions to reduce healthcare disparities that can holistically support Black women's health.

> Well, it's kind of like, you have to act a certain way. You have to act like you know exactly what's going on, or they will talk to you any type of way, and they will talk to you stupid.

> And so they're telling me the facts, and I'm sitting there thinking they're telling me from a broad perspective, like it's common, this happens. Oh, it's like treating my carpal tunnel like it's morning sickness. Some doctors can look at you like you're just a number. Like you're not a person. I've had experiences when calling the nurses on the phone. Like, 'hey, this is what I'm feeling. Um, what do y'all think we should do?' And they're like, "Oh, you're fine. Oh, that's normal."
>
> They'll analyze you and your symptoms but if they don't feel like it's important enough, they won't say or do anything until it's the last minute, until you come back in months later and they actually see the problem or when it's an emergency....maybe. I mean you'll wait in the room for hours. And then, the doctor will come into the room and it's like they don't give you any hope. It's depressing to be ignored consistently.

The case of Gloria clearly highlights invalidation and invisibility. The next case segment further illustrates this.

> After the miscarriage at 36, Gloria and Robert were very open to conceiving again. Gloria was also aware that she was considered advanced maternal age. While the couple decided not to pursue medical intervention to

> promote fertility, they did decide to maintain optimal health to improve their chances and preparation to care for an infant and keep up with a toddler. At age 38, when Gloria was told that she had PCOS for a year, unbeknownst to her, she felt as if her limited opportunity of naturally conceiving had been stolen and her chances of potentially conceiving were diminished even further. In session, Gloria reported that this experience was devastating, and Robert shared that he felt powerless to help his wife. When the phone disconnected, he could not reach his wife for several hours. He called family and friends to ask if they had heard from her and recounted what he knew about the appointment.

Gloria felt dismissed when the provider left the room without closing out the appointment or the door. She also felt invisible as the physician shut down her questions and was nonchalant about the diagnosis while asserting that Gloria had been informed of it when she had not. Additionally, for this couple, the consequences of invalidation were considerable and traumatic.

Potential Solutions to Reduce Healthcare Disparities and Support Black Women

Although some African Americans hold distrust of the healthcare system, many ask for strategies to reduce healthcare disparities, improve care provision, and increase their comfort with medical providers. This section will discuss the necessity of increasing provider allyship and advocacy in the medical care experiences of Black women.

Increasing Allyship in the Healthcare System

African American women in Hotz's study (2021) shared a common concern related to their experiences in the U.S. Healthcare system. This concern was the absence of allyship in the patient to doctor relationship with their medical providers and healthcare teams. According to Acheson (2018), an **ally** stands up against the exclusion and discrimination of marginalized identities and actively works towards increasing inclusion through positive and conscious intervention. An ally for Black women in the U.S. healthcare system would be someone who provides and maintains a safe space, is empathic, recognizes the existence of stereotypes, and promotes holistic healthcare intervention and education.

- Advocate for others
- Allocate opportunities for growth
- Call out systemic inequalities and microaggressions
- Validate marginalized groups
- experiences
- Be respectful, listen, provide support, and change

Action is what creates *allyship.* Specifically, allyship is a fluid process that requires trust, accountability, and consistent positive actions that support marginalized groups (Acheson, 2018). According to Acheson (2018) there are necessary steps one must engage in to become vetted as an ally (see inset). Participants in Hotz's (2021) qualitative study pleaded for a support person on their treatment team. The necessity of community allyship is essential in the fight to dismantle systemic racism. To effectively create change and lean into allyship, healthcare providers need to work on implicit biases and the promotion of accountability.

An example of allyship for Black women in their medical treatment is a physician who notices a nurse using microaggressions when interacting with a Black woman patient. The physician could immediately intervene and support the patient by validating, listening, and collaboratively problem-solving to reduce their distress. After leaving the room, the physician could ask to speak with the nurse about the interaction they observed. Then, the physician could research resources to share with the care team so that Black women feel supported in their practice.

An absence of allyship means that Black women are left vulnerable and subject to invalidation and dismissal in their medical care. Active allyship from healthcare providers would help Black women feel more comfortable and inclined towards professional help-seeking. The physical and psychological consequences of a lack of allyship in Black women's healthcare include unattended symptoms leading to chronic illness (i.e., Chron's disease, infertility, pregnancy complications), depression, anxiety, emotional dysregulation, hypertension, increased stress, and emotional guardedness.

Increasing the Self-Advocacy of Black Women

Hotz's (2021) study also highlighted the significance of self-advocacy as a way of addressing medical racism. The participants demonstrated strength and self-reliance when they continued to seek medical treatment from providers who committed microaggressions and unintentionally created a space of adversity and awkwardness. This perseverance speaks to Black women's desires towards enhancing wellness, longevity, and increasing survival odds. Below is an example of the necessity of self-advocacy for Black women in their medical care.

> But I feel like because I'm a Black woman, I've had to advocate for myself more than I think somebody else would. A couple of times I had a thought like, 'It's crazy.' It's crazy that you got to advocate for yourself. But, I don't know that I wouldn't advocate for myself if I was a white female? I ask my OB's like, 'what are you doing to make sure that this doesn't don't happen to me?'

Persistence is a primary factor in self-advocating and directly intervening with providers and staff. Black women are often required to advocate for themselves. To do this, Hotz (2021) found that many Black women conduct a self-assessment of their physical and psychological symptoms, concerns, and distress. In psychotherapy, it is crucial to process the cost and the associated societal and cultural pressures of strength such as seeing oneself or being perceived as 'super-human' or 'infinitely strong'. When Black women fulfill these stereotypes, such as the image of the *Strong Black Woman*, it is often done to serve as a method of persistence and protection (Ferdinand, 2016). However, in doing so, they may also be inadvertently putting their health last. In Hotz's (2021) study, some negative consequences of self-advocacy were mental and physical exhaustion, feeling drained, burdened, chronic physical symptoms, anxiety, rumination, sadness, loneliness, and isolation. The following section will address the benefits of supporting Black women clientele in psychotherapy and will identify therapeutic strategies to enhance self-advocacy while minimizing the negative consequences. Black Feminist Therapy will be discussed as a way of supporting these efforts.

Decreasing Implicit Bias in Health Care Professionals

For health care providers, one environment that is deemed as influential is their educational experience and training. One study that focused on medical student training reported that students who were trained by a doctor with high implicit bias were more likely to adopt the same biases and attitudes as their supervising doctor (Boscardin, 2015). This means future doctors could be acting on biases learned during their medical training. Providing training that will reduce implicit bias in those who play a role in educating the health professionals of our future is imperative. By ensuring our educators are not passing on their biases to future health professionals, we would be reducing the experiences of invalidation, discrimination, and medical racism that Black women often fall victim to.

Black Feminist Therapy

Utilizing strategies from Black Feminist Therapy and the Balance, Reflection, Energy, Association, Transparency, Healing, and Empowerment (BREATHE) Model can also increase the overall wellness of Black women because of its non-patriarchal concepts and culturally appropriate framework (Evans, Bell, & Burton, 2017). A foundational strategy drawn from Black Feminism would be teaching the "three core themes." These include exposing multiple oppression (i.e., personally, at home, in career), developing positive self-talk and ignoring traditional stereotypes, and battling oppression to increase empowerment (Collins, 2015).

Black Feminist Therapy positively enhances psychological wellbeing because it teases apart the oppression and societal pressures that Black women experience. Essentially, the theory exposes systems of oppression and hones in on the group's ability to thrive among societal barriers by teaching skills to reduce psychological distress, increase self-actualization, and empowerment (Guy-Sheftall, & Guy-Sheftall, 2011). African American women in the healthcare system need skills to self-soothe after dealing with oppression in their medical care. In Hotz's (2021) study, participants were left to singularly process their negative experiences and had little opportunity to reflect due to their schedules. Black women are left susceptible to increased emotional dysregulation due to their social vulnerability and the many societal "isms" that serve to harm (Coleman et al., 2006).

In psychotherapy, clinicians can work with Black women on implementing Black Feminist strategies into their lives. These include processing negative messages about gender role expectations and behaviors, teaching assertiveness techniques and active coping skills, discussing socio-political forces and their mental health consequences, and supporting action against oppression (Greene, 1994; Evans, Bell, & Burton, 2017). When facing healthcare disparities, Black women often assume blame for their conditions and symptoms (Robinson & Keith, 2003). This can lead to distorted thinking, emotional dysregulation, an increase in cultural mistrust, adoption of stereotypes (i.e., *Strong Black Woman*), and avoidance of help-seeking (Hotz, 2021). These Black Feminism strategies support the deconstruction of heteronormative, patriarchal, and societal expectations and stereotypes of Black women. Using these strategies in their medical care can promote a desire for Black women to self-advocate which may ultimately improve overall health and longevity.

Redefining the self is the most crucial component of Black Feminism therapy and is ultimately the central goal (Evans, Bell, & Burton, 2017). It is appropriate to help Black women interacting with the healthcare system to examine psychosocial, societal, ad contextual factors during their period of rediscovery. This examination assists with externalizing the stressors instead of internalizing the problem (Williams, 2000). According to Woods-Giscombe (2010), the *Strong Black Woman* schema is the most consistent stereotype that Black women utilize to combat stress because of its ability to support caretaking, independence, and affect regulation. However, this schema can negatively impact health, as evidenced in the previous literature and Hotz's (2021) study. Teaching Black women mind-body interventions that redefine the importance of cultivating an inner strength supported by holistic wellness, wholeness, and authenticity is critical (Woods-Giscombe, 2010; Evans, Bell, & Burton, 2017).

Supporting Black women in psychotherapy by teaching adaptive strategies can help to reduce the heaviness of race-related and personal stressors. According to Donovan & West (2015), African Americans are more likely to internalize stress, leading to chronic illness. Black women are the most impacted by chronic health issues like cardiovascular disease, hypertension, and obesity and utilize poor coping strategies (i.e., alcohol or substance abuse, emotional guardedness, isolation) (Lewis & Van Dyke, 2018).

Spirituality Spiritual Strategies Social Support Physical Strategies Support Groups Therapy

Adaptive strategies support Black women in their interactions with medical providers because of their ability to target emotional dysregulation and controllability. Here are the recommended adaptive strategies that therapists should encourage Black women to lean into to support their holistic wellbeing (Evans, Bell, & Burton, 2017):

Spirituality and prayer are some of the main adaptive strategies that support Black women and protect them from suicidal ideation and attempts, while improving coping and managing psychological illness and physical health symptoms (Waite & Killian, 2008; Reed & Neville, 2014). When Black women lean into consistent prayer, they can release their worries and place anguish and burdens onto an external power. Black women in Hotz's (2021) study spoke about utilizing prayer and their religious beliefs as methods of coping with challenging news from their providers and living in continued distress. A participant shared the following:

> All I can really do is pray about it or at least think that things will get better one day. My family encourages me to be more involved with scripture. I don't know. I'm not religious but would say my spirituality helps when others let me down.

Spirituality provides an undeniable sense of comfort for Black women. According to Woods-Giscombe et al., (2016), Black women can derive meaning and key into their purpose through spiritual beliefs, prayer, meditation, and additional coping methods. Meditation is a popular self-care intervention that accesses both physical and spiritual activities. Therapists can gauge Black women's interest in utilizing spirituality as a protective coping method. Additionally, clinicians can encourage leaning into routine spiritual activities such as meditation and yoga, which could help improve relaxation, enhance self-care, and build personal and physical growth and strength. Spirituality practices are the foundation for Black women to build their adaptive strategies toolkit. Yoga, walking, and other low-impact exercises decrease cardiovascular issues, stress, mental health concerns, and other health conditions (Bland & Sharma, 2017). Black women could also connect with a family member, friend, or neighbor to walk and access support (Evans, Bell, & Burton, 2017).

Social support is the next adaptive strategy that can support Black women when interacting with the healthcare system and their medical providers. Accessing social support has been an essential factor for Black women because it provides both internal and external protection from harm and race-related stress, and provides a space to process traumas (Evans, Bell, & Burton, 2017). Social support reduces mortality and morbidity rates (Chatters et al., 2014). In Hotz's study, Black women would process their experiences with racism and discrimination and the resultant emotional fatigue with personal support systems like family, partners, friends, and the Black community. This utilization of culturally based coping supports the existing literature on African Americans needing close-knit support to combat racism and protect their physical and psychological wellbeing (Davis, 2019; Howard et al., 2020).

Support groups are another adaptive coping strategy that therapists should encourage Black women to utilize. Support groups could help Black women process their experiences in the U.S. Healthcare system, race-related stress, and other stressors. Accessing a shared community for Black women is vital because it is affirming and reduces the perpetuation of silencing (Evans, Bell, & Burton, 2017). Some hospitals, community centers, and clinics might run no-cost groups and online searches could help access specific groups or "meet-ups" with other Black women dealing with chronic illness.

Practicing from an Integrative therapeutic approach and teaching these adaptive strategies provides culturally appropriate interventions, which supports the holistic wellbeing of Black women. When therapists draw from Feminist and Multicultural frameworks, this moves towards dismantling systemic racism, and redefining patriarchal role expectations, and personalizing identity, strength, and coping mechanisms. These interventions build up and support Black women by teaching them to pour into the self, utilize engagement coping strategies positively, improves attitudes, and increase the motivation for self-advocacy in their medical care. Below is a Black woman's opinion on the importance of self-advocacy in medical treatment.

> I think when people are aware of how you feel, they definitely take that into consideration when they're trying to give you the best care. If something still ain't sitting right, you know, say the doctor said something, we're not blindly trusting them, if it don't feel right to us. I definitely think that we

should be informed and we should have our own information and do our own research, so we can ask better questions in those appointments. It puts the burden on us, but at the end of the day, you gotta take care of yourself. If we already got to be these advocates, and you got to go in and you got to go hard;, and you got to make sure the doctors and staff are doing right. Black women who advocate for themselves with white providers can say like, 'I know this is uncomfortable, but hey, these are the staggering statistics.'

Conclusion

Gloria sought out a 2nd opinion and met with a Reproductive Endocrinologist (REI). She could not find an African American provider. However, she did ask around and found someone she believed would be culturally competent and aware. The REI did thorough testing for PCOS, validated Gloria's concerns about the previous appointment, and affirmed her interest and right in seeking a 2nd opinion and advocating for herself. Gloria and Robert felt good about reconnecting with their therapist for emotional support and are glad they advocated for Gloria and sought a 2nd opinion with a culturally aware and competent REI. The couple has decided to pursue some options to enhance their probability of conceiving for the next 12 months. Gloria is not interested in conceiving in her 40s and Robert agrees. Additionally, the couple is spiritual and religious and have also decided that if Gloria has not conceived by age 40, they are meant to pursue a child-free and meaningful life. They feel good about where they are in life and plan to continue to enjoy it with family and friends. While they hope not to have any additional negative medical experiences, they also feel prepared to seek allyship and advocate for themselves as needed.

In the U.S. Healthcare system, Black women continue to face systemic racism, implicit bias, and invalidation. These issues seep into professional school curricula leading to false beliefs that translate into direct patient care. In their treatment experiences, Black women call for professional allyship with their healthcare providers to help them increase longevity, survival odds, and improve holistic wellness. Black women are explicitly asking to be seen and heard in the U.S. Healthcare system. The strategies mentioned in this chapter call on U.S. society, the medical community, and mental health professionals to increase their allyship by leaning into active efforts that promote the dismantling of systemic racism to protect the wellbeing of Black women. Additionally, when clinicians adhere to these strategies, this provides a safe and non-judgmental space for Black women in psychotherapy.

References

American Public Health Association. (2020). *Racism and health.* https://www.apha.org/topics-and-issues/health-equity/racism-and-health.

Atcheson, S. (2018). *Allyship - The Key To Unlocking The Power Of Diversity*. Forbes. https://www.forbes.com/sites/shereeatcheson/2018/11/30/allyship-the-key-to-unlocking-the-power-of-diversity/?sh=4caebc7849c6.

Bland, V., & Sharma, M. (2017). Physical activity interventions in African American women: A systematic review. *Health promotion perspectives*, *7*(2), 52–59. https://doi.org/10.15171/hpp.2017.11.

Boscardin, C. K. (2015). Reducing implicit bias through curricular interventions. *Journal of Internal Medicine.* 30, 1726-1728. https://doi.org/10.1007/s11606-015-3496-y.

Chatters, L. M., Nguyen, A. W., Taylor, R. J., & Hope, M. O. (2018). Church and family support networks and depressive symptoms among African Americans: Findings from The National Survey of American Life. *Journal of Community Psychology*, *46*(4), 403–417. https://doi.org/10.1002/jcop.21947.

Coleman, M., Cannon, K., Razak, A., Monroe, I., Majeed, D., Skye, L., Stephanie Y. Mitchem, West, T. (2006). Roundtable Discussion: Must I Be Womanist? *Journal of Feminist Studies in Religion*, 22(1), 85-134.

Collins, H. P. (2015). *Black feminist thought*. Routledge.

Cooper-Owens, D. (2018). *Medical bondage: Race, gender, and the origins of American gynecology*. University of Georgia Press.

Davis, S. M. (2019). When sistahs support sistahs: A process of supportive communication about racial microaggressions among Black women. *Communication Monographs*, *86*(2), 133–157.

Donovan, R. A., & West, L. M. (2015). Stress and mental health: Moderating role of the strong Black woman stereotype. *Journal of Black Psychology*, *41*(4), 384–396.

Evans, S. Y., Bell, K., & Burton, N. K. (2017). *Black women's mental health. Balancing strength and vulnerability*.

Ferdinand, R. (2016). I am not your mammy: The penalty for failing to be a stereotype. *Journal of Mother Studies*, *1*.

Giurgescu, C., Zenk, S. N., Templin, T. N., Engeland, C. G., Kavanaugh, K., & Misra, D. P. (2017). The impact of neighborhood conditions and psychological distress on preterm birth in African-American women. *Public Health Nursing*, *34*(3), 256–266.

Greene, B. (1994). African American women. In L. Comas-Diaz & B. Greene (Eds.), *Women of color: Integrating ethnic and gender identities in psychotherapy* (pp. 10-29).

Greenwood, B. N., Hardeman, R. R., Huang, L., & Sojourner, A. (2020). Physician–patient racial concordance and disparities in birthing mortality for newborns. *Proceedings of the National Academy of Sciences*, *117*(35), 21194-21200.

Guy-Sheftall, B., & Guy-Sheftall, B. (2011). *Words of Fire An Anthology of African-American Feminist Thought*. New Press.

Hagiwara, N., Dovidio, J. F., Stone, J., & Penner, L. A. (2020). Applied racial/ethnic healthcare disparities research using implicit measures. *Social cognition*, *38*(Supplement), s68-s97.

Hall, W. J., Chapman, M. V., Lee, K. M., Merino, Y. M., Thomas, T. W., Payne, B. K., Eng, E., Day, S. H., & Coyne-Beasley, T. (2015). Implicit Racial/Ethnic Bias Among Health Care Professionals and Its Influence on Health Care Outcomes: A Systematic Review. *American journal of public health*, *105*(12), e60–e76. https://doi.org/10.2105/AJPH.2015.302903.

Hotz, A. (2021). *A Phenomenological Investigation of African American Women's Views on the United States of America's Healthcare System* (Unpublished doctoral dissertation). Tennessee State University.

Howard, S., Sultana, S., & Snell, C. L. (2020). Social isolation among young Black women: Implications for social work. *Social Work Education*, 1–14.

Howell, E. A. (2018). Reducing disparities in severe maternal morbidity and mortality. *Clinical Obstetrics and Gynecology*, *61*(2), 387.

Jones, L. V., & Guy-Sheftall, B. (2017). *Black feminist therapy as a wellness tool.* In S. Y. Evans, K. Bell, & N. K. Burton (Eds.), *Black women's mental health: Balancing strength and vulnerability* (p. 201–213). State University of New York Press.

Lewis, J. A., Williams, M. G., Peppers, E. J., & Gadson, C. A. (2017). Applying intersectionality to explore the relations between gendered racism and health among Black women. *Journal of Counseling Psychology*, *64*(5), 475.

Lewis, T. T., & Van Dyke, M. E. (2018). Discrimination and the health of African Americans: The potential importance of intersectionalities. *Current Directions in Psychological Science*, *27*(3), 176–182.

Penner, L. A., Dovidio, J. F., West, T. V., Gaertner, S. L., Albrecht, T. L., Dailey, R. K., & Markova, T. (2010). Aversive racism and medical interactions with Black patients: A field study. *Journal of experimental social psychology*, *46*(2), 436-440.

Penner, L. A., Dovidio, J. F., Gonzalez, R., Albrecht, T. L., Chapman, R., Foster, T., ... & Eggly, S. (2016). The effects of oncologist implicit racial bias in racially discordant oncology interactions. *Journal of clinical oncology*, *34*(24), 2874.

Penner, L. A., Harper, F., Dovidio, J. F., Albrecht, T. L., Hamel, L. M., Senft, N., & Eggly, S. (2017). The impact of Black cancer patients' race-related beliefs and attitudes on racially-discordant oncology interactions: A field study. *Social science & medicine (1982)*, *191*, 99–108. https://doi.org/10.1016/j.socscimed.2017.08.034.

Ray, K. (2019). The power of black patients' testimonies when teaching medical racism. *Teaching Health Humanities*, 129.

Reed, T. D., & Neville, H. A. (2014). The Influence of Religiosity and Spirituality on Psychological Well-Being Among Black Women. *Journal of Black Psychology*, *40*(4), 384–401. https://doi.org/10.1177/0095798413490956.

Roberts, A., Jackson, M. S., & Carlton-Laney, I. (2000). Revisiting the need for feminism and Afrocentric theory when treating African American female substance abusers. *Journal of Drug Issues, 30,* 901–918.

Robinson-Brown, D., & Keith, V. (2003). *In and out of our right minds the mental health of African American women*. Columbia University Press.

Street Jr., R. L., Makoul, G., Arora, N. K. & Epstein, R. M. (2009). How does communication heal? Pathways linking clinician-patient communication to health outcomes. *Patient Education and Counseling*, 74(3), 295–301. https://doi.org/10.1016/j.pec.2008.11.015.

Waite, R., & Killian, P. (2008). Health beliefs about depression among African American women. *Perspectives in Psychiatric Care, 44*,185-195.

Whaley, A. L. (2001). Cultural mistrust and mental health services for African Americans: A review and metanalysis. *The Counseling Psychologist, 29,* 513–531.

Weisz, C., & Quinn, D. M. (2018). Stigmatized identities, psychological distress, and physical health: Intersections of homelessness and race. *Stigma and Health, 3*(3), 229–240.

Williams, D. R. (2000). Race, Stress, and Mental Health: Findings from the Commonwealth Minority Health Survey. In C. Hogue, M. A. Hargraves, & K. S. Collins (Ed.), *Minority Health in America: Findings and Policy Implication From the Commonwealth Fund Minority Health Survey* (pp. 209-243). Baltimore, MD, Johns-Hopkins University Press.

Woods-Giscombé, C. L. (2010). Superwoman Schema: African American Women's Views on Stress, Strength, and Health. *Qualitative Health Research, 20*(5), 668–683. https://doi.org/10.1177/1049732310361892.

Woods-Giscombe, C., Robinson, M., Carthon, D., Devane-Johnson, S., & Corbie-Smith, G. (2016). Superwoman Schema, Stigma, Spirituality, and Culturally Sensitive Providers: Factors Influencing African American Women's Use of Mental Health Services. *Journal of Best Practices in Health Professions Diversity, 9*(1), 1124-1144.

Zielinski, M. J., & Veilleux, J. C. (2018). The Perceived Invalidation of Emotion Scale (PIES): Development and psychometric properties of a novel measure of current emotion invalidation. *Psychological assessment, 30*(11), 1454–1467. https://doi.org/10.1037/pas0000584.

Chapter 15

By My Own Bootstraps: Career Success, the Sacrifice of African-American Women, and the "American Dream"

Pia L. Scott[1,*], PhD
and Shane´J. Gill[2], PhD
[1]P.L. Scott Group, LLC, Charleston, South Carolina, USA
[2]Regent University, Virginia Beach, Virginia, USA

Abstract

From the days of chattel slavery onward, the contributions of Black women have been and continue to be the backbone of American society. Despite women's advancement in the workplace, Black women continue to encounter glass ceilings as they grapple with underrepresentation, microaggressions, and oppression in the workplace. As they race towards achieving the "American Dream," Black women continue to encounter racial and gender discrimination, segregation in the workplace, caregiver roles, and fulfilling duties expected by their respective communities. The consequences of managing this dual and often conflicting role in the workplace and household despite their contributions and qualifications. Of significance are the statistics that Black women in C-Suite or corporate level positions encounter; some of the experiences these women encounter are unique to Black women. Research suggests that Black women are likely to demonstrate ambition and be interested in corporate America promotions; However, Black women are less likely to have mentors and opportunities to advance or receive recognition despite their education and qualifications. Systemic racism in the workplace and

* Corresponding Author's Email: drpscott2016@gmail.com.

In: How Did We Survive?
Editor: Tina Marie Glover
ISBN: 979-8-88697-918-3

corporate America must be considered in exploring the implications of race and gender in career success and advancement in working-class Black women. This chapter will explore the issue at hand using critical race theory and relational cultural identity Theory. Furthermore, this chapter will discuss the historical roles of African American women, cultural assumptions and expectations about Black women in the workplace, and the implications of these factors in how Black women are reshaping how they define success and identity.

Introduction

Roots

Economically, black people have historically contributed to the economic development of the United States and internationally. Research points out that African Americans have been negatively impacted by the experiences of oppression through trans-generational slavery, including modern-day racism, which influenced social injustice, discrimination, and stigmatization. Despite the accomplishments and contributions by African American women in our society, the stigma of whom they are perceived to represent (i.e., Jezebel) is rooted in racism and sexism, and this often encourages the hindrance of social mobility while expecting African American women to deny their true greatness and accept negative perceptions of their self-worth. Black women lack access to social capital, sponsorship, and additional resources needed to acquire leadership roles. The (2004) Catalyst Workplaces that Work for Women report found that Black women were often shut out of influential networks and were less likely to have a mentor or sponsor than white women. These experiences go back to invisibility during slavery, in which Black women were subjected to mental, physical, and emotionally unhealthy spaces. Some of the remnants of Slavery and the hierarchy of racial trauma are something that Black women still experience today.

The Hierarchy of Slavery

The history of Black people from West African societies through the American slavery experience of the historical racial violence, racial bias, and racial stereotypes have been and continue to be problematic for African

Americans, particularly women who have observed these acts against African American men and children but also were even more victims themselves by these racist acts against them. African American women are susceptible to experiencing racism more than any other racial/ethnic group (Comas-Diaz et al., 2019; Stevens-Watkins et al., 2014). African American women are among the most diverse ethnic groups, disproportionately in health, medical, socioeconomic, poverty, trauma and violence, substance use disorders, and psychological problems (D'Orio et al., 2015; Jihanjee, 2014; Meyers & Zane, 2013).

The Intersection of Race and Gender

Race or persons that share physical features and characteristics has been used to marginalize and reinforce discriminatory practices (Carter, 2007). The effects of marginalization have reverberated throughout history and are ever-much present in the African American community. Referred to historical trauma, this reverberation has manifested itself as narratives that include discrimination, genocide, slavery, and persecution (Mohatt, Thompson, Thai, & Tebes, 2014). For individuals that have experienced complex trauma, alterations in affect regulation, attention, attachment, and self-perspective can be altered (Curtois, 2014). However, discrimination or perpetuation of negative attitudes and beliefs that infringe on the rights and freedoms of African Americans has been associated with poorer mental and physical health, increasing their risk of other diseases and difficulty coping with chronic stressors associated with socioeconomic differences (Myers et al., 2015). Intersectionality theory seeks to explore the implications of race, history, class, and gender on one's overall experience (Samuels & Ross-Sheriff).

Stress is a physical and emotional response to a significant event that overwhelms one's ability to cope effectively. Stress can contribute to maladaptive behavior and detrimental consequences without adequate coping mechanisms. Stress has been attributed to one of two factors, including isolated events and continuous events over an extended period (Pearlin, Menaghan, Lieberman, and Mullan, 1981). Socially, stress develops as a result of many factors, including but not limited to the individual, family, community, life transitions, and social relationships (Pearlin et al., 1981). The environment can significantly influence the type and severity of stress an individual experiences. For women, the workplace is one such environment.

In fact, for almost two-thirds of women, the experience of micro-aggressions in the workplace is familiar (Krivkovich, Robinson, Starikova, Valentino, and Yee, 2017).

Black women's experience of micro-aggression and differences in their experiences in the workplace calls into question the intersection between race and gender in the workplace for Black women. Micro-aggressions are defined as brief but common and accepted practices of verbal and behavioral assaults that are intentional or unintentional and attack a person or group of a particular race (Holder, Jackson, and Ponterotto, 2015). Racism has significant effects on Blacks' mental health and wellness, such as depression and anxiety that stems from an overall negative self-concept as they attempt to assimilate into the dominant culture while rejecting their culture of origin (Franklin & Boyd-Franklin, 2000; Holder et al., 2015). In the workplace, women are under immense stress as they attempt to defy expectations and challenge societal assumptions that they are hostile, aggressive, over sexual and immoral, and incompetent. Authenticity lessens as the traits and characteristics that shape their identity are sacrificed to appease and submit to the dominant culture. Loss of identity can be a traumatic experience that contributes to emotional and mental dysfunction with long-term consequences, including a threat to one's self-esteem for Blacks (Banovic & Bjelajac, 2012; Courtois & Gold, 2009; Franklin, 1999; Olff, 2012).

Trauma and Identity of African American Women: A Comparative Analysis

Womanhood and Black identity are viewed through their personal experiences, work, relationships, and family roles. Although Black and White women share the identity of womanhood, the experiences and perceptions of what it means to be a woman have defining differences based on race that make the experiences of Black women significantly different. Black and White women may experience gender bias. However, Black woman is more likely to experience racial bias based on race too. A Black woman looking to advance in her career in the workplace is judged based on two things that are devalued, race and gender, whereas a White woman is devalued based on gender.

A 2004 study by the Catalyst Workplaces That Work for Women highlighted that African-American women suffer from barriers stemming from many areas of discrimination, including negative, race-based stereotypes; more frequent questioning of their credibility and authority; and a lack of institutional support (2004). Another study conducted (2011) by the Catalyst Workplaces That Work for Women found that negative stereotyping and exclusion from influential networks influenced how diverse women experience workplaces limiting diverse women's access to trusting relationships (Catalyst, 2011). While White women are part of an oppressed group based on gender, they are still considered to have the privilege that Black women do not benefit from.

Western society is dominated by white cultural standards in which White women are rewarded. White women have been depicted to be the foundation of purity, chastity, and virtue; women of Color have historically been caricatured by the negative stereotypes and the historical lower status position associated with their racial communities in American society (Hernandez & Rehman, 2002; Collins, 2000; Lorde, 1984; Hooks, 1981).

African American women have endured significant trauma and have taken on the identity of the "Strong Black Woman" stereotype. Societal views of black women stem from years of oppression and negative charactertures that plague the community. During the slave trade, slavery, Jim Crow, and segregation, black women's roles were the jezebel (hypersexual), the Sapphire (an angry black woman), or the nurturing Mammy taking care of White families. In the 1960s, black women who allegedly abused the system receiving welfare funds came to be known as the single mother on welfare, aka the "Welfare Queen." The Strong Black Woman has surfaced in recent years to describe the modern Black woman. Beauboeuf-Lafontant (2005) and Harris-Lacewell (2004) theorize that the Strong Black Woman developed as the alternative to negative stereotypes of African American women, as discussed above. The evolution of the "Strong Black Woman" perpetuates the independent woman as the sole provider, emotionally strong, and traits that counter the negative stereotypes, which have some negative associations such as anxiety.

The Black woman has to mask her feelings and often deprive herself of her needs. "Strong Black Woman" is a mantra for so much a part of U.S. culture that it is seldom realized how great a toll it has taken on the emotional well-being of the African American woman. As much as it may give her the illusion of control, it keeps her from identifying what she needs and reaching out for help Romero (2000, p. 225). These stereotypes have perpetrated cultural assumptions and expectations of how Black women act.

Cultural Assumptions and Expectations of Black Women

Society assumes that Black women are "strong" and exhibit a strength where they are expected to perform in many roles. Strength is characterized by the determination to succeed, self-control, independence, and work ethic. In contrast, caregiving is exhibited by prioritizing others' needs, being self-sacrificing, and supporting families/communities (e.g., Woods-Giscombé, 2010). The Strong Black Woman (SBW) is a race-gender schema that prescribes culturally specific feminine expectations for African American women, including unyielding strength, assumption of multiple roles, and caring for others (e.g., Beauboeuf-Lafontant, 2007; Settles, Pratt-Hyatt, & Buchanan, 2008). This notion has caused significant emotional damage, perceptions, and an expectation that suggests Black women can do it all or be the "Superwomen."

Black women's needs are even discounted in the medical space. Black women have been refused medical treatment while giving birth because of the "Strong Black Woman" Stereotype. Medical treatment for Black women encompasses discrimination and racist practices dating back to Slavery, Jim Crow, and the Civil Rights Era, where medical treatments were administered without medications. Enslaved women had limited access to healthcare, and the available "care" often involved medical experimentation. James Marion Sims, the "Father of Modern Gynecology" and former president of the American Medical Association, performed many reproductive experimental surgeries without anesthesia to treat various childbirth illnesses among enslaved African American women (Washington, 2006). There is an intersection of gender and race in history as Black women's jobs were to bear children for the purpose of economic advantages for the slave master. Black women were viewed as property and had no rights to their own bodies.

Cultural assumptions that Black women are nurturing caregivers like Mammy or the Angry Black Woman are damaging to their mental health and self-worth. This stigma of the caregiver in the workplace puts significant pressure on Black women to care for everyone or not speak up for fear of being labeled the "Angry Black Woman." In an attempt to defy stereotypes, Black women work even harder to be promoted or be successful in their careers if they maintain the status quo. Black women express navigating their careers to include code-switching, changing their natural hair to fit the European look, and often question their ability to do the job they have been hired for. Research has highlighted Black women's negative experiences in the workplace and society. Although they have suffered and sacrificed, they continue to be successful and reach achievements.

Case Study-Achievement, Success, and the American Dream

Ashley is a 29-year-old single heterosexual African American female. She identifies as middle class. Ashley is a graduate of a historically Black college and is from Atlanta, Georgia. She began her career in the food industry, which evolved into retail and, later, a position in a corporate insurance company. Despite her education and nearly a decade of experience, Ashley encountered severe microaggression in the workplace, discrimination, and sexual harassment by her male counterparts. Ashley initially reported to treatment, identifying depression as the chief complaint. As the sessions progressed, it was determined that Ashley's sense of identity was not fully integrated; As a Black woman, Ashley contorted herself, in speech, dress, attitude, and overall behavior, to submit to White assumptions and expectations about Black culture and women, while attempting to meet expectations of her family and community.

In the workplace, Ashley reported that she was "expected to be submissive, docile, and accept the subliminal things they [White colleagues] say. It can be about whether my hair is real, my body, indirect comments about sex, and jungle fever. I want to move up. So that is that." She often reported the conflict between workplace and family and community expectations. She stated, "this is the complete opposite of home. I go by my nickname when I am home or in the neighborhood. My hair is down; I do not need the wigs and all the extra shit. I curse, can get loud, use my slang, and it is normal. I must water myself down to get promoted and 'act White.' It is just so many barriers. It is people honestly getting promoted before me. I want the white picket fence, the money, cars, all of that. I have to sell out to get it."

In this excerpt, Ashley attests to the dual nature of the Black identity of women. Like Ashley, Black men must negotiate their sense of self and identity influenced by cultural expectations and requirements while attempting to meet the dominant culture's expectations (Franklin & Boyd-Franklin, 2000). Failing to socialize or assimilate often has severe mental, emotional, and social consequences. Black men have been categorized and portrayed as being violent, threatening, incapable of higher-order functioning such as logic and reason, and overtly sexual; Identity in Black men has been polarized, with men being identified as "good" or "bad" depending on their compliance with expectations of White culture and rejection of their customs and values (Curry, 2018).

In conceptualizing this case, one must consider how Ashley and other Black women negotiate their identity to achieve the "American Dream." The "American Dream," or TAD, was a term in which the definition was based on the core tenant that opportunities were based on an individual's abilities and achievements (Combs, 2015). Material wealth and acumen were also indicators of success and having accomplished the American Dream. Based on this definition, one would assume that Ashley, for example, would have accumulated material wealth and acumen by following the prescribed path of obtaining an education. However, Ashley reported that she would have to "sell out" to obtain the "white picket fence, cars, and the money." The assumption of having to "sell out" is of significance, which is consistent with Black men and women's experience in the workplace. To "sell out" has often been compared to "acting White" and assuming character traits that are more subservient and docile and less threatening to Whites. However, her role in the family and community, one in which she is expected to serve, care, and tend to other persons, significantly impacts her career choice and progression, an all too common barrier for Black women in the workforce and those that aspire to achieve success while avoiding the anxiety of failure (Allen, 1979).

Womanhood and Blackness are two barriers that Ashley must overcome, with Blackness overshadowing her education, experience, and potential in her respective career and field. Of importance are the mental health consequences that Black women, including Ashley, who reported depression, experience. Poverty, crime, chronic incarceration, lack of access to adequate resources and educational opportunities, and other factors significantly increase the likelihood of barriers in adulthood for Black women in the absence of female role models that represent success and an integrated identity (Allen, 1979). Ashley, like many Black men and women, succumb to the effects of systemic oppression that are often dismissed when considering barriers to surpassing the glass ceiling in the workplace and corporate America. The consequences are severe, with Black women and men experiencing rage, anxiety, and depression, among other symptoms, as the effects of racism exceed their ability to cope (Franklin & Boyd-Franklin, 2000). Therefore, one must first acknowledge the role of stigma and separatism based on race that reduces the equity in the workplace for Black women in addressing the trauma these women experience.

Stigma, Race, and Separatism

Systems of race, class, and oppression structure African American women. The strong Black women concept perceives that Black or African American women are often the backbone of the family; they have strong family and nurturing bonding, strong work ethic, and strong community and social ties through the church (Danzer et al., 2016). The practice of African American women taking on family and social roles may influence an overwhelming responsibility that refers to them as "Superwoman." The superwoman can also be a double-edged sword of deviance and resilience to counteract economic disadvantage and racial/ethnic and gender inequality (Woods-Giscombe, 2010).

African American women's experience of stereotyping, malicious remarks, or discrimination practices may leave them vulnerable to stress, frustration, and living in racist systems to experience dissonance between their "real self" and "ideal self," emotional suppression about unfair treatment, and they may shift to being liabilities of experiencing adverse physical and mental health and substance use problems (Jerald et al., 2017; Prather et al., 2016; Wood-Giscombe, 2010). Research indicated that insensitive comments or insults regarding the cultural value and intelligence and negative stereotype images of African American women related to "Jezebel" (hypersexual or seductive) and "Sapphire" (nagging or angry Black women) are rooted in American culture and are justification for structural racism (Jerald et al., 2017; Lewis et al., 2016). The stigma on African American women may prevent appropriate cultural knowledge by service providers and the larger society to fairly provide care and rightful opportunity in every aspect of living. Consequently, the stigmatization can be internalized by some African American women, and they may experience maladapting coping (e.g., risky sexual behavior and substance use) as a mechanism (Jerald et al., 2017).

For centuries, African Americans have been plagued by race and racism. Race is theorized to have established superiority between Europeans and Non-Europeans. At the same time, racism may be defined differently and include individual, institutional, structural, cultural, and intragroup levels. Racism is rooted in negative beliefs and attitudes (i.e., stereotypes) and is the mechanism used as a powerful social construct to rank people into systematically hierarchically distinct and inferior groups. Racism affected, and still affect, millions of African Americans, and it is more than scattered episodes of discrimination. It involves widespread racist ideology and the power to oppress other racial groups the opportunities, rewards, freedoms, and dignity

(Carter, 2007; Lewis et al., 2015). The research found that racism can impede appropriate medical and preventive health services for African Americans (Alang, 2019). The high exposure to racism, including racial discrimination, can have a negative psychological, emotional, and physical impact on Black women (Black et al., 2015; Prather et al., 2016). For example, African American women may experience a range of adverse consequences, including work, academic, emotional, police involvement, and other related social problems (Klein et al., 2016; Pittman & Kaur, 2018).

Critical Race Theory and Relational Cultural Theory

To gain some understanding of the broad aspects of stigma, race, racism, and trauma in the United States, the use of Critical Race Theory (CRT) emphasized that human and civil rights are supposed to give empowerment and support individuals and racial groups, but when rights are quickly taken away, ignored, or defeated by oppressive perspectives, this suggested that rights are not guaranteed, but of superficial hope or enlightenment to social corrections or change. Since the 1990s, critical race theory has expanded the groundwork for legal studies, and CRT has been widely used in legal research in the activist role in social justice, oppression, racial inequalities, and reforms that can affect the value of lives across social, racial/ethnicity, economic, cultural, and political perspectives. Tenets such as storytelling, daily bias, identifying racism as a social construct, interest convergence, and intersectionality are used to explore in-depth meaning and worldview relevant to gender, identity, and cultural differences (Bracey II, 2015; Hall & Fields, 2015). Overall, through the lens of CRT, the insensitivity of racism that influences disparities and inequalities in education, economics, health, and society is often downplayed by White America. As such, this can be demonstrated through limited or no resources or access to opportunities of quality living that threaten the safety and security of African Americans and evoke strain on the relationships between them and White America (Bracey II, 2015). The relational theory explains that there is often a need to address the psychodynamics of cultural differences relevant to the complexity of gender-specific models for women whose trust, autonomy, and worth are challenged and experienced through oppression, abuse, injustice, and treatment (Quinn et al., 2015).

Reshaping the Definition and Narrative of Identity and Success of Black Women

The cultural context of the Black experience can be reshaped and redefined through economic empowerment, self-worth, and valuing their emotional needs. Black women's contributions to the United States and globally have historically been overlooked, ignored, and discounted. Women gained the right to vote under the 19th Amendment. However, this did not apply to Black women. The Black woman was essential to the movements to change the landscape of not only Black women but the rights of the Black community. They participated in movements such as the Women's Suffrage Movement, Civil Rights Movement, and present-day with B.L.M. Each of these movements provided the opportunity for Black women to change the current landscape of injustices and inequalities, fighting for the rights of Black women to vote and more. Reshaping womanhood through healthier perceptions and a positive sense of self-worth allows Black women to reclaim their womanhood without apology. Black women have neglected their well-being and often their mental health to appease a system of oppression. Specifically, they are met with significant challenges in the workplace and mobility in their careers. Redefining success for many Black women consists of self-evaluation, self-worth, and acceptance.

Conclusion

The remnants of slavery and Jim Crow laws continue to reverberate throughout history. When considering differences in achievement and success, one must first explore the intersection of race and gender while simultaneously considering how these demographics have been used to perpetuate the oppression of persons of color, specifically Black persons. In a patriarchal and White society, women are dehumanized, being deduced into objects of gratification. For Black women, race is used to further deduce them to property, with their value associated with their physical attributes and qualities. In the workplace, trauma is likely to develop from a system that perpetuates these stereotypes and repeatedly assaults the self-esteem of Black women, contributing to limited aspirations and negative beliefs about the ability to accomplish a dream that, at its inception, was never designed or intended for them to achieve. The workplace has a fundamental role in trauma and related outcomes for Black women. It is therefore tasked with reassessing the essence of equality and opportunities for equity to deconstruct the very system society has created.

References

Alang S. M. (2019). Mental health care among blacks in America: Confronting racism and constructing solutions. *Health Services Research*, 54(2), 346–355. https://doi.org/10.1111/1475-6773.13115.

Allen, W. R. (1979). Family roles, occupational statuses, and achievement orientations among black women in the United States. *Signs: Journal of Women in Culture and Society*, *4*(4), 670–686. http://www.jstor.org/stable/3173365.

Beauboeuf-Lafontant, T. (2005). Keeping up appearances, getting fed up: The embodiment of strength among African American women. *Meridians: Feminism, Race, Transnationalism*, 5, 104–123. doi:10.1177/0022487105282576.

Black, L. L., Johnson, R., & VanHoose, L. (2015). The relationship between perceived racism/discrimination and health among black American women: A review of the literature from 2003 to 2013. *Journal of racial and ethnic health disparities*, 2(1), 11–20. https://doi.org/10.1007/s40615-014-0043-1.

Bracey II, G. E. (2015). Toward a critical race theory of state. *Critical Sociology*, 41(3), 553 –572. https://doi.org/ 10.1177/0896920513504600.

Carter, R. T. (2007). Racism and psychological and emotional injury: Recognizing and assessing race-based traumatic stress. *The Counseling Psychologist*, *35*(1), 13–105. doi: 10.1177001100006292033.

Catalyst Workplace That Work for Women. (2004). *Advancing African-American Women in the Workplace: What Managers need to Know.*(Report). https://www.catalyst.org/research/advancing-african-american-women-in-the-workplace-what-managers-need-to-know/

Collins, P. H. (2000). *Black Feminist Thought (2nd ed.).* New York: Routledge.

Comas-Diaz, L., Hall, G., N., & Neville, H. A. (2019). Racial trauma: Theory, research, and healing: Introduction to the special issue. *American Psychologist,* 74(1), 1–5. http:/doi.org/10.1037/amp0000442.

Combs, S. L. (2015). The American dream: Divisible economic justice for all. Race, *Gender, & Class*, 22, 228–235.

Courtois, C.A. (2008). Complex Trauma, Complex Reactions: Assessment and Treatment. *Psychotherapy: Theory, Practice, Training, 41*(4), 412–425. doi: 10.1037/0033-3204.41.4.412.

Curry, T. J. (2018). Killing boogeymen: Phallicism and the misandric mischaracterizations of Black males in theory. *Res Philosophica*. doi: 10.11612/resphil.1612.

Danzer, G., Rieger, S. M., Schubmehl, S., & Cort, D. (2016) White psychologists and African Americans' historical trauma: Implications for practice, *Journal of Aggression, Maltreatment & Trauma*, *25*(4), 351–370. http://doi.org/10.1080/10926771.2016.1153550.

D' Orio, B. M., Thompson, M. P., Lamis, D. A., Heron, S., & Kaslow, N. (2015). Social support, attachment, and drug misuse in suicidal African American women. *Journal of Addiction Research & Theory, 23*(2), 170–176. http://doi.org/10.3109/16066359.2014.966096.

Franklin, A. J. (1999). Invisibility syndrome and racial identity development in psychotherapy and counseling African American men. *The Counseling Psychologist, 27*(6), 761–793. doi: 10.1177/0011000099276002.

Franklin, A. J., & Boyd-Franklin, N. (2000). Invisibility syndrome: A clinical model of the effects of racism on African-American males. *American Journal of Orthopsychiatry, 70*(1), 33–41. doi: 10.1037/h0087691.

Giscombe, K.(2011). Catalyst Workplace That Work for Women. *Building Trust Between Managers and Diverse Women Direct Reports* (Report). https://www.catalyst.org/research/building-trust-between-managers-and-diverse-women-direct-reports/

Hall, J. M., & Fields, B. (2015). "It's killing us!" narratives of Black adults about microaggression experiences and related health stress. *Global Qualitative Nursing Research,* 2(2333393615591569), 1–14. https://doi.org/10.1177/2333393615591569.

Harris-Lacewell, M. (2004). *Barbershops, bibles, and BET: Everyday talk and Black political thought.* Princeton, NJ: Princeton University Press.

Hernandez, D. & Rehman, B. (2002). Colonize This!" Young Women of Color on Today's Feminism. Emeryville: Seal Press.

Hooks, B. (1981). *Ain't I A Woman?: Black Women and Feminism.* Boston: South End Press.

Jerald, M. C., Cole, E. R., Ward, L. M., & Avery, L. R. (2017). Controlling images: How awareness of group stereotypes affects black women's well-being. *Journal of Counseling Psychology, 64*(5), 487- 499 http://dx.doi.org/10.1037/cou0000233.

Jihaniee, S. (2014). Evidenced based psychosocial interventions in substance use. *Indian Journal of Psychology Medicine. 36*(2), 112-118. http://doi.org/10.4103/0253-7176.130960.

Klein, H., Sterk, C. E., & Elifson, K. W. (2016). The prevalence of and factors associated with alcohol-related problems in a community sample of African American women. *Journal of Addiction, Article ID 7513827*, 1-11. http://doi.org/10.1155/2016/7513827.

Lewis, T. T., Cogburn, C. D., & Williams, D. R. (2015). Self-reported experiences of discrimination and health: Scientific advances, ongoing controversies, and emerging issues. *Annual Review of Clinical Psychology, 11*, 407-440. http://doi.org/10.1146/annurev-clinpsy-032814-112728.

Lewis, J. Mendenhall, R., Harwood, S. A., & Huntt, M. B. (2016). Ain't I a Woman?": Perceived gendered racial microaggressions experienced by black women. *The Counseling Psychologist 2016, 44*(5), 758–780. http://doi.org/10.1177/ 00110000 16641193.

Liao KY-H, Wei M, Yin M. The Misunderstood Schema of the Strong Black Woman: Exploring Its Mental Health Consequences and Coping Responses Among African American Women. *Psychology of Women Quarterly*. 2020;44(1):84-104. doi:10.1177/0361684319883198

Meyer, O. L., & Zane, N. (2013). Race and ethnicity influence clients' experiences of mental health treatment. *Journal of Community Psychology, 4*(17), 884-901. http://doi.org/10.1002/jcop.21580.

Mohatt, N. V., Thompson, A. B., Thai, N. D., & Tebes, J. K. (2014). Historical trauma as public narrative: A conceptual review of how history impacts present-day health. *Social Science & Medicine, 106*, 128-136. doi: 10.1016/j.socscimed.2014.01.043.

Myers, H. F., Wyatt, G. E., Ullman, J. B., Loeb, T. B., Chin, D., Prause, N., ... & Liu, H. (2015). Cumulative burden of lifetime adversities: Trauma and mental health in low-SES African Americans and Latino/as. *Psychological Trauma: Theory, Research, Practice, and Policy*, *7*(3), 243. doi: 10.1037/a0039077.

Olff, M. (2012). Bonding after trauma: On the role of social support and the oxytocin system in traumatic stress. *European Journal of Psychotraumatology*, *3*(1), 18597. doi: 10.3402/ejpt.v3i0.18597.

Pittman, D. M., & Kaur, P. (2018). Examining the role of racism in the risky alcohol use behaviors of black female college students *Journal of American College Health, 66*(4), 310-316. https://doi.org/10.1080/07448481.2018.1440581.

Prather, C., Fuller, T. R., Marshall, K. J., & Jeffries, W. L. (2016). The impact of racism on the sexual and reproductive health of African American women. *Journal of Women's Health, 25*(7), 664-671. http://doi.org/10.1089/jwh.2015.5637.

Quinn, C. R., & Grumbach, G. (2015). Critical race theory and the limits of relational theory in social work with women. *Journal of Ethnic & Cultural Diversity in Social Work*, *24*(3), 202–218. https://doi.org/10.1080/15313204.2015.1062673.

Stevens-Watkins, D., Perry, B., Pullen, E., Jewell, J., & Oser, C. B. (2014). Examining the associations of racism, sexism, and stressful life events on psychological distress among African-American women. *Cultural diversity & ethnic minority psychology*, *20*(4), 561– 569. https://doi.org/10.1037/a0036700.

Washington H. (2006). *Medical Apartheid: the Dark History of Medical Experimentation on Black Americans from Colonial Times to the Present*. New York: Doubleday.

Woods-Giscombé, C. L. (2010). Superwoman schema: African American women's views on stress, strength, and health. *Qualitative Health Research*, 20, 668–683. doi:10.1177/1049732310361892.

Chapter 16

Institutional and Systemic Racism and the Traumatic Experiences of African-American Women

Layla J. Bonner[1,*], PhD
Gimel Rogers[2]
Agnes Lover[3]
and Tamiko Webb[4], PhD

[1]LMFT, NCC, Assistant Professor, M.A. in Mental Health Counseling Program, Belmont University, Nashville, Tennessee, USA
[2]Psy.D., ABPP, F.I.R.E. Igniting Lives, Owner; Faculty/Associate Director Online MAP/MACLP Programs, Pepperdine University, Los Angeles, California, USA
[3]MBA, M.Div., D.Min. Saint Paul African Methodist Episcopal Church, Lead Pastor
[4]Inpatient Coordinator; Adjunct Professor, Tennessee State University, Nashville, Tennessee, USA

Abstract

The United States has a long history of engaging in White supremacist ideologies and the oppression of people of color. These ways of thinking have become ingrained in many of American culture's norms, practices, and even laws. Historically, the lives of marginalized groups have been significantly affected. Black Americans, in particular, have had to manage overt racism and discrimination daily. Black women are especially vulnerable as they are a part of two marginalized groups. The intersection of race and gender involves multiple oppressions. Black women, especially, must contend with the impact of gendered and racial

* Corresponding Author's Email: layla.bonner@belmont.edu.

In: How Did We Survive?
Editor: Tina Marie Glover
ISBN: 979-8-88697-918-3

discrimination in their communities, education, profession, and religious institutions.

Keywords: African American women, Black women, institutional racism, systemic racism, women in America

Introduction

Growing up, many Christian children who attended private schools and Christian camps learned a song, "Jesus Loves the Little Children." The song says that Jesus loves all the children of the world red, brown, yellow, black, and white. However, some of the same individuals that taught the song did, in fact, discriminate against people of color. Discrimination may adversely impact one's sense of identity, value, esteem, and worth. Race based trauma affects a child's mental, physical, emotional, and spiritual development. This adverse impact is worsened when it is perpetrated by perceived trusted adults. Children of color are particularly vulnerable because they are still in the early stages of psychological and moral development. For example, Erik Erikson, who developed the psychosocial development model, indicated that teachers and peers take on increasing importance on school aged children (i.e., six to 12-years-old). According to Erikson, if this stage is favorable, then the child will be able to exercise his or her abilities and intelligence in the world, and to affect the world in the way that the child desires. If the stage is unfavorable, then the child ~~has~~ develops a sense of inadequacy, a sense of inability to act in a competent manner, and low self-esteem. The virtue, i.e., targeted outcome for this stage, is competence. If a child is subjected to race-based trauma in an environment that is perceived to be safe such as an educational or religious institution, then it affects self-esteem and self-worth, especially when their skin color is weaponized against them. Furthermore, Rogers (2020) wrote, "Often, sociocultural factors are not examined when assessing a youth affected by violence, and the youth's presentation is misattributed or mislabeled" (p. 4). This in return produces long-term detrimental repercussions on how one lives in society. This is why trauma, by design, perpetuates oppression and undoubtedly why systems are allowed to continue to oppress people of color, especially women.

Institutional and systemic racism refers to the pervasive cultural bias and discriminatory practices, policies, and procedures that are deeply ingrained in society's social structures, systems, and institutions (Delgado & Stefancic,

2001; Walter et al., 2017). According to Jones (2002), institutionalized racism is defined "as the structures, policies, practices, and norms resulting in differential access to the goods, services, and opportunities of society by race." These structures include social, economic, educational, and political domains that foster inequalities for non-dominant groups, especially African Americans (Walter et al., 2017). In the United States, historical inequalities and racist attitudes and ideologies are shaped and embedded into the foundation of contemporary systems, structures, customs, and laws that disadvantage African Americans and position them as inferior (Jones, 2002; Pine & Hilliard, 1990; Winfield, 2007). Furthermore, when African Americans fight against policies that are causing massive suffering in their community, the ultra-wealthy Corporate America and Wall Street executives fund organizations that actively oppose those efforts (Freeman, 2021). Thereby, creating a smoking mirror that ignorance was the driving force of systemic racism when, in fact, money and power is propelling racial injustice. Some refer to this institutionalized racism as "The New Racism" as it is more subtle and invisible in many ways (Lynch, 2019). The oppressive experiences of African-American women are especially unique due to the intersection of race, gender, and class (Thomas, 2004), and their intersectionality by nature put them at risk for substantial oppression. As a result of multiple identities, Black girls, and women experience "interactive oppressions" as they are Black and female (King, 1988, p. 42; Spates, Evans, James, & Martinez, 2020), and this has been coined as "gendered racism" (Lewis et al., 2017). Gendered racism is often seen in institutions; therefore, it is critical to understand how the institutions and systems with which Black girls and women interact on a regular basis inflict damage and trauma. This chapter will explore gendered racism of African American women in the context of the community (i.e., violence, healthcare, and social services) educational/academic setting, workplace, and religious institutions. Of note, African American and Black will be used interchangeably to be inclusive of the whole African Diaspora.

Community

Perry (2003) wrote, "Each year in the United States, five million children are exposed to abuse, violence, and other traumatic events. Unlike the veterans from Vietnam, most of these children don't rotate out of the war zone after a year" (p.11). Community violence most often occurs in rural and urban low socioeconomic communities, and it includes indirect or direct violence or violence related events. Violence such as bullying, school shootings, gang violence, human and drug trafficking, or physical altercations in the parks, grocery stores, and in front of homes. Rogers (2014) wrote, "Community violence not only predisposes African-American women to the preceding traumas, particularly (IPV), but it also makes them vulnerable to family violence, violence that is proximal to an individual's development." Ultimately, exposure to community violence can adversely impact both work and school performance as well as social relationships, and this impact can lead to posttraumatic stress symptoms. Likewise, research indicates that community violence exposure is highly correlated with aggression and posttraumatic stress versus anxiety and depression (McDonald & Richmond, 2008). These compounded traumatic experiences can lead to health complications and premature death especially due to a lack of quality healthcare and/or interaction with the legal system and/or child welfare services (CWS).

Black women are subjected to a lack of quality healthcare due to disparities in access and equity of healthcare and community services rooted in systemic racist practices. This means a greater risk of poor maternal health, maternal mortality, and pre-term birth for Black women. Taylor (2020) asserts "that structural racism is a powerful social determinant of maternal health that has roots in a historical system of oppression and devaluing of women of color and persists today in more subtle health care policies and practices" (p. 506). White women have had the privilege of living in a White-dominated society that nullifies their womanhood in the oppression, especially in the healthcare system. For example, historically "the advent of the study of obstetrics and gynecology with the use of enslaved Black women's bodies; forced sterilization and promotion of birth control among low-income Black women as a condition of social welfare programs; and ignoring Black women's pain" (Taylor, 2020, p. 507), are absent to White women's experiences. While these practices are not as pervasive, some still exist, and subtle disparities remain. Thus, health does not exist outside of social context, and the social context that Black women have lived in is inequitable and costly.

Similar to the poor outcomes in the healthcare system, Black women face unique challenges in the legal system and CWS. Willingham (2018) underscored that Black women face the intersecting oppressions of race, gender, and justice in a society that was never designed to protect them. Willingham (2018) asserted that "state-sanctioned violence that Black women and girls experience is a manifestation of their continued survivorization, dehumanization, and social exclusion, and is a function of the systemic racism that permeates the American criminal injustice system" (p. 77). The same is held true for Black women who are involved with the CWS. Research has indicated that disparities in Black families have Black children in the CWS system at alarming rates and are more likely to end up in the foster system (Rogers & Bryant-Davis, 2020). For some women who have not been exposed to or affected by community violence and systematic oppression of the healthcare, legal system, and CWS, other structures remain in place that continue to oppress African-American women. Such systems include educational and academic settings.

History of Racism and Discrimination in Education

Historical events that have shaped inequalities within the educational system propagated a belief in the inferiority of Blacks and can be traced back to attitudes, customs, and laws that were established as far back as slavery. Between 1740 and 1834, many southern slave states enacted Anti-Literacy Laws that deemed it illegal for anyone to teach enslaved or free Blacks to spell, read, or write. For example, The Alabama Slave Code of 1833 declared that anyone who violated the law would be fined up to $500 (Smithsonian American Art Museum, 2021; Akin Digest of Laws, n.d.). These states utilized forced illiteracy as a tool to maintain dominance and social control over slaves as they feared that educating Blacks might encourage them to communicate with one another, run away, or revolt (Abercrombie, 2020; Tolley, 2016; Smithsonian American Art Museum, 2021).

While the 14th amendment to the United States Constitution established equal legal rights and protections for Blacks, states continued to enact anti-Black laws that delineated Blacks as inferior and Whites as superior in every aspect of life. Between 1877 and the 1960's, the Jim Crow system, established a racial caste system that further normalized and, albeit, created a cultural standard of discrimination against Blacks (Ferris University, 2021; USC, 2021). In 1896, the U.S. Supreme Court provided legal support for such normative practices in Plessy vs. Ferguson. The Plessy vs. Ferguson court decision legitimized separate but equal treatment of Blacks (Ferris State University, n.d.). Hence, Blacks were then permitted to obtain an education so long as it was in separate schools and did not involve comingling with Whites (USC Gould School of Law, 2021). The ruling perpetuated inequities in access to and quality of education for Blacks (Abercrombie, 2020). During that time, materials "were frequently outdated, books handed down from the White schools. Black teachers had larger class sizes, less equipment and were paid significantly less than White teachers" (Abercrombie, 2020, para. 5). These laws may also have set the stage for the Black-White achievement gap (Abercrombie, 2020). In 1954, the U.S. Supreme Court overturned its ruling in Plessy v. Ferguson deeming it unconstitutional.

The Brown v. The Board of Education of Topeka court decision ended legal segregation in public schools. Other states issued legal challenges to school segregation at that time, and social scientists supported their objections by arguing that segregated schools created a sense of inferiority among Black school children and negatively impacted their self-esteem, psyche, and emotional well-being (Akin, n.d.). Despite this forced desegregation, racist or anti-Black attitudes persisted, and many Whites resisted desegregation even to the point of violence (Harris, 2015). Just over 25 years ago, in 1994, some social scientists were still attempting to proclaim intellectual inferiority of Blacks. Charles Murray and Richard Herrnstein, a psychologist, co-authored and published a controversial text entitled, *The Bell Curve* (Southern Poverty Law Center [SPLC], 2021). The authors claimed that Blacks were genetically less intelligent than whites. He also made claims about affirmative action policies that painted Blacks as being unqualified for jobs (SPLC, 2021). These are the sorts of practices and policies that have historically shaped the dominant worldview and expectations of African Americans.

Laws may have changed but the residue of anti-Black discrimination, laws, norms, and practices has left an impact on the ways in which White teachers and administrators teach, conceptualize, and perceive Black students. It also impacted the way in which Black students experience and interact with the educational system. The history of and cumulative advantage of White supremacy, dominance, and privilege in American educational practices, laws, and social norms provide context to the contemporary experiences of Black girls and women in educational settings (DiPrete & Eirich, 2006; Ricks, 2014).

Similar to the healthcare settings' subtle oppressive barriers, racism and discrimination continue to create structural and psychological barriers in education (Torres et al., 2010; Tourse et al., 2018). Institutionalized racism in education manifests as differences in the access to and quality of educational opportunities, information, and resources (Jones, 2002; Massey 1975). Deficit teaching models, racial stereotypes, and more contemporary yet subtle forms of racism such as racial and gendered microaggressions persist and promote the false narrative that Black women are intellectually inferior, incapable, and unqualified (Solorzano & Yosso, 2001; Torres, Driscoll, & Burrow, 2010).

Contemporary Experiences of Black Girls in K-12

Literature suggests that deficit thinking in teaching pedagogy and low expectations of African-American school age students present barriers to their early academic success and emotional well-being (Joseph, Viesca, & Bianco, 2016; Massey et al., 1975). Additional barriers include inequalities in school funding, quality of teachers, and inadequate college preparatory curriculum at predominantly African American schools (Joseph et al., 2016). For young women in particular, some authors note that certain career fields like Science, Technology, Engineering, and Mathematics (STEM) have historically been characterized as more masculine fields yielding recruiting outcomes that are less equitable for girls and women (Joseph et al., 2016). Lastly, authors cite differential outcomes in disciplinary actions and penalties for Black students both male and female. Blacks are more likely to be suspended or expelled, and disciplinary approaches and policies fail to consider "issues of race, racism, or racial justice" (Joseph et al., 2016, p. 5). Inequalities are also represented in the differential dropout rates of African American students (Joseph et al., 2016).

Black schoolgirls are often objectified in a stereotypical fashion (Joseph et al., 2016). For example, some from the dominant culture label them as "loud, hot mamas, and…having an attitude" (Joseph et al., 2016, p. 5). These stereotypical labels represent a failure on the part of educators and researchers who cannot or refuse to acknowledge the coping strategies employed by Black girls to manage feelings of invisibility (Evans-Winters, 2005; Koonce, 2012; Ricks, 2014). Black female adolescents also described experiences with White peers and even White adults in their community as inappropriate like touching their hair without consent (Seaton & Tyson, 2019). Such behaviors are degrading and devaluing of African American bodies much like during slavery when Black women were made powerless and treated as property with no human rights (Collins, 2000; as cited in Joseph et al., 2016; Seaton & Tyson, 2019; Melaku & Beeman, 2020). Experiences of marginalization have a strong impact on the experiences of Black schoolgirls and those entering emerging adulthood alike (Mirza, 2015).

Contemporary Experiences of Young Black Women in College

During qualitative interviews with Black undergraduate college students, some participants reported feelings of isolation, self-doubt, feelings of invisibility in the classroom, and low self-efficacy as a result of racial micro-aggressions in class and on campus (Solorzano et al., 2000). They described double standards in behavioral expectations of them in comparison to White students. Some also reported feeling utter exhaustion from the onslaught of negative assumptions made about them because of their race. For example, a Black female college student noted that her White counterparts often made assumptions that many Black students had been admitted solely as result of affirmative action (Solorzano et al., 2000). Other Black women described experiencing feelings of helplessness and poor academic performance even to the point of withdrawing from their academic institution because of the constant need to manage racial microaggressions. One young woman ultimately made the decision to transfer from her Predominantly White Institutions (PWI) to a Historically Black College and University (HBCU). The cumulative experience that some Black women have with racial microaggressions leaves little desire for them to continue the struggle with learning at institutions of higher education that only serve to challenge their worth, aptitudes, and abilities (Solorzano et al., 2000).

Negative perceptions of African-American women as less than persist even as they pursue advanced and terminal degrees. In a sample of doctoral students composed primarily of Black women who had previously or were currently attending PWI's, participants reported multiple race related barriers to achieving their education. Those barriers included the "Assumption of Criminality/Second Class Citizen" and the "Underestimation of Personal Ability" (Torres et al., 2010, p.12-13). According to Sue et al. (2007), these racial microaggressions qualify as microinsults which suggest to persons of color that they are somehow unqualified, underqualified, or made qualified only as a result of quote or affirmative action. One participant reported that she felt the need to "prove herself" to overcompensate for the negative assumptions made by faculty members about her competence and abilities (Torres et al., 2010). Furthermore, the participant in the study noted her expectation that this subtle form of racism would continue even after obtaining her doctorate. These high achievers also reported that they frequently felt isolated and alienated as a result of their marginalization in their academic programs and institutions (Torres et al., 2010). Contending with these subtle slights adds an unnecessary and complicated level of stress that these scholars experience in an already complex and complicated endeavor. Additionally, results indicated that the stress induced by racial microaggressions were also related to participant reports of depressive symptomatology (Torres et al., 2010). Similar to the exasperation of Black women in college, Black female faculty also feel exhausted with their experiences of discrimination, White dominance, and White privilege (Smith, 2008).

Contemporary Experiences of Black Female Faculty

In 2021, Pulitzer Prize winner Nikole Hannah-Jones applied for tenure and promotion at The University of Chapel Hill. Though the acclaimed journalist and professor was herself an alumnus at the university and successfully served on the faculty for many years, the Board of Trustees denied her application. Many speculated that her tenure had been denied because of her outspokenness about racial injustice and her critical investigation about the truths of slavery and racism in America in her 1619 Project podcast. That speculation was, perhaps, confirmed for some with reports that one of the university's and Hussman School of Journalism and Media's most prominent multimillion-dollar donors, Walter Hussman Jr., objected to her tenure due to perspectives she shared through her 1619 Project podcast. Mr. Hussman, a well-connected and successful White male in the community, further made is his objections known to the Chancellor of the university before a final decision had been made about her tenure (Flaherty, 2021; Folkenflik, 2021). Upon her tenure denial, Hannah-Jones described the experience as humiliating, painful, and enraging (Clayson & McMahon, 2021). She expressed the embarrassment of being rejected by the institution with which she had a long-standing academic and professional relationship. In fact, this institution (her alma mater), had just publicly applauded her excellence in media and journalism by inducting her into their Hall of Fame (Clayson & McMahon, 2021). In one interview, Hannah-Jones concluded that, "I've spent my entire life proving that I belong in elite White spaces that were not built for Black women" (Wamsley, 2021, para. 18). Hannah-Jones's experience illustrates the subtle yet deeply painful experiences of discrimination, betrayal, and disillusionment that some Black women have shared about their interactions with some of the PWI's in which they are employed. While the university reversed its decision, Hannah-Jones chose to resign and teach at Howard University, a Historically Black College and University. Her resignation should come as no surprise as Black scholars who are confronted with racial discrimination and hostility often end up resigning from their positions (Melaku & Beeman, 2021; Smith, 2011).

Though very public, Professor Hannah-Jones's narrative is simply one of many documented cases of the negative experiences of Black faculty in academia. Black faculty report having their authority, credentials, and competence questioned not only by students in the classroom but also by faculty colleagues and staff (Constantine, Smith, Redington, & Owens, 2008). They report experiences with microaggressions and gendered racism (Constantine et al., 2008). Some have reported being denied tenure and promotion, receiving unfair and biased evaluations, and working in racial climates that left them feeling isolated and invisible (Daniel, 2019; Patton & Catching, 2009; Smith & Calasanti, 2005; Turner & Gonzalez, 2011). Dr. Hannah-Jones's experience makes clear the lack of psychological safety that Black female academics experience at White academic institutions (Melaku & Beeman, 2020).

Black women in higher education contend with a number of institutional and systemic factors that negatively influence their personal and professional well-being. Despite efforts at diversity and inclusion, many Black female professors remain underrepresented in the Academy (Alexander & Moore, 2008; Williams-June & O'Leary, 2021). Due to this lack of representation and tokenism, many have felt simultaneously invisible and hypervisible (Constantine et al. 2008; Dickens et al., 2020; Dickens, Womack, & Dimes, 2019). As a result of their status, feelings of isolation sometimes ensue. This also adds to internal pressure to make shifts in their identity and ways of being to mitigate any stereotypes that others have of Black women (Jones & Shorter-Golden, 2003). Literature has referred to this phenomenon as "double consciousness" (Du Bois, 1903; Spates et al., 2020). Black women shift their identities publicly and wear a figurative mask out of fear that their authentic Black female self might breed negative consequences (Jones & Shorter-Gooden, 2009; Spates et al., 2020).

They also experience what has been referred to as cultural taxation where, due to their marginalized status, Black faculty are often tasked with added responsibilities in furthering the mission of diversity and inclusion at their university and with mentoring students who are also from marginalized backgrounds (Consantine et al., 2008; Padilla, 1994; Reid, 2021). In fact, Black female faculty in particular are tasked with "other mothering" (Giuffrida, 2005). This additional labor, while recognized as a sociocultural necessity by some, adds to their already overtaxed schedules and takes away from the time needed to engage in activities that are necessary to advance in the profession such as writing and publishing (Constantine et al., 2008).

Black women also experience institutional slights, for example, when White students complain about their teaching. Institutions end up supporting the privileged positions of White students as opposed to supporting Black faculty. For example, using the autoethnographic approach, Cobb-Roberts (2011) described her experience with a White male student who felt uncomfortable being challenged on his position of colorblindness in a diversity course that she taught. While she made purposeful attempts to make all students feel safe to express themselves during classroom discourse, this student felt attacked when peers critiqued some of his comments that reflected White privilege. This particular student issued his concerns of unfair treatment to university administration. The administration, then, supported the student by suggesting the presence of a third party or police officer during class as he made a classroom presentation all without the professional courtesy of a prior discussion with the faculty member (Cobb-Roberts, 2011).

Privilege, i.e., power over resources and protection from consequences is another, is another challenge for faculty of color. One example of privilege in an academic institution is the prioritizing of White supremacist ideology supported by students that negatively impact the professional advancement of Black professors. The narrative of the student in Cobb-Robert's (2011) autoethnography is an illustration of how some students wield White male privilege to find protection from the discomfort of engaging in racial discourse and having their biases objectively challenged within the classroom setting by peers and their Black professors (Liu, 2017). Institutions serve as power-governors who maintain racism and legitimize White privilege when they blindly accept racially tinged objections to the classroom instruction and management of faculty of color without critical reflection (Liu, 2017). People of color are expected to acculturate or accommodate to White norms, values, and expectations. Acculturative processes are rooted in White Supremacy, "the ideological belief that biological and cultural Whiteness is superior" (Howard & Sommers, 2021; Liu et al., 2017). Acculturation legitimizes, protects, and reinforces White dominance and White privilege (Hindriks et al., 2014; Liu et al., 2017). Our systems and the individuals therein might think more reflectively and more critically upon how much of the way in which people of color are evaluated educationally and professionally is rooted in a systemically racist and discriminatory system. The biased perspectives of such students often end up in faculty evaluations which may have a negative impact on their tenure and promotion (Arnold, Crawford, & Khalifa, 2016).

Left to manage the physical and emotional toll of microaggressions, racial insults, and discrimination, some Black female faculty experience racial battle fatigue (Arnold et al., 2016; Chancellor, 2019; Cobbs-Roberts, 2011). Psychological injuries such as traumatic stress, depressive symptoms, anxiety, and suicidal ideation are also connected to reported experiences with racial discrimination by women of color (Donovan et al., 2013; Polanco-Roman et al., 2019). Community, mentoring, and faith are often protective factors and should be considered in any support initiatives provided to professional Black women.

Workplace Discrimination of Black Women in Non-Academic Settings

Much focus has been given to the subject of racial diversity in the workplace as society confronts numerous concerns that are emerging as a result of an increasingly diverse workforce. These concerns set the foundation for environmental justice undertakings from the civil rights movements to current day social justice movements like, Black Lives Matter (Bullard, 2020). Furthermore, American society continues to be confronted with a demoralizing array of social and political challenges in the workplace (Johnson, 2020). Likewise, the pandemic has increasingly devastated society by revealing pre-existing race and class-based inequalities in health and income (Johnson, 2020).

Black women continue to report the perception that they have less access to professional resources and opportunities than their White female counterparts and in comparison to Black or White men (Spates et al., 2020). Conditions for today's pay inequities were set in motion long ago with the United States' history and practice of racial segregation in education and in the job market. The racial wage gap furthers overall income inequality (Paul et al., 2018). In spite of legislation such as the Equal Pay Act of 1963 and the Civil Rights Act of 1964, labor market research suggests that discrimination may be a causal factor in the wage gap between Blacks and Whites (Paul et al., 2018; Hamilton 2000). For Black women, the intersection of race and gender further creates a unique threat to pay equity (Paul et al., 2018).

The National Partnership for Women and Families (NPWF; 2021) shared a number of statistics regarding Black women and the racial wage gap. The organization noted that women earned 82 cents for every dollar earned by a man. However, Black women earned 63 cents to every dollar earned by a man. The average yearly salary for Black women was $41,098 compared to $65,208 for White men. Paul et al., (2018) proposed a framework in which the gender and racial pay gap converge to explain the disparity for Black women. In their examination of the relationship between multiple identities and economy-wide wage comparisons, the authors found that the annual wage for Black women equaled 44% less than that of White men and 20% less than White women. The authors attempted to explain this wage gap via statistical analyses. They investigated whether labor market characteristics such as educational attainment, age, occupation, and industry accounted for the wage differences or discrimination. Results indicated that unexplained factors such as discrimination based on the intersection of race and gender rather than labor market characteristics accounted for more of the difference in wage earnings. Many Black women are the primary source of income in their households. The loss in wages means that they have less money for healthcare, childcare, educational pursuits, debt relief, to provide overall support to their families, and to establish generational wealth (NPWF, 2021).

Over the years, literature has examined the nature of racial differences within the U.S. workforce (Hibbler, 2002). Conversely, there is one variable that has remained largely unchanged, the underrepresentation of African-American women in executive positions (Beckwith, Carter, & Peters, 2016). As noted in the literature, it is imperative to explore and identify what barriers, perceived or real, prevent African-American women from being promoted to leadership positions within various organizations (Beckwith, Carter, & Peters, 2016). Notwithstanding the progress the country has made in relation to gender and racial equality, there continues to be a widespread lack of African-American women in prominent leadership positions (Beckwith, Carter, & Peters, 2016). The data is undeniable and in many ways disheartening. Despite lawmaking and affirmative action, there has been little improvement (Beckwith, Carter, & Peters, 2016).

For instance, Title II of the Civil Rights Act of 1991 created the 21-member, dual-party Federal Glass Ceiling Commission (Department of Labor, 1995). The Commission's order is to study the barriers to the advancement of minorities and women of color within corporate hierarchies (the problem known as the glass ceiling), to issue a report on its findings and conclusions, and to make recommendations on ways to disassemble the glass ceiling. The Commission assumed an extensive research and information collecting effort, including surveys of chief executive officers, public hearings, and dialogues with focus groups (Department of Labor, 1995). Glass ceiling barriers continue to deny countless numbers of trained people the opportunity to compete for and hold executive level positions in the workplace. Minorities and women of color are still consistently underrepresented at the highest levels of corporate America (Department of Labor, 1995). For instance, 97 percent of the leading managers of Fortune 1000 Industrial and Fortune 500 companies are White, and 95 to 97 percent are male; in the Fortune 2000 Industrial and Service corporations, only 5 percent of senior executives are women, and almost all of them are White. African-American men with professional degrees earn 21 percent less than their White colleagues holding the same level of education in the same job categories (Department of Labor, 1995).

Accordingly, a number of theories have been presented about the current state of discrimination against African-American women in the workplace (Hibbler, 2002). According to Morrison and Von Glinow (1990), many of these theories fall into three universal categories. For instance, there are those that assume that personal differences deter women and people of color from achieving specific goals. These theories posit that personal distinctions in under-represented groups are largely responsible for their disparity and treatment in the workplace (Morrison & Von Glinow, 1990). In addition, some theories cite discrimination by the majority culture as the cause of disparities. For example, concerns surrounding partiality and stereotyping on the part of White males in power form the basis for the slow progress of woman of color and experiences of workplace discrimination (Morrison &Von Glinow, 1990). Morrison and Von Glinow (1990) argue that census-based research steadily documents that African-American women's roles and wages are much lower than that of White males in the workplace. Morrison and Von Glinow (1990) also conjectured that women of color have lower credentials than White men, even when they have the same level of education.

The final category involves theories of systemic discrimination. These theories postulate that widespread policies and practices in the social system maintain discriminatory treatment of African American woman and people of color (Morrison & Von Glinow, 1990). Beckwith, Carter, & Peters, (2016) argue that the main origin of the disproportion of women being promoted to leadership positions in the workplace is due in part due to the fact that males created many of the workplace guidelines, standards, and practices which are designed for men and out of the experiences of men. As a result, the interests and needs of women continue to be underrepresented. For instance, the manner in which organizations define and evaluate leadership competences are based largely upon male-dominated traits (Beckwith, Carter, & Peters,

2016). This is noteworthy because of the increased underrepresentation of African-American woman experiencing discrimination in the workplace.

Sims (2009) explored the impact of African-American skin tone bias in the workplace and implications for critical human resource development by examining the impact of skin tone bias among African-American men and woman. Results indicated that skin tone bias was a mutual workplace phenomenon that resulted in negative behaviors, both intentional and unintended (Sims, 2009). During qualitative interviews with African Americans from the Chicago chapter of the Black Data Processing Associates (BDPA), participants described tense employee relations and an uncomfortable work environment as the result of skin tone bias. Some participants reported that they witnessed segregated work environments where dark-skin and light-skin African Americans separated themselves from one another. They also reported that darker skinned individuals received fewer promotions (Sims, 2009). Results indicated that participants experienced discrimination and feelings of inferiority when in the workplace (Sims, 2009).

Double Standards in the Workplace

Undoubtedly, workplace discrimination has become a nationalized issue. From a cultural standpoint, as well as with the increase in racial superiority that began to emerge in the second part of the 20th century. African-American women are faced with contradictory values; whether to dress in ways that are a likeness of their ethnicity or to conform to the traditional workplace dress standards. African-American women are distinguished in part by simultaneous membership in two different oppressed groups: African American and women (Etter-Lewis, 1994).

Hughes and Dodge (1997) explored relationships between job conditions, racial bias in the workplace, and perceived job quality. They examined relationships between African-American women's exposure to a range of occupational stressors, including two types of racial bias—institutional discrimination and interpersonal prejudice—and their evaluations of job quality. Results indicated that institutional discrimination and interpersonal prejudice were more important predictors of job quality among these women than were other occupational stressors. Further, racial bias in the workplace was most likely to be reported by workers in predominantly White work settings. In addition, African-American women who worked in service, semiskilled, and unqualified occupations reported significantly more institutional discrimination such as lower wages and minimal promotional opportunities when compared to other majority ethnic groups within the workplace (Hughes & Dodge, 1997).

Another study examined racial stereotyping in violation of Title VII by examining hair grooming policies for African American women and found that such policies disproportionately impacted them (Bennett-Alexander & Harrison, 2015). The authors sought to establish that natural hair is an indisputable characteristic, as is all hair, made changeable by social policies that enforce an acceptable standard of beauty, which mainly focused on the mainstream of beauty such as straight and or manageable hair types (Bennett-Alexander & Harrison, 2015). Bennett-Alexander and Harrison (2015) argued that such social policies are a continuation of race-based policies that creates discrimination and stereotyping towards woman of color. Another similar article explored biases, employment discrimination, and Black women's hair in the workplace with regard to workplace grooming policies. The authors found that such policies also created ongoing hair dilemmas and discrimination towards African-American women and further created economic disparities that negatively impacted promotions in the workplace (Powell, 2018). In addition, hair discrimination is a social injustice characterized by unfairly modifying policies and insulting individuals based on the appearance of their hair (Mbilishaka, Clemons, Hudlin, Warner, & Jones, 2020). This is the unfortunate experience of many people of color in various settings across the country which continues to place emphasis on the denial of employment opportunities based on grooming policies that outlaw Black hair (Hamilton, 2021). Furthermore, the role of state and local administrations in protecting civil rights has recently been highlighted through the increase in the number of hair discrimination laws passed to protect African American's, namely Black women (Hamilton, 2021).

Title VI which prohibits employment discrimination based on race, color, religion, sex and national origin (Powell, 2018). One can argue that certain hair styles and grooming practices are directly related to one's national origin, race, and color (Powell, 2018). Although there are current laws supporting equal opportunity for people of color, overt discrimination has been viewed as socially unacceptable. Notwithstanding, these signs of limited advancement continue to cause a dilemma of workplace discrimination which then promotes double standards towards African-American women.

Religious Institutions

African-American women are the backbone of the Black church and continue to leave their footprint in the church. Their support is evident through financial giving and mounting hours of weekly volunteer service. Various statistical studies bear out that, though they are the dominant congregants in the pews, they are subservient in leadership positions. Thus, women are more likely to fall prey to spiritual abuse and gender inequality. Undeniably, the use of gender to control and deny access in the church is spiritual abuse. Womanist Theologians would argue that Black women are still survivors of abuse due to their gender.

> Womanist thinkers and liberationist theologians agree that power is the weapon used against women as a way of controlling and limiting their participation in influential roles. This holds true for public and private spheres. The institution of sexism as it lives and breathes today is fueled by the misappropriation of power; and when it is used to deny access, to abuse survivors, or to protect wrongdoing, then that power becomes a vehicle for discrimination and a weapon for oppression. (Jones, 1971, p. 68-69)

Historically, women are not unfamiliar with church abuse. As a result of the 1816 formation of the African Methodist Episcopal (A.M.E.) Church, the first A.M.E. Doctrine and Discipline was produced in 1817. Although women notably were a part of the congregation, the representations of their voices at conferences were limited. Records reflect the following policy, "The General Conference or Convention shall be composed of one delegate for every two hundred members belonging to our society, who shall be nominated by the Quarterly Meeting Conference, and appointed by the male members of society." (AME, 1871, p. 56)

It clearly states in the 1817 Doctrine and Discipline that only the male' members of society' constituted the delegation. It would be 131 years later, in the 1948 General Conference, that legislation was introduced for women to be allowed to serve on the lesser of the ordination tracts (Something within.com, 2015). Although significant strides have been made, even in the twenty-first century, an ordained A.M.E. female minster stated, "What can be more violent than the humiliation of being declared unworthy to serve... having to fight for an appointment to a church for which you are more than qualified, while less qualified males receive choice assignments?" (Jones, 1971. p. 61).

Spiritual abuse boils down to a misuse of spiritual authority. The misuse of authority may be by clergy, church leaders, and even church membership. The survivors of spiritual abuse become confused because authority figures who represent God or a community of believers and promise healing and restoration have betrayed their sacred trust. Consequently, the abuse diminshes "that person's sense of self. Spiritual abuse crosses religious boundaries and may be subtle, overt, mild, or traumatic" (Childers, 2012, p.37). Abuse in any form is about power and control.

The church's struggle for power and control polarizes members and often drives some to leave. Some church members are critical of the involvement and ministry contribution of others. Thus, survivors voice their feelings through anonymous letters or verbal complaints or air complaints (complaints to family, friends, or other members). However, remaining anonymous in their complaints may be perceived as cowardly and equivalent to throwing a rock and hiding a hand. Retaliatory efforts suchs as writing anonymous threatening letters, withholding money, turning off utilities, and concentrating power and leadership positions on a select few are all abusive characteristics..

The loss is devastating and often unrecoverable. The survivors of spiritual abuse either stay and conform or perhaps leave and stray from the body of Christ altogether. "Individuals who have experienced unhealthy religion likely have multiple layers of loss,...loss of innocence, loss of trust, loss of world view, loss of relationships — including a perceived loss of relationship with God — and loss of self" (Childers, 2012, p.37). Abusive behavior has limited some members' willingness to get involved and serve in the church. If the spiritual abuse is not addressed, it will be to the detriment of the congregation. However, if the leadership is sensitized to spiritual abuse and has a willingness to change, perhaps the spiritual health of the church may improve.

After abuse has occurred, survivors may be fearful, in denial, or even blame themselves. It is grievous when spiritual abuse impacts the survivor's spiritual beliefs and relationship with God. Survivors "are not only in pain emotionally and psychologically, but they are full of fear about God, thinking that they are in trouble because they haven't gotten it right, or been good enough, or been Christian enough" (Van Vonderen, 2015). Some survivors cope with abuse through delusion or distortions of reality. "Conscious denial has to exist in a spiritual abuse situation in order to convince others that everything is fine, and also to fix blame away from the person or system." (Johnson and Van Vonderen, 1991). Survivors also are likely held captive by being irrational in their thought process (Johnson and Van Vonderen, 1991).

Even though the abuse is obvious, the survivor is often trapped and will continue to be victimized whether they stay or whether they leave.

Jeff VanVonderen (2015) confirms that the survivors fear losing their investment in the system. There is more to lose by leaving than staying. There is a loss of the energy, time, and money they have invested as well as their connections to others and emotions (VanVonderen, 2015). Leaving is complicated and feelings of anger become a normal response to abuse. "However, even legitimate anger if not properly channeled and dealt with, can degenerate into bitterness and cynicism toward everything spiritual" (Henke, 2015).

Conclusion

People of color are expected to acculturate or accommodate to White norms, values, and expectations. Acculturative processes are rooted in White Supremacy and the idea that biological and cultural Whiteness are superior (Howard & Sommers, 2021; Liu et al., 2017). Acculturation legitimizes, protects, and reinforces White dominance and White privilege (Hindriks et al., 2014; Kunst et al., 2015; Liu et al., 2017). Simply put, White is right. At least, that is what White supremacist ideology would lead one to believe. Nevertheless, White is not always right, and our systems and the individuals therein might think more reflectively and more critically about how much of the way in which people of color are evaluated educationally and professionally is rooted in a systemically racist and discriminatory system.

The oppression, as mentioned earlier, is strategic racism and manifests in the form of power and control. The Power and Control Wheel of Historical Trauma (PCWHT) is a guide to assist lay persons and professionals to understand, explore and process contemporary trauma within the context of historical trauma. According to Rogers and Bryant-Davis (2020), the PCWHT is "Similar to the original power and control wheel, the main category describes the different forms of power and control, and the subcategories are tactics used by perpetrators" (p. 8). However, the tactics described in this wheel exemplify the manifestation of oppression within microsystems and macrosystems. The PCWHT is divided into eight categories (a) physical violence, (b) systematic resource denial, (c) economic abuse, (d) appropriation of cultural resources, traditions, and knowledge, (e) spiritual abuse, (f) race socialization via cultural abuse, (g) psychological abuse, and (h) sexual violence. Each of the preceding categories has subcategories which are detailed in Rogers and Bryant-Davis (2020). Mental health professionals can present the wheel to their clients and ask if they have experienced any tactics. The professional can use the information to understand better the oppression the client has experienced in her life and inform treatment planning. These categories and subcategories can be used to ignite the healing process and continue to understand the gendered racialized trauma.

Although the issue of racial and ethnic diversity in the workplace has been widely researched in other fields, relatively few studies have explored workplace discrimination of African-American women (Hibbler, 2002). James's (2015) recent article brought attention to this significant and timely subject matter. James's in-depth work aimed to explore current policies based on workplace inclusion theories and best practices for a diverse workplace to provide evidence supporting the benefit of collaboration, respect, and dialogue across culturally diverse groups within organizations. Recommendations aimed to fill any gaps confronted, integrate ethical codes and standards to improve current policies and to guide the change process within the workplace for people of color (James, 2015). The findings indicated that organizations that fail to effectively achieve diversity lost the occasion to take advantage of the potential of their workforce, and such indecision prohibited organizational growth and sustainability under the growing complex circumstances (James, 2015).

Education on spiritual abuse is a necessary step to prevention. A psycho-ecclesial program will help leadership understand spiritual abuse and evaluate the negative effects of spiritual abuse. Psychologist Lenore Walker defined a Survivor Therapy Empowerment Program (STEP), which is a psychoeducation program for women who suffered intimate partner violence (IPV) (Walker, 2017). The psychoeducation program "deals with how people think about what has occurred and how it affects their feelings and their behavior" (Walker, 2017, p. 435). Since STEP is a psychoeducation program non-mental health care professionals may facilitate the study in small groups, bible study even women support groups and workshops.

Spiritual abuse closely mirrors intimate partner violence, therefore certain STEPs are adaptable to spiritual abuse. With adaptations for spiritual abuse, the following STEPs have been redefined:

- STEP One, Definition of Spiritual Abuse;
- STEP Six, Three types of violence: structural, symbolic and direct;
- STEP Eight, Grieving the End of a Relationship; and
- STEP Eleven, Building Healthy Congregation Relationships.

Exposing survivors to a psycho-ecclesial program equips them with information that helps survivors understands abuse and the reality of what has happen to them. It also helps the survivor to process their feelings of anger and take steps to move from being a survivor. Facilitating workshops in a group setting is valuable because it allows survivors to share feelings in a safe setting and it also reinforces learning new information in a discussion setting. It is important to incorporate the survivors "'voice': to create an environment where they can speak, to listen to the silence and understand that it may conceal a narrative, and to ask different and open questions about abusive experiences" (Wijma, et al., 2007, p. 159). A group setting may make it easier to share because survivors will address their shame and understand they are not alone in their abuse. A discussion on a healthy congregation would be beneficial because it provides a benchmark to compare their current experiences.

Adaptation of Lenore Walker's psychoeducation STEP program may prove beneficial to religious organizations. Creating awareness of spiritual abuse through review of characteristics and examples may sensitize pastors, church leaders and members to the seriousness of the abuse. Some churches may negate spiritual abuse especially if the act is not sexual or a result of direct violence however in an episcopal form of church government it is needful to defined structural and symbolic violence as sources of spiritual abuse as well. Finally, caution should be taken when using spiritual coping techniques in the recovery process for they may prove healing, or they may also prove detrimental if the survivor feels they have failed in their faith. Intervention in instances of spiritual abuse is important. It may help stop the revolving doors of churches, help survivors recover and create a healthier church environment for members to thrive and grow spiritually.

Conclusively, oppression of Black women is combated through mind, body, and spirit practices. Luam Keflezgy said, "Dance provides a sacred space for Black women, one where we can be totally free, where we can be completely uninhibited" (Bond, 2018, p. 151). Another way to combat oppression is through activism. Patrisse Cullors, cofounder of Black Lives Matter stated, "Black Lives Matter is not just an affirmation for us, and it is not just about black people living inside the United States. It is about blackness as a philosophy, as a way of life across the diaspora" (Bond, 2018, p. 89). Moreover, community, mentoring, programming, and faith are often protective factors and should be considered in any assistance provided to Black women. If you are an advocate, ally, practitioner, or preacher, note that,

Black women are noticeably powerful which is why oppression, abuse, and trauma will inevitably be the barrier to overcome; and it will be overcome.

References

Abercrombie, J. C. (2020, February 6). Anti-literacy laws: There were laws against teaching Blacks to read? Amazing Black History. https://amazingblackhistory.com/2020/02/06/anti-literacy-laws-would-you-believe-there-were-laws-against-teaching/.

Acuff, J. (2018). Confronting racial battle fatigue and comforting my blackness as an educator. *Multicultural Perspectives*, *20*(3), 174-181.

African Methodist Episcopal Church. (1817). *The Doctrine and Discipline of the African Methodist Episcopal Church First Edition, 1817*. Philadelphia, PA: John H. Cunningham, 1817. Accessed May 5, 2015. http://docsouth.unc.edu/church/ame/ame.html.

Alexander, R., & Moore, S. E. (2008). The benefits, challenges, and strategies of African American faculty teaching at predominantly White institutions. *Journal of African American Studies*, *12*(1), 4-18.

Akin., J. D. (n.d.), A Digest of the Laws of the State of Alabama – 1833. Alabama Department of Archives and History, Montgomery, Alabama. https://archives.zalabama.gov/teacher/slavery/lesson1/doc1-9.html.

Allen, A., Scott, L. M., & Lewis, C. W. (2013). Racial microaggressions and African American and Hispanic students in urban schools: A call for culturally affirming education. *Interdisciplinary Journal of Teaching and Learning*, *3*(2), 117-129.

Arnold, N. W., Crawford, E. R., & Khalifa, M. (2016). Psychological heuristics and faculty of color: Racial battle fatigue and tenure/promotion. *The Journal of Higher Education*, *87*(6), 890-919.

Barbro, "Cycles of Abuse," 159.

Beckwith, A. L., Carter, D. R., & Peters, T. (2016). The Underrepresentation of African American Women in Executive Leadership: What's Getting in the Way? *Journal of Business Studies Quarterly, 7,* 116-134.

Bennett-Alexander, D. D. & Harrison, L. F. (2015). My Hair is Not Like Yours: Workplace Hair Grooming Policies for African American Women as a Racial Stereotyping in Violation of Title VII. *Cardoza & Gender, 437,* 438-460.

Bullard, R.D. (2020). From Civil Rights to Black Lives Matter in Lessons in Environmental Justice: From Civil Rights to Black Lives Matter and Idle No More. Sage Publications.

Chancellor, R. L. (2019). Racial battle fatigue: The unspoken burden of Black women faculty in LIS. *Journal of Education for Library and Information Science*, *60*(3), 182-189.

Childers, M. (2012). Holy Havoc: Chaplains as First Responders in Healing Spiritual Abuse." *Chaplaincy Today (Online)* 28,(2) *ATLA Religion Database with ATLASerials*, EBSCO*host.*

Clayson, J. & McMahon, S. (2021, July 7). Nikole Hannah-Jones explains difficult decision to reject UNC tenure after humiliating denial. WBUR. https://www.wbur.org/hereandnow/2021/07/07/nikole-hannah-jones-tenure.

Cobb-Roberts, D. (2011). Betwixt safety and shielding in the academy: Confronting institutional gendered racism—Again. *The Negro Educational Review*, *62*(1-4), 89.

Cokley, K. (2006). The impact of racialized schools and racist (mis) education on African American students' academic identity. *Addressing racism: Facilitating cultural competence in mental health and educational settings*, 127-144.

Constantine, M. G., Smith, L., Redington, R. M., & Owens, D. (2008). Racial microaggressions against Black counseling and counseling psychology faculty: A central challenge in the multicultural counseling movement. *Journal of Counseling & Development*, *86*(3), 348-355.

Dade, K., Tartakov, C., Hargrave, C., & Leigh, P. (2015). Assessing the impact of racism on Black faculty in White academe: A collective case study of African American female faculty. *Western Journal of Black Studies*, *39*, 134-146.

Daniel, B. J. (2019). Teaching while black: Racial dynamics, evaluations, and the role of White females in the Canadian academy in carrying the racism torch. *Race Ethnicity and Education*, *22*, 21-37.

Darling-Hammond, L. (1028, April 11). Kerner at 50: Educational equity still a dream deferred. The Learning Policy Institute. https://learningpolicyinstitute.org/blog/kerner-50-educational-equity-still-dream-deferred?gclid=CjwKCAjw_o-HBhAsEiwANqYhp_Tb1DV3w-7_fb4YxVVC_4zw4JibfrFGTLgVqwbNF_sDJz9S7pYY5RoCinMQAvD_BwE.

Davis, S., & Brown, K. (2017). Automatically Discounted: Using Black Feminist Theory to Critically Analyze the Experiences of Black Female Faculty. *International Journal of Educational Leadership Preparation*, *12*(1), 27-34.

Delgado, R., & Stefancic, J. (2001). *Critical race theory: An introduction*. New York: New York University Press.

DeMatthews, D. (2020). Addressing racism and ableism in schools: A DisCrit leadership framework for principals. *The Clearing House: A Journal of Educational Strategies, Issues, and Ideas*, *93*(1), 27-34.

Dickens, D., Jones, M., & Hall, N. (2020). Being a Token Black Female Faculty Member in Physics: Exploring Research on Gendered Racism, Identity Shifting as a Coping Strategy, and Inclusivity in Physics. *The Physics Teacher*, *58*(5), 335-337.

Dickens, D. D., Womack, V. Y., & Dimes, T. (2019). Managing hypervisibility: An exploration of theory and research on identity shifting strategies in the workplace among Black women. *Journal of Vocational Behavior*, *113*, 153-163.

DiPrete, T. A., & Eirich, G. M. (2006). Cumulative advantage as a mechanism for inequality: A review of theoretical and empirical developments. *Annual Review of Sociology*, *32*, 271-297.

Donovan, R. A., Galban, D. J., Grace, R. K., Bennett, J. K., & Felicié, S. Z. (2013). Impact of racial macro-and microaggressions in Black women's lives: A preliminary analysis. *Journal of Black Psychology*, *39*(2), 185-196.

Du Bois, W. E. B. (1903). *The souls of black folk: Essays and sketches.* A. G. McClurg & Co.

Evans-Winters, V. (2005). *Teaching black girls: Resiliency in urban classrooms.* Peter Lang.

Ferris State University (n.d.). What was Jim Crow? https://www.ferris.edu/jimcrow/what.htm.

Flaherty, C. (2021, June 1). UNC donor lobbied against Hannah-Jones, and her lawyers set deadline. Inside Higher Ed. https://www.insidehighered.com/quicktakes/2021/06/01/unc-donor-lobbied-against-hannah-jones-and-her-lawyers-set-deadline.

Folkenflik, D. (2021, June 21). UNC Journalism school tried to give Nikole Hannah-Jones Tenure. A top donor objected. National Public Radio. https://www.npr.org/2021/06/21/1007778651/journalism-race-and-the-fight-over-nikole-hannah-jones-tenure-at-unc.

Garrison-Wade, D. F., Diggs, G. A., Estrada, D., & Galindo, R. (2012). Lift every voice and sing: Faculty of color face the challenges of the tenure track. *The Urban Review, 44*(1), 90-112.

Griffin, K. A., Pifer, M. J., Humphrey, J. R., & Hazelwood, A. M. (2011). (Re) defining departure: Exploring Black professors' experiences with and responses to racism and racial climate. *American Journal of Education, 117*(4), 495-526.

Guiffrida, D. (2005). Other mothering as a framework for understanding African American students' definitions of student-centered faculty. *The Journal of Higher Education, 76,* 701-723.

Hamilton, A. (2021). Untangling Discrimination: The Crown Act and Protecting Black Hair. *University of Cincinnati Law Review, 89,* 483-508.

Harris, L. M. (2015, March 26). The long ugly history of racism at American universities. The New Republic. https://newrepublic.com/article/121382/forgotten-racist-past-american-universities.

Henke, D. "Spiritual Abuse." Watchman Fellowship. Accessed March 10, 2015. http://www.watchman.org/profiles/pdf/spiritualabuseprofile.pdf.

Henke, D. "Spiritual Abuse in the Bible." Watchman Fellowship. Accessed December 21, 2015. http://www.watchman.org/articles/cults-alternative-religions/spiritual_abuse-in-the-bible/.

Hibbler, D. K. (2002). African American's Perceptions of Workplace Equity: A Starting Point. *Journal of Park and Recreation Administration, 20,* 42-60.

Hughes, D. & Dodge, M. A. (1997). African American Women in the Workplace: Relationships Between Job Conditions, Racial Bias at Work, and Perceived job Quality. *American Journal of Community Psychology, 25,* 581-599. doi: 10.1023/A:1024630816168.

James, J. (2015). Linking African Americans to the Workplace. *International Journal of Business and Social Science, 6,* 256-263.

Johnson, D. & VanVonderen, J. (1991). *The Subtle Power of Spiritual Abuse*. Bloomington, MN: Bethany House Publishers.

Johnson, O. (2020). An Opening: Advocating for Equity in a Polarized America. *Poverty and Race Research Action Council, 29,* 1-16.

Jones, C. P. (2002). Confronting institutionalized racism. *Phylon (1960-)*, 7-22.

Jones, Lawrence N. "They Sought a City: The Black Church and Churchmen in the Nineteenth Century." *Union Seminary Quarterly Review* 26, no. 3 (March 1, 1971):

253-272. Accessed May 6, 2015. *ATLA Religion Database with ATLASerials*, EBSCO*host*.

Jones, M. C., & Shorter-Gooden, K. (2009). *Shifting: The double lives of Black women in America*. Harper Collins.

Joseph, N. M., Viesca, K. M., & Bianco, M. (2016). Black female adolescents and racism in schools: Experiences in a colorblind society. *The High School Journal*, *100*(1), 4-25.

Kelly, B. T., & McCann, K. I. (2014). Women faculty of color: Stories behind the statistics. *The Urban Review*, *46*(4), 681-702.

King, D. K. (1988). Multiple jeopardy, multiple consciousness: The context of a Black feminist ideology. *Signs: Journal of women in culture and society*, *14*(1), 42-72.

Koonce, J. B. (2012). Oh, those loud Black girls!": A phenomenological study of Black girls talking with an attitude. *Journal of Language and Literacy Education*, *8*(2), 26-46.

Lewis, J. A., Mendenhall, R., Harwood, S. A., & Huntt, M. B. (2013). Coping with gendered racial microaggressions among Black women college students. *Journal of African American Studies*, *17*(1), 51-73.

Lewis, J. A., Mendenhall, R., Harwood, S. A., & Browne Hunt, M. (2016). "Ain't I a woman?" Perceived gendered racial microaggressions experienced by Black women. *The Counseling Psychologist*, *44*, 758-780.

Liu, W. M. (2017). White male power and privilege: The relationship between White supremacy and social class. *Journal of Counseling Psychology*, *64*(4), 349-358.

Liu, W. M., Liu, R. Z., Garrison, Y. L., Kim, J. Y. C., Chan, L., Ho, Y., & Yeung, C. W. (2019). Racial trauma, microaggressions, and becoming racially innocuous: The role of acculturation and White supremacist ideology. *American Psychologist*, *74*(1),143-155.

Louis, D. A., Rawls, G. J., Jackson-Smith, D., Chambers, G. A., Phillips, L. L., & Louis, S. L. (2016). Listening to our voices: Experiences of Black faculty at predominantly White research universities with microaggression. *Journal of Black Studies*, *47*(5), 454-474.

Lynch, M. (2019, October 9). History of institutional racism in U.S. public schools. The Edvocate. https://www.theedadvocate.org/history-of-institutional-racism-in-u-s-public-schools/.

Massey, C. G., Scott, M. V., & Dornbusch, S. M. (1975). Racism without racists: Institutional racism in urban schools. *The Black Scholar*, *7*(3), 10-19.

Mbilishaka, A. M., Clemons, K., Hudlin, M., Warner, C., & Jones, D. (2020). Don't get it twisted: Untangling the psychology of hair discrimination within Black communities. *American Journal of Orthopsychiatry, 90,* 590-599. doi: 10.1037/ort0000468.

McGowan, J. M. (2000). Multicultural teaching: African American faculty classroom teaching experiences in predominantly White colleges and universities. *Multicultural Education*, *8*(2), 19.

Melaku, T. & Beeman, A. (2020, June 25). Academia isn't a safe haven for conversations about race and racism. Harvard Business Review. https://hbr.org/2020/06/academia-isnt-a-safe-haven-for-conversations-about-race-and-racism.

Mirza, H. S. (2014). Decolonizing higher education: Black feminism and the intersectionality of race and gender. *Journal of Feminist Scholarship*, *7*(7), 1-12.

Moody, A. T., & Lewis, J. A. (2019). Gendered racial microaggressions and traumatic stress symptoms among Black women. *Psychology of Women Quarterly*, *43*(2), 201-214.

Morrison, A. M. & Glinow, M. A. (1990). Women and Minorities in Management. *American Psychologist, 45,* 200–208. doi.org/10.1037/0003-066X.45.2.200.

Padilla, A. M. (1994). Research news and comment: Ethnic minority scholars; research, and mentoring: Current and future issues. *Educational Researcher*, *23*(4), 24-27.

Patton, L. D., & Catching, C. (2009). 'Teaching while black': Narratives of African American student affairs faculty. *International Journal of Qualitative Studies in Education*, *22*, 713-728.

Cobb-Roberts, D. (2011). Betwixt safety and shielding in the academy: Confronting institutional gendered racism—Again. *The Negro Educational Review*, *62*(1-4), 89.

Perry, B. D. P. (2003). Effects of Traumatic Events on Children.

Polanco-Roman, L., Anglin, D. M., Miranda, R., & Jeglic, E. L. (2019). Racial/ethnic discrimination and suicidal ideation in emerging adults: the role of traumatic stress and depressive symptoms varies by gender not race/ethnicity. *Journal of Youth and Adolescence*, *48*(10), 2023-2037.

Powell, C. (2018). Bias, Employment Discrimination, and Black Women's Hair: Another Way Forward. *Brigham Young University Law Review, 2,* 933-968.

Pine, G. J., & Hilliard, A. G. (1990). Rx for racism: Imperatives for America's schools. Phi Delta Kappan, 71(8), 593-600.

Reid, R. A. (2021). Retaining Women Faculty: The problem of invisible labor. *PS: Political Science & Politics*, *54*, 504-506.

Ricks, S. A. (2014). Falling through the cracks: Black girls and education. *Interdisciplinary Journal of Teaching and Learning*, *4*(1), 10-21.

Rogers, G. (2014). African American Women Coping with Trauma. In Bryant-Davis, T., Austria, A. M., Kawahara, D. & Willis, D. J. (Eds.), *Religion and Spirituality for Diverse Women: Foundations of Strength and Resilience* (pp. 71-82)**.** Santa Barbara, CA: Praeger.

Rogers, G. (2020). Youths 'exposure to violence in the family. In Geffner, R., White, J. W., Rogers, G., & Bryant-Davis, T. (2020). Historical and contemporary racial trauma among Black Americans: Black Wellness Matters. In Geffner, R., White, J. W., Hamberger, L. K., Rosenbaum, A., Vaughan-Eden, V., & Vieth, V. I. (Eds.) *Handbook of Interpersonal Violence and Abuse Across the Lifespan*. New York: Springer International Publishing.

Sims, C. (2009). The Impact of African American Skin Tone Bias in the Workplace: Implications for Critical Human Resource Development. *Journal of Workforce Education and Development, 3,* 1-17.

Smith, W. A. (2008). Higher education: Racial battle fatigue. In R. T. Schaefer (Ed.), *Encyclopedia of race, ethnicity, and society* (pp. 615–618). Thousand Oaks, CA: Sage.

Smith, J. W., & Calasanti, T. (2005). The influences of gender, race, and ethnicity on workplace experiences of institutional and social isolation: An exploratory study of university faculty. *Sociological Spectrum*, *25*, 307-334.

Smith, W. A., Yosso, T. J., & Solórzano, D. G. (2011). Challenging racial battle fatigue on historically White campuses: A critical race examination of race-related stress. In Christine A. Stanley (Ed.), *Faculty of Color: Teaching in predominantly White colleges and universities*. Stanley (pp. 211-237). Anker Publishing.

Smithsonian American Art Museum (2021, July 3). Literacy as freedom. https://americanexperience.si.edu/wp-content/uploads/2014/09/Literacy-as-Freedom.pdf.

Solorzano, D. G., & Yosso, T. J. (2001). From racial stereotyping and deficit discourse toward a critical race theory in teacher education. *Multicultural education*, *9*(1), 2-8.

Something Within.com, "These All Died in Faith: Women in the AME Church," accessed May 18, 2015, http://www.somethingwithin.com/archive-amewomen.htm.

Southern Poverty Law Center (2021, July 3). Charles Murray. https://www.splcenter.org/fighting-hate/extremist-files/individual/charles-murray.

Spates, K., Evans, N. T., James, T. A., & Martinez, K. (2020). Gendered racism in the lives of Black women: A qualitative exploration. *Journal of Black Psychology*, *46*(8), 583-606.

Sue, D. W., Capodilupo, C. M., Torino, G. C., Bucceri, J. M., Holder, A., Nadal, K. L., & Esquilin, M. (2007). Racial microaggressions in everyday life: implications for clinical practice. *American psychologist*, *62*(4), 271.

Thomas, V. G. (2004). The psychology of Black women: Studying women's lives in context. *Journal of Black Psychology*, *30*(3), 286-306.

Tolley, K. (2016). Slavery. In J. Angulo (Ed.) *Miseducation: a history of ignorance-making in America and abroad*. (pp. 13-33). Johns Hopkins University Press.

Torres, L., Driscoll, M. W., & Burrow, A. L. (2010). Racial microaggressions and psychological functioning among highly achieving African Americans: A mixed-methods approach. *Journal of Social and Clinical Psychology*, *29*(10), 1074-1099.

Tourse, R. W., Hamilton-Mason, J., & Wewiorski, N. J. (2018). The infrastructure of racism: The institutional dimensions. In R. W. Tourse, J. Hamilton-Mason, & N. J. Wewiorski (Eds.), *Systemic racism in the United States. Scaffolding as a social construction*. (pp. 79-99). Springer International Publishing.

Trejo, J. (2020). The burden of service for faculty of color to achieve diversity and inclusion: The minority tax. *Molecular biology of the cell*, *31*, 2752-2754.

Turner, C. S. V., & González, J. C. (2011). Faculty women of color: The critical nexus of race and gender. *Journal of Diversity in Higher Education*, *4*, 199-211.

University of Southern California. USC Gould School of Law (n.d.). A brief history of Jim Crow laws. https://onlinellm.usc.edu/a-brief-history-of-jim-crow-laws/.

U.S. Department of Labor. (1995). Good For Business: Making Full Use of The Nation's Human capital: report from the Federal Glass Ceiling Commission. Retrieved from http://www.dol.gov/oasam/programs/history/reich/reports/ceiling2.pdf.

Van Vonderen, J. "Spiritual Abuse: An Interview with Jeff VanVonderen." Spiritual Abuse Recovery Resource, Christian Recovery International. Accessed March 5, 2015. http://www.spiritualabuse.com/?page_id=58.

Walker, L.E.A. (2017). *The Battered Woman Syndrome (4th Ed.)*. New York, NY: Springer.

Walter, A. W., Ruiz, Y., Tourse, R. W. C., Kress, H., Morningstar, B., MacArthur, B., & Daniels, A. (2017). Leadership matters: How hidden biases perpetuate institutional racism in organizations. *Human Service Organizations: Management, Leadership & Governance*, *41*(3), 213-221.

Wamsley, L. (2021, July 6). After tenure controversy, Nikole Hannah-Jones will join Howard faculty instead of UNC. National Public Radio. https://www.npr.org/2021/07/06/1013315775/after-tenure-controversy-nikole-hannah-jones-will-join-howard-faculty-instead-of.

Wijma, B., Thapar-Björkert, S., Hammarström, N. C., & Swahnberg, K. (2007). Cycles of Abuse Nurtured by Concealment: A Clinical Report. *Journal of Psychosomatic Obstetrics and Gynecology,28*(3), pp. 155-160.

Williams-June, A. & O'Leary, B. (2021, May 27). How many Black women have tenure on your campus? Search here. The Chronicle of Higher Education. https://www.chronicle.com/article/how-many-black-women-have-tenure-on-your-campus-search-here.

Winfield, A. G. (2007). Eugenics and education in America: Institutionalized racism and the implications of history, ideology, and memory 155-160.

About the Authors

Treatment Practices of Black/African American Women Dealing with Race-Based Trauma

Dr. Tina Marie Glover is originally from San Diego, California. She received her doctorate from Oregon State University in Counselor Education and Supervision. She is a repeat Alumni of Portland State University, receiving a Master's in Counseling with an emphasis on Rehabilitation and Community Counseling and a Bachelor of Science in Sociology and Psychology. Dr. Glover is a Nationally Certified Rehabilitation Counselor, a State and Nationally Certified Addictions Counselor, and a License Professional Counselor in multiple states. Dr. Glover has held numerous leadership positions that help promote and elevate the counseling field. She is an active Zeta Phi Beta Sorority, Incorporated member and a community leader.

Dr. Glover has worked in the human service field for over two. Some of her work includes working closely with adolescent and adult gang members, domestic violence intervention and prevention, and working with the Coalition for Human Sex Trafficking, aiding victims with the transition. She has over a decade of experience addressing and training individuals around multicultural and social justice issues. She believes infusing diversity, equity, and inclusion into her work on multiple levels strengthens her practice. Dr. Glover's belief system allows her to address prevention, intervention, and stabilization of mental health and addiction issues.

Etiology of Trauma in African-American Women

Tiffany Brannon is a native of Lexington, KY. She has her doctorate from the University of the Cumberlands in the Counseling Education and Supervision program. She received her Bachelor's degree in Psychology with a concentration in Juvenile Justice from Eastern Kentucky University. She graduated with honors from Lindsey Wilson College with a Master of Clinical Counseling in Education.

Tiffany has over ten years post master's clinical experience and is a practicing clinical director, adjunct professor, and program manager working with adult males with significant mental health diagnoses in a residential facility. Tiffany also specializes in substance abuse, domestic violence (offenders and victims), trauma (sexual abuse/violence), anger management, generalized anxiety, and other mental health diagnoses in youth and adult populations.

Tiffany is a wife and mother of four children. She is an active member of Zeta Phi Beta Sorority, Incorporated member, and is the organization's International Domestic Violence Program Manager.

The Trauma of Colorism Across the Lifespan

Dr. Kerri Legette McCullough is a National Certified Counselor, a Certified Clinical Trauma Professional, a Licensed Professional Counselor in Virginia & District of Columbia, and a Licensed Clinical Professional Counselor in Maryland. She works with children, adolescents, adults, and families who have experienced various traumas. She has over nine years of professional experience, including community mental health, program evaluation & creation, and providing direct services to children, adolescents, adults, and families. She earned her Master of Arts in Clinical Mental Health Counseling and an Ed. D in Counselor Education and Supervision from Argosy University.

Black Women and Girls and the Culture of Silence in the Aftermath of Sexual Violence

Kristal Miller is a second-year Kean University, Union, New Jersey doctoral student. She previously attended Lincoln University, PA, earning a Bachelor's degree in Political Science, and Montclair State University, NJ, where she obtained her Master's degree in Counseling. Kristal's counseling career spans more than 20 years. She has worked with various populations in various treatment settings, including men, women, children, the justice-involved population, substance abuse, and mental health.

The African American Woman's Historical Trauma: Our Inability to Heal

Dr. Nakpangi Thomas is a National Certified Counselor, Licensed Professional Counselor for the State of Michigan, Clinical Traumatologist, and Approved Clinical Supervisor. She was the CEO of a small private practice and owns the Thomas Traumatology Institute in Detroit. Dr. Thomas has over 21 years of experience in social justice and advocacy, radio, and behavioral/mental health field working with youth and adults.

Dr. Tezonia Morgan, also known as "The Forgiveness Doctor," owns Wings of Virtue Counseling and Research Institute, where she counsels, conducts clinical supervision and consultation, and develops research. She is passionate about the mental health field, forgiveness, and mental freedom in the African-American community. Outside of forgiveness, her research interests include racial microaggression, the breakdown of the African American home, and the deaf and hard-of-hearing culture.

Deconstructing Negative Stereotypes about Black Women: Implications for Clinical Treatment

Portia Allie-Turco is a Clinic Director, Program Coordinator, and Lecturer at the State University of New York Plattsburgh. She is a former chief diversity officer, family court mediator, and consultant for the Department of Social Services. She specializes in racial, historical, and generational trauma.

Untangling Black Hair: Black Women's Eternal Search for Self and Beauty

Katrina Pinkney is a licensed counselor and educator passionate about BIPOC communities' mental and physical well-being. She has worked in diversified industries, including non-profit, public health, healthcare, and higher education sectors. Katrina is a doctoral candidate in the CACREP-accredited counselor education and supervision (CES) program at the University of the Cumberlands. Her research interests are multiculturalism, health disparities, marginalized populations (specifically Black Americans), provider implicit bias in mental health, and gendered racism.

Mindfulness-Based Stress Reduction as a Treatment for Traumatic Stress for African-American Women

Dr. Tiffany Williams is an Assistant Professor of Psychology at Tennessee State University. She serves as faculty for the master's and doctoral counseling psychology programs. She received a BA in Psychology and Sociology, an MEd in Clinical Mental Health Counseling, and a Ph.D. in Urban Education: Counseling Psychology from Cleveland State University. Dr. Williams is licensed as a Psychologist in Ohio and Tennessee.

Paigean Jones is a second-year student in the social work doctoral program at Howard University. She received a Master of Social Work from Georgia State University in 2019. Ms. Jones is a licensed master's level social worker, a registered yoga teacher at the 200-hr level, and a certified trauma specialist. She specializes in mindfulness, self-care, maternal health disparities, and Black women's mental health.

Chomba Muwele is a doctoral student in the counseling psychology program at Tennessee State University. She received a BS from the University of San Francisco, where she studied Kinesiology, Psychology, Child and Youth Studies, and an MA in Mental Health Counseling from Boston College.

Misdiagnosing and Underdiagnosing African American Women: Implications for Trauma-Informed Care

Theresa Libios is a Counselor Education and Supervision doctoral student at Walden University. She earned an M.A. in Clinical Mental Health Counseling from Southern New Hampshire University. She is a licensed professional counselor associate in Texas. Theresa has private and public classroom instruction experience working with disadvantaged and special education students. My special interests are working with the unique mental concerns of women and special programs for research to address mental health disparities for people of color. Theresa was invited to serve on the Association for Play Therapy's Research Committee, the University of Texas AMEN project, and the AGE of Central Texas' She Thrives Conference Committee.

Openness and Depth: Gender and Racially Sensitive Clinical Practice Through the Lens of Afrocentricity, Black Feminism, and Transformative Trauma-Informed Care Approaches

Dr. Lauren Elizabeth Downey has built her counseling career around helping marginalized and underserved populations from all walks of life make meaning of their trauma experiences. The co-author is a Licensed Professional Clinical Counselor and Supervisor (LPCC-S) in Kentucky and a nationally certified trauma-focused cognitive behavioral counselor. She possesses a master's degree from the University of Kentucky in rehabilitation counseling and a doctorate in counselor education and supervision from Eastern Kentucky University. She has counseled marginalized men, women, and children in many settings. In 2018, her passion for counseling individuals who have experienced trauma grew into her private practice, the Trauma-Informed Counseling Center (TICC).

Ariel Dew, LPCC, has worked within targeted Black communities for approximately ten years, providing advocacy and counseling to underserved neighborhoods. As a Licensed Professional Clinical Counselor in Kentucky, the co-author serves as a Treatment Director for Specialized Alternatives for Families and Youth, a non-profit organization providing intensive in-home therapy to preserve and reunify families involved with child protective services. In addition, Ariel Dew manages a private practice providing counseling to individuals and families, utilizing certifications in trauma-focused cognitive behavior therapy and family systems advanced trauma therapy. As a Chicago School of Professional Psychology graduate, she earned a master's degree in clinical counseling psychology with a trauma-informed concentration.

Let the Healing Begin: Black Women's Spirituality in Times of Trauma

Dr. Awa Jangha is an Assistant Professor of Counselor Education in the Clinical Mental Health Counseling program at the Seminary of the Southwest. Her dissertation research focused on experiences of power in the identity development of African-American female pastoral counselors in training and utilized art to explore. She is a Licensed Professional Counselor and a Board-

Certified Art Therapist and offers both spiritually integrated counseling and art therapy in her private practice, Art and Spirit Counseling.

Dr. Latoya Moss is the Director of Counseling and Student Support Services at the Savannah College of Art and Design, Atlanta location. Her dissertation research was titled Survivors of Personal and Professional Trauma: Exploring the Lived Experience of Clergy Women Diagnosed with Cancer. She holds the credentials of Nationally Certified Counselor, Licensed Professional Counselor, and Certified Professional Counselor Supervisor. Dr. Moss incorporates the topics of Religion and Spirituality in her clinical and supervisory work.

Counseling African American Women: A Person-Centered Spiritual Approach

Cerise Lewis is a Licensed Marriage and Family Therapist. She earned a Master of Science in Marriage and Family Counseling Therapy and is pursuing a Ph.D. in Counselor Education and Supervision at Capella University. Lewis's dissertation research studies counselor educators' experiences teaching students to integrate faith and spirituality into clinical work. She works primarily with African-American individuals, couples, and families experiencing relationship interaction problems, infidelity, trauma, depression, and anxiety.

Black Women: Pregnancy and Trauma

Dr. Kimberley Dockery, LMFT, was born in Memphis, TN. After completing her bachelor's in psychology at Christian Brothers University, she worked as a continuing education coordinator at the University of Tennessee Cancer Institute. Because of her involvement in cancer research and education, she decided to pursue her master's at Kansas State University in Family Therapy. She relocated to South Florida to complete her doctorate in Family Therapy at Nova Southeastern University. Dockery works on helping women. Her clinical interest includes working with patients dealing with infertility, pregnancy, pregnancy loss, menopause, parenting, anxiety, adjustment issues, and patients dealing with gender identity and sexuality. She is dedicated to facilitating positive change by exploring the patient's story within their context, interactions, and relationships. She enjoys spending time with her family and friends, baking, and relaxing at the beach.

"Reclaiming Connection" Interpersonal Healing in African American Women Assailed by Relational Trauma.

Ryan Wright is a Licensed Graduate Professional Counselor currently working at a community mental health agency in Washington, D.C., where he serves as an intake coordinator and therapist. Ryan obtained a master's in Rehabilitation counseling from the University of the District of Columbia (CACREP-Accredited). Ryan received his bachelor's degree in psychology from Lafayette College, where he attended on a Posse scholarship. Ryan is a member of the American Counselor Association and a subdivision member of the Association of Humanistic Counseling.

"I Want to Live!" Exploring the Inequities in the U.S. Healthcare System

Allison Hotz is a Doctoral Candidate at Tennessee State University (TSU) and is slated to graduate in August 2022. She will work in the Clinical Health Psychology track at the Memphis VA Medical Center. She earned her Bachelor's and M.S. degrees from the University of Memphis. Her research interests focus on dissecting race-based trauma, service learning, graduate education, integrative behavioral health, and conceptualizing the psychological well-being of marginalized populations.

Dr. Oatis-Ballew earned her B.A. from Fisk University and her M.S. and Ph.D. degrees from Howard University. She is a Professor and Coordinator of the Ph.D. in Counseling Psychology at Tennessee State University in Nashville, TN. Her research interests are cultural competency in Health Services Psychology and inclusive learning environments. She is also a Licensed Psychologist and has maintained a practice for 20 years.

Dr. Esther Lynch received her M.S. and Ph.D. from Tennessee State University (TSU) and is an assistant professor at TSU. She is a core faculty member in the graduate program. Her research interest includes integrated behavioral health, trauma, and romantic relationships. All these interests intentionally focus on marginalized populations as she strives to highlight prevalent issues not commonly explored or discussed through her courses, research, and clinical work.

By My Own Bootstraps: Career Success, Sacrifice of African American Women, and the "American Dream"

Dr. Pia L. Scott is a licensed professional counselor and certified career development facilitator. She is the CEO of the P L Scott Group, LLC, focusing on the 3C's approach: Counseling, Coaching, and Consulting. She provides counseling, coaching, and consulting services, developing training for counselors. As a professor, she incorporates career and professional development into the curriculum. She has experience providing assessments, job placement services, labor market research, career transition, and transferable skills analysis, having previous experience as a career counselor.

Dr. J. Denise Bowman is pursuing her license. She has education and experience in social work, prevention, criminal justice, legal, and addiction. Dr. Bowman provides counseling, mentoring, and consulting services to diverse individuals and age groups. She embraces life through her spirituality and learning and enjoys inspiring others to embrace their greatness.

Dr. Shane Gill is a Counselor Education and Supervision student at Capella University. Intrigued with research and program evaluation, Shane´ opted to pursue a degree that would aid her in developing competence in identifying culturally appropriate counseling models and theories specific to minority populations. A dedicated advocate and learner, Shane dedicates her career to Black studies and the role of counselors in advocacy, social justice, and multiculturalism in education and research.

Black Women in the Ivory Tower: Institutional Oppression and Intersectionality

Injung Lee, Ph.D., is an assistant professor in the Department of Counseling and Higher Education at Northern Illinois University. Her primary research interest centers on the professional identity development of counselors-in-training, ethnic/cultural minority populations in counselor education, and trauma-informed teaching in counselor education. She is a Nationally

Certified Counselor (NCC) with clinical experience in school and mental health counseling.

Eunae Han, M.A., is a doctoral student in the Counselor Education and Supervision program at the University of Iowa. Her research interests include the feminist approach to counselor education and trauma-informed counseling and supervision. Before pursuing her doctoral degree, she worked as a professional licensed counselor for three years in South Korea. She worked as a counselor supporting survivors of sexual misconduct, which has impacted her academic journey to advocate for women.

Institutional and Systemic Racism and the Traumatic Experiences of African American Women

Layla Bonner, Ph.D., LMFT, NCC, is an Assistant Professor in the Master of Arts degree program in Mental Health Counseling at Belmont University. She earned her doctorate in Clinical Counseling, Teaching, and supervision from Trevecca Nazarene University in 2018. She is also a licensed marriage and family therapist in Tennessee (LMFT), a Nationally Certified Counselor (NCC), and an Approved Supervisor with the American Association for Marriage and Family Therapy.

Gimel Rogers, Psy.D., *ABPP,* is a licensed psychologist and is Board Certified in Clinical Psychology by the American Board of Professional Psychology. With over ten years of clinical, professional speaking, and training experience, she owns F.I.R.E. Igniting Lives. She earned her doctorate from Pepperdine University and has provided trauma-focused care to many clients. She is an expert witness and assists clients in criminal, family, and civil cases involving various forensic issues. She is the Faculty and the Associate Director of the Online MAP/MACLP Programs at Pepperdine University. Her inaugural book is the "21-Day Relationship Healing Devotional and Journal," a poetry-based devotional that promotes restoration through reflection. She is the content developer of the Power and Control Wheel of Historical Trauma.

Reverend Doctor Agnes M. Lover serves as Lead Pastor at Saint Paul African Methodist Episcopal Church in Montgomery, Alabama, Rosa Parks Home Church, and is committed to passionate worship, community-focused ministry, and the anointed preaching of God's Holy Word. Rev. Dr. Lover received the Doctor of Ministry from United Theological Seminary. Her doctoral project, "From Preying to Praying: Exposing the Effects of Spiritual Abuse in the Church," establishes a psycho-ecclesial model to equip church leaders with the necessary knowledge concerning spiritual abuse and utilizes a biblical behavioral model to illustrate how church leadership should implement spiritual authority. She received a Master of Divinity from Candler School of Theology, a Master of Business Administration from St. Peters College, a Master of Science in Computer Science from Stevens Institute of Technology, and a Bachelor of Science in Mathematics and Computer Science from Xavier University.

Index

D

E

F

G

H

I

T

U

V

W